Affirmative Action

Primary Documents in American History and Contemporary Issues

The Abortion Controversy
Eva R. Rubin, editor

The AIDS Crisis
Douglas A. Feldman and Julia Wang Miller, editors

Capital Punishment in the United States
Bryan Vila and Cynthia Morris, editors

Constitutional Debates on Freedom of Religion
John J. Patrick and Gerald P. Long, editors

Drugs and Drug Policy in America
Steven Belenko

The Environmental Debate
Peninah Neimark and Peter Rhoades Mott, editors

Equal Protection and the African American Constitutional Experience
Robert P. Green, Jr., editor

Founding the Republic
John J. Patrick, editor

Free Expression in America
Sheila Suess Kennedy, editor

Genetic Engineering
Thomas A. Shannon, editor

The Gun Control Debate
Marjolijn Bijlefeld, editor

Major Crises in Contemporary American Foreign Policy
Russell D. Buhite, editor

The Right to Die Debate
Marjorie B. Zucker, editor

The Role of Police in American Society
Bryan Vila and Cynthia Morris, editors

Sexual Harassment in America
Laura W. Stein

States' Rights and American Federalism
Frederick D. Drake and Lynn R. Nelson, editors

U.S. Immigration and Naturalization Laws and Issues
Michael LeMay and Elliott Robert Barkan, editors

Women's Rights in the United States
Winston E. Langley and Vivian C. Fox, editors

AFFIRMATIVE ACTION

A Documentary History

Edited by JO ANN OOIMAN ROBINSON

Primary Documents in American History and Contemporary Issues

GREENWOOD PRESS
Westport, Connecticut • London

Library of Congress Cataloging-in-Publication Data

Affirmative action : a documentary history / edited by Jo Ann Ooiman Robinson.
    p. cm.—(Primary documents in American history and contemporary issues,
  ISSN 1069–5605)
  Includes bibliographical references (p.   ) and index.
  ISBN 0–313–30169–7 (alk. paper)
    1. Civil rights—United States—History—Sources.   2. Affirmative action
  programs—United States—History—Sources.   3. Discrimination—United States—
  History—Sources.   4. Reverse discrimination—United States—History—Sources.   I.
  Robinson, Jo Ann, 1942–   II. Series.
  JC599.U5A346853   2001
  331.13'3'0973—dc21   00–049508

British Library Cataloguing in Publication Data is available.

Library of Congress Catalog Card Number: 00–049508
ISBN: 0–313–30169–7
ISSN: 1069–5605

First published in 2001

Greenwood Press, 88 Post Road West, Westport, CT 06881
An imprint of Greenwood Publishing Group, Inc.
www.greenwood.com

Printed in the United States of America

Copyright Acknowledgments

In Memory of
Cleo M. Stipp (1912–1994)
and
John L. Stipp (1909–1995)

Contents

THE 1930s

WORLD WAR II

THE KENNEDY ERA

PART V. 1981–2000: **Affirmative Action Entrenched**
and Embattled

THE REAGAN–BUSH YEARS

THE ADMINISTRATION OF WILLIAM JEFFERSON CLINTON

Contents

Contents

Series Foreword

This series is designed to meet the research needs of high school and college students by making available in one volume the key primary documents on a given historical event or contemporary issue. Documents include speeches and letters, congressional testimony, Supreme Court and lower court decisions, government reports, biographical accounts, position papers, statutes, and news stories.

The purpose of the series is twofold: (1) to provide substantive and background material on an event or issue through the texts of pivotal primary documents that shaped policy or law, raised controversy, or influenced the course of events, and (2) to trace the controversial aspects of the event or issue through documents that represent a variety of viewpoints. Documents for each volume have been selected by a recognized specialist in that subject with the advice of a board of other subject specialists, school librarians, and teachers.

To place the subject in historical perspective, the volume editor has prepared an introductory overview and a chronology of events. Documents are organized either chronologically or topically. The documents are full text or, if unusually long, have been excerpted by the volume editor. To facilitate understanding, each document is accompanied by an explanatory introduction. A selected bibliography of related sources appears at the end of this volume.

It is the hope of Greenwood Press that this series will enable students and other readers to use primary documents more easily in their research, to exercise critical thinking skills by examining the key documents in American history and public policy, and to critique the variety of viewpoints represented by this selection of documents.

Preface

The first step toward completing this project was to develop a basic outline of the origins and evolution of affirmative action. I was guided in this by the scholarship of Herman Belz, Hugh Davis Graham, Joan Hoff, Paul Moreno, and Richard Scotch. I am indebted to each of them. Once the outline was drawn up, the job of searching for appropriate documentary materials began. Over a three-year period, in addition to my own labors, this task involved the skills and persistence of six individuals. Early library forays by Elinor Robinson and Matthew Wernsdorfer provided necessary start-up data. Between them, Jane Sellman and Sean Brimm found about one-third of the materials that I eventually selected for use. Wendy Gates and Baiyina Muhammad also contributed needed items. I am grateful to each of these individuals and especially appreciative of Sean Brimm's cheerful doggedness in finding documents on which the rest of us had given up. These assistants and I all owe a hearty vote of thanks to the unsung professional librarians who helped us at the Morris B. Soper Library, Morgan State University; the University of Baltimore Law School Library; the Enoch Pratt Central Library in Baltimore City; the Milton Eisenhower Library at Johns Hopkins University; and the Morris Library of the University of Delaware, Newark. We also benefited from two Internet "libraries": Cornell Law School's Legal Information Institute and "Findlaw" originating in Mountain View, California.

As I compiled the documents, Kristen Anchor kept track of their length and set up a system for requesting permissions and staying on top of the responses. She also checked citations and helped me in myriad other ways, for which I am most grateful. Twelve Morgan State University graduate students enrolled in my seminar on affirmative action in the spring of 1999, when this documentary history was still very much a work in progress. Their critical reading pointed up several mistakes in the rough manuscript, and their thoughtful responses helped me improve the work. I extend special thanks to students Willa McClain, Spencer Tyrus, and the late Elizabeth Rhodes for bringing to my attention materials that I added to the manuscript.

Lucinda Burgess, also a Morgan State graduate student, bore a substantial part of the tedium of compiling the table of contents and bibliography, and I value her help. As per my contract with Greenwood Publishing Group, I selected an advisory committee when I began. Members of this committee have helped in various ways. Jerry Thornberry of Gilman School in Baltimore City shared his clipping files; Vivian Fisher, director of special collections at Morgan's Soper Library, also provided me with sources; Lucy Thornton Berry, who teaches in the Baltimore City public schools, reviewed the original outline and made helpful suggestions; Elinor Robinson critiqued the introduction, to its definite improvement; and Debra Newman Ham, my colleague on the history faculty at Morgan State, read the entire manuscript. She saved me from careless mistakes and made many insightful suggestions. Thanks to each committee member, and special thanks to Debra Ham for her generosity.

Encouragement and moral support count for a great deal in getting through any major undertaking. I am fortunate in having multiple sources of such backing. At each stage of the publication process I have received expert guidance from the staff at Greenwood Press. Acquisitions editor, Emily Michie Birch, has given me consistently sound advice, but I particularly appreciate her deep reserves of patience and goodwill. I am also grateful to Maureen Melino for her counsel on permissions and her generous assistance as I scrambled to obtain the final okays. I value the sharp eye of copy editor, Carol Lucas, and the thoroughness of production editor, Heidi L. Straight. Thanks are also in order to Alex Petri for his marketing skills. When the need for lawyerly expertise arose, I was very fortunate to be directed to Nancy Gregor and am thankful for her services. Whenever I've vented my impatience with this protracted project, friends have helped me keep some perspective and sense of humor. I've come to count on my 1960s college suitemate, Jane Campbell, and her weekly e-mail notes of empathy and cheer from Wisconsin. My longtime friend and colleague Rosalyn Terborg-Penn has never failed to show interest and support. Also essential to keeping up my spirits have been my witty and compassionate "fitness" program partners, Linda Forlifer and Karen Olson. Without the friendship of the Kohl-Garbart team I would never have finished. I am immeasurably grateful for Deborah Kohl's sage advice and endless acts of practical assistance and Hadley Garbart's patient and expert guidance through this brave new world of computers and cyberspace. Along with depending on these friends, I have leaned on my family—daughter Elinor, son Joseph, daughter-in-law Melissa Robinson. Their ways of helping are too numerous to list and too essential to be noted with a simple thank-you. Yet, that and my love will have to suffice.

Near the time that this project was first conceived came the deaths of Cleo and John Stipp, to whom I've dedicated the book. Cleo was working in the Admissions Office when I entered Knox College in Galesburg, Illinois, in 1960. She mothered me through the undergraduate years and ever after. John, professor emeritus of history, was my mentor. The central themes of affirmative action—fairness and justice—were close to their hearts, just as their legacy of love and goodness will always be close to mine.

Note to the Reader

In keeping with the format of the series to which this book belongs (Primary Documents in American History and Contemporary Issues), the documents that follow are organized chronologically. To aid the reader who may want to follow each thread of "race," "gender," and "disability" separately, the documents are also labeled **r, g,** and **d** according to their contents.

Introduction

Affirmative action is an effort to develop a systematic approach to open the doors of education, employment, and business development opportunities to qualified individuals who happen to be members of groups that have experienced long-standing and persistent discrimination.
—William Jefferson Clinton, July 19, 1995

Affirmative action can have a shallow or a deep meaning.
—Charles R. Lawrence III and Mari J. Matsuda

Most books about affirmative action concentrate on the category of race, particularly the African American experience; some examine gender; and a few give attention to disability. Little notice has been given to the parallels, convergences, and conflicts among those who find themselves defined by these categories and whose quests for self-definition and social justice have both helped to shape and been shaped by affirmative action. By the same token, most books about affirmative action focus on the present and treat the subject as a phenomenon belonging entirely to the last half of the twentieth century. But the history of affirmative action is intertwined with struggles for basic human rights and equal political and economic opportunity reaching back to the founding of the United States. While this documentary history does not provide that complete historical context, it seeks to avoid a "shallow meaning" by beginning in the nineteenth century, bringing together material by and about African Americans, women, and the disabled, and taking into account the development of social and political movements that gave rise to, and remain connected to, affirmative action.

African Americans, women, and individuals with disabilities are certainly not the only groups that have, in President Clinton's words, "experienced long-standing and persistent discrimination," but these particular groups have been historical bellwethers. The racism, sexism, and cruel stereotyping that they experienced are emblematic of how, throughout U.S. history, the ruling majority has excluded and labeled "inferior" all groups that did not conform to the dominant (predominantly white, male, Protestant) culture. Put in the bluntest of terms, this has meant, according to author Daniel C. Maguire, that from its beginnings "the United States has been operating under a rigid quota system. This quota system has insisted on and got a 90 to 100 percent monopoly for white males in all the principal centers of power in government, business, and the professions, and in the competition for jobs at every level" (Maguire 1980, 3).

Economic and cultural differences within and among the three groups examined here illustrate the multilayered nature of prejudice and discrimination in the United States. Gender stereotypes were only part of the oppression borne by women who were also African American and/or disabled. Similarly, disabled African Americans of both sexes suffered from racial discrimination as well as from prejudices against disability. Furthermore, racism not only was a characteristic of the white male establishment but also infected social movements for women's rights and the rights of the disabled. At the same time, the nature and impact of discrimination were affected by material circumstances. For example, affluent women, though treated as inferior, still had economic and social advantages over individuals who were enslaved, institutionalized, or living in unremitting poverty.

From wherever they were launched, the prolonged battles against injustice and subordination in which the disabled, women, and African Americans played major roles not only won significant gains for these groups but also served as models for others seeking to resist oppression. They moved the nation closer to its purported ideals of "liberty and justice for all." Nevertheless, none of the groups featured here have completely prevailed over the labels of "inferiority" and the exclusions from the rights of citizenship and equal opportunity that have burdened them for so long. Their hard-won gains have never been guaranteed to last. As numerous documents in this book illustrate, advances that required immeasurable courage and perseverance to achieve were invariably challenged and, in many cases, undermined before they had time to take root. Even those that managed to survive proved disappointing because they were not adequately supported and enforced.

This book provides a sampling of documents related to affirmative action and its historical roots and context, beginning in the mid-nineteenth century and continuing into the year 2000. Before approaching these documents, it may be useful to broaden the scope and briefly look at the experience and status of African Americans, women, and the disabled, beginning with the founding of the United States.

At the time of the first national election under the U.S. Constitution (1790) approximately 750,000 African Americans lived in the United States, all but about 8 percent of whom were enslaved. Although the word "slavery" appears nowhere in the Constitution, that document legitimated the institution of slavery in three separate provisions. Article 1, Section 2, known as the "three-fifths compromise," determined that representation in the House of Representatives and direct taxes would be apportioned among the states according to the number of free persons in those states and "three fifths of all other persons"—a veiled, yet obvious, reference to slaves. Section 9 of the same article permitted the importation of "such Persons as any of the States . . . shall think proper to admit" up to the year 1808 (allowing the Atlantic slave trade to continue for another two decades). Finally, Article 4, Section 2 mandated that anyone owing service or labor in one state who fled to another state must be returned to the person due the owed service. This provision regarding those whom slave owners referred to as "fugitive slaves" was twice reinforced before the Civil War, in laws of 1793 and 1850. These measures, which accorded no legal protection to individuals who were captured or, for that matter, to anyone who spoke for them, left even "free persons of color" vulnerable to being kidnapped and enslaved.

Undergirding the institution of slavery was "the precept of inferiority," which, as noted by the late federal judge A. Leon Higginbotham Jr.,

posed as an article of faith that African Americans were not quite altogether human. . . . From the time the Africans first disembarked here in America, the colonists were prepared to regard them as inferior. (Higginbotham 1996, 9)

That precept was evident in the thinking of nearly all the figures who played prominent parts in the conception and building of the United States. The same Thomas Jefferson who immortalized the assertion that "all men are created equal" wrote of African Americans:

In memory they are equal to the whites; in reason much inferior, as I think one could scarcely be found capable of tracing and comprehending the investigations of Euclid; and . . . in imagination they are dull, tasteless, and anomalous. (quoted in Jordan 1968, 436)

Three years before the Civil War, Roger Taney, chief justice of the United States Supreme Court, asserted in the well-known *Dred Scott* decision that African Americans had always been regarded as beings of an inferior order, and altogether unfit to associate with the white race, either in social or political relations; and so far inferior, that they had no rights which the white man was bound to respect. (quoted in Higginbotham 1996, 65)

Although Abraham Lincoln, with great presence and compassion, managed to preserve the nation as a federal union when bitter divisions over slavery nearly destroyed it, and although he became the symbolic Great Emancipator, he, too, had internalized the precept of inferiority with regard to African Americans, as he had made clear in his 1858 campaign for the U.S. Senate when he told an Illinois audience:

There is a physical difference between the white and black races which I believe will for ever forbid the two races living together on terms of social and political equality. And inasmuch as they cannot so live, while they do remain together there must be the position of superior and inferior, and I as much as any other man am in favor of having the superior position assigned to the white race. (quoted in Higginbotham 1996, 172)

Documents included in Part I of this book provide a glimpse of the laws and constitutional amendments passed in the era of Reconstruction that challenged the precept of inferiority and briefly nudged the country toward fulfillment of the stated goals of its own Declaration of Independence and Constitution. But the forces of racism, supported by economic priorities associated with rapid industrialization, soon prevailed. Southern "Redeemers," with the cooperation of the federal government and northern capital, struck down the laws, circumvented the amendments, and reinforced the precept of inferiority by such instruments as lynching, economic exploitation, and a rigid and brutally enforced system of segregation.

Documents included in Parts II through IV of this history highlight the numerous organized attacks on racism that African Americans initiated through religious and civic associations and, in the mid-twentieth century, through a massive grassroots civil rights movement. The outcome of these struggles bears the stamp of the courts and the Congress, the White House, and other governmental institutions, but every court ruling, law, executive order, and enforcement guideline concerning civil rights also bears the mark of the relentless African American quest for freedom and justice.

In the earlier stages of that quest, before the civil rights era, which came to fruition in the 1960s, some proposed reforms and some public policies included measures that proved to be similar to the affirmative action remedies of subsequent decades. This is particularly true of certain programs associated with the New Deal of President Franklin Roosevelt.

The New Deal encouraged a view of government as an activist body responsible for ensuring that citizens enjoyed the basics of a good life, including a living wage, a home, and retirement security. Making certain that African Americans received their fair share of these citizenship entitlements became a priority for African American leaders, including governmental appointees such as Lawrence Oxley, William Hastie, and Robert Weaver. By introducing the practice of "proportional hiring" in Roosevelt's Public Works Administration (PWA), they took a step toward addressing the economic disadvantage of African American workers. Simultaneously, however, other new Deal programs discriminated against African Americans, as did many segments of the labor union movement, which the New Deal had greatly empowered. Thus, at the end of World War II, as historian Thomas Sugrue has written, "whole sectors of the American economy were still largely closed to" African Americans. While white workers pursued job and income security through their unions, African Americans intensified their quest for equal opportunity through the courts and, as time went on, in the streets (Sugrue 1998, 886–897).

The civil rights struggles beginning in the era of World War II and continuing into the 1970s began with demands for equality and hopes for a racially integrated society. However, even the most heralded responses to those demands fell short. The nature of these shortfalls can be seen in the *Brown* decisions of the Supreme Court, included in Part II of this study, and in the Civil Rights Act of 1964 and the enforcement agency created by that act, the Equal Employment Opportunity Commission, detailed in Part III. In both cases the will to establish justice for all came up against, and was extensively compromised by, white resistance. That resistance was grounded in the enduring "precept of inferiority" and fueled by fear that equality for all would undermine security for whites.

Affirmative action was one response to the failure of civil rights legislation to establish equality. This failure, argue the authors of affirmative action, proves that inequality and injustice are too deeply embedded in American society to be removed by legislative or judicial fiat alone. They have urged that leaders in both the public and the private sectors become proactive in creating opportunities for the historically subordinated to partake of education, employment, advancement, and involvement in all areas of society. Only in this way, they insist, can systemic discrimination be uprooted. As Supreme Court justice Harry Blackmun put it in his opinion on the *Bakke* case (Doc. 235) "In order to get beyond racism we must first take account of race."

Other responses to the failure of civil rights legislation have been nonviolent civil disobedience, Black Nationalist and separatist movements, and periodic, violent explosions of rage. The turn toward affirmative action by mainstream leaders took some impetus from these responses, as may be seen in this book's material on the eras of Lyndon Johnson and Richard Nixon. Particularly significant was the development of the Philadelphia Plan, which forced some of the strongest white, male bastions of organized labor to begin to open their ranks to minorities and, eventually, women.

The extent to which Americans seemed to be stuck fast in the racist patterns of their history and in need of a fresh approach was emphasized by sociologist Kenneth Clark in testimony to the National Advisory Commission on Civil Disorders, which Lyndon Johnson established after major rioting in Detroit and Newark in the summer of 1967 (Doc. 147). Clark reminded the commissioners of their numerous predecessors:

> I read that report . . . of the 1919 riot in Chicago, and it is as if I were reading the report of the investigating committee on the Harlem riot of '35, the report of the investigating committee on the Harlem riot of '43, the report of the McCone Commission on the Watts riot [of 1965].
> I must again in candor say to you . . . —it is a kind of Alice in Wonderland— with the same moving picture re-shown over and over again, the same analysis, the same recommendations, and the same inaction. (*National Advisory Commission on Civil Disorders* 1968, 483)

Fourteen years later, after a decade and a half of affirmative action, Eleanor Holmes Norton, who had served under President Carter as head of the Equal Employment Opportunity Commission, concluded that systemic discrimination had made affirmative action essential. Testifying in 1981 at hearings of the U.S. Commission on Civil Rights, she stated:

> [T]he public has little appreciation for what the process was in reaching these remedies [affirmative action] finally. Lesser remedies were tried for many years with virtually no success. . . . If the sad history of remedy-failure is laid out clearly, I believe most Americans will come to see why the Congress, the State legislators, and the courts have all finally unanimously embraced these remedies. The alternative was simply unthinkable: permanent second class status for minorities and women. . . .
> . . . These patterns [of discrimination] were built in leadened attitudes and practices centuries in the making. They must be taken apart step by step. It is a labor of the whole society. ("Consultation on the Affirmative Action Statement of the U.S. Commission on Civil Rights" 1981, 75)

Even as Norton spoke, the administration of President Ronald Reagan was working to undo the "embrace" of affirmative action. Documents on the Reagan years are found in Part V of this book.

In those same remarks before the Civil Rights Commission, Eleanor Holmes Norton claimed that the "worst remaining patterns" of discrimination were "female ones because of the strong prevalence of virtually all-female occupations." Women, she said, were "concentrated in about 20 occupations, men in about 230." Job segregation is one part of the long history of the subordination of women in American society. That subordination, like the institution of slavery, was a "given" for the men who wrote the Constitution of the United States. From a woman's point of view the most striking characteristic of the Constitution is that, as legal scholar Joan Hoff has emphasized, "women are not mentioned at all." The government established by the Constitution, Hoff concludes, was "an exclusively masculine system of justice based on English common law and eighteenth-century ideals of liberty, justice and equality" (Hoff 1991, 117).

In the common-law tradition the basic rights of citizenship—signing contracts, owning property, using one's own earnings as one saw fit, engaging in political actions such as voting—were denied to married women. The English law asserted, "Man and wife are one person. . . . A woman, as soon as she is married, is called *covert*, in Latin, *nupta*, that is, *veiled*, as it were, clouded and over-shadowed. . . . To a married woman her new self is her superior, her companion, her master" (1632 legal text quoted in Flexner 1970, 7–8). While this tradition underwent some modification in the American colonies, the basic precept of inferior female status did not change.

Religious teachings helped to maintain it. In most early American settlements male leaders drew on the Judeo-Christian tradition to validate their superior status and authority. Instrumental in this regard was the Old Testament view of woman as created from a rib of the first man and destined to be submissive to him. The Garden of Eden story laid the responsibility on woman for introducing sin into the world. Thus, women bore careful watching and had to be restricted to fulfilling the female duties of housekeeping, childbearing, and child raising. The worlds of politics and commerce belonged to their male relatives. While some women who never married and some widows did engage in business, they were going against the grain. For most always-single women the opprobrium of being a "spinster" was harsh.

Women who yearned for education or sought to engage in discourse on the substantive issues of the day often came up against what historian Eleanor Flexner has noted as the almost universal belief "that a woman's brain was smaller in capacity and therefore inferior in quality to that of a man" (Flexner 1970, 23). Thomas Jefferson rebuffed a woman who wrote him with questions about the new Constitution; he told her that "the tender breasts of ladies were not formed for political convulsion" (quoted in Sochen 1974, 73).

Certain women were exempted from these forms of paternalism and subjected instead to harsh exploitation. The most viciously exploited were African American women, particularly those who were enslaved and whose owners engaged in slave breeding. According to historian John Hope Franklin, "breeding was so profitable that many slave girls became mothers at thirteen and fourteen years of age. By the time they were twenty some women had given birth to as many as five children." Slave masters bragged about having women in bondage who were "uncommonly good breeders" (Franklin 1980, 126). The mentality that accepted this practice was often equally capable of justifying as a "property right" the rape of the women whom they controlled.

Although racism and sexism cannot be simply equated, the connections between the social movements that opposed the subordination of human beings because of their skin color and/or their anatomy are worth examining. An early connection was forged in the abolitionist movement of the mid-nineteenth century. On the one hand, that movement was a vehicle for public action by women associated with both the antislavery and women's rights movements. On the other hand, abolitionist organizations harbored assumptions about female inferiority that sparked the first organized women's revolt in the United States. When Elizabeth Cady Stanton and Lucretia Mott attended an 1840 antislavery convention in London, they and other women were barred from participating in the proceedings on the main floor and were forced to observe from a balcony. Later Mrs. Stanton wrote of the cumulative effect on her of this and other experiences, including her personal situation as a wife and mother isolated in the little town of Seneca Falls, New York:

My experiences of the World Anti-Slavery Convention, all I had read of the legal status of women, and the oppression I saw everywhere, together swept across my soul, intensified now by many personal experiences. . . . I could not see what to do or where to begin—my only thought was a public meeting for protest and discussion. (quoted in Flexner 1970, 73–74)

In the summer of 1848, Mrs. Stanton, Mrs. Mott, and three friends wrote an announcement and submitted it to their local newspaper, inviting "the public generally" to "a convention to discuss the social, civil and religious rights of woman." At the ensuing Seneca Falls Convention an intrepid band of believers in the rights of women, including the great abolitionist orator Frederick Douglass, revised Thomas Jefferson and submitted to the world their own "Declaration of Principles," which asserted "that all men and women are created equal" and protested that "the history of mankind is a history of repeated injuries and usurpations on the part of man toward woman, having in direct object the establishment of an absolute tyranny over her" (Flexner 1970, 74–75).

The women's movement grew in the years before the Civil War. Activists organized state and national conventions and targeted state legislatures with petition campaigns, such as the one led by Susan B. Anthony in 1854–1855. She delivered 6,000 signatures to New York lawmakers, petitioning for property rights, the right to child custody after divorce, and the right to vote. With the outbreak of war in 1861, women's rights advocates channeled their energies to the Union cause and continued to press for the abolition of slavery. Through the National Women's Loyal League they collected 400,000 signatures in support of the Thirteenth Amendment, outlawing slavery.

Documents in Part I of this book highlight the schism that occurred over the Fourteenth and Fifteenth Amendments, establishing full citizenship and the right to vote for African American males. Focusing on race meant the postponement of the issue of women's citizenship. The schism eventually became a clear division of the woman's rights movement into two organizations—the American Woman Suffrage Association (AWSA) and the National Woman Suffrage Association (NWSA). The AWSA continued in the tradition of the prewar Republican Party and abolitionist movement to promote universal suffrage. The NWSA represented, as historian Rosalyn Terborg-Penn has described it, "the woman suffrage-first faction," which "pitted Black men against women in a racist way" (Terborg-Penn 1998, 27). While the AWSA concentrated solely on gaining the suffrage for women, primarily by a state-by-state strategy, the NWSA entertained a variety of women's issues and advocated a federal suffrage amendment. The two organizations merged in 1890, forming the National American Woman Suffrage Association (NAWSA). The forces of the NAWSA triumphed in 1919–1920 with passage and ratification of the Nineteenth Amendment, guaranteeing women's right to vote.

As observed in Part II of this book, the right to vote did not guarantee economic and social equality for women as a group anymore than the Reconstruction amendments had protected African Americans from injustice. For both groups labor shortages during times of war created economic opportunities that inevitably shrank with the signing of peace agreements and the return of servicemen expecting to resume their prewar jobs. In the case of women, wartime employment in traditionally male occupations gave the lie to the notion that they were incapable of performing "men's work." However, that notion revived quickly at each war's end. The fact that women themselves were divided over whether they needed special laws to protect them in the workplace and whether another constitutional amendment (the proposed Equal Rights Amendment [Doc. 36]) was required to ensure their full citizenship weakened women as an organized force in the labor market. As a political and social force, women were also divided by class and race, each person's loyalty and status significantly affected by her ties to male kin.

As indicated in Part III, both the women's movement and the civil rights movement became forces to reckon with in the 1960s and 1970s.

Part III also illustrates some of the ways in which the women's movement both lagged behind, and drew inspiration and momentum from, the civil rights revolution. Similarly, affirmative action on behalf of women followed after legal and judicial affirmative action initiatives for African Americans. As historian Melvin Urofsky has noted with regard to the courts:

[R]acial classification had been assumed, at least since World War II, to be malign and discriminatory; gender classification, on the other hand, had been assumed, at least until the 1970s, to be benign. (Urofsky 1997, 51–52)

In gender-related cases highlighted in Parts III and IV, particularly *Johnson v. Santa Clara* (Doc. 304), the courts began to validate women's right to equal opportunity. However, judges held sex and gender discrimination subject only to "intermediate scrutiny," rather than the "strict scrutiny" that they applied to racial discrimination.

Women's rights advocates—many of whom had adopted the "feminist" label by the 1970s—pressed their case in Congress and the courts. They identified the inferior social, political, and economic status of women as systemic oppression, originating in the same patriarchal system that oppressed and brutalized racial and ethnic minorities. Just as civil rights advocates had determined that dismantling the structure of racism required the race-conscious remedies of affirmative action, so feminists called for gender-conscious affirmative action. Without denying differences among women based on class and race, they pointed to pervasive patterns of discrimination in employment and earnings, women's universal vulnerability to rape and physical abuse, and widespread stereotyping of women as intellectually and physically inferior to men. "Women suffer group disadvantage and ending this group disadvantage requires group-remedy," insisted scholars Charles Lawrence and Mari Matsuda. They concluded:

If our culture and history place women outside the corridors of power, we must find ways to bring them in through affirmative action. (Lawrence and Matsuda 1997, 157–158)

Examples of the practical efforts to follow this reasoning are found in Parts III through V of this book.

While the travail of women and African Americans in the United States began with their exclusion from the arenas of politics and governance, a few disabled individuals participated in both the ratification of the Declaration of Independence and the writing of the Constitution. Among the signers of the Declaration was Stephen Hopkins, believed to have had cerebral palsy. He was quoted as saying when he affixed his signature, "My hand trembles but my heart does not" (quoted in Lenihan 1976/1977, 12). One of New York's delegates to the Constitutional Convention of 1787, Gouverneur Morris, was an amputee, having lost a leg in a carriage accident. However, these examples of active service and political and social status are exceptions to the general pattern that defined disability as a state of dependence on either one's family or the local community. In this regard the disabled shared with women the lingering effects of British legal traditions—in the case of the disabled, the English poor laws, which placed responsibility for care of the infirm and indigent in the hands of local authorities.

By the early nineteenth century population growth was putting more pressure on local welfare systems than they could handle. Reform efforts included enlisting the resources of private philanthropy and state governments and new policies of sending the able-bodied poor to work-houses and the physically and mentally disabled to almshouses. Over time such institutions became vile places to live. In the 1850s reformer Dorthea Dix led a nationwide campaign to improve conditions, especially for the mentally ill. After personally investigating the care of mentally disabled people in her home state of Massachusetts, Dix publicly decried "the present state of insane persons confined in this Commonwealth, in cages, closets, cellars, stalls, pens! Chained, naked, beaten with rods, and lashed into obedience" (quoted in Blum 1977, 240). She called for the use of federal funds to build new facilities for disabled citizens. The first items in this documentary history depict the outcome of her appeal to the federal government.

Both reformers such as Dix and the lawmakers and welfare administrators whose policies the reformers sought to improve conceived of all disabled people as entirely dependent upon others, requiring one form or another of custodial care. It seems never to have occurred to them that this view was, in the words of legal scholar Jacobus tenBroek, "the product of cultural definition—an assumptive framework of myths, stereotypes, aversive responses and outright prejudices" (tenBroek 1966a, 814). A major task of the disability rights movement has been to challenge and begin to break apart that framework, which was constructed with another version of "the precept of inferiority." This version manifested itself in many ways, from misguided charity, to simple meanness: the segregation of individuals in institutions; the stereotypes of utter helplessness portrayed in charitable fund drives and telethons; immigration policies that refused admission to the United States to individuals with disabling mental or physical conditions; laws passed in many states forbidding the disabled to marry; the eugenics movement, which flourished in the early twentieth century, calling for the creation of a stronger human race by forcing the sterilization of "misfits" and "defectives"; and a category of "ugly laws," some of which remained in effect as late as the mid-1970s. Typical of such laws was the provision in the Chicago Municipal Code that stipulated:

No person who is diseased, maimed, mutilated or in any way deformed so as to be an unsightly or disgusting object or improper person to be allowed in or on the public ways or other public places in this city, shall therein or thereon expose himself to public view, under a penalty of not less than one dollar nor more than fifty dollars for each offense. (Burgdorf and Burgdorf, 1975, 863)

The thoroughness with which Americans internalized the concept of disability as a mark of inferiority can be seen in the case of Franklin D. Roosevelt, president of the United States, 1933–April 1945. Paralyzed from the waist down by a bout with polio in the 1920s, FDR cultivated a public image of physical fitness. He seldom used a wheelchair in public, and often when moving from one point to another in full view he moved between two aides who actually were carrying him as he lifted himself on their arms and appeared to be walking. Thus, even the leader of one of the most powerful nations in the world found it necessary to downplay his disability and avoid the stigma commonly attached to it (Gallagher 1985).

Set against Roosevelt's denial, the demands made on his administration by members of the League of the Physically Handicapped (highlighted in Part II) are striking. Refuting the stereotype of "helpless," they asserted their right to be treated by the federal government on the same basis as other citizens and in so doing called attention to heretofore unexamined prejudices and false assumptions about disability. League members were forerunners of the disability rights movement, which coalesced in the last half of the twentieth century to challenge old definitions of "normal" and to improve the social, economic, and physical environment for all Americans. As Lawrence and Matsuda have observed, "All human beings are vulnerable to disability, and all will experience at least part of our lives with physical challenges, including the vulnerability of infancy, illness, and aging" (Lawrence and Matsuda 1997, 261). In fighting for accessible buildings, public transportation, reasonable accommodations in the workplace, and learning environments that allow all students to reach their full potential, the disability rights movement fostered widespread benefits.

As documents in Parts IV and V demonstrate, Congress did not pass the legislation that first made such benefits conceivable until 1973 (Doc. 242). The landmark bill for disability rights—the Americans with Disabilities Act—took another seventeen years to become law (Doc. 333). The documents also indicate the degree to which interactions between civil rights and disability rights advocates were significant factors in the emergence of a politically effective lobby for the disabled. Starting from groundwork established by the civil rights movement, the disability rights movement of the 1970s and 1980s passed quickly through the transition from seeking the end of discrimination to calling for remedies bearing the stamp, if not the language, of affirmative action. As Lawrence and Matsuda have written:

The Americans with Disabilities Act is the most radical affirmative action program in the nation's history. It goes well beyond the principle of nondiscrimination, requiring businesses to spend money and change their operations to accommodate the disabled. This was an affirmative command: change business as usual, alter old concepts of merit, to include and welcome those who were previously kept out. (Lawrence and Matsuda 1997, 108)

By the 1990s the term "affirmative action" was a lightning rod for public controversy. Opponents associated it with "quotas," "preferential treatment," "reverse discrimination," and the victimization of white students and workers. They proved impervious to counterarguments that affirmative action plans that included goals and timetables were not quotas and that no law or court order had ever forced an employer or an admissions officer to hire, promote, or admit unqualified applicants. Those who attacked affirmative action also brushed aside the concept of systemic discrimination. While denouncing race- and gender-conscious measures as threats to standards of excellence in the academic and business worlds, they did not inquire into the effect on standards of the policy common within the white male establishment, summarized in the age-old saying "it's not what you know but whom you know."

At the same time that its foes nurtured the perception that affirmative action was rapidly displacing whites, particularly white men, on campuses and in workplaces, studies such as the Republican-initiated *Glass Ceiling Report* demonstrated that, as of 1995, white males constituted 43 percent of the workforce and held 95 percent of the top positions in politics, universities, the legal profession, and the media and on the boards of major corporations (Doc. 345).

Those who saw affirmative action as a necessary (though imperfect and not by itself sufficient) tool in the continuing struggle against persistent inequalities and injustices in American life invoked two concepts—"fairness" and "the general welfare." A parable attributed to California politician Willie Brown by the director of the Lawyers' Committee for Civil Rights in San Francisco, Eva Paterson, captures what they meant by fairness:

Brown . . . compared American history to a four hundred-year-old poker game in which one side always cheated. At some point, the cheating stopped, and one player had one chip and another had one million. Suddenly the player who had been cheating died, and his grandson took over and promised never to cheat again. "If you just keep playing poker, this person with one little chip is never going to catch up," reasoned Paterson, "unless some of those chips, which are ill-gotten gains, are given to the person who was cheated." (quoted in Cose 1997, 126–127)

Inherent in this way of viewing history is another concept, that of "unearned privilege." University of Texas journalism professor Robert Jensen has described this as "the dirty secret that we white people carry around with us every day . . . some of what we have is unearned." Where one lives, the quality of the schools one attends, the contacts one has ("whom you know . . ."), physical appearance, marital and parental status—all of these factors tend to favor whites over minorities, men over women, the able-bodied over the disabled in myriad and usually unnoticed ways. "When I seek admission to a university, apply for a job, or hunt for an apartment," wrote Jensen, ". . . almost all of the people evaluating me for those things look like me. . . . They see in me a reflection of themselves—and in a racist world that is an advantage. . . . My flaws are more easily forgiven because I am white . . ." (*Baltimore Sun,* July 19, 1998).

"Promoting the general welfare" is another fundamental purpose of affirmative action. As the population of the United States became increasingly diverse, employers and economic forecasters recognized the necessity of ensuring that all citizens have access to education, employment, professional development, and promotional opportunities. Their awareness in this regard was heightened by studies such as that published by the Hudson Institute, a conservative think tank. Released in 1987, *Workforce 2000* projected a future in which half of all workers would be women, and one-third would be people of color. As public dissatisfaction grew over rising welfare costs, other studies showed that billions of dollars per year could be saved in welfare payments if the estimated 82 percent of people with disabilities who were able to work were employed (*Congressional Record,* September 7, 1989, 10713). To advocates of affirmative action, the implications of such statistics seemed clear. Lawrence and Matsuda summarized them simply:

Using the strength of each of us, promoting multiple talents and virtues, bringing into the center those previously left out, is a recipe for economic revitalization as well as public mental health. (Lawrence and Matsuda 1997, 265)

However simple the words, the possible consequences of thinking in these terms were profound—more profound than some Americans were ready to accept. The poet and essayist Kathleen Norris has observed of religious prophecy that "it takes our measure with regard [to the status quo]: the discomfort we feel when the boundaries shift is the measure of our allegiance to the way things are" (Norris 1996, 214). The demands of affirmative action are not unlike those of the biblical prophets; they require the shifting of boundaries, and not everyone is willing for those shifts to occur. On the other hand, some who represent "those previously left out" believe that affirmative action measures have not gone far enough and that reparations (compensation for past losses) should be exacted—especially for those unearned privileges bought by the brutal system of slavery. Among supporters of the reparations concept is john a. powell of the American Civil Liberties Union, who maintains:

Mainstream approaches, such as affirmative action, will not, regardless of how well they are applied, begin to address the underlying inequalities confronting African Americans in our dominant white society. Playing fair now is not enough to put African Americans in a comparable position to accumulate wealth today. . . . (powell in Hartman 1997, 192)

Those who call for reparations estimate that the indebtedness of white Americans for the cumulative effects of slavery, segregation, and all other manifestations of race discrimination throughout U.S. history amounts to trillions of dollars. With regard to the feasibility of such sums ever being paid, they cite precedents such as the payments and official apology made by the U.S. government to Japanese Americans who were held in internment camps during World War II and the monetary compensation and apology made by the state of Florida to the African American families whose small town of Rosewood had been destroyed by racists in the 1920s. Richard America, author of *Paying the Social Debt: What White America Owes Black America*, asserts that the debt "should be paid primarily through investment in human capital—education and training over two to three generations. It should also be repaid through investments in targeted housing, capital formation and business creation" for African Americans (America, quoted in Hartman 1997, 195. See also Robinson 2000). When placed in this perspective, the reparations argument of the 1990s does not differ that much from the call of Martin Luther King Jr. and others in the 1960s for "a domestic Marshall Plan" (Doc. 127).

While reparations remain in the realm of speculation, affirmative action has a history of a little more than three decades. Evaluating the effects of that history is part of the job of those who study this book. The relative weight that readers give to the advances and to the disappointments in the long struggle for social justice leading up to affirmative action will help determine their views of it. Readers who perceive discrimination based on gender, race, and disability to be misguided aberrations in an otherwise sound democratic system may find affirmative action remedies to be excessive. If they interpret the substantial transformations that have occurred over time—for example, the abolition of slavery, the enfranchisement of the unenfranchised, the end of legalized segregation, the establishment of nationwide standards of access to public accommodations, transportation, education, and the workplace—as evidence of a national consensus on behalf of civil and human rights for everyone, they may question the need for additional measures that give special weight to such characteristics as disability, gender, and race.

On the other hand, readers who find that superior–inferior distinctions among groups are so deeply rooted in U.S. history that none of the aforementioned transformations have yet succeeded in uprooting them might regard affirmative action as a logical step. Those who are bothered by the degree to which such distinctions have historically been legitimated in American laws, court rulings, and public policies are likely to conclude that there was, and is, a need for race- and gender-conscious remedies and for mandates that require consciousness of the rights of disabled citizens.

While seeking to define their individual positions on affirmative action, readers should examine it from various points of view—those of the lawmakers and judges, those of monitors, managers, and enforcers, and those whose lives and livelihoods were changed by it. Each point of view reveals a different facet of any given affirmative action program. For example, from the perspective of the Equal Employment Opportunity Commission (EEOC) and the courts, the consent decrees initiated by the EEOC in the 1970s against large corporations (examined in Part IV) were major breakthroughs against racism and sexism. To many white, male employees they were violations—"discrimination in reverse." The women of both races and African American men on whose behalf the decrees were ordered were often frustrated and disappointed by the limited opportunities that the decrees actually provided. Depending on the corporation, such consent decrees brought substantive change over time, so that later generations of workers benefited more. In other cases enforcement was never strong enough for minorities and women to ever realize their intended benefits. In the light of such variability, some analysts have argued that "affirmative action cannot be deemed either good or bad. It all depends on the goals sought and the means chosen." This is the position adopted by legal scholar Erwin Chemerinsky, who insists that "discussions about affirmative action should not be at the general level concerning its overall desirability, but rather about specific practices under particular circumstances" (Higham, 101).

Thus, readers must give careful attention to factors of time and to the diversity of approaches and responses to affirmative action. As advocates regularly point out, the thirty-some years over which affirmative action has evolved represents a small fraction of the time in which injustices and inequities have been entrenched in American society. Pitted against this solid entrenchment, affirmative action has been an ever-changing mélange of laws, rulings, guidelines, decrees, and voluntary plans (overseen by various and sundry departments and agencies in both the public and private sectors). Even its strongest supporters have recognized that, lacking coordination and consistency, affirmative action is a flawed instrument. "Mend it; don't end it," urged President William Jefferson Clinton in July 1995 (Doc. 351). Five months later African American businessman Ward Connerly began a well-orchestrated and increasingly widespread campaign to outlaw affirmative action in state-by-state referenda (Doc. 363). Having followed the history of affirmative action from its nineteenth-century precedents to the end of the twentieth century, readers will be left to evaluate the respective merits of the Clinton and Connerly positions. They will also be prepared to answer the following basic questions:

- What is the most historically accurate definition of "affirmative action"?
- How and why did affirmative action originate?
- What are the connections and differences among
  1. social movements seeking equality?
  2. legal efforts aimed at ending intolerance and discrimination?
  3. public policies and practices of affirmative action?
- What path of development has affirmative action followed?
- Why does that path have so many twists, turns, branches, and byways?
- What are the implications of affirmative action for all racial and ethnic minorities?
- What are the implications of affirmative action for such groups as senior citizens and homosexuals?
- From where in U.S. society has affirmative action drawn support? From where has it drawn opposition?
- What events or trends have encouraged its support?
- What events or trends have strengthened its opponents?
- What changes in U.S. society can be attributed directly to affirmative action?

Part I

1854–1900:
Affirmations of, and Limitations on, the Citizenship Status of African Americans, Women, and the Disabled, in Legislative Action, Judicial Rulings, and Public Policy Decisions

"Affirmative action is the name given to an array of policies designed to create greater equality of opportunity in American society" (Knight and Wing 1995, 210). It rests on the assumption that the federal government bears a substantial measure of responsibility for designing and enforcing such policies. Across the centuries of U.S. history that assumption gained support among American policymakers; however, it has never enjoyed universal consent. A significant struggle between the executive and legislative branches of government occurred over this issue in the 1850s. In response to the ardent campaign of reformer Dorothea Dix on behalf of government support for the mentally ill, Congress passed a law that would have transferred land from the public domain to all states that agreed to sell the land and use the proceeds to build hospitals for "the indigent insane." President Franklin Pierce vetoed the law.

{d}DOCUMENT 1: Speech of Senator Solomon Foot Regarding a Bill for the Benefit of "Indigent Insane Persons," 1854

The bill was introduced by Senator Solomon Foot of Vermont. His arguments on its behalf included his rebuttal to opponents who maintained that federal action of the sort that he proposed was an intrusion on the rights and responsibilities of the individual states.

* * *

[T]his bill . . . has been pending before Congress for the last five or six years, and has passed each House by decisive majorities at different terms. . . .

By the last census, it appears there are over thirty thousand persons in the United States laboring under the most fearful and terrible of all inflictions, mental alienation or insanity. . . .

[T]o restore them, so far as it may be done, to reason, to usefulness, and to happiness, is no secondary object of public interest or of national concern. . . .

It is no argument against this proposition to tell us that it is the duty and the proper business of the States to provide for and to take care of their indigent insane. We do not propose to take from them that duty, but . . . rather to encourage and aid them in the discharge of it.

Source: The Congressional Globe 23, Pt. 1 (February 21, 1854): 455–456.

{d}DOCUMENT 2: Veto Message of President Franklin Pierce, May 3, 1854

Franklin Pierce's veto message reflected his ties to southern states' rights advocates and his belief in limiting the powers of the federal government.

* * *

I have been compelled to resist the deep sympathies of my own heart in favor of the humane purpose sought to be accomplished, and to overcome the reluctance with which I dissent from the conclusions of the two houses of Congress. . . .

[I]f Congress have power to make provision for the indigent insane . . . it has the same power to provide for the indigent who are not insane, and thus to transfer to the Federal Government the charge of all the poor in all the States. It has the same power to provide hospitals and other local establishments for the care and cure of every species of human infirmity. . . . The whole field of public beneficence is thrown open to the care and culture of the Federal Government. . . .

I cannot find any authority in the Constitution for making the Federal Government the great almoner of public charity throughout the United States.

Source: Veto Messages of the Presidents of the U.S. (49th Congress, 2d Session, Senate Misc. Document 53, 1886), Serial Set 2451: 211–213.

Supporters of the bill railed against Pierce's veto but were unable to gather the votes to override it. In historical perspective his action became "a landmark precedent limiting federal interventions in welfare matters for the next half century" (Lenihan 1976/1977, 22).

Providing the mentally disabled with opportunity for "usefulness and happiness" was but one item on the agenda of mid-nineteenth-century reformers. Abolishing slavery and extending the rights of citizenship to African Americans and women were the paramount causes of that era. Conflicts and controversies unresolved then remained at the root of the continuing struggle over affirmative action as the twentieth century drew to a close.

Although passage of the Thirteenth Amendment in 1865 rendered the brutal system of slavery unconstitutional, it did not establish rights of citizenship for former slaves, nor did it address the multiple forms of discrimination faced by all African Americans, including those who had not been enslaved. With the law of 1865 establishing a Bureau of Refugees, Freedmen, and Abandoned Lands and the Civil Rights Act of 1866, Congress sought to address these issues.

{r}DOCUMENT 3: The First Freedmen's Bureau Bill, March 3, 1865

With the Freedmen's Bureau Bill of March 1865, Congress established what has been called "the original federal civil rights agency" (Lowery and Marszalek 1992, 302). The bureau provided federally funded assistance—in the form of housing, employment, food, legal aid, and schooling—to white refugees who supported the Union and especially African Americans released from slavery. Although the first enabling legislation stipulated that assistance could include the distribution to refugees and freedmen of abandoned, confiscated, or purchased land in acre parcels, President Andrew Johnson returned most of such land to the original Confederate owners.

* * *

Be it enacted by the Senate and House of Representatives of the United States of America in Congress assembled, That there is hereby established in the War Department, to continue during the present war of rebellion, and for one year thereafter, a Bureau of Refugees, Freedmen, and Abandoned Lands. . . . The said bureau shall be under the management and control of a Commissioner to be appointed by the President. . . .

[T]he Commissioner . . . shall have authority to set apart, for the use of loyal refugees and freedmen, such tracts of land within the insurrectionary States as shall have been abandoned, or to which the United States shall have acquired title by confiscation or sale, or otherwise, and to every male citizen . . . there shall be assigned not more than forty acres of such land, and the person to whom it was so assigned shall be protected in the use and enjoyment of the land for . . . three years at an annual rent not exceeding six per centum upon the value of such land. . . . At the end of said term . . . the occupants of any parcels so assigned may purchase the land and receive such title thereto. . . .

Source: Appendix to the Congressional Globe 35, Pt. 2 (March 3, 1865): 141.

{r}DOCUMENT 4: Congressional Opponents of the Freedmen's Bureau Act of 1866

Reformers in Congress sought to extend the life of the Freedmen's Bureau with a new bill—the 1866 Freedmen's Bureau Act. By this time the end of the Civil War rendered references in the bill to white refugees virtually meaningless, and, as the first report of the director of the Freedmen's Bureau had made clear, nearly all bureau services were directed toward African Americans. Thus, the act was an example of race-conscious legislation. The debate that it occasioned in Congress has a familiar ring a century later in a society caught up in debates over affirmative action and controversies regarding "reverse discrimination." Representative Nathaniel G. Taylor (Republican from Tennessee) and Senator James A. McDougal (Democrat from California) were among the opponents of the act who resisted what Taylor called "class legislation."

* * *

Congressman Taylor: This sir, is what I call class legislation—legislation for a particular class of the blacks to the exclusion of all whites. . . .

Such partial legislation . . . seems to me to be in opposition to the plain spirit pervading nearly every section of the Constitution that congressional legislation should in its operation affect all alike.

Senator McDougal: This bill undertakes to make the negro in some respects their [whites'] superior . . . and gives them favors the poor white boy in the North cannot get.

Source: Congressional Globe 35, Pt. 1 (January 24 and January 31, 1866): 544, 401.

{r}DOCUMENT 5: President Andrew Johnson's Veto Message on the Freedmen's Bureau Bill of February 1866

Supporters of the 1866 act overcame the opposition and passed the bill only to have President Johnson veto it. He also spoke against its race-conscious provisions.

* * *

The third section of the bill authorizes a general and unlimited grant of support to the destitute and suffering refugees and freedmen and their wives and children. . . . The Congress of the United States has never heretofore . . . founded schools for any class of our own people. . . . It has never deemed itself authorized to expend the public money for the rent or purchase of homes for the thousands, not to say millions of the white race who are honestly toiling from day to day for their subsistence. A system for the support of indigent persons in the United States was never contemplated by the authors of the Constitution; nor can any good reason be advanced why, as a permanent establishment it should be founded for one class or color of our people more than for another. . . . The idea on which the slaves were assisted to freedom was that on becoming free they would be a self-sustaining population. Any legislation that shall imply that they are not expected to attain a self-sustaining condition must have a tendency injurious alike to their character and their prospects.

Source: The Papers of Andrew Johnson 10 (February–July 1866): 122–123.

{r}DOCUMENT 6: Reply of Senator Lyman Trumbull to President Johnson's Veto of the 1866 Freedmen's Bureau Bill

Senator Lyman Trumbull (Republican from Illinois) provided a point-by-point rebuttal to Johnson's message. With regard to the president's complaint that never before had the government made provisions for a particular class of citizens, Trumbull stressed the unique history of the enslavement of African Americans.

* * *

[N]ever before in the history of this Government have nearly four million people been emancipated from the most abject and degrading slavery ever imposed upon human beings; never before has the occasion arisen when it is necessary to provide for such large numbers of people thrown upon the bounty of the Government, unprotected and unprovided for. . . . Can we not provide for those among us who have been held in bondage all their lives, who have never been permitted to earn one dollar for themselves, who by the great constitutional amendment declaring freedom throughout the land, have been discharged from bondage to their masters who had hitherto provided for their necessities in consideration of their services?

Source: Congressional Globe 35, Pt. 1 (February 20, 1866): 939.

{r}DOCUMENT 7: The Civil Rights Act of 1866

Although civil rights supporters in Congress were temporarily thwarted by the president's veto of the Freedmen's Bureau Act, they succeeded in passing the Civil Rights Act of 1866 and, in this case, overriding another Johnson veto.

* * *

Be it enacted by the Senate and House of Representatives of the United States in Congress assembled, That all persons born in the United States and not subject to any foreign power, excluding Indians not taxed, are hereby declared to be citizens of the United States; and such citizens of every race and color, without regard to any previous condition of slavery or involuntary servitude, except as a punishment for crime whereof the party shall have been duly convicted, shall have the same right, in every State and Territory of the United States, to make and enforce contracts, to sue, be parties, and give evidence, to inherit, purchase, lease, sell, hold, and convey real and personal property, and to full and equal benefit of all laws and proceedings for the security of person and property as is enjoyed by white citizens, and shall be subject to like punishments, pains, and penalties, and to none other, any law, statute, ordinance, regulation or custom to the contrary notwithstanding.

Source: U.S. Statutes at Large 4 (April 9, 1866): 27.

Congress revised and passed a second Freedmen's Bureau Bill, which Johnson again vetoed, arguing against special treatment for "any favored class of citizens." This time the votes were marshaled to pass the bill over his veto.

The same lawmakers who supported the Freedmen's Bureau and the Civil Rights Act of 1866 were responsible for passage of the Fourteenth Amendment to the U.S. Constitution. There is evidence that they saw the amendment as a way "to provide a constitutional basis for the Freedmen's Bureau Act" (Schnapper 1985, 785). Contemporary supporters of affirmative action cite this historical context as evidence that the Fourteenth Amendment was intended from the beginning to uphold race-conscious remedies as a part of "equal protection" (Schnapper 1985, 785).

{r}DOCUMENT 8: The Fourteenth Amendment to the Constitution of the United States, 1866

Disregarding the comprehensive language of the Civil Rights Act of 1866 was a ruling by Justice Noah Swayne in a case involving the rights of African Americans to testify in court. Swayne ruled that the 1866 act conferred "only certain civil rights" on African Americans leaving political rights open to question. This reasoning and the Black Codes, which southern states had substituted for slave codes, prompted civil rights supporters to seek a fourteenth amendment (Higginbotham 1978, 77–78, 81). The second sentence of Section 1 (the Equal Protection Clause) would become a basic point of reference in future affirmative action cases.

* * *

Section 1. All persons born or naturalized in the United States and subject to the jurisdiction thereof, are citizens of the United States and of the State wherein they reside. No State shall make or enforce any law which shall abridge the privileges or immunities of citizens of the United States; nor shall any State deprive any person of life, liberty or property, without due process of law, nor deny to any person within its jurisdiction the equal protection of the laws.

Source: Constitution of the United States.

{r}DOCUMENT 9: The Fifteenth Amendment to the Constitution of the United States, 1869

Reconstruction efforts to affirm and protect the citizenship rights of African Americans also included the Fifteenth Amendment, promising the right to vote to African American men.

* * *

Section 1. The right of citizens of the United States to vote shall not be denied or abridged by the United States or by any State on account of race, color, or previous condition of servitude.

Source: Constitution of the United States.

{d}DOCUMENT 10: *Davenport v. Ruckman*, New York Court of Appeals, January 1868

Although President Pierce's 1854 veto put federal action with regard to the disabled "on hold" through the end of the nineteenth century, state courts and legislatures did address their status from time to time. Of particular significance was a ruling by Chief Justice Hunt in the New York Court of Appeals in 1868.

The 1868 New York decision, *Davenport v. Ruckman*, dealt with the case of Clara A. Davenport, who was partially blind. She was injured when she fell into an excavated area outside a building on which Elisha Ruckman held the lease. She sued both the city of New York, which was responsible for the excavation, and Mr. Ruckman, maintaining that the site should have been barricaded to prevent accidents. Attorneys for the city and Ruckman argued that Davenport should be found negligent for walking outside without an escort. When a lower court jury decided the case in favor of Davenport, city officials and Ruckman carried it to the state court of appeals, where Davenport's position was upheld.

* * *

The streets and sidewalks are for the benefit of all conditions of people, and all have the right, in using them, to assume that they are in good condition, and to regulate their conduct upon that assumption. A person may walk or drive in the darkness of the night, relying upon the belief that the corporation has performed its duty and that the street or the walk is in a safe condition. He walks by a faith justified by law, and if his faith is unfounded and he suffers an injury, the party in fault must respond in damages. So, one whose sight is dimmed by age, or a nearsighted person whose range of vision was always imperfect, or one whose sight has been injured by disease, is each entitled to the same rights, and may act upon the same assumption.

Source: 37 New York, 568 at 573 (1868).

{d}DOCUMENT 11: Jacobus tenBroek, Looking Back on the 1868 *Davenport* case

A century later the distinguished legal scholar Jacobus tenBroek, who was himself blind, interpreted, from the standpoint of the disabled, *Davenport* and a substantial body of similar cases occurring into the mid-twentieth century.

* * *

The discussion [in *Davenport v. Ruckman* and similar cases] . . . proved a valuable starting point for the courts in seeing that the duty of the defendant is not confined to the able-bodied. Its . . . role was thus historic in . . . imposing upon cities and abutting property owners an obligation to maintain the streets, highways, bridges and other public places in a condition safe for the disabled traveler.

Source: tenBroek 1966b, 869, 870.

{r/g}DOCUMENT 12: Elizabeth Cady Stanton, February 1869

The language of the Fourteenth and Fifteenth Amendments was cause for bitter disappointment on the part of some women's rights advocates. The word "male" in "Section Two" of the Fourteenth Amendment—which reduced the number of congressional representatives to which a state was entitled if that state "in any way abridged" the citizenship rights of any eligible male voter—raised the question of whether women were citizens. The Fifteenth Amendment, by listing "race, color, or previous condition of servitude" and remaining mute on "sex," was equally troubling to one segment of women suffragists, of whom Elizabeth Cady Stanton was representative.

* * *

The proposed amendment for "manhood suffrage" not only rouses woman's prejudices against the negro, but on the other hand his contempt and hostility toward her as an equal. . . . the republican cry of "manhood suffrage" creates an antagonism between black men and all women, that will culminate in fearful outrages on womanhood, especially in the southern states. While we fully appreciate the philosophy that every extension of rights prepares the way for greater freedom to new classes and hastens the day for liberty to all, we, at the same time, see that the immediate effect of class enfranchisement results in greater tyranny and abuse of those who have no voice in the government.

Source: Elizabeth Cady Stanton, "Women and Black Men," *The Revolution* 3, no. 6 (February 11, 1869).

{r/g}DOCUMENT 13: Susan B. Anthony, May 1869

The heated debate over whether victims of racism and victims of sexism are equally entitled to legal protection continued unresolved for more than a century and was often characterized by racist assumptions such as those implied by Stanton and in the following remarks by her close ally, Susan B. Anthony.

* * *

The old anti-slavery school says women must stand back and wait until negroes should be recognized. But we say if you will not give the whole loaf of suffrage to the entire people, give it to the most intelligent first. If intelligence, justice, and morality are to have precedence in the Government, let the question of woman be brought up first and that of negro last.

Source: Susan B. Anthony, Debate during Anniversary of American Equal Rights Association, May 12, 13, 1869, in *History of Woman Suffrage*, edited by Elizabeth Cady Stanton, Susan B. Anthony, and Matilda Joslyn Gage, vol. 2 (Rochester, NY: Charles Mann Printing, 1881): 383.

{r/g}DOCUMENT 14: Frederick Douglass, May 1869

Before and after the era of the Reconstruction amendments, abolitionist, orator, editor, and political spokesman Frederick Douglass advocated the vote for women. Indeed, he had played a crucial role in the decision to include suffrage in the declaration of the first woman's rights convention at Seneca Falls, New York, in 1848. But in 1869 political and social realities required, in his view, that precedence be given to establishing voting rights for African American men.

* * *

When women, because they are women, are dragged from their homes and hung upon lamp-posts; when their children are torn from their arms and their brains dashed to the pavement; when they are objects of insult and outrage at every turn; when they are in danger of having their homes burnt down over their heads; when their children are not allowed to enter schools; then they will have an urgency to obtain the ballot equal to black men.

Source: Quoted in Benjamin Quarles, "Frederick Douglass and the Woman's Rights Movement," *Journal of Negro History* 25, no. 1 (January 1940): 41.

{r/g}DOCUMENT 15: Frances Ellen Watkins Harper, 1869

Sharing the views of Douglass and equally outspoken against those of the Anthony–Stanton faction was African American abolitionist and author Frances Ellen Watkins Harper.

* * *

When it was a question of race, she [Harper] let the lesser question of sex go. But the white women all go for sex, letting race occupy a minor position. . . . If the nation could handle only one question, she would not have the black women put a single straw in the way, if only the men of the race could obtain what they wanted.

Source: Frances Ellen Watkins Harper paraphrased in *History of Woman Suffrage*, edited by Elizabeth Cady Stanton, Susan B. Anthony, and Matilda Joslyn Gage, vol. 2 (Rochester, NY: Charles Mann Printing, 1881): 391, 392.

{g}DOCUMENT 16: U.S. Government Expenses Appropriation, July 12, 1870

Congress took up aspects of woman's rights beyond the vote in the era of Reconstruction. To legislate "equal pay for equal work irrespective of sex" was the purpose of a rider attached to an appropriations bill debated in both houses of Congress in the summer of 1870.

* * *

Be it enacted by the Senate and House of Representatives of the United States of America in Congress assembled, That the following sums be, and the same are hereby, appropriated . . . for the fiscal year ending the thirtieth of June, eighteen hundred and seventy-one. . . . [The rider followed a list of appropriations for each government department.]

Sec. 2. *And be it further enacted*, That the heads of the several departments are hereby authorized to appoint female clerks, who may be found to be competent and worthy, to any of the grades of clerkships known to the law, in the respective departments, with the compensation belonging to the class to which they may be appointed.

Source: U.S. Statutes at Large 16 (July 12, 1870): 230, 250.

{g}DOCUMENT 17: Speech in the House of Representatives Supporting Equal Pay for Equal Work, Congressman Charles W. Willard of Vermont, June 11, 1870

Among the defenders of women's right to equal pay was Representative Charles W. Willard of Vermont.

* * *

I hold that this government owes it to women of the country . . . that they shall no longer be held in a subordinate position and treated as inferiors; that it shall say to them there shall be hereafter no position under this Government for which they are fitted which shall not be open to them equally with men; that when they do the work of any of their brothers in any office under the Government, they shall have the same pay their brothers have; that their brains are worth as much, that their labor, their energy, their industry are all worth as much as the labor, the industry, the energy and the brains of anybody. . . . If the women of the country had the ballot today—as I believe they ought to have it—then this House would be found voting unanimously for this proposition.

Source: The Congressional Globe 42, Pt. 5 (June 11, 1870): 4355.

{r}DOCUMENT 18: "Petition from Colored Citizens" Presented by Charles Sumner to the U.S. Senate, December 19, 1873

For African Americans, full citizenship implied equal treatment in public places and on public conveyances. In 1870 Massachusetts senator Charles Sumner introduced a bill that was intended to protect African Americans' rights in public accommodations, as well as guarantee their right to serve on juries and have equal access to public education. It provoked bitter debate in both houses of Congress.

African Americans, through various organized efforts, including a national convention movement, pressured politicians who were in sympathy with them to gain passage of a civil rights act. The petition presented by Charles Sumner in the following excerpt was part of a flood of petitions from African Americans considered by Congress in the early 1870s.

* * *

MR. SUMNER. I also offer the memorial of the national convention of colored persons recently assembled here in Washington, praying to be protected in their civil rights. . . . It sets forth the denial of rights to which they are now subjected, the indignities to which they are exposed in travel, in the school-room, in public institutions, and in the court-house through the denial of an impartial jury; and it asks for the adoption of a thorough civil rights law.

Source: Congressional Record 2, Pt. 1 (December 19, 1873): 325.

{r}DOCUMENT 19: Congressmen Harris and Ransier on the Proposed Civil Rights Act, January 5, 1874

The following exchange between the white Democratic representative from Virginia, John Harris, and the African American Republican representative from South Carolina, Alonzo Ransier, suggests the degree of racial antagonism present in the debates on Sumner's bill.

* * *

Mr. HARRIS. [T]his bill . . . is based upon the purpose, the theory, of the absolute equality of the races. It seeks to enforce by law a doctrine which is not accepted by the minds nor received in the hearts of the people of the United States—that the negro in all things is the equal of the white man. And I say there is not one gentleman upon this floor who can honestly say he really believes that the colored man is created his equal.

Mr. RANSIER. I can.

Mr. HARRIS of Virginia. Of course you can; but I am speaking to the white men of the House; and, Mr. Speaker, I do not wish to be interrupted again by him. . . .

I know the objection that will occur to the mind of every gentleman on the other side of the House. . . . They will say this is prejudice—unjust prejudice. Admit that it is prejudice, yet the fact exists, and you as members of Congress and legislators are bound to respect that prejudice. It was born in the children of the South; born in our ancestors, and born in your ancestors in Massachusetts—that the colored man was inferior to the white.

Mr. RANSIER. I deny that.

Mr. HARRIS, of Virginia. I do not allow you to interrupt me. Sit down; I am talking to white men; I am talking to gentlemen.

Source: Congressional Record 2, Pt. 1 (January 5, 1874): 376, 377.

{r}DOCUMENT 20: Congressman Ransier on the Entitlement of African Americans to Equal Rights

Later, during the same debate, Congressman Ransier minced no words in describing the entitlement of African Americans to full equality. In the process he indicated his contempt for the prejudice of the racists among his colleagues.

* * *

Mr. RANSIER. . . . Five millions of people, citizens of our country who bode you no evil, suffer to-day the most humiliating discriminations, in the matter of the most ordinary privileges attaching to them as human beings, because of their color and previous condition of imposed servitude. . . . [T]hese people, one of whom I am, are a part of the nation. . . . They have contributed largely toward her wealth and bared their breasts in the face of her enemies, foreign and domestic. . . . They have established their loyalty beyond dispute; have given evidence of their fitness for political rights, and will be satisfied with nothing short of their equal civil rights, such as are enjoyed by other citizens. . . .

The colored people ask of the country no peculiar privileges. But it is feared by the gentleman from Kentucky and those he represents in this matter of civil rights, that if we colored people are put upon a plane of civil equality with them in law—going into the same schools, hotels, and places of amusement, and into the jury-box and the cemetery—we, by virtue of our intellectual superiority and our moral and physical force, if not numbers, will absorb the race to which he and they belong. This is the logical deduction from the apprehensions to which he has given expression. Let me thank him in the name of the colored people of the country, for the compliment he has, perhaps unconsciously, paid them; but I must deny that that would necessarily follow civil equality in this country, or that there is any serious intention on our part to thus destroy . . . the race to which he belongs. We are known, Mr. Speaker, to be too magnanimous for that. . . .

The bugbear of "social equality" is used by the enemies of political and civil equality for the colored man in place of argument. There is not an intelligent white man or black man who does not know that that is the sheerest nonsense; and I would have it distinctly understood that I would most certainly oppose the passage of the pending bill . . . if I believed that its operation would be to force upon me the company of the member from Kentucky, for instance, or any one else. . . .

Mr. Speaker, all [we] ask is an equal chance in the race of life, and the same privileges and protection meted out to other classes of people in our land. We cannot engage in the industrial pursuits, educate our children, defend our lives and property in the courts, receive the comforts provided in our common conveyance necessary to our wives and little ones . . . and in short engage in the "pursuit of happiness" as rational beings, when we are circumscribed within the narrowest possible limits on every hand, disowned, spit upon, and outraged in a thousand ways.

Source: Congressional Record 2, Pt. 1 (January 5, 1874): 382, 383.

{r}DOCUMENT 21: The Civil Rights Act of 1875, Enacted March 1, 1875

Opponents of the act continued to denounce it as unwarranted federal interference and unconstitutional imposition of social equality. The outcome of long debate was a considerably weaker bill than the act originally proposed by Charles Sumner. The section on education was entirely removed. Voted into law a year after Sumner's death, the act of 1875 would be nullified by Supreme Court rulings in the civil rights cases of 1883 (Doc. 24).

* * *

Be it enacted by the Senate and the House of Representatives of the United States of America in Congress assembled, That all persons within the jurisdiction of the United States shall be entitled to the full and equal enjoyment of the accommodations, advantages, facilities and privileges of [public establishments, transportation, and entertainment] subject only to the conditions and limitations established by law, and applicable alike to citizens of every race and color, regardless of any previous condition of servitude.

Source: U.S. Statutes at Large 28, Pt. 3 (March 1, 1875): 336.

{g}DOCUMENT 22: *Minor v. Happersett*, U.S. Supreme Court, 1875

In the early 1870s women began to test their status under existing laws by attempting to vote and taking action in court when the attempts were blocked. The best-known case was that of Susan B. Anthony, who registered, voted, and was arrested and tried in Rochester, New York. Anthony's pretrial lecture tours and the drama of the trial itself ended in anticlimax with a verdict of "guilty" (for willfully defying the state law, which prohibited women from voting) and a fine, which the plaintiff never paid. Of more consequence was the case brought by Francis Minor and his wife, Virginia, against a registrar in St. Louis who had blocked Mrs. Minor's attempt to vote. Her husband, a lawyer, argued that by declaring "all persons born or naturalized in the United States . . ." to be citizens, the Constitution automatically conferred the right to vote on women, and state laws such as the one invoked by the registrar in St. Louis could not contravene that constitutional right. The lower courts did not agree and were upheld by the Supreme Court (Hoff 1991, 169–172). Chief Justice Morrison Waite delivered the unanimous decision.

* * *

There is no doubt that women may be citizens. They are persons, and by the fourteenth amendment . . . are expressly declared to be "citizens of the United States. . . ." But . . . it did not need this amendment to give them that position. . . .

[S]ex has never been made one of the elements of citizenship in the United States. . . . The same laws precisely apply to both [men and women]. The fourteenth amendment did not affect the citizenship of women any more than it did of men. . . .

[I]t cannot for a moment be doubted that if it had been intended to make all citizens of the United States voters, the framers of the Constitution would not have left it to implication. . . .

For nearly ninety years the people have acted upon the idea that the Constitution when it conferred citizenship, did not necessarily confer the right of suffrage. . . .

If the law [against women voting] is wrong it ought to be changed; but the power for that is not with us.

Source: 88 U.S. 162 at 165, 178 (1874).

{g}DOCUMENT 23: Declaration of Rights, Delivered by Susan B. Anthony, 1876

In the wake of her own case and the *Minor* decision, Susan B. Anthony sounded a resounding note of outrage on the occasion of the U.S. Centennial.

* * *

The history of our country the past hundred years has been a series of assumptions and usurpations of power over woman in direct opposition to the principles of just government. . . .

[T]he violation of these fundamental principles [include] . . .

Unequal codes for men and women. . . . The fact of sex, not the quantity or quality of work, in most cases decides the pay and position. . . .

Special legislation for woman has placed us in a most anomalous position. . . . In some States women may enter the law schools and practice in the courts; in others they are forbidden. In some universities girls enjoy equal educational advantages with boys, while many of the proudest institutions in the land deny them admittance, though the sons of China, Japan and Africa are welcomed there. . . . [O]ur most sacred rights have been made the football of legislative caprice. . . .

We ask justice, we ask equality, we ask that all the civil and political rights that belong to citizens of the United States, be guaranteed to us and our daughters forever.

Source: "1876 Declaration of Rights," in *History of Woman Suffrage*, edited by Elizabeth Cady Stanton, Susan B. Anthony, Matilda J. Gage, vol. 3 (New York: Fowler & Wells, 1881): 31–34.

{r}DOCUMENT 24: Civil Rights Cases of 1883

The civil rights cases of 1883 reached the Supreme Court in that year as a set of appeals from suits filed by African Americans under the Civil Rights Acts of 1875 in five different states (Kansas, Missouri, California, New York, and Tennessee). In each case the plaintiff had been denied access to public accommodations. The Supreme Court ruled against all of them and against the Civil Rights Act of 1875. Defining access to public accommodations as a "social," as opposed to a civil, right, the Court argued that Congress did not have the power to legislate "private rights." The author of the Court ruling, Justice Joseph Bradley, suggested that blacks were asking for legal favors. Dissenting from the majority, Justice John Marshall Harlan championed civil rights law as constitutional and essential.

* * *

A. Justice Joseph Bradley

It is obvious that the primary and important question in all the cases is the constitutionality of [the Civil Rights Act of 1875]. . . .

Has Congress constitutional power to make such a law? . . .

On the whole, we are of opinion that no countenance of authority for the passage of the law in question can be found in either the thirteenth or fourteenth amendment of the constitution; and no other ground of authority for its passage being suggested, it must necessarily be declared void. . . .

When a man has emerged from slavery, and by the aid of beneficent legislation has shaken off the inseparable concomitants of the state, there must be some stage in the progress of his elevation when he takes the rank of a mere citizen, and ceases to be the special favorite of the laws, and when his rights as a citizen, or a man, are to be protected in the ordinary modes by which other men's rights are protected.

B. Dissent of Justice John Marshall Harlan

My brethren say that when a man has emerged from slavery, and by the aid of beneficent legislation has shaken off the inseparable concomitants of the state, there must be some stage in the progress of his elevation when he takes the rank of a mere citizen and ceases to be the special favorite of the laws. . . . It is, I submit, scarcely just to say that the colored race has been the special favorite of the laws. What the nation, through congress, has sought to accomplish in reference to that race is, what had already been done in every state in the Union for the white race, to secure and protect rights belonging to them as freemen and citizens; nothing more. . . . The difficulty has been to compel a recognition of their legal right to take that rank. . . . At every step in this direction the nation has been confronted with class tyranny. . . . To-day it is the colored race which is denied . . . rights fundamental in their freedom and citizenship. At some future time it may be some other race that will fall under the ban. . . . The supreme law of the land has decreed that no authority shall be exercised in this country upon the basis of discrimination, in respect of civil rights, against freemen and citizens because of their race, color, or previous condition of servitude. To that decree . . . every

one must bow, whatever may have been, or whatever now are, his individual views as to the wisdom or policy, either of the recent changes
in the fundamental law, or of the legislation which has been enacted to
give them effect.

For the reasons stated I feel constrained to withhold my assent to the
opinion of the court.

Source: 109 U.S. 3 at 9, 25, 26, 61–62 (1883).

{r}DOCUMENT 25: *Plessy v. Ferguson,* 1896

The erosion of the rights and protections legislated by Congress in
relation to African Americans during Reconstruction was completed in
the 1896 Supreme Court ruling on *Plessy v. Ferguson,* which validated
"separate but equal" racial policies and practices. The subject of the
case was a challenge to segregated transportation raised by Homer
Plessy, described by the Court as "seven-eighths Caucasian and one-
eighth African blood." He had argued that "the reputation of being
white" was a valuable form of property, "the masterkey to the golden
door of opportunity." While denying that segregation imposed an inferior status on African Americans, the Court majority responded that
he was not legally entitled to such "property." Justice John Marshall
Harlan, in a famous dissent, argued otherwise.

* * *

A. Majority Opinion Delivered by Justice Henry Billings Brown

It is claimed by the plaintiff . . . that, in an [*sic*] mixed community, the
reputation of belonging to the dominant race, in this instance the white
race, is "property," in the same sense that a right of action or of inheri-
tance is property. Conceding this to be so, for the purposes of this case,
we are unable to see how this statute deprives him of, or in any way
affects his right to, such property. If he be a white man, and assigned to
a colored coach, he may have his action for damage against the company
for being deprived of his so-called "property." Upon the other hand, if
he be a colored man, and be so assigned, he has been deprived of no
property, since he is not lawfully entitled to the reputation of being a
white man. . . .

We consider the underlying fallacy of the plaintiff's argument to consist in the assumption that the enforced separation of the two races
stamps the colored race with a badge of inferiority. If this be so, it is not
by reason of anything found in the act, but solely because the colored

race chooses to put that construction upon it. . . . The argument also assumes that social prejudices may be overcome by legislation, and that equal rights cannot be secured to the negro except by an enforced commingling of the two races. We cannot accept this proposition. If the two races are to meet upon terms of social equality, it must be a voluntary consent of individuals . . . Legislation is powerless to eradicate racial instincts or to abolish distinctions based upon physical differences, and the attempt to do so can only result in accentuating the difficulties of the present situation. If the civil and political rights of both races be equal one cannot be inferior to the other civilly or politically. If one race be inferior to the other socially, the constitution of the United States cannot put them upon the same plane.

B. Dissent by Justice John Marshall Harlan

The white race deems itself to be the dominant race in this country. And so it is, in prestige, in achievements, in education, in wealth and in power. So, I doubt not, it will continue to be for all time, if it remains true to its great heritage and holds fast to the principles of constitutional liberty. But in the view of the constitution, in the eye of the law, there is in this country no superior, dominant ruling class of citizens. There is no caste here. Our Constitution is color-blind. . . . The law regards man as man, and takes no account of his surroundings or of his color when his civil rights as guaranteed by the supreme law of the land are involved. It is therefore to be regretted that this high tribunal . . . has reached the conclusion that it is competent for a State to regulate the enjoyment by citizens of their civil rights solely upon the basis of race. . . .

We boast of the freedom enjoyed by our people above all other peoples. But it is difficult to reconcile that boast with a state of law which, practically, puts the brand of servitude and degradation upon a large class of our fellow citizens, our equals before the law. The thin disguise of "equal" accommodations for passengers in railroad coaches will not mislead any one, nor atone for the wrong this day done.

Source: 163 U.S. 537 at 551, 559, 562 (1896).

Part II

1901–1963: "Affirmative Action," Early Usage of the Term and Foreshadowings in Executive Orders, Judicial Rulings, and State and Federal Laws

Issues unresolved in the Reconstruction era persisted into the twentieth century. Two such issues concerned the role of the federal government in promoting social reforms and the methods used to attack injustices. How extensively should the government intervene in promoting "liberty and justice for all"? Should laws and public policies be revised to ensure that disadvantaged groups will be treated no differently than all other members of society? Or do the historically disadvantaged need to be addressed as distinct classes, entitled to one form or another of special protection? Between the Progressive era of Theodore Roosevelt and the New Frontier of John F. Kennedy, Americans repeatedly confronted these questions, and their courts, legislatures, and executives wrestled with them.

PROGRESSIVISM AND WORLD WAR I

DOCUMENT 26: The Republican Roosevelt (U.S. President 1901–1909) on Government Leadership, Which Proceeds "Actively and Affirmatively"

"Progressivism" emerged around the turn of the century. Progressives attacked corruption and supported laws to protect exploited groups, especially women and children. President Theodore Roosevelt was a leader in this movement. Although his version of reform was tainted by racism and antagonism toward more radical reformers, he, nonetheless, espoused a view of active government leadership that contrasted sharply with "let alone" practices of earlier eras.

* * *

My view was that every executive officer, and above all every executive officer in high position [in government] was a steward of the people bound actively and affirmatively to do all he could for the people.

Source: Theodore Roosevelt, an Autobiography (New York: Da Capo Paperback, 1913): 372.

{g}DOCUMENT 27: *Muller v. Oregon*, 1908

Woman's rights activists contributed to Progressive reform as they continued the quest for a federal suffrage amendment and undertook new economic initiatives, including laws establishing maximum hours and other protections for women workers. The constitutionality of these laws was called into question by a Supreme Court ruling in the 1905 case *Lochner v. New York*, when the Court struck down a law limiting the working hours of male bakery employees.

In 1908 the Supreme Court ruled on the case of Curt Muller, an employer who ordered female employees to work beyond the ten-hour limit mandated by Oregon law. The Oregon decision, based on a view of women as a separate class of workers, would influence employment practices until it was invalidated by Title VII of the Civil Rights Act of 1964 (Docs. 121, 122) (Hoff 1991, 194–201).

* * *

[H]istory discloses . . . that woman has always been dependent upon man. . . . She is properly placed in a class by herself, and legislation designed for her protection may be sustained, even when like legislation is not necessary for men, and could not be sustained.

Source: 208 U.S. 412 at 422 (1908).

{r}DOCUMENT 28: Proceedings of the National Negro Conference, 1909

At the same time that women were pressing for political and economic justice, African Americans continued their struggle against racism and denials of their citizenship rights. W. E. B. Du Bois emerged as a spokesman for vigorous and forthright pursuit of those rights. He instigated the Niagra Movement in 1905, when he and other African American leaders gathered and encouraged protest against racism in all its manifestations. Four years later, at their founding conference, Du Bois and an interracial team of leaders for the National Association for the Advancement of Colored People (NAACP) demanded government action on behalf of racial justice.

* * *

As first and immediate steps toward remedying . . . national wrongs so full of peril for the whites as well as the blacks of all sections, we demand of Congress and the Executive:

(1) That the Constitution be strictly enforced and the civil rights guaranteed under the Fourteenth Amendment be secured impartially to all.

(2) That there be equal educational opportunities for all and in all the States and that public school expenditure be the same for the Negro and the white child.

(3) That in accordance with the Fifteenth Amendment the right of the Negro to the ballot on the same terms as other citizens be recognized in every part of the country.

Source: Quoted in *Black Protest Thought in the Twentieth Century*, edited by August Meier, Eliot Rudwick, and Francis Broderick (Indianapolis: Bobbs-Merrill Educational, 1971): 66.

{r}DOCUMENT 29: The *Chicago Defender*, August 1919

U.S. entry into World War I accelerated change for all Americans, but especially African Americans and women. The war increased the "Great Migration" of African Americans leaving the South in pursuit of northern jobs. Although there were no "White" and "Colored" signs in northern cities, churches and social clubs were segregated, and housing codes relegated them to specific areas, where city services were scarce. Following the war, job openings rapidly declined. In addition, African Americans were repeatedly the targets of violence on the part of whites who felt they were competing for jobs and housing. In 1919 more than twenty cities experienced racial outbreaks. The worst occurred in Chicago. The *Chicago Defender* observed that a new generation of African Americans was prepared to fight back against racist attacks.

* * *

The *Chicago Defender*, edited by and for negroes, frankly admits that . . . : "The younger generation of black men are not content to move along the line of least resistance, as did their sires. . . . Industrially our position has been benefited by the war. Socially it has grown decidedly worse. On all sides we have been made to feel the humiliating pressure of the white man's prejudice."

Source: Quoted in *The Literary Digest* (August 9, 1919): 11.

{g}DOCUMENT 30: War Labor Conference Board Report, March 1918

The economic effects of World War I were not as extensive with regard to sex and gender. Nonetheless, war industries recruited women workers to "nontraditional" jobs, and they advocated equal compensation—but without passing equal pay laws.

* * *

If it shall become necessary to employ women on work ordinarily performed by men, they must be allowed equal pay for equal work.

Source: War Labor Conference Board Report, March 1918, quoted in Jo Freeman, *The Politics of Women's Liberation* (New York: David McKay, 1975): 175.

THE 1920s

{g}DOCUMENT 31: Mary Anderson on Sex Discrimination against the Women's Bureau, 1920s

One consequence of the use of women in war industries was the creation of special agencies such as the Women's Bureau, for which Congress voted permanent status in 1920. Its first director was Mary Anderson, who later recalled how sex discrimination bedeviled the very agency charged with advancing economic opportunity for women.

* * *

In all the phases of our work during the whole time I was with the Women's Bureau we had to be on the alert to fight discriminations against women. . . . Sometimes these discriminations hit us in the bureau itself. . . .

One of the most serious situations we had to face came in the very early days, . . . when Senator Reed Smoot of Utah put a proviso in our appropriation bill saying that only two people on the staff could be paid more than two thousand dollars a year. He said that no woman on earth was worth more than that. I was aghast at this, knowing how it would affect us, because we had several people, our most valued workers, who were paid more than two thousand dollars. I went to Mr. Smoot myself. . . . He laid his hand on my shoulder and said, "You needn't worry. You won't lose anyone. After the war we'll have so much unemployment they'll take the positions at any price." As it happened, he was right.

Source: Mary Anderson, *Woman at Work, the Autobiography of Mary Anderson as Told to Mary N. Winslow* (Minneapolis: University of Minnesota Press, 1951): 151.

{g}DOCUMENT 32: The Nineteenth Amendment (Passed June 4, 1919, Ratified August 18, 1920)

The senator's intransigence on the matter of fair wages would not have surprised veterans of the woman's suffrage movement, who had battled male intransigence on the vote for some fifty-two years. Two months after Congress approved the Women's Bureau bill, the Nineteenth Amendment affirming that voting right was finally ratified.

* * *

The right of citizens of the United States to vote shall not be denied or abridged by the United States or by any State on account of sex.

Source: Constitution of the United States.

{d}DOCUMENT 33: Vocational Rehabilitation Act Amendment of July 11, 1919

As a result of World War I, Congress established another new federal agency, a bureau for veterans, with emphasis on rehabilitation for those disabled by the war. Because medicine had improved, wounded soldiers survived World War I in unprecedented numbers. In response, Congress passed new laws, including vocational rehabilitation acts and a veteran bureau's bill. The original vocational rehabilitation act of 1918 was amended a year later.

* * *

Every person . . . having a disability incurred, increased or aggravated while a member of [the armed forces], or later developing a disability contracted while serving with such forces, and who in the opinion of the federal Board for Vocational Education is in need of vocational rehabilitation . . . shall be furnished . . . such course of vocational rehabilitation as the [Federal Board for Vocational Education] shall prescribe and provide.

Source: Quoted in *Annual Report of the Director, United States Veterans Bureau for Fiscal Year Ended June 30, 1922* (Washington, DC: U.S. Government Printing Office, 1922): 4.

{d}DOCUMENT 34: Public Law No. 47: An Act to Establish a Veterans' Bureau, August 9, 1921

In June 1920 Congress extended the federal coverage of disability programs to citizens injured in industrial settings. On August 9, 1921,

Congress established the U.S. Veterans' Bureau. Up to this point veterans had to shuttle among three separate agencies for treatment and settlement of claims. The Veterans' Bureau consolidated these functions.

* * *

There is hereby established an independent bureau under the President to be known as the Veterans' Bureau, the director of which shall be appointed by the President.

Source: Statutes at Large 42 (August 9, 1921): 147.

{g}DOCUMENT 35: *Adkins v. Children's Hospital,* April 19, 1923

Just as the post–Civil War amendments provided an essential foundation for, but did not guarantee equal opportunity for, African Americans, so the Nineteenth Amendment provided means for women to pursue equality but did not in itself eliminate gendered inequalities. Just as the Supreme Court had argued in the civil rights cases of 1883 (Doc. 24) that it was time for African Americans to assume "the rank of a mere citizen," so a later group of justices argued in 1923 in *Adkins v. Children's Hospital* that women were now nearly equal to men and no longer required the protection of a gender-based minimum wage law.

* * *

In view of the great—not to say revolutionary—changes which have taken place . . . in the contractual, political and civil status of women, culminating in the Nineteenth Amendment, it is not unreasonable to say that these differences [between the sexes] have now come almost, if not quite, to the vanishing point. . . . [W]e cannot accept the doctrine that women of mature age . . . require or may be subjected to restrictions upon their liberty of contract which could not lawfully be imposed in the case of men under similar circumstances.

Source: 261 U.S. 525 at 553 (1923).

{g}DOCUMENT 36: Proposed Equal Rights Amendment, Introduced 1923

While followers of Susan B. Anthony and her successor, Carrie Chapman Catt, believed that women should receive special consideration in laws governing the workplace, another body of woman's rights activists in the National Woman's Party (NWP), led by Alice Paul, took a different view. They demanded equality for women in every aspect of public life. The NWP drafted an equal rights amendment and arranged for its introduction in Congress in 1923.

* * *

Section 1. Men and women shall have equal rights throughout the United States and every place subject to its jurisdiction.

Source: Congressional Record-Senate (December 10, 1923): 150.

THE 1930s

{r}DOCUMENT 37: Hiring of African Americans in Public Works Administration Projects in Selected Cities Based on 1930 Occupational Census

Faith in prosperity in the 1920s gave way to economic collapse in the 1930s. In this era African Americans initiated direct action campaigns against white-owned firms whose customers were predominantly black. These campaigns forced legislatures and courts to address racial discrimination. A few state legislatures enacted employment antidiscrimination laws. As a result of concerted pressure brought to bear on the Roosevelt administration by African American leaders, the federal government made fair employment initiatives part of some public works programs in the New Deal. As a precedent-setter for affirmative action the Public Works Administration (PWA) is especially significant. Its director, Harold Ickes, instituted a policy of proportional hiring, a concept that originated with the African American leaders, including Ickes' race relations adviser, Robert Weaver. Weaver's white colleague Clark Forman suggested the system, which became PWA policy. It required contractors to employ at least the same percentage of African American workers as recorded in the 1930 census for each city (Moreno 1997, 58).

* * *

City	Census % Unskilled African American Construction Workers	% Unskilled African American Construction Workers on PWA Project Payroll	Census % Skilled African American Construction Workers	% Skilled African American Construction Workers on PWA Project Payroll
Birmingham	83.8	80.68	23.81	25.4
Indianapolis	58.2	62.6	4.9	2.6
Philadelphia	60.2	80.4	6.1	6.0
Washington, D.C.	84.6	90.1	12.5	6.2

Source: Adapted from "Appendix" in Marc W. Kruman, "Quotas for Blacks: The Public Works Administration and the Black Construction Worker," *Labor History* 16, no. 1 (Winter 1975): 50–51.

{r}DOCUMENT 38: Enforcement of Order Issued by Secretary of Interior Harold Ickes Banning Discrimination in All Projects of the Public Works Administration, September 1, 1933

Employers and unions resisted proportional hiring, but Ickes held firm.

* * *

Spring 1935

Secretary Ickes has definitely informed us that unless some arrangement is made for the employment of a minimum number of skilled negro workers on P.W.A. projects in Chicago he would refuse to approve any further allocation of funds for any project whatsoever in your city.

Source: Isador Lubin, commissioner of the Bureau of Labor Statistics, to Victor Olander, secretary of the Illinois Federation of Labor, 1935, quoted in Marc W. Kruman, "Quotas for Blacks: The Public Works Administration and the Black Construction Worker," *Labor History* 16, no. 1 (Winter 1975): 42.

{r}DOCUMENT 39: Robert Weaver, Writing in *Opportunity,* Summer 1936

Robert Weaver praised the PWA policy in an article for the journal of the Urban League.

* * *

I am convinced that [the proportional hiring program] is a workable solution to a difficult problem. In this instance the Federal Government has done more than make a gesture in the direction of effectively preventing discriminations against colored workers. Here is a program which does not correct an abuse after the project is completed—as is usually the case when Negroes' rights are being protected—but it sets up a criterion which is *prima facie* evidence of discrimination. If the contractor does not live up to this requirement it is accepted—until disproved—that he is discriminating against colored workers. Instead of the Government's having to establish the existence of discrimination, it is the contractor's obligation to establish the absence of discrimination.

Source: Robert Weaver, "An Experiment in Negro Labor," *Opportunity* 14 (1936): 298.

DOCUMENT 40: National Labor Relations Act, July 5, 1935

The term "affirmative action" appeared for the first time in federal law in the National Labor Relations Act (NLRA). Affirming the obligation of the federal government to protect workers' rights to unionize, the NLRA authorized the National Labor Relations Board to investigate and act upon workers' complaints. Subsequent laws attacking racial discrimination were modeled on the NLRA. Ironically, the labor unions that benefited from the NLRA frequently practiced the very kinds of discrimination that the later affirmative action orders would proscribe.

* * *

Whenever it is charged that any person has engaged in . . . any . . . unfair labor practice, the Board, or any agent or agency designated by the Board . . . shall have power to issue and cause to be served upon such person a complaint stating the charges ... and containing a notice of hearing before the Board. ...

If upon the preponderance of the testimony taken the Board shall be of the opinion that any person named in the complaint has engaged in or is engaging in any such unfair labor practice, then the Board shall state its findings of fact and shall issue and cause to be served on such person an order requiring such person to cease and desist from such unfair labor practice, and to take such affirmative action including reinstatement of employees with or without back pay, as will effectuate the policies of this Act.

Source: U.S. Code, 1935, Vol. 29, secs. 160b, 160c.

{g}DOCUMENT 41: Report by Mary Elizabeth Pidgeon on Women in the Economy of the United States, 1937

In 1937 Mary Elizabeth Pidgeon prepared a study for the Women's Bureau on the effect of the New Deal on women. She noted that labor codes mandated by the 1933 National Industrial Recovery Act often set women's wages below those of men.

* * *

Effects of labor legislation on Conditions of Women's Work

The National Industrial Recovery Act sought to secure for both sexes shortened hours, increased wages and further protection of collective bargaining rights. ...

That the powerful force of tradition keeps women's wages down even under legislation applying to both sexes shows that there still is need of special measures to assist women in attaining adequate standards.

Source: Mary Elizabeth Pidgeon, *Women in the Economy of the United States of America, a Summary Report* (Washington, DC: Women's Bureau, 1937): 8.

{d}DOCUMENT 42: The Social Security Act of 1935

Among the longest-lasting initiatives of the New Deal was the Social Security Act of 1935. It established, for the first time in U.S. history, a permanent program of assistance for disabled adults.

* * *

To provide for the general welfare by establishing a system of Federal old-age benefits, and by enabling the several States to make more adequate provision for aged persons, blind persons, dependent and crippled children, maternal and child welfare, public health, and the administration of their unemployment compensation laws. . . .

TITLE X—GRANTS TO STATES FOR AID TO THE BLIND

For the purpose of enabling each State to furnish financial assistance, as far as practicable under the conditions in such State, to needy individuals who are blind, there is hereby authorized to be appropriated for the fiscal year ending June 30, 1936, the sum of $3,000,000, and there is hereby authorized to be appropriated for each fiscal year thereafter a sum sufficient to carry out the purposes of this title.

Source: U.S. Statutes at Large 49 (1935): 531, 555.

{d}DOCUMENT 43: *Washington Post* Report on League of the Physically Handicapped, May 10, 1936

The Social Security Act was one of several New Deal policies affecting the disabled community. Recognizing the importance of being organized and proactive, disabled advocacy groups pressured the government to include their constituencies in federal job programs and social welfare legislation. The American Foundation for the Blind, founded in 1921, was instrumental in having a separate title for the blind included in the Social Security law. A smaller and short-lived organization—the League of the Physically Handicapped (LPH)—pressed the Works Progress Administration (WPA) on the issues of employability and access to jobs for handicapped individuals. The league emerged from spontaneous demonstrations in the spring of 1935, targeting federal Emergency Relief Bureau (ERB) offices in New York City. "The Crippled Pickets"—as they were characterized by headline writers—declared on their signs, "We Don't Want Tin Cups, We Want Jobs" and "We Are Lame but We Can Work." That fall the league again picketed the New York ERB, demanding "a just share of the millions of jobs being given out by the government." Dissatisfied with the results of local protest, an LPH delegation traveled to Washington, D.C. The *Washington Post* followed the delegation's activities there (Longmore and Goldberger, 2000, 907).

* * *

Sylvia Flexer, one of the group, explained its aim. . . . "They class us as unemployables, despite the fact that our members include college and trained teachers, chemists, bacteriologists, physicists and others who are professionally skilled.

"We are going to stay here until Mr. [Harry] Hopkins [WPA director] does see us. . . ." [P]ermission was granted the petitioners to remain in the building overnight. . . .

Source: "Crippled Group on Jobs Quest 'Camps' at WPA," *Washington Post* (May 10, 1936): 4.

{d}DOCUMENT 44: *New York Times* Report on "New York Group Camping in Washington," August 1937

Finally, the LPH members met with Hopkins, who reportedly told them to prepare a "thesis" regarding their allegations that federal programs discriminated against the disabled (*Washington Post*, May 12, 1936). Three months later the league sent a ten-page "Thesis on Conditions of Physically Handicapped" to Hopkins and FDR, with copies to the press. The document provided data showing that New York City relief rolls included 12,000 disabled individuals, 5,000 of whom were employable and only 1,500 of whom held WPA jobs.

While no reply arrived from Washington, on September 12, 1936, the New York director of the WPA announced that 7 percent of all WPA jobs in the city would be earmarked for handicapped workers. The WPA instituted nationwide layoffs the following spring, resulting in hundreds of disabled workers losing their jobs and a return trip to Washington by LPH representatives. Again, the press followed their efforts.

* * *

Thirty-two members of the New York League of Physically Handicapped, who arrived here Saturday . . . presented their charges and proposals today to Aubrey Williams, acting administrator, and will see him again tomorrow. . . .

Saturday they camped on the small lawn at WPA headquarters. Last night they slept on the Washington Monument grounds, with blankets provided by the Volunteers of America.

Source: "Plea by Disabled Put to WPA Chief," *New York Times* (August 17, 1937): 7.

Meetings with WPA leaders proved fruitless, and the delegation returned home. Within a year the organization ceased to exist. Though short-lived, the League of the Physically Handicapped made its mark as a harbinger of policies enacted at the end of the century. As historians Paul Longmore and David Goldberger have noted, members of the league "attributed their economic disadvantages, not to their disabilities, but to . . . unjust policies" (Longmore and Goldberger 2000, 908).

{d}DOCUMENT 45: Robert Irwin, 1932 Origins of the "Talking Book"

The American Foundation for the Blind and its executive director from 1929 to 1950, Dr. Robert Irwin, advocated independence for blind people and limited federal assistance. Irwin was instrumental in harnessing WPA resources to manufacture the special recording machines needed for "Talking Books." The next selection is Dr. Irwin's account of the start of a viable "Talking Book" program.

* * *

In 1932, with the help of the Carnegie Corporation, the American Foundation for the Blind started a laboratory for the development of a phonograph record satisfactory for circulating library purposes. . . .

After considerable persuasion the W.P.A. inaugurated a project for the manufacture of Talking Book machines. This . . . resulted in the construction of more than 23,000 instruments which became the property of the Library of Congress. They were lent to blind people throughout the country through the State agencies for the blind. . . .

The Talking Book has brought the ability to read at will within the reach of a large percentage of blind people who were formerly entirely dependent upon their seeing associates for their reading.

Source: Robert B. Irwin, "The Talking Book," in *Blindness, Modern Approaches to the Unseen Environment*, edited by Paul A. Zahl (Princeton, NJ: Princeton University Press, 1950): 346, 350, 352.

{d}DOCUMENT 46: George W. Veditz, "The Relative Value of Sight and Hearing," 1937

While blind activists pressed for the Talking Book, deaf scholar and teacher George W. Veditz was among those who worked to establish the means by which the nonhearing could live with a maximum of independence. Chief among these means was sign language, as opposed to the lip reading that was the established instructional goal in most schools for the deaf. In the following essay from 1937 Veditz invited his readers to contemplate a world without sound.

* * *

Civilization in a deaf world would eventually be the same as it is now. Every form of modern convenience with the exception of the telephone and radio, the phonograph and other contrivances depending on the . . . sense of hearing would come into existence. . . .

There would be no Mozarts . . . no Carusos . . . no Beethovens, though Beethoven was deaf, but every branch of art except the one of . . . music would flourish. . . . Some deaf Columbus would in time discover America; some deaf Galileo would fashion his telescope; some Fahrenheit his thermometer.

Source: George W. Veditz, "The Relative Value of Sight and Hearing," *American Annals of the Deaf* 82, no. 2 (March 1937): 124.

{d}DOCUMENT 47: The New Deal and Blind Vendors

Two other New Deal laws that benefited the disabled authorized arrangements similar to "set-asides" in later affirmative action initiatives for minorities and women. In both cases the beneficiaries were blind vendors.

* * *

A. Randolph-Sheppard Act, June 20, 1936

In authorizing the operation of vending facilities on federal property, priority shall be given to blind persons licensed by a State agency as provided [herein].

B. Wagner-O'Day Act, June 25, 1938

There is established a committee to be known as the Committee for Purchase from the Blind and Other Severely Handicapped. . . .

[I]n the purchase by the Government of commodities produced and offered for sale by qualified nonprofit agencies for the blind or such agencies for other severely handicapped, priority shall be accorded [to such agencies].

Source: Statutes at Large, vol. 49 (June 20, 1936): 1559; vol. 52 (June 25, 1938): 1196.

{r}DOCUMENT 48: Charles Hamilton Houston, "A Challenge to Negro College Youth," 1938

As the blind and other disabled groups sought to conform New Deal reforms to their rights and needs, the NAACP was mounting a series of challenges to the "separate but equal" doctrine as applied to higher education. State universities in, and bordering, the South denied admission to African American students. Directing the legal attack on this practice was Charles Hamilton Houston, chief counsel for the NAACP. In the following "Challenge" Houston urged African American students to demand equal opportunity.

* * *

A Negro has handicaps enough without having to pay taxes to support the education of white students to learn how to suppress him. The opportunities of education are not equal now; but if the Negro college youth of this generation accept the challenge, they can go far toward making educational opportunity equal, if not for themselves, then for the little Negro children now in primary and secondary schools.

Source: Charles H. Houston. "A Challenge to Negro College Youth," *The Crisis* (January 1938): 14–15.

WORLD WAR II

World War II, fought by the Allied powers in the name of freedom and self-determination for all people, intensified the efforts of minorities and women to realize those same goals on the American home front. Likewise, the wartime theme of unity echoed within the United States as a new organization emerged among the blind.

{d}DOCUMENT 49: Presidential Address of Jacobus tenBroek at the Founding of the National Federation of the Blind, November 1940

In November 1940, sixteen individuals from seven states gathered in Wilkes-Barre, Pennsylvania, for the founding conference of the National Federation of the Blind. They elected Jacobus tenBroek (Doc. 11) as their first president. In his inaugural address, he called for collective action against Title X of the Social Security Act (Doc. 42), which included a provision requiring that blind workers' earnings be deducted from their Social Security payments.

* * *

Have Our Blind Social Security?

[A]s far as the blind are concerned the Social Security Act has not only failed to attain its plainly expressed goals but it has been used as a weapon. . . .

[A]ccording to the Social Security Board, a needy blind person is one whose need is the same as that of paupers, indigents, and the aged. . . .

A needy blind person has a greater need. . . . [H]is need consists in some fair utilization of his productive capacity. This can only be obtained by restoring him to economic competence in a competitive world.

Source: Reprinted in Floyd W. Matson, *Walking Alone and Marching Together* (Baltimore: National Federation of the Blind, 1990): 18, 20.

{r}DOCUMENT 50: President Franklin Roosevelt, Executive Order 8802, June 25, 1941

African Americans sought a "double victory" in World War II—democracy not only abroad but also at home. This point of view prevailed even before the United States entered the war. On September 27, 1940, labor leader A. Philip Randolph, Walter White (head of the NAACP), and T. Arnold Hill of the National Urban League met with President Franklin Roosevelt on the issues of segregation and discrimination in the armed forces and national defense industries. The president promised to investigate their concerns, but when he offered no tangible remedies, Randolph appealed for 10,000 African Americans to de-

scend on the nation's capital under the slogan "We Loyal Negro Amer-
ican Citizens Demand the Right to Work and Fight for Our Country."
Randolph did not call off the march until the president issued Executive
Order 8802.

* * *

I do hereby reaffirm the policy of the United States that there shall be
no discrimination in the employment of workers in defense industries
or government because of race, creed, color, or national origin, and I do
hereby declare that it is the duty of employers and of labor organizations,
in furtherance of said policy and of this order, to provide for the full
and equitable participation of all workers in defense industries, without
discrimination because of race, creed, color, or national origin.

Source: Code of Federal Regulations, Title 3 (1938–1943 compilation): 957.

Executive Order 8802 also mandated nondiscriminatory policies in
defense industry vocational and training programs; required that all
defense contracts contain nondiscrimination clauses; and established
the Committee on Fair Employment Practice, to be administered from
the Office of Production Management.

{g}DOCUMENT 51: *The Employment Security Review*, April 1942

While maneuvering to head off the March on Washington Movement, the Roosevelt administration was also mounting an aggressive
campaign to recruit women into war production industries.

* * *

Adequate staffing of arms factories will depend not only on the employment of all women presently unemployed, but also on the recruitment
of hundreds of thousands of women not now in search of work.

Source: "Women in War Jobs," *Employment Security Review* (April 1942): 11.

{g}DOCUMENT 52: War Manpower Commission Policy on Women, October 1942

In October 1942 the U.S. War Manpower Commission (WMC), guided by its Women's Advisory Committee (WAC), issued a statement of policy on women war workers.

* * *

To promote the rapid and orderly induction of women into the labor market and to insure their subsequent employment and training opportunities, the War Manpower Commission hereby declares as basic national policies . . .

1. *Recruitment and Referral of Women Workers*:
   a. Qualified women who are unemployed and who are registered in local offices of the United States Employment Service be referred to employment and training opportunities on a basis of equality with men. . . .

2. *Training of Women Workers* . . . :
   b. Women be admitted on a basis of equality with men to enrollment in the Engineering, Science, and Management War Training Program conducted by colleges, universities, and technical schools in cooperation with the United States Office of Education. . . .
   d. Women participate equally with men in plant training programs. . . .

3. *Employment of Women Workers* . . . :
   d. Wage rates, including the entrance rate, be determined for all workers on the basis of the work performed, irrespective of sex.

Source: "WMC Policy on Wartime Employment of Women," *Employment Security Review* (December 1942): 6–7.

{g}DOCUMENT 53: Dorothy Thompson, "Women and the Coming World," 1943

However forward-looking, the WMC policy promised more than its authors could deliver. Without laws to enforce them, government promises of equal pay and child care were regularly ignored by industry. Employers paid lower starting wages to women and reclassified jobs to maintain a dual pay scale. While the number of women in the U.S. labor force jumped from 12 million to 19 million between 1940

and 1945, the gap between women's earnings in industry and those of
men remained the same, with women paid 65 percent of what men
were paid. Nonetheless, women expanded their roles and their hori-
zons during the war. The implications of this expansion would not be
fully apparent until the 1960s, but prescient observers such as journalist
Dorothy Thompson realized their significance.

* * *

The war has created a pressing demand for labor, and it has demonstrated that there is no field of human activity in which women cannot
substitute for men.

There is no example . . . in which a class or group of people who have
once succeeded in expanding the area of their lives is ever persuaded
again to restrict it.

Source: Dorothy Thompson, "Women and the Coming World," *Ladies Home Journal* (October 1943): 6.

{d}DOCUMENT 54: Theodore Brimm, "Hiring the Handicapped," April 1942

Government mobilization for World War II also encompassed physically disabled citizens. Government spokesmen appealed to employers to assess "handicapped" workers' individual skills and avoid
preconceptions about their abilities.

* * *

War has made it clear that if our vast, expanding victory program is to
be sustained, there must be a full use of the skill, training, and experience
of every available worker, including not only the Negro, the older men,
and women, but also the handicapped worker. . . .

How to overcome employer attitudes towards the employment of the
handicapped is a real challenge to us all. . . .

There was a time when even placement officials looked at all one-
legged men as watchmen, all blind persons as broom-makers, and all
tuberculous persons as able to do "light, outdoor work" only. . . .

All the individual's potentialities must be considered.

Source: Theodore Brimm, "Hiring the Handicapped," *Employment Security Review*
(April 1942): 22.

{d}DOCUMENT 55: *Monthly Labor Review* Report on Federal Wage Guidelines for Handicapped Workers, October 1942

Federal officials established wage guidelines for handicapped workers. Despite wartime eagerness to utilize such workers, officials relegated them to "subminimum" pay rates.

* * *

All determinations of prevailing minimum wages, issued by the Secretary of Labor under the Public Contracts Act and in effect on August 12, 1942, were amended effective September 15, 1942, to provide for handicapped or superannuated workers the same subminimum rates of pay ... as are applicable for them under the Fair Labor Standards Act.

Source: Monthly Labor Review (October 1942): 843–844.

{d}DOCUMENT 56: *Science Digest* Report on War Jobs for the Handicapped, March 1943

Some areas of private industry, at least the automobile plants owned and operated by the Ford Motor Co., implemented policies and wage scales for handicapped workers that were more progressive than the government's. In the following discussion, the editors of *Science Digest* describe Ford's policies.

* * *

Today, with labor shortages growing more acute, employment of the handicapped is an economic operating necessity. In our first year of war, a far larger number of sailors and soldiers have been returned to civilian life because of battle injuries than is generally known. . . .

The Ford Motor Co. . . . has been solving [the problem of training disabled workers] for 20 years. . . .

Today, 11,652 disabled persons are full-time employees at [the] River Rouge [Ford plant in Michigan]. In this group are 687 blind; 66 are deaf and dumb; 42 partially incapacitated by infantile paralysis; 112 are epileptics; 101 have organic heart ailments; 80 have only one arm; one has no arms; 96 have spine curvatures.

All of these people are receiving standard wages. Their employment is dictated by neither charity nor altruistic humanitarianism. Each is expected to give full value for his wages.

Source: Science Digest (March 1943): 57–58.

{d}DOCUMENT 57: Barden LaFollette Act, July 6, 1943

In July 1943 Congress took a major step in the area of vocational rehabilitation with passage of the Barden LaFollette Act, which substantially increased federal funding for state rehabilitation programs and expanded the use of such funding beyond education to cover other needs of the disabled.

* * *

From the sums made available . . . the Secretary of the Treasury shall pay to each State which has an approved plan for vocational rehabilitation . . .

(1) the necessary cost . . . of providing vocational rehabilitation . . . to disabled individuals certified by the State . . . as war disabled civilians;

(2) one-half of necessary expenditures under such plan . . . for rehabilitation, training, and medical examinations . . . of other disabled individuals; and

(3) one-half of necessary expenditures under such plan . . . for rehabilitation services specified [in the following] . . . to disabled individuals (not including war disabled civilians) found to require financial assistance with respect thereto. . . .

(a) corrective surgery or therapeutic treatment. . . .

(b) necessary hospitalization. . . .

(c) transportation, occupational licenses and customary occupational tools and equipment. . . .

(d) prosthetic devices as are essential to obtaining or retaining employment.

(e) maintenance . . . including the cost of any necessary books and other training material.

Source: U.S. Statutes at Large, 57, Pt. 1 (1943): 376.

While Congress and various federal wartime agencies took action on the employment of women and the disabled, the Committee on Fair

Employment Practice monitored policies affecting African Americans. The committee determined that the executive order under which they operated did not forbid segregation. In contrast to the proportional hiring policy employed earlier in the Roosevelt administration (Docs. 37–39), the Committee on Fair Employment Practice explicitly ruled out quotas as remedies for underrepresentation of minorities in defense work. Reorganized three times, the committee operated until Congress withdrew its funding in 1946.

{r}DOCUMENT 58: Thomas Sancton, "The Race Riots," *The New Republic*, July 1943

Social tumult and tension formed the backdrop for the Fair Employment Practice Committee. An estimated 240 racial disturbances erupted in the summer of 1943. The most destructive was in Detroit. Observers, such as journalist Thomas Sancton, called for Franklin Roosevelt to take more aggressive action against racial injustice.

* * *

Why, in these months, when the peril of open race war hung upon the air, hasn't Mr. Roosevelt come to us with one of his greatest speeches, speaking to us . . . of a country where all are created equal? . . .

The United States never needed more gravely than it does today a strong and intelligent federal policy on the race issue.

Source: Thomas Sancton, "The Race Riots," *The New Republic* (July 5, 1943): 12, 13.

{r}DOCUMENT 59: *An American Dilemma*, Spring 1944

The Carnegie Corporation had commissioned Swedish economist Gunnar Myrdal to conduct an intensive examination of American race relations, beginning in the late 1930s. The result of his research—conducted with a team of over 100 American scholars, black and white—was published in the spring of 1944. In a chapter on "Economic Inequality" Myrdal pinpointed the persistence of the precept of inferiority.

* * *

Southerners still think of Negroes as their former slaves. . . . To Northerners, the Negro is . . . just an alien, felt to be particularly difficult to assimilate into the life of the community.

Source: Gunnar Myrdal, *An American Dilemma* (New York: Harper and Row, Twentieth Anniversary Edition, 1962): 219.

{r/g}DOCUMENT 60: *An American Dilemma*, Appendix 5 on Women, 1944

Myrdal attached to his study of race an appendix on women. Though generally ignored at the time, his interpretation of the history of African Americans and females as interrelated would emerge again when the civil rights and women's liberation movements surged a quarter of a century later.

* * *

Appendix 5. A PARALLEL TO THE NEGRO PROBLEM
As in the Negro problem, most men have accepted as self-evident, until recently, the doctrine that women had inferior endowments in most of those respects which carry prestige, power, and advantages in society. . . .
[W]omen are still hindered in their competition by the function of procreation; Negroes are laboring under the yoke of the doctrine of unassimilability. . . . The second barrier is actually much stronger than the first in America today. But the first is more eternally inexorable.

Source: Gunnar Myrdal, *An American Dilemma* (New York: Harper and Row, Twentieth Anniversary Edition, 1962): 1077, 1078.

{r}DOCUMENT 61: *Smith v. Allwright*, April 3, 1944

An example supporting Myrdal's assertion that many white southerners maintained a slaveholder's mentality toward African Americans was the "white primary"—laws in southern states barring African Americans from voting in party primary elections. Since the primary vote usually determined the outcome of the regular election, this practice undermined black voting power. In Texas an African American dentist, Lonnie Smith, initiated a court challenge on this issue. It reached the Supreme Court in April 1944. In a previous decision (*Grovey v. Townsend*, 1935) the Court had decided that a political party could conduct a primary on whatever terms it chose. In the *Smith* decision the Court reversed itself. Civil rights advocates were jubilant. In addition to scuttling the "white primary," the Court also affirmed its duty to reexamine previous decisions when circumstances indicate flaws in such decisions. This affirmation would take on immense importance in 1954 (Doc. 84).

* * *

The United States is a constitutional democracy. Its organic law grants to all citizens a right to participate in the choice of elected officials without restriction by any State because of race. This grant to the people of the opportunity for choice is not to be nullified by a State through casting its electoral process in a form which permits a private organization to practice racial discrimination in the election. Constitutional rights would be of little value if they could be thus indirectly denied. . . .

In reaching this conclusion we are not unmindful of the desirability of continuity of decision in constitutional questions. However, when convinced of former error, this Court has never felt constrained to follow precedent. . . .

Grovey v. Townsend is overruled.

Source: 321 U.S. 649 at 664, 665, 666 (1944).

{r}DOCUMENT 62: *Steele v. Louisville and Nashville Railroad Co.*, December 1944

In 1944 the Supreme Court heard two other cases brought by African Americans. The plaintiffs included railway firemen Bester William Steele and Tom Tunstall. The all-white Brotherhood of Locomotive Firemen and Enginemen not only excluded all blacks from union membership but also prohibited their promotion to engineers and sought to drive them out of their firemen's jobs. When Steele and Tunstall's employers ignored Fair Employment Practices Committee (FEPC) rulings in their favor, they sued—Steele in the Alabama state courts and Tunstall in the federal courts of Virginia. Both men's cases reached the U.S. Supreme Court in 1944 and were ruled on in December. The majority decision left the union free to discriminate in its criteria for admitting workers to membership but required it to represent all workers, including nonmembers, in collective bargaining agreements.

* * *

While the statute [the Railway Labor Act] does not deny to such a bargaining labor organization the right to determine eligibility to its membership, it does require the union, in collective bargaining and in making contracts with the carrier, to represent nonunion or minority union members of the craft without hostile discrimination, fairly, impartially, and in good faith.

Source: 323 U.S. 192 at 204 (1944).

POSTWAR ERA

{r}DOCUMENT 63: Servicemen's Readjustment Act, June 22, 1944

As World War II drew to a close, Congress prepared for the return of men and women in the armed services to civilian life, including more than 1 million African Americans. Along with Executive Order 8802 (Doc. 50), Public Law 346, popularly known as the "GI Bill," created major opportunities for employment and education. For African Americans these were the first such opportunities since the era of Reconstruction. Among the provisions of the law were guarantees that all returning veterans with honorable discharges would have access to federally funded health care, college or vocational education, assistance in obtaining jobs, and loans for home buying and the opening of businesses.

The impact of the GI Bill on postwar America was transformative. An entire generation used its advantages to gain college degrees, pursue job opportunities, and become homeowners. In a later era, the GI Bill would become a frequent point of reference for supporters of economic set-asides and targeted college admissions programs. They found in the law of 1944 an analogy to the affirmative action policies of the late 1960s and after. The following selection focuses on the education provisions of the GI Bill.

* * *

To provide Federal Government aid for the readjustment in civilian life of returning World War II veterans. . . .

Title II, Chapter IV—Education of Veterans

2. Any . . . eligible person shall be entitled to education or training, or a refresher or retraining course, at an approved educational or training institution, for a period of one year. . . . Upon satisfactory completion of such course . . . such person shall be entitled to an additional period or periods of education or training, not to exceed the time such person was in the active service. . . .

5. The Administrator [of Veterans' Affairs] . . . shall pay to the educational or training institution, for each person enrolled in full time or part time course of education or training the customary cost of tuition and such laboratory, library, health, infirmary, and other similar fees as are customarily charged and may pay for books, supplies, equipment and other necessary expenses. . . .

6. While enrolled in and pursuing a course . . . such person . . . shall be paid a subsistence allowance of $50 per month, if without a dependent or dependents, or $75 per month if he has a dependent or dependents.

Source: U.S. Statutes at Large 58, Pt. 1 (1944): 284, 288, 289.

{r/g}DOCUMENT 64: University of Wisconsin *Catalog*, June 1945

Many schools granted the veterans special consideration—lower entrance requirements, tutorial support, refresher courses, college credit for work accomplished in the military, and other assistance. The men (and some women) who took advantage of these benefits surprised college faculties and administrations by performing at higher levels than their younger, traditional fellow students. (On women and the GI Bill see Willenz 1994, 41–46.) According to scholar Reginald Wilson, "the veterans' academic performance . . . proved for the first time that tests of ability are not predictive of academic performance when motivation and expectations are high" (Wilson 1994, 36).

Even before the GI Bill had become law, universities were preparing to enroll veterans. At the University of Wisconsin, for example, a special faculty committee was established to plan for "all matters of policy relating to . . . war veterans. . . ." The policy that it outlined was spelled out in the university *Catalog* issued in June 1945.

* * *

Veterans who are admitted to the University and who qualify with the Veterans' Administration . . . will receive a monthly subsistence allowance in addition to tuition, fees, books, and necessary supplies. . . .

The University has modified its entrance requirements so that veterans

of World War II who do not possess all the requirements for admission
may be admitted to the University upon giving satisfactory evidence that
they are prepared to take advantageously the subjects open to them. . . .

For the veteran who has been long absent from the classroom, refresher courses have been established in English and mathematics. Further assistance through special quiz sections or additional refresher
courses will be instituted when there is sufficient demand. . . .

Counseling and testing services are available to all students in meeting
their special educational and vocational problems.

Source: Bulletin of the University of Wisconsin, General Announcement of Courses
(June 1945): 16–17.

{r}DOCUMENT 65: Engineer Robert Eubanks and the GI Bill after World War II

Quoting Harvard president James B. Conant, *Life Magazine* maintained in June 1946 that the GI Bill was fostering "the democratic process of 'social mobility' . . . piercing the class barriers which even in
America, have tended to keep a college education the prerogative of
the few" (Murphy 1946, 22). In keeping with that view, Reginald Wilson has called attention to the large part played by the GI Bill in "developing a tiny group of [African American] professionals into the large,
stable, and growing 'black bourgeoisie' " that existed by the end of the
century (Wilson 1994, 38). An example of this professional class is
Robert A. Eubanks. A distinguished engineer, he practiced his profession in the field and then as a full professor at the University of Illinois.

* * *

Accepted at Howard University with a tuition-only scholarship, Eubanks couldn't afford to go. He joined the Army and heard about the GI
Bill by word of mouth when he mustered out in 1946.

He went to school year-round at the Illinois Institute of Technology
(ITT), earning a degree in theoretical and applied mechanical engineering
in January 1950. Because "employers weren't hiring black engineers," he
stayed at ITT, earning a master's and then a doctorate by 1953. . . .

"It's very hard to explain now what things were like in the 1940s,"
[Eubanks recalled]. . . . "[R]estrictions on blacks then were rough. The GI
Bill gave me my start to being a professional instead of a stock clerk."

Source: University of Illinois at Urbana-Champaign *News Bureau*, quoted in Wilson 1994, 38.

{r}DOCUMENT 66: Entertainer Harry Belafonte Looking Back on the GI Bill of 1944

In a 1996 television documentary, entertainer and stalwart civil rights supporter Harry Belafonte also recalled how important the GI Bill was for African Americans. His reference to Isaac Woodward was a reminder of the surge of racial violence characterizing the end of World War II, much of it directed against African American veterans like Woodward, who was in army uniform in February 1946, when his attackers destroyed his eye sockets by thrusting a club into each one.

* * *

The GI Bill was extremely critical for all of us. . . . We returned to a nation where the Ku Klux Klan was on the rise. Many of us were devastated that, after all we had done, America was still that way. Do you know the story of Isaac Woodward? He was the great black hero, highly decorated. When he came back they gouged out his eyes because he wouldn't sit in the back of the bus. All the doors which should have been open to us weren't. Had it not been for the GI Bill, we would have been severely shut out.

Source: Unpublished manuscript by Karen Thomas for television documentary, quoted in Michael J. Bennett, *When Dreams Come True* (Washington, DC, and London: Brassey's, 1996): 272.

{r}DOCUMENT 67: *James v. Marinship Corp.*, 1945

While veterans of all economic and racial backgrounds took advantage of congressional largesse, civil rights groups continued to press for economic justice through the courts. A significant challenge to the discriminatory practices of unions occurred in the courts of California when an African American boilermaker, Joseph James, filed suit on behalf of himself and "approximately one thousand other Negro workers similarly situated." While the suit focused on the Marinship Corporation, the real target was the International Brotherhood of Boilermakers, which had successfully pressured the shipyard owners to fire African American workers who refused to pay dues for membership in the "auxiliary lodges" that the union reserved for them. In

the case of James, a Marinship employee, the California Supreme Court
upheld a lower court injunction prohibiting his employer from enforcing the union policy. "Local No. 6" of the International Brotherhood
was the union chapter representing the white workers at Marinship,
while African American workers were relegated to "Auxiliary A-41."

* * *

The auxiliary . . . has no voice nor vote in the affairs of Local No. 6.
. . . [W]here grievances arise in which whites and Negroes have different
interests, it is clear that the Negroes will not be adequately represented
and the opportunity for discrimination is obvious. . . .

Marinship . . . has at least indirectly assisted the union in carrying out
its discrimination against plaintiff.

The judgment [of the lower courts against Marinship] is affirmed.

Source: 155 P. 2d 329 at 338, 340–341, 342 (1945).

{r}DOCUMENT 68: The New York State Law against Discrimination (Ives–Quinn), 1945

While the courts wrestled with cases such as *James*, the seven members of the FEPC sought to make a final statement before Congress cut
off their funding. They requested and obtained from President Truman
Executive Order 9664. Issued December 18, 1945, the order authorized the FEPC to "receive and investigate complaints" in industries that
were converting from war to peace production. In so doing, the committee hoped to establish that federal opposition to discrimination
would not end with the war.

At the same time as Executive Order 9664 was issued, state legislatures began to create local agencies to combat employment discrimination. New York took the lead in 1945 with a law on which
twenty-five other states would model FEPCs by the early 1960s. The
Ives–Quinn law established a five-member commission to receive, investigate, and remedy complaints of discrimination. In detailing the
commission's authority to impose remedies, authors of the bill employed the term "affirmative action."

* * *

Section 132. . . . If . . . the commission shall find that a respondent has engaged in any unlawful employment practice . . . the commission shall

state its findings of fact and shall issue and cause to be served on such respondent an order requiring such respondent to cease and desist from such unlawful employment practice and to take such affirmative action, including (but not limited to) hiring, reinstatement or upgrading of employees, with or without back pay, or restoration to membership in any respondent labor organization, as, in the judgment of the commission, will effectuate the purposes of [the law].

Source: McKinney's Consolidated Laws of New York, Book 18, Cumulative Annual Pocket Part (1950): 73.

{g}DOCUMENT 69: Proposed Equal Pay for Equal Work Law for Women, June 1945

At neither the state nor the federal level was there substantial interest in the question of legislation attacking discrimination based on sex. Nonetheless, as the war came to an end, equal pay for equal work was a live issue for women factory workers who were forced to yield their jobs to returning GIs and were seeking to retrain for white-collar positions and remain in the workforce. At the end of 1945 equal-pay bills were introduced in both houses of Congress (by Senators Claude Pepper and Wayne Morse and Representative Mary Norton). Both failed to pass. For the next eighteen years similar legislation would be voted down.

* * *

The Congress hereby finds that the existence in industry of differentials based on sex is an inequality in compensation standards which constitutes an unfair wage practice.

Source: Congressional Record 91, Pt. 12 (June 21, 1945): 6411.

{g}DOCUMENT 70: ERA Supporter Alma Lutz Commenting on Equal Pay, 1946

While women's organizations were united in opposing differential wage standards for men and women, they remained divided regarding differential standards of protection. Advocates of the Equal Rights Amendment (ERA) sought to eliminate all separate standards. Opponents of the ERA insisted that women be treated as a special class in regard to working hours and safety conditions. In the following commentary, Alma Lutz (who favored the ERA) described the position of its opponents as a "paradox."

* * *

To some of us, espousal of the Equal Pay bill and opposition to the Equal Rights Amendment seems like a paradox, for we believe that the Equal Pay bill needs the Equal Rights Amendment to make it effective. . . .

[T]he traditional argument that women are inferior, weaker workers is to the advantage of some employers who want to keep available a class of cheap labor. They find ways of labeling jobs as women's jobs and men's jobs, implying that men's jobs require more skill or strength and therefore higher wages.

Source: Alma Lutz, "Which Road, Women Workers?" *Christian Science Monitor Magazine Section* (February 2, 1946): 2.

{r}DOCUMENT 71: *Morgan v. Virginia*, June 3, 1946

While women's groups wrangled over the ERA, national civil rights organizations became involved in an unanticipated legal suit brought in 1944 by Irene Morgan against the state of Virginia. The suit laid the foundation for subsequent campaigns against segregated public accommodations. It was triggered when a Greyhound bus driver ordered Mrs. Morgan and a fellow African American passenger to move to the last row of the bus on which they were traveling and allow white passengers to take their seats. Mrs. Morgan's refusal and follow-up legal action challenged the state law that the driver had invoked. When the Virginia Supreme Court of Appeals upheld that law, Mrs. Morgan and her NAACP lawyers took their case to the U.S. Supreme Court. There the Virginia law was ruled unconstitutional, insofar as its application to interstate public transportation was concerned.

* * *

It seems clear to us that seating arrangements for the different races in interstate motor travel require a single, uniform rule to promote and protect national travel. Consequently, we hold the Virginia statute in controversy invalid.

Source: 328 U.S. 373 at 386 (1946).

{r}DOCUMENT 72: Presidential Letter Appointing a Commission on Higher Education, July 1946

After assuming the presidency in April 1945, Harry Truman repeatedly urged Congress to create a permanent fair employment committee. Behind these urgings was unremitting pressure from African American leaders, including A. Philip Randolph. However, every attempt to pass such legislation was thwarted. A total of seventy bills introduced in both houses between 1942 and 1952 failed. Therefore, Truman continued the practice of his predecessor, exercising the powers of the executive to address issues of fair employment. He used the same method to draw attention to the issue of equal opportunity in higher education.

* * *

As veterans return to college by the hundreds of thousands, the institutions of higher education face a period of trial which is taxing their resources and their resourcefulness to the utmost. . . .

These matters are of such far-reaching national importance that I have decided to appoint a Presidential Commission on Higher Education . . . composed of outstanding civic and educational leaders.

Source: Higher Education for American Democracy, a Report of the President's Commission on Higher Education (New York: Harper and Brothers, 1948). The "Letter of Appointment" over the signature of Harry Truman is unnumbered.

{r}DOCUMENT 73: *To Secure These Rights: The Report of the President's Committee on Civil Rights*, October 29, 1947

Truman's committee on civil rights reported its findings in October 1947. It had reached a strong consensus supporting the rights of racial and other minorities and calling for bold action on their behalf.

* * *

Four basic rights have seemed important to this Committee. . . .

1. *The Right to Safety and Security of the Person.* . . .
2. *The Right to Citizenship and its Privileges.* . . .
3. *The Right to Freedom of Conscience and Expression.* . . .
4. *The Right to Equality of Opportunity.* . . .

Too many of our people still live under the harrowing fear of violence or death at the hands of a mob or of brutal treatment by police officers.

The committee also placed heavy stress on the disabling effects of economic inequalities and injustices.

The opportunity of each individual to obtain useful employment and to have access to services in the fields of education, housing, health, recreation and transportation . . . must be provided with complete disregard for race, color, creed, and national origin.

The committee concluded its report with thirty-five recommendations, including withholding federal funds from institutions that practiced discrimination and passage of new legislation.

To strengthen the right to safety and security of the person, the President's Committee recommends: . . .
The enactment by Congress of an antilynching act. . . .
To strengthen the right to equality of opportunity, the President's Commission recommends:
The conditioning by Congress of all federal grants-in-aid and other forms of federal assistance to public or private agencies for any purpose on the absence of discrimination and segregation based on race, color, creed or national origin. . . .

The enactment of a federal Fair Employment Practices Act prohibiting all forms of discrimination in private employment, based on race, color, creed, or national origin.
The federal act should apply to labor unions and trade and professional associations, as well as to employers.

Source: President's Commission on Civil Rights, *To Secure These Rights* (Washington, DC: U.S. Government Printing Office, 1947): 6–8, 9, 157, 166, 167.

{r}DOCUMENT 74: The Effect of Discrimination on Americans' Standard of Living, Illustrated by the President's Committee on Civil Rights, 1947

Truman's civil rights panel linked equal opportunity to national prosperity.

* * *

DISCRIMINATION IN EMPLOYMENT MEANS...

INEFFICIENT USE
OF OUR LABOR FORCE....

LESS PURCHASING POWER

....AND A LOWER
LIVING STANDARD FOR ALL

LESS
CONSUMER DEMAND

LESS PRODUCTION

FAIR EMPLOYMENT PRACTICES WOULD HELP BRING ...

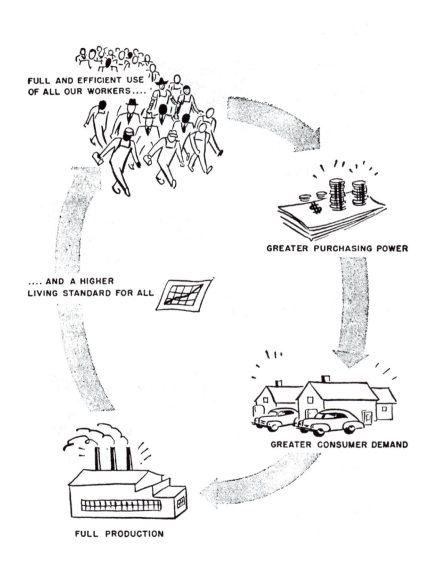

FULL AND EFFICIENT USE OF ALL OUR WORKERS....

GREATER PURCHASING POWER

.... AND A HIGHER LIVING STANDARD FOR ALL

GREATER CONSUMER DEMAND

FULL PRODUCTION

Source: President's Committee on Civil Rights, *To Secure These Rights* (Washington, DC: U.S. Government Printing Office, 1947): 142–143.

{r}DOCUMENT 75: Report of the President's Commission on Higher Education, December 1947

Two months after the Civil Rights Committee completed its work, the President's Commission on Higher Education submitted its findings under the title *Higher Education for American Democracy*.

* * *

Discrimination in Higher Education

It is vital to stress that discrimination in one or another form . . . is a national phenomenon. . . . Its consequences are felt throughout the land by such diverse religious and racial groups as Negroes, Jews, Catholics, Puerto Ricans, Mexicans, Latin Americans, Italians, and Orientals. . . .

Racial Discrimination

The Negro is the most frequent victim of racial discrimination because prejudice on the basis of color is dominant in the American community. . . .

The Impact of Segregation on Higher Education for Negroes

Negroes represent approximately 10 percent of the total population of the United States. Yet enrollments of Negroes in institutions of higher education during the school year 1947 accounted for only 3.1 percent of the total. An estimated 75,000 students of Negro descent were enrolled; of these approximately 85 percent were enrolled in 105 segregated institutions. . . .

Discrimination by Graduate and Professional Schools

Negro students receive a much smaller proportion of advanced degrees. . . .

Table 5 well summarizes the situation in several important professional fields.

Table 5
**Comparison of Number of Negroes and Whites in Selected Professions in
Comparison to Negro Population and White Population in Segregated Areas**

Profession	Ratio of Practitioners to Population	
	Negro	White
Doctors	1:4,409	1:843
Dentists	1:12,101	1:2,795
Pharmacists	1:22,815	1:1,714
Lawyers	1:24,997	1:702
Social Workers	1:11,537	1:2,654
Engineers	1:130,700	1:1,644

To End Racial Discrimination

This Commission concludes that there will be no fundamental correction of the total condition until segregation legislation is repealed.

Source: Higher Education for American Democracy. A Report of the President's Commission on Higher Education, vol. 2 (New York: Harper and Brothers, 1948): 29, 32, 34, 35.

Four of the education commission's twenty-seven members (the presidents of the University of Arkansas, Emory University, and Washington University, joined by Richmond editor and historian Douglas Southall Freeman) dissented from the recommendation to end segregation. They received backing from other southern and border state educators.

{r}DOCUMENT 76: President Truman's Special Message to Congress on Civil Rights, February 2, 1948

Three months after receiving the report of his civil rights committee, President Truman delivered a special address before Congress in support of the committee's recommendations. Some historians have found in it—when taken with the civil rights committee report—the framework for civil rights initiatives of succeeding decades. They have also noted that during the remainder of his own term the president achieved none of the objectives declared in his message.

* * *

I recommend . . . that the Congress enact legislation at this session directed toward the following specific objectives:

1. establishing a permanent Commission on Civil Rights, a Joint Congressional Committee on Civil Rights, and a Civil Rights Division in the Department of Justice.
2. Strengthening existing civil rights statutes.
3. Providing Federal protection against lynching.
4. Protecting more adequately the right to vote.
5. Establishing a Fair Employment Practice Commission to prevent unfair discrimination in employment.
6. Prohibiting discrimination in interstate transportation facilities.

Source: Public Papers of the Presidents. January 1 to December 31, 1948: 122.

{r}DOCUMENT 77: Executive Order 9981, July 26, 1948

In his address to Congress, Truman had promised to take further executive action. He did so in July 1948, issuing Executive Order (EO) 9980, establishing a Fair Employment Board in the Civil Service Commission, and EO 9981, establishing a Committee on Equality of Treatment and Opportunity in the Armed Services. The new Fair Employment Board sought to coordinate fair employment policies among federal agencies. It was not authorized to enforce such policies and did not have much impact. Implementation of 9981, intended to desegregate the armed forces, was slow. However, this measure has been ranked as "Truman's most significant civil rights accomplishment" (Lowery and Marszalek 1992, 175).

* * *

It is hereby declared to be the policy of the President that there shall be equality of treatment and opportunity for all persons in the armed services without regard to race, color, religion or national origin. This policy shall be put into effect as rapidly as possible, having due regard to the time required to effectuate any necessary changes without impairing efficiency or morale.

Source: Federal Register 13 (July 28, 1948): 4313.

{d}DOCUMENT 78: Presidential Proclamation on National Employ the Handicapped Week, August 27, 1947

In the same period in which he was pursuing executive action on racial equality, President Truman also helped to set in motion new machinery for advocacy on behalf of disabled citizens by supporting a congressional resolution establishing a national week focused on employment of the handicapped.

* * *

WHEREAS, the people of this Nation are profoundly conscious of the limitless debt they owe to their fellow citizens who count the costs of wars in terms of physical handicaps; and . . . each year the toll of industrial and other accidents increases the number of handicapped persons seeking work. . . .

NOW THEREFORE, I . . . do hereby call upon the people of the United States to observe the week of October 5–11, 1947 as National Employ the Physically Handicapped Week.

Source: Statutes at Large 61 (1947): 1086.

{d}DOCUMENT 79: The Strachan Proposal Presaging Affirmative Action for the Disabled, January 1946

The origins of National Employ the Physically Handicapped Week lay with Paul Strachan, founder and leader of the American Federation of Handicapped Persons. Disabled through a train accident and burdened with a number of debilitating illnesses, Strachan lobbied persistently for the right of disabled individuals to participate in the economy and maintain as much self-sufficiency as possible. Having gained federal sponsorship for the national week of emphasis on handicapped employment, Strachan went on to enlist Alabama congressman John Sparkman as the sponsor of a bill that—as scholar Edward Berkowitz has observed—"we would now call an affirmative action plan" (Berkowitz 1987, 72). Sparkman introduced Strachan's proposal in the House of Representatives in January 1946. Strachan's plan was defeated, but the philosophy of self-determination that lay behind it would emerge again in future decades.

* * *

Mr. SPARKMAN. I am . . . introducing a bill to establish a Federal Commission for the Physically Handicapped. . . .

Title II [of the proposed bill].
Sec. 201. [E]mployers in industry having contracts with the Federal Government . . . [shall] place and retain in employment fixed proportions of persons qualified to work, but handicapped by disablement. . . . [T]hat such employers . . . shall be advised and aided in the introduction of work methods and the adjustment of tools, appliances and machinery necessary to accommodate certain types of disablement. . . .

Title III.
Sec. 301. The Commission shall establish and maintain a register of qualified disabled persons. . . .

Title IV.
Sec. 402. It shall be the duty of every employer, in filling vacancies, to take into employment registrants to the number ascertained to be his quota. . . .

Standard percentages shall be fixed by the Commission and shall be: For plants, industries or offices or other businesses employing less than 100 persons, not less than 1 percent of the total number of persons employed . . . for . . . businesses employing over 100 but less than 1,000 persons, no less than 1 1/2 percent of the total number employed . . . for . . . businesses employing over 1,000 persons, not less than 2 percent of the total number employed.

Source: Congressional Record 92, Pt. 9, Appendix (January 22, 1946): A175, A176–A177.

{d}DOCUMENT 80: Public Law 617, June 10, 1948

While Congress avoided the Strachan plan, it continued to take limited steps to eliminate barriers for the disabled. Such steps included an annual appropriation for National Employ the Handicapped Week (approved in 1949) and a 1948 amendment to the Civil Service Act.

* * *

An Act to amend the Civil Service Act [by adding the following]:

[N]o person shall be discriminated against in any case because of any physical handicap, in examination, appointment, reappointment, reinstatement, reemployment, promotion, transfer, retransfer, demotion, or removal, with respect to any position the duties of which, in the opinion of the Civil Service Commission, may be efficiently performed by a person with such a physical handicap: *And provided further*, That such employment will not be hazardous to the appointee or endanger the health or safety of his fellow employees or others.

Source: Public Law 617, *U.S. Statutes at Large* 62, Chap. 434, 351 (1948).

{r}DOCUMENT 81: *Hughes v. Superior Court*, May 8, 1950

As the 1940s came to an end, an important civil rights lawsuit was making its way through the state courts of California to the U.S. Supreme Court. The suit was filed by the Lucky Stores grocery chain against protesters who demanded the hiring of black workers in proportion to the number of blacks who shopped at the Lucky store in Richmond, California. The management obtained an injunction against picketers led by a group calling themselves the Progressive Citizens of America (PCA). The injunction was granted by the county superior court on the grounds that picketing for racial quotas was unlawful. After picketers, including PCA member John Hughes, defied the injunction and were arrested and fined, the PCA, backed by the NAACP, carried the case to an appeals court, which lifted the injunction. Lucky Stores then appealed to the California Supreme Court, where the injunction was again upheld. On November 8 and 9, 1949, the U.S. Supreme Court heard arguments on the case. Lawyers for John Hughes argued that PCA was seeking only the level of employment for blacks that they would enjoy at Lucky Stores if the grocery chain did not discriminate. In a debate that would sound very familiar in a later era of affirmative action, PCA lawyers responded to the charge that the proportional hiring that they demanded was in itself discriminatory. They maintained, "Special consideration does not become 'discrimination' where its beneficiaries are a uniquely oppressed and exploited social group." The Supreme Court issued its decision on May 8, 1950, finding against John Hughes and PCA.

* * *

To deny to California the right to ban picketing in the circumstances of this case would mean that there could be no prohibition of the pressure of picketing to secure proportional employment on ancestral grounds of Hungarians in Cleveland, of Poles in Buffalo, of Germans in Milwaukee, of Portuguese in New Bedford, of Mexicans in San Antonio, of the numerous minority groups in New York, and so on through the whole gamut of racial and religious concentrations in various cities. . . . The differences in cultural traditions instead of adding flavor and variety to our common citizenry might well be hardened into hostilities by leave of law.

Source: 339 U.S. 460 at 464 (1950).

{r}DOCUMENT 82: *Sweatt v. Painter*, 1950

In upholding California's opposition to "arbitrary discrimination upon the basis of race and color alone," the U.S. Supreme Court dealt defeat to advocates of proportional hiring but reinforced the grounds for litigation against racial segregation. A succession of challenges to "separate but equal" policies in state professional schools had prepared this ground. The challengers were represented by NAACP lawyers, headed by Charles Houston (Doc. 48) and Thurgood Marshall. Earlier challenges had been won against the law schools of the University of Maryland (1935), the University of Missouri (1938), and the University of Oklahoma (1948). In April 1950 the Supreme Court ruled on the cases of Herman Sweatt, who was seeking admission to the University of Texas at Austin, and John McLaurin, an applicant to the doctoral program in the School of Education at the University of Oklahoma. Thurgood Marshall argued and won both cases.

Herman Sweatt was a veteran who applied to the University of Texas Law School at Austin in 1946. The Texas State Board of Regents denied him admission, citing state law that mandated the segregation of schools. The following year the Regents created a law school for black students at a black college in Houston. State courts found that this school met the standards for "separate but equal." Refusing to attend the new school, Sweatt appealed to the Supreme Court. Both Sweatt and the state of Texas pressed the High Court to revisit the *Plessy* decision (Doc. 25). The Court majority, in ruling that Sweatt had a right to attend the Austin law school, declined to reexamine the decision of 1896. The *Sweatt* case resurfaced forty-six years later, when a race-conscious admissions program designed to remedy the effects of historical discrimination (illustrated by Sweatt's experience) was challenged in the courts (Doc. 353).

* * *

Whether the University of Texas Law School is compared with the original or the new law school for Negroes, we cannot find substantial equality in the educational opportunities offered white and Negro law students by the State. . . .

[W]e cannot agree with respondents that the doctrine of *Plessy v. Ferguson* . . . requires affirmance of the judgment [in this case]. Nor need we reach petitioner's contention that *Plessy v. Ferguson* should be reexamined in the light of contemporary knowledge respecting the purposes of the Fourteenth Amendment and the effects of racial segregation.

We hold that the Equal Protection Clause of the Fourteenth Amendment requires that petitioner be admitted to the University of Texas Law School.

Source: 339 U.S. 629 at 633, 636 (1950).

THE ADMINISTRATION OF DWIGHT EISENHOWER

{r}DOCUMENT 83: Executive Order 10479, August 18, 1953

The Eisenhower years were pivotal in the history of American race relations, but not because of presidential action. Rather, the Supreme Court triggered far-reaching change, while the executive branch of government proceeded cautiously on all matters of race. Eisenhower's earliest initiative, Executive Order 10479, replaced the Committee on Government Contract Compliance (created by Truman at the very end of his administration) with a new President's Committee on Government Contracts (PCGC). This committee analyzed the racial composition of federal workers in various cities and brought some pressure to bear on employers to hire African Americans.

* * *

There is hereby established the Government Contract Committee . . . composed of fourteen members. . . .

The Committee shall make recommendations to the contracting agencies for improving and making more effective the nondiscrimination provisions of government contracts.

Source: Executive Order 10479, *Federal Register* 18, no. 161 (August 13, 1953): 4899.

{r}DOCUMENT 84: *Brown v. Board of Education,* May 17, 1954

In December 1952 the Supreme Court heard opening arguments on five cases calling into question the "separate but equal" doctrine in public education. The five suits were consolidated under the title of the case that came first alphabetically, *Brown v. Board of Education.* Thurgood Marshall headed the team of lawyers for the plaintiffs. The final decision in May 1954 overturned *Plessy* and inspired intensified activism among civil rights advocates and their opponents.

* * *

Does segregation of children in public schools solely on the basis of race . . . deprive the children of the minority group of equal educational opportunities? We believe that it does. . . .

We conclude that in the field of public education the doctrine of "separate but equal" has no place.

Source: 347 U.S. 483 at 495 (1954).

{r}DOCUMENT 85: Reactions to the *Brown* Decision, Spring/Summer 1954

Early public response to the *Brown* ruling ranged from elation to threats of "massive resistance," as the comments of editor Carey McWilliams, lawyer Louis Redding, and Senator James Eastland demonstrate.

* * *

A. Carey McWilliams, editor of *The Nation*
The dead no less than the living must have rejoiced [when Chief Justice Earl Warren delivered the decision.] Among the ghosts that smiled with pleasure . . . [was] Homer Adolph Plessy. . . . Another beaming ghost would be Justice John Marshall Harlan [Doc. 25].

Source: Carey McWilliams, "The Climax of an Era," *The Nation* (May 29, 1954): 453–454.

B. NAACP Lawyer Louis L. Redding
[T]ravail . . . will ensue before the court's rejection of separate, inferior status for Negro children is reflected in all the schoolrooms of the nation.

Source: Louis L. Redding, "Evasions Barred," *The Nation* (May 29, 1954): 454.

C. Mississippi Senator James Eastland
The Court holds that the segregation of white and colored children in public schools has a detrimental effect upon the colored children. What about the white children? Do they not, also, have rights? Will not the commingling of the races in public schools have a detrimental effect upon white children? . . .

[A]t no time in the foreseeable future will there be a single racially integrated school in the State of Mississippi. That . . . is something that the white race will not permit under any conditions; and there is not the power of compulsion on the part of the Federal Government to compel it.

Sources: Congressional Record 100, Pt. 1 (May 27, 1954): 7252; (July 23, 1954): 11524–11525.

{r}DOCUMENT 86: *U.S. News & World Report* (December 1954), Inquiry on Enforcement of Executive Order 10557

In the year between the 1954 *Brown* decision and the Court's ruling on its implementation, Congress amended the Vocational Rehabilitation Act (Doc. 33), establishing a new advisory council on vocational rehabilitation. Eisenhower also issued two additional executive orders on employment, 10557 concerning the meaning of "compliance" and 10590 establishing yet another committee on fair employment. While the language of EO 10557 was detailed, what it meant in practical terms for employers was a widely asked question. Three months after Eisenhower issued the order, *U.S. News & World Report* asked unnamed "government officials" to answer that question.

* * *

So that employers and individuals may know what is going on . . . *U.S. News & World Report* asked specific questions of Government officials concerned with interpreting and enforcing the rules. . . .

Q. **Exactly what is the Federal Government trying to do?**
A. It is trying, by use of its vast spending power, to make all employers end racial or religious discrimination in hiring and firing. . . .

Q. **Does this mean that a company must hire a certain percentage of Negroes [and other groups] to get Government business?**
A. No. No quotas are established. No employer is told that he must have a certain percentage of any group in his factory. . . .

Q. **This committee has direct power to enforce employment rules?**
A. No. It can only make recommendations to the regular federal agencies that deal with the businessmen. . . .

Q. **[N]o really "tough" compliance initiative is on?**
A. Not as yet.

Source: "One More Color Line Ruled Out, Employers Told to End Race Bias in Hiring," *U.S. News & World Report* (December 17, 1954): 46–47.

The committee established in Eisenhower's order of August 1953 (Doc. 83) operated within the Civil Service Commission. With Executive Order 10590 the president created the President's Committee on Government Employment Policy, which answered directly to him, thereby indicating that the full authority of his office was behind enforcement of equal opportunity policy. Nonetheless, his administration was characterized by hesitancy to exercise that authority.

{r}DOCUMENT 87: *"Brown II,"* May 31, 1955

Four months after the new employment committee was established, the Supreme Court issued its ruling on enforcement of the *Brown* decision. The 1955 decision, sometimes referred to as *Brown II,* dashed the celebratory spirits with which the NAACP lawyers and their supporters had greeted the initial ruling. By turning over the process of implementation to local governments, the Court left school desegregation in the hands of those who most opposed it.

* * *

Brown v. Board of Education, Enforcement Decree
Because of their proximity to local conditions and the possible need for further hearings . . . we believe it appropriate to remand these cases to . . . the courts which originally heard [them]. . . . The District Courts [are therefore ordered to proceed] to admit to public schools on a racially nondiscriminatory basis with all deliberate speed the parties to these cases.

Source: 349 U.S. 294 at 299, 301 (1955).

{d}DOCUMENT 88: Social Security Amendments of 1956 (Statement of Purpose)

In the judgment of scholar Jacobus tenBroek, one of the most significant developments for the disabled in this period was the passage by Congress of amendments to the Social Security Act of 1935. "There is no single landmark event in the social history of the disabled comparable to the Supreme Court decision in the *Brown* case," he wrote. "There are, however," he added, "a number of episodes and actions which are similar in portent if not in scope." He offered the Social Security Amendments of 1956 as a prime example because of a strong emphasis on "self-support" and "self-care" (tenBroek 1966a, 833–834).

* * *

To promote the well-being of the Nation by encouraging the States to place greater emphasis on helping to strengthen family life and helping needy families and individuals to attain the maximum economic and personal independence of which they are capable.

Source: U.S. Statutes at Large 70 (1956): 848.

{r}DOCUMENT 89: The Southern Manifesto, March 12, 1956

Meanwhile, "Massive Resistance" to school integration was spreading not only in southern towns and cities but also in the halls of Congress. Seventy-seven members of the House of Representatives (joined later by another five colleagues) and nineteen senators (all the southern senators, except Estes Kefauver of Tennessee and Lyndon Johnson of Texas) signed and distributed a document that soon became known as the Southern Manifesto. It carried no force of law. However, the influence of those who signed it and the responses of those who opposed it—ranging from mild statements of support for desegregation to avoiding the issue altogether—helped to legitimate defiance of the *Brown* rulings.

* * *

We regard the decision of the Supreme Court in the school cases as a clear abuse of judicial power. . . .

In the case of *Plessy v. Ferguson* in 1896 the Supreme Court expressly declared that . . . no person was denied any of his rights if the States provided separate but equal public facilities. . . .

This interpretation, restated time and again, became a part of the life of the people of many of the States and confirmed their habits, customs, traditions, and way of life. . . .

We . . . decry the Supreme Court's encroachments on rights reserved to the States and to the people. . . .

We commend the motives of those States which have declared the intention to resist forced integration by any lawful means. . . .

We pledge ourselves to use all lawful means to bring about a reversal of this decision.

Source: Congressional Record 102, Pt. 1 (March 12, 1956): 4459–4464.

{r}DOCUMENT 90: Circuit Judge Richard Rives on *Browder v. Gayle,* June 5, 1956

The *Brown* decisions against segregated schools implied, but did not directly mandate, the end of segregation in other public venues. The ruling that finally demolished *Plessy v. Ferguson* grew out of the Montgomery, Alabama, bus boycott, undertaken by the African American citizens of that city between December 5, 1955, and December 21, 1956. The protest was sparked by the arrest on December 1, 1955, of Mrs. Rosa Parks, who, having taken a seat in the middle section of the bus (which by company policy was unreserved), refused to yield the seat to a white passenger when the driver ordered her to do so. The superbly disciplined boycotters— mobilized by the Montgomery Improvement Association (MIA) and inspired by the leadership of the twenty-six-year-old Baptist minister Martin Luther King Jr.—employed car pools and shoe leather to get to work, leaving the city buses virtually empty. The MIA filed a lawsuit in federal court against Montgomery city officials and the owners of the bus company on behalf of four other women who had been arrested under circumstances similar to those experienced by Mrs. Parks. Filed in federal district court, the case was ruled on by a panel of three federal judges in May. Martin Luther King Jr. assured the Montgomery protesters that "we are not wrong in what we are doing. If we are wrong," he proclaimed, "the Supreme Court of the nation is wrong. If we are wrong the Constitution of the United States is wrong. . . . If we are wrong, justice is a lie . . ." (Carson 1997, 71). Reverend King's confidence was affirmed by the Fifth Circuit Court.

* * *

[T]here is now no rational basis upon which the separate but equal doctrine can be validly applied to public carrier transportation within the City of Montgomery and its police jurisdiction. The application of that doctrine cannot be justified as a proper execution of the state police power.

Source: 142 F. Supp. 707 (M.D. Ala., 1956).

{r}DOCUMENT 91: Supreme Court Decision on *Browder v. Gayle*, November 1956

On November 13 the U.S. Supreme Court upheld the District Court ruling in *Browder v. Gayle*. In one short sentence, the highest court eviscerated *Plessy v. Ferguson* in any and all of its possible applications.

* * *

The motion to affirm is granted and the judgment is affirmed.

Source: Browder v. Gayle, 352 U.S. 903 (1956).

{r}DOCUMENT 92: Eisenhower Press Conference, July 17, 1957

President Eisenhower avoided entanglement with the Montgomery protest and in the summer of 1957 reassured the southern status quo regarding federal intervention in civil rights struggles.

* * *

I can't imagine any set of circumstances that would ever induce me to send Federal troops . . . into any area to enforce the orders of a Federal court, because I believe that [the] common sense of America will never require it.

Source: Dwight D. Eisenhower, *Public Papers of the Presidents* (1957): 546.

{r}DOCUMENT 93: The Civil Rights Act of 1957

The Eisenhower administration did lend support to efforts in Congress on behalf of a new civil rights bill. In September Congress passed the Civil Rights Act of 1957. The first federal civil rights legislation since Reconstruction, the 1957 act created a six-member Civil Rights Commission and placed enforcement authority for civil rights violations in the Justice Department.

* * *

Part I—Establishment of the Commission on Civil Rights

Sec. 101. (a) There is created in the executive branch of the Government a Commission on Civil Rights. . . .

DUTIES OF THE COMMISSION
Sec. 104. (a) The Commission shall—

(1) investigate allegations in writing under oath or affirmation that certain citizens of the United States are being deprived of their right to vote. . . .

Part IV—To Provide Means of Further Securing and Protecting the Right to Vote

Sec. 131. . . .

Whenever any person has engaged . . . in any act or practice which would deprive any other person of [the right to vote] . . . the Attorney General may institute for the United States . . . a civil action or other proper proceeding.

Source: Laws of the 85th Congress 1 (1957): 703, 705, 707.

{r}DOCUMENT 94: Illinois Senator Paul Douglas' Assessment of the Civil Rights Act of 1957

Most supporters of civil rights found the 1957 bill to be sorely lacking, as the following comment by Senator Douglas indicates.

* * *

[The act is no more than] soup made from the shadow of a crow which had starved to death.

Source: Quoted in Bruce Schulman, *Lyndon B. Johnson and American Liberalism* (New York: St. Martin's Press, 1995): 53.

{r}DOCUMENT 95: Texas Senator Lyndon Johnson's Assessment of the Civil Rights Act of 1957

Lyndon Johnson viewed the act differently—from the perspective of practical politics.

* * *

I got all I could on Civil Rights in 1957. Next year I'll get a little more, and the year after that a little more. The difference between me and some of my northern friends is that I believe you can't force these things on the South overnight. You advance a little and consolidate; then you advance again.

Source: Quoted in Bruce Schulman, *Lyndon B. Johnson and American Liberalism* (New York: St. Martin's Press, 1995): 53.

Passage of the Civil Rights Act coincided with the opening of the 1957–1958 school year. In Little Rock, Arkansas, a plan for gradual desegregation, beginning with admission of a small number of African American students to Little Rock High School, had been approved by the federal district court and was to be implemented by the School Board. When Arkansas governor Orval Faubus defied the court order, President Eisenhower overcame his antipathy to intervention and sent federal troops to Little Rock. With their backing the "Little Rock Nine" integrated the high school. The following year Faubus closed all the Little Rock schools.

{d}DOCUMENT 96: Jacobus tenBroek, "The Cross of Blindness," 1957

While African Americans in cities such as Montgomery and Little Rock challenged the racist status quo, disabled citizens were also going up against barriers cemented in foundations of law, custom, and prejudice. When Jacobus tenBroek addressed the seventeenth annual convention of the National Federation of the Blind in 1957, he listed sixteen recent events exemplifying discrimination against blind people. His examples included the following.

* * *

Where is the need for all this organization and militant activity? Why can't the blind let well enough alone?

These are reasonable questions. . . . I believe that the answer may best be given by reciting a list of sixteen specific events which have taken place recently in various parts of the country. The events are:

1. A blind man . . . was denied a room in a well-known YMCA [Young Men's Christian Association] in New York City . . . on the ground that he was blind.
2. A blind man was rejected as a donor by the blood bank in his city . . . on the ground that he was blind. . . .
4. A blind man was rejected for jury duty in a California city . . . on the ground that he was blind. . . .
9. A blind high school student who was a duly qualified candidate for student body president was removed from the list of candidates by authority of the principal and faculty of the school . . . on the ground that he was blind. . . .
11. A blind man, who had been a successful justice court and police court judge in his community for eleven years, ran for the position of superior court judge in the general election of 1956. . . . The voters . . . elected him handily. At the next session of the state legislature a bill was introduced disqualifying blind persons as judges. . . .
12. More than sixty blind men and women . . . were recently ordered by the building and safety authority of a large city to move out of their hotel-type living quarters . . . on the ground that as blind people they were subject to the code provisions regarding the "bedridden, ambulatory, and helpless. . . ."
15. A blind person, duly convicted of a felony and sentenced to a state penitentiary, was denied parole when he became eligible . . . on the ground that he was blind.

Source: Jacobus tenBroek, "The Cross of Blindness," 1957, reprinted in Floyd W. Matson, *Walking Alone, Marching Together* (Baltimore: National Federation of the Blind, 1990): 96–99.

As tenBroek expressed the yearning of the blind "to compete on equal terms," (*New Yorker*, January 1958), the civil rights movement was gaining momentum. A major catalyst for college-age citizens was the sit-ins directed against segregated lunch counters. To consolidate their efforts, participants in the sit-in movement established the Student Nonviolent Coordinating Committee (SNCC) in April 1960. Adding increased boldness and impatience to the quest for civil rights, SNCC evolved quickly into one of the major civil rights organizations of the era. Other key groups promoting direct action were the Southern Christian Leadership Conference (SCLC), which had grown out of the Montgomery Improvement Association, and the Congress of Racial Equality (CORE), which had pioneered nonviolent protest in the era of World War II.

{r}DOCUMENT 97: Civil Rights Act, May 6, 1960

From the vantage point of those who were directly challenging segregation, the strategy that Senator Lyndon Johnson had identified in 1957 as the most practical (Doc. 95) seemed woefully inadequate. But it did serve the purposes of the politicians who managed in 1960 to get another civil rights act through Congress. The law of 1960 provided a small measure of federal support for victims of voting rights violations. As had happened with the 1957 Civil Rights Act, removed from the original version of the 1960 bill were enforcement powers granted to the Justice Department. Also as in 1957, Lyndon Johnson was universally credited with engineering the compromises that secured passage of the new law. Soon, as vice president and then president of the United States, Johnson would play a decisive role in advocating "affirmative action" and making it a central issue in American life.

* * *

Title VI

Sec. 60. . . . [S]ection 131 of the Civil Rights Act of 1957 . . . is amended as follows:
(a). Add the following . . .
". . . in the event the court finds that any person has been deprived on account of race or color of any right or privilege [related to voting] . . . the court shall, upon request of the Attorney General . . . make a finding whether such deprivation was or is pursuant to a pattern or practice. If the court finds such pattern or practice, any person of such race or color resident within the affected areas shall . . . until the court subsequently finds that such pattern or practice has ceased, be entitled upon his application therefore, to an order declaring him qualified to vote. . . .

Source: Laws of 86th Congress, 2nd Session 1 (1960): 97, 102.

{r}DOCUMENT 98: Senator Paul Douglas' Assessment of the 1960 Civil Rights Act

The latest civil rights legislation was again found wanting by liberals such as Senator Douglas.

* * *

Like the mountain that labored and brought forth a mouse, the United States Congress after eight weeks of Senate debate and weeks of House debate, passed what can only by courtesy be called a civil rights bill.

Source: Paul H. Douglas, "Trends and Developments, the 1960 Voting Rights Bill: The Struggle, the Final Results and the Reasons," *Journal of Intergroup Relations* 1, no. 3 (Summer 1960): 82.

{r}DOCUMENT 99: *Boynton v. Virginia*, 1960

Of longer-term effect than the 1960 Civil Rights Act was the Supreme Court decision of the same year, extending to public transportation terminals the prohibition established in *Morgan v. Virginia* (Doc. 71) against segregated public transportation. In the *Boynton* case an African American law student traveling from Washington, D.C., to Montgomery, Alabama, was arrested when he requested service in the "whites only" section of the bus terminal restaurant in Richmond, Virginia. His conviction in the local police court for trespassing was upheld by the Hustings Court of Richmond and the Virginia Supreme Court but overturned by a majority of the U.S. Supreme Court.

* * *

Mr. Justice Black delivered the opinion of the Court. . . .

Interstate passengers have to eat. . . . Such passengers in transit on a paid interstate Trailways journey had a right to expect that this essential transportation food service voluntarily provided for them under such circumstances would be rendered without discrimination prohibited by the Interstate Commerce Act.

Source: 364 U.S. 454 at 455, 463 (1960).

THE KENNEDY ERA

{r}DOCUMENT 100: Attorney General Robert Kennedy on Civil Rights Enforcement, March 1961

Civil rights became a pivotal issue in the election of 1960 between the Democratic contenders for the White House, John F. Kennedy and Lyndon Johnson, and their Republican opponents, Richard Nixon and Henry Cabot Lodge. During the election campaign Martin Luther King Jr. was sentenced to prison and hard labor for a minor traffic violation. Telephone calls placed by John Kennedy to King's wife and by the candidate's brother, Robert Kennedy, to the judge who had sentenced him obtained not only the civil rights leader's release but also about 75 percent of the black vote for the Democratic ticket. Those black votes helped to secure the narrow margin by which John Kennedy became president. Even before the telephone calls, Kennedy made campaign pledges that he would use the powers of the presidency to issue an executive order on fair housing, promote civil rights legislation in Congress, and urge all Americans to obey "the moral imperative" of racial justice.

However, once in office, the Kennedy administration failed to keep the campaign promises. The disappointment of his movement supporters began when he devoted one short sentence to civil rights in his first State of the Union message. Their misgivings were hardly allayed when the president's brother, Attorney General Robert Kennedy, reprised the Eisenhower policy regarding enforcement of civil rights law.

* * *

I don't think we would ever come to the point of sending troops [into a state]. . . . I cannot conceive of this administration's letting such a situation deteriorate to that level.

Source: Peter Maas, "Robert Kennedy Speaks Out on Civil Rights," *Look* 25, no. 7 (March 28, 1961): 24.

{r}DOCUMENT 101: *New York Times* Report, May 10, 1961

During the presidential campaign the Kennedys had delegated to Pennsylvania senator Joseph Clark and New York congressman Emanuel Celler the task of drafting legislation to match campaign promises on civil rights. In May 1961 Clark and Celler presented that legislation to Congress, only to have the administration disavow it.

* * *

The White House disassociated itself today from civil rights legislation introduced by two Democrats yesterday in Congress. . . . Pierre Salinger, President Kennedy's press secretary, said that "the President has made it clear that he does not think it is necessary at this time to enact civil rights legislation."

Source: "White House Doubts Need of New Rights Laws Now," *New York Times* (May 10, 1961): 1.

{r}DOCUMENT 102: Executive Order 10925, March 6, 1961

On one issue—job discrimination—the Kennedy administration did move forward. With a publicity blitz in March 1961, the president issued Executive Order 10925 and declared that his administration was committed to equal opportunity in employment by the federal government and its contractors. EO 10925 established another contract compliance committee with authority over not only government contractors, as with the committees of Truman and Eisenhower (Docs. 76, 77, 83, 86), but also labor unions whose members worked for government contractors. In a "color-blind" context the Kennedy order employed the term "affirmative action."

* * *

III. A
Section 301
The contractor will not discriminate against any employee or applicant for employment because of race, creed, color or national origin. The contractor will take affirmative action to ensure that applicants are em-

ployed, and that employees are treated during employment, without
regard to race, creed, color, or national origin.

Source: Federal Register 26 (1961): 1977.

{r}DOCUMENT 103: James Farmer's Memory of the Kennedy Administration and the Freedom Rides of 1961

By the end of 1961, the Kennedy administration was trying to quell
an explosive chain of events set off when the Congress of Racial Equality (CORE) determined to test *Boynton v. Virginia* (Doc. 99) by sending
integrated teams of "Freedom Riders" on Greyhound and Trailways
buses into bus terminals in the Deep South. After racist mobs attacked
the riders, Robert Kennedy called for a "cooling-off period" and was
rebuffed by CORE leader James Farmer.

* * *

I . . . said, . . . Please tell the attorney general that we have been cooling
off for 350 years. If we cool off any more, we will be in a deep freeze.
The Freedom Ride will go on.

Source: James Farmer, *Lay Bare the Heart, an Autobiography of the Civil Rights Movement* (New York: Arbor House, 1978): 206.

{r}DOCUMENT 104: *New York Times*, November 2, 1961

With reinforcement from SNCC, the rides continued, along with the
violence, involving more than 1,000 volunteers. By the fall of 1961 the
Kennedy administration had directed the Interstate Commerce Commission (ICC) to put an end to all forms of segregated interstate transportation. In November the ICC issued an order to that effect.

* * *

[All "common carriers" must post signs reading], "Seating aboard this
vehicle is without regard to race, color, creed, or national origin."

Source: New York Times, November 2, 1961, 1.

{g}DOCUMENT 105: Executive Order 10980, December 15, 1961

If civil rights supporters were impatient with the Kennedy adminis-tration's cautious stance toward their movement, backers of the emerg-ing women's movement were aggravated by what one scholar has described as the administration's "benign neglect masquerading as pseudo concern" for women's issues (Hoff 1991, 231). John Kennedy took the advice of Vice President Johnson and Women's Bureau direc-tor Esther Peterson and appointed a commission on the status of women. In the executive order creating the new commission, President Kennedy employed the phrase "affirmative steps . . . to assure non-discrimination on the basis of sex." He appointed former First Lady Eleanor Roosevelt to chair the commission. When she died within a year, the president selected Esther Peterson as her successor.

* * *

Part I. Establishment of the President's Commission on the Status of Women

Sec. 101. There is hereby established the President's Commission on the Status of Women. . . .

Part II. Duties of the President's Commission on the Status of Women. . . .

Sec. 201. The Commission shall review progress and make recommen-dations as needed for constructive action in [six areas, including] . . .

(f) The employment policies and practices of the Government of the United States with reference to additional affirmative steps which should be taken through legislation, executive, or administrative action . . . to enhance constructive employment opportunities for women.

Source: Federal Register 26, no. 242 (December 16, 1961): 12059.

{r}DOCUMENT 106: Civil Rights Worker Charles McDew and Robert Kennedy in the Early 1960s

Nonviolent direct action, as demonstrated in the sit-ins and Freedom Rides, was pushing everyone to move faster on civil rights. As civil rights workers continued to risk—and, in some cases, lose—their lives, relations between them and the government reached a breaking point. When Herbert Lee, the first African American to register to vote in Amite County, Mississippi, since World War II, was murdered, and Robert Kennedy refused to provide federal protection for African American witnesses to the murder, SNCC field-worker Charles McDew exploded.

* * *

I remember calling Bobby Kennedy a bunch of names and saying, "You guys have lied to us. You don't intend to do shit and you're not going to protect the rights of Negro voters as you promised." . . . We understood that clearly we were out there by ourselves.

Source: Quoted in Mark Stern, *Calculating Visions* (New Brunswick, NJ: Rutgers University Press, 1992): 68.

{r}DOCUMENT 107: John F. Kennedy's Address to the Nation, September 30, 1962

The impression that the administration's heart was not in civil rights action was further reinforced by its laconic sponsorship of a bill to outlaw literacy tests for voter registration. The bill would have established a sixth grade education as a sufficient qualification for voting and would have abolished the literacy test, which *Time* described as "the South's most effective device for denying the vote to Negroes" (*Time*, May 18, 1962). The bill was killed by a southern filibuster, against which the administration mounted no real defense.

However much the Kennedys desired to remain low-key in relation to civil rights, the press of events, fueled by advocates and resisters, forced them to act more decisively. When Mississippi governor Ross Barnett and his lieutenant governor Paul Johnson personally blocked the federal court-ordered admission of African American James Meredith to the University of Mississippi, John Kennedy ordered 300 federal marshals to the campus and extracted from the governor a pledge that state law enforcement would work with the marshals to protect Meredith. The president addressed the nation via radio and television.

* * *

[I]n a government of laws and not of men, no man, however prominent or powerful, and no mob, however unruly or boisterous, is entitled
to defy a court of law.

Source: Public Papers of the Presidents (January 1 to December 31, 1962): 727.

{r}DOCUMENT 108: *Pittsburgh Courier* Editorial, December 1, 1962

The president was upstaged as he spoke by the very kind of "boisterous" mob that he sought to forestall by his speech. To make matters
worse, he was betrayed by Governor Barnett, who allowed the Mississippi State Police to withdraw from the melee and offered no protection
for Meredith and no support for the marshals. Fifteen hours of rioting
ensued, quelled finally by 5,000 federal troops and federalized National Guardsmen. While the Kennedys had demonstrated resolve in
this episode, their enthusiasm for decisive action on civil rights was
still not consistently apparent. In November 1962 John Kennedy finally
issued the long-promised executive order on fair housing (EO 11063).
In a press conference devoted primarily to the Cuban missile crisis,
he sandwiched a reference to EO 11063 between a lengthy discourse
on the recent standoff with the Soviet Union and the conflict in progress
between China and India. The short shrift given the fair housing order irked African Americans, as noted by the editor of the *Pittsburgh
Courier.*

* * *

Negroes are getting very weary of tokenism hailed as victories.

Source: Pittsburgh Courier (December 1, 1962).

{d}DOCUMENT 109: Vocational Rehabilitation Commissioner Mary Switzer, 1962

The heady mix of impatience, expectation, and sense of entitlement
that characterized social protest movements in the 1960s was apparent
among the disabled and their organizations. The commissioner of the
Office of Vocational Rehabilitation from 1950 until 1967, Mary Swit-

zer, observed in 1962 that a major shift in thinking had occurred within the ranks of the disabled.

* * *

[There exists] a tremendous demand on the part of handicapped people, their families and friends. . . . Today large numbers of people have become aware that something can be done about disability through modern rehabilitation programs and they expect the public programs to respond to this need.

Source: Quoted in Marvin B. Sussman, *Sociology and Rehabilitation* (Washington, DC: American Sociological Association, 1965): 20.

{d}DOCUMENT 110: Executive Order 10994, 1962

Not only were demand and awareness among the disabled growing, but definitions of disability rights were expanding. A presidential executive order in 1962 contributed to the expansion by ordering that the word "physically" be removed from the name of the President's Committee on Employment of the Handicapped.

* * *

There is hereby established the President's Committee on Employment of the Handicapped. . . .
[A]ll members, employees, records, property, funds and pending business of the President's Committee on Employment of the Physically Handicapped . . . shall . . . become members, employees, records, property, funds, and pending business of the Committee established by this order.

Source: Federal Register 27 (1962): 1447.

{r}DOCUMENT 111: Martin Luther King Jr., "Letter from a Birmingham Jail," 1963

Martin Luther King Jr. and the Southern Christian Leadership Conference took nonviolent protest to new levels of mass participation and intensity in Birmingham, Alabama, in the spring of 1963. In common cause with the Alabama Christian Movement for Human Rights (ACMHR), King mobilized the African Americans of Birmingham, including more than 1,000 school children. When the local police chief ordered attacks on the demonstrators by firehoses and police dogs, his inhumanity was condemned throughout the nation and around the world.

Martin Luther King was jailed and for a time held incommunicado. During this incarceration King composed his famous "Letter from a Birmingham Jail." Prompted by criticism from white clergy who called the Birmingham demonstrations "untimely and unwise," King's indignant rejoinder carried a special message for the "white moderate."

* * *

I have been gravely disappointed with the white moderate. I have almost reached the regrettable conclusion that the Negroes' great stumbling block in the stride toward freedom is not the White Citizens' Councilor or the Ku Klux Klanner, but the white moderate who is more devoted to "order" than to justice . . . who paternalistically feels that he can set the timetable for another man's freedom. . . . Shallow understanding from people of good will is more frustrating than absolute misunderstanding from people of ill will.

Source: James M. Washington, ed., *A Testament of Hope, the Essential Writings and Speeches of Martin Luther King, Jr.* (New York: Harper, 1986): 295.

{r}DOCUMENT 112: Historian Arthur Schlesinger Jr. Recounts a May 1963 Confrontation between African Americans and Robert Kennedy

King's caustic reflections on the "white moderate" were echoed in a highly charged encounter between Robert Kennedy and a group of African Americans selected by author James Baldwin to participate in a private discussion of civil rights issues. The meeting took place in Kennedy's apartment in New York City on May 24, 1963. Most of the guests were "notables"—psychologist Kenneth Clark; Chicago Urban League director Edwin Berry; SCLC attorney Clarence Jones; playwright Lorraine Hansberry; and singers Lena Horne and Harry Belafonte. Also present was CORE field secretary Jerome Smith, whose rage at the nation's failure to come to grips with racial injustice quickly became the focal point of the meeting. Historian Arthur Schlesinger Jr. reconstructed the meeting from accounts of various participants.

* * *

Lorraine Hansberry said to Kennedy, "Look, if *you* can't understand what this young man [Jerome Smith] is saying, then we are without any hope at all because you and your brother are representatives of the best that a white America can offer; and if *you* are insensitive to this, then there's no alternative except our going in the streets . . . and chaos. . . ."

Kennedy said . . . that his grandparents had encountered discrimination and now, two generations later, his brother was President; a Negro would be President within forty years. Baldwin replied furiously, "Your family has been here for three generations. My family has been here far longer than that. Why is your brother at the top while we are still so far away? That's the heart of the problem." . . .

Source: Arthur M. Schlesinger Jr., *Robert Kennedy and His Times* (New York: Ballantine Books, 1979): 356–360.

{g}DOCUMENT 113: The Equal Pay Act of 1963

In the also sensitive—but, in this period, not so volatile—area of woman's rights the Kennedy administration gained some favor when the president signed the Equal Pay Act of 1963. As an amendment to the Fair Labor Standards Act of 1938, it covered only the workers covered by that original act, leaving out high-salaried professional and executive workers and low-salaried domestic and agricultural workers.

* * *

(d) Prohibition of sex discrimination

(1) No employer having employees subject to any provisions of this section shall discriminate . . . on the basis of sex by paying wages . . . at a rate less than the rate at which he pays wages to employees of the opposite sex . . . for equal work on jobs the performance of which requires equal skill, effort, and responsibility and which are performed under similar working conditions, except where such payment is made pursuant to (i) a seniority system; (ii) a merit system; (iii) a system which measures earnings by quantity or quality of production; or (iv) a differential based on any other factor other than sex. . . .

(2) No labor organization, or its agents . . . shall cause or attempt to cause . . . an employer to discriminate against an employee in violation of paragraph (1) of this subsection.

Source: U.S. Code 29, sec. 206-d (1963).

{r}DOCUMENT 114: President Kennedy's Report to the American People on Civil Rights, June 11, 1963

Very soon John and Robert Kennedy were faced with another southern racial crisis. African American students Vivian Malone and James Hood had applied for admission to the summer session at the University of Alabama at Tuscaloosa. A federal district court had enjoined Alabama governor George Wallace from blocking their enrollment. The governor, declaring that he was "the embodiment of the sovereignty of this state," promised to preserve segregation. However, in this instance, neither the White House nor the Department of Justice temporized. The moment that George Wallace turned back Hood and Malone from the registrar's office, John Kennedy federalized the Alabama National Guard. When the federalized Guard appeared on the university campus, the governor left, and the two students were registered. The same evening the president delivered a nationally televised address, which placed the issue of civil rights in a moral framework.

* * *

We are confronted primarily with a moral issue. It is as old as the scriptures and is as clear as the American Constitution.

The heart of the question is whether all Americans are to be afforded equal rights and equal opportunities, whether we are going to treat our fellow Americans as we want to be treated. . . .

It is a time to act in the Congress, in your State and local legislative body and, above all, in all of our daily lives. . . .

Next week I shall ask the Congress of the United States to act, to make a commitment it has not fully made in this century to the proposition that race has no place in American life or law.

Source: Public Papers of the Presidents. January 1 to November 22, 1963 (1963): 469.

Kennedy's stirring affirmation of racial justice was again overshadowed the very night that he spoke, this time by the assassination of the head of the Mississippi NAACP, Medgar Evers. A tireless organizer for voting rights and against segregation, Evers had long been a target of the Ku Klux Klan. Evers' killer went free at the time, though when the case was reopened some thirty years later, a guilty verdict was finally returned, and the aging and unrepentant murderer was sentenced to jail.

{r}DOCUMENT 115: Speech of John Lewis at the March on Washington, August 1963

President Kennedy was anxious about demonstrations in the streets, and the angry crowd that nearly rioted at the end of Medgar Evers' funeral intensified his worries. When A. Philip Randolph announced that a march on Washington would occur at the end of the summer, Kennedy and his advisers attempted to persuade civil rights leaders to call it off. After all such attempts failed, the president endorsed it as being in "the great American tradition."

On August 28, 1963, a quarter of a million Americans gathered under the Washington Monument calling for "Freedom, Jobs, and Justice—Now." Among the many speeches delivered that day, the most provocative was that of John Lewis, president of SNCC.

* * *

In good conscience we cannot support the Administration's civil rights bill, for it is too little, too late. . . .

We won't stop now. . . . The next time we march we won't march on Washington, but will march through the South, through the Heart of Dixie the way Sherman did. We will make the action of the past few months look petty.

Source: "Pre-edited Draft," SNCC Papers, reprinted in Peter B. Levy, ed., *Let Freedom Ring, a Documentary History of the Modern Civil Rights Movement* (Westport, CT: Praeger, 1992): 120–122.

{r}DOCUMENT 116: Martin Luther King's Speech at the March on Washington, August 1963

The most memorable speech that day was Martin Luther King's "I Have a Dream" oration.

* * *

When the architects of our republic wrote the magnificent words of the Constitution and the Declaration of Independence, they were signing a promissory note to which every American was to fall heir. This note was a promise that all men would be guaranteed the unalienable rights of life, liberty and the pursuit of happiness.

It is obvious today that America has defaulted on this promissory note insofar as her citizens of color are concerned. . . . But we refuse . . . to believe that there are insufficient funds in the great vaults of opportunity of this nation. So we have come to cash this check. . . .

Even though we must face the difficulties of today and tomorrow I still have a dream . . . that one day this nation will rise up and live out the true meaning of its creed: We hold these truths to be self-evident; that all men are created equal.

Source: James M. Washington, ed., *A Testament of Hope, the Essential Writings and Speeches of Martin Luther King, Jr.* (New York: Harper, 1986): 217, 219.

Among participants in the March on Washington the overpowering oratory of Martin Luther King and the empowering emotions of common purpose and strength in numbers seemed to swallow up the anger and bitterness to which John Lewis had given voice. However, eighteen days later anger and bitterness erased whatever euphoria still lingered from the march. On Sunday, September 15, 1963, racists set off a bomb in the Sixteenth Street Baptist Church of Birmingham. Services were in progress, and four little girls attending Sunday school were killed. Two other African American youths died in the street violence that followed. Pressure on the Kennedy administration to get a strong civil rights bill through Congress intensified.

{g}DOCUMENT 117: *American Women*, the Report of the President's Commission on the Status of Women, October 1963

At the same time, appointees to the President's Commission on the Status of Women were winding up their deliberations. On October 11 Esther Peterson submitted their report. While envisioning far-reaching changes in education and employment opportunity for women, the commissioners eschewed the ERA, defended existing protective labor laws, and followed conventional assumptions about women's family roles.

* * *

CONSTITUTIONAL RECOGNITION

Since the Commission is convinced that the United States Constitution now embodies equality of rights for men and women, we conclude that a constitutional amendment need not now be sought in order to establish this principle.

RECOMMENDATIONS OF THE PRESIDENT'S COMMISSION ON THE STATUS OF WOMEN . . .

WOMEN AND EMPLOYMENT

Equal opportunity for women in hiring, training, and promotion should be the governing principle in private employment. . . .

LABOR STANDARDS

The federal Fair Labor Standards Act . . . should be extended to employment subject to federal jurisdiction but now uncovered. . . .

SECURITY OF BASIC INCOME. . . .

Paid maternity leave or comparable insurance benefits should be provided for women workers.

Source: American Women: The Report of the President's Commission on the Status of Women and Other Publications of the Commission (New York: Charles Scribner's Sons, 1965): 66, 210–211, 212.

{g}DOCUMENT 118: Earnings and Employment Graphs from *American Women*, 1963

The commission illustrated the importance of equity and security in regard to women's salaries with numerous statistics, including the following graphs.

* * *

Women's Earnings Are Less Than Men's and . . .

MEDIAN WAGE OR SALARY INCOME

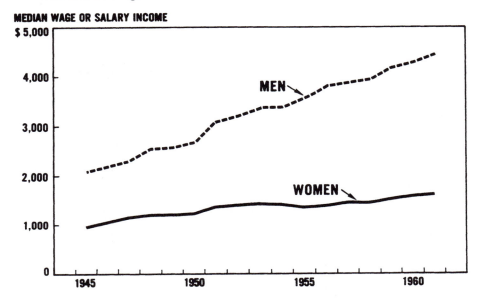

Hourly Pay in Retail Trade Illustrates Why

THOUSANDS OF EMPLOYEES

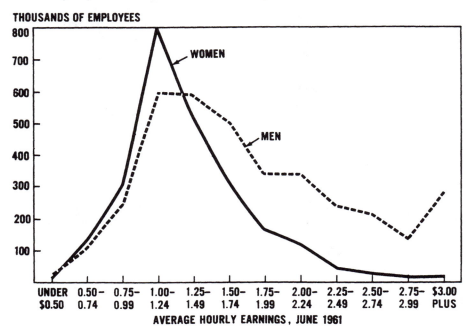

Every Third Worker Is a Woman (percent of all workers)

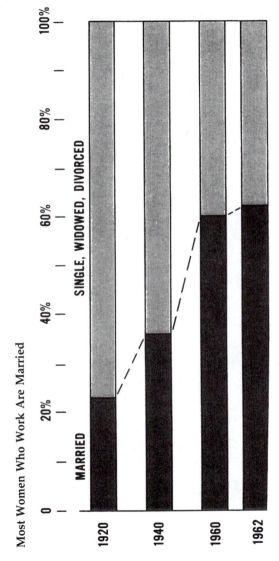

Most Women Who Work Are Married

Source: American Women: the Report of the President's Commission on the Status of Women and Other Publications of the Commission (New York: Charles Scribner's Sons, 1965): 46, 47, 56, 57.

Except for the Equal Pay Act (Doc. 113), which was signed before the commission issued its final report, no legislation followed directly from *American Women*. Nonetheless, the commission's work helped to focus attention on women's issues and inspired the establishment of state and local commissions throughout the country. Within four years every state in the nation had a women's commission in some form, addressing women's concerns at the grass roots.

On November 22, 1963, an assassin ended John F. Kennedy's life, bringing his presidential administration to an abrupt close and placing in the hands of Lyndon B. Johnson the fate of pending civil rights legislation. In that legislation lay the seeds of the presidential orders, congressional mandates, and court rulings on affirmative action that are traced in the next three sections of this history.

Part III

1964–1972: Evolution of a Complex and Ambiguous Body of Congressional Law, Rules of Executive Enforcement, and Court Decisions

The laws and policies that came to formally and specifically define "affirmative action" took root in the Civil Rights Act of 1964. They branched out from there in many directions, creating a complicated and sometimes tangled growth of mandates, regulations, plans, and controversies. For minorities, women, and (gradually) disabled citizens on whom they were focused—and without whose activism they would not exist—these laws and policies inspired an intensified quest for equality, justice, freedom, and independence. For those who stood to gain least from, or who believed they would lose ground because of, affirmative action, the laws and policies provoked dissent, anger, and, increasingly, organized resistance.

THE ADMINISTRATION OF LYNDON JOHNSON

{r/g}DOCUMENT 119: Contents of the Civil Rights Act of 1964, Passed July 2, 1964

The Civil Rights Act of 1964 was divided into ten sections.

* * *

TITLE I—VOTING RIGHTS

TITLE II—INJUNCTIVE RELIEF AGAINST DISCRIMINATION IN PLACES OF PUBLIC ACCOMMODATION

TITLE III—DESEGREGATION OF PUBLIC FACILITIES

TITLE IV—DESEGREGATION OF PUBLIC EDUCATION

TITLE V—COMMISSION ON CIVIL RIGHTS

TITLE VI—NON-DISCRIMINATION IN FEDERALLY ASSISTED PROGRAMS

TITLE VII—EQUAL EMPLOYMENT OPPORTUNITY

TITLE VIII—REGISTRATION AND VOTING STATISTICS

TITLE IX—INTERVENTION AND PROCEDURE AFTER REMOVAL IN CIVIL RIGHTS CASES

TITLE X—ESTABLISHMENT OF COMMUNITY RELATIONS SERVICE

Source: Laws of the 88th Congress, 2nd session (July 2, 1964): 287–319.

{r}DOCUMENT 120: Title VI of the Civil Rights Act of 1964

For the future of affirmative action policy, Titles VI and VII would prove to be of most import. Federal courts would return again and again to these statutes as they evaluated disputes between opponents and proponents of affirmative action. Repeatedly, they would examine congressional debates on Titles VI and VII, turning over the question of whether the intent of the law was to impose a "color-blind" standard for all methods of ending present discrimination and the lingering effects of past discrimination, or if the law permitted voluntary "race-conscious" strategies.

* * *

Sec. 601. No person in the United States shall, on the ground of race, color, or national origin, be excluded from participation in, be denied the benefits of, or be subjected to discrimination under any program or activity receiving Federal financial assistance.

Source: Laws of the 88th Congress, 2nd Session (July 2, 1964): 301.

{r}DOCUMENT 121: Title VII of the Civil Rights Act of 1964, Before It Was Amended

Originally, the wording of Title VII paralleled that of Title VI, prohibiting discrimination on the basis of race, nationality, and religion. However, Congressman Howard Smith of Virginia, in order to impede passage of the Civil Rights Act, tried to trivialize the bill by attaching a sex discrimination amendment to Title VII. His plan backfired.

* * *

Title VII Sec. 703
(a) It shall be an unlawful employment practice for an employer—
    (1) to ... discriminate against any individual with respect to his compensation, terms, conditions, or privileges of employment, because of such individual's race, color, religion or national origin.

Source: Laws of the 88th Congress, 2nd Session (February 8, 1964): 304.

{g}DOCUMENT 122: The Smith Amendment to Title VII of the Civil Rights Act of 1964, Offered February 8, 1964

When Congressman Smith offered the amendment, he read from a letter that he had allegedly received from one of his female constituents.

* * *

The clerk read as follows: Amendment offered by Mr. Smith of Virginia . . .
    After the word "religion" insert the word "sex."
MR. SMITH of Virginia. . . . Now I am very serious about this amendment. . . .
    I want to read you an extract from a letter that I received the other day. . . .

The census of 1960 shows that we had 88,331,000 males living in this country, and 90,992,000 females, which leaves the country with an "imbalance" of 2,661,000 females. . . .

[S]hutting off the "right" of every female to have a husband of her own is, . . . I am sure you will agree . . . a grave injustice. . . .

I read that letter just to illustrate that women have some real grievances and some real rights to be protected. I am serious about this thing.

Source: Congressional Record 110, Pt. 1 (February 8, 1964): 2577.

{r/g}DOCUMENT 123: House Debate on the Smith Amendment, February 8, 1964

The Smith amendment not only inspired exchanges between feminists and their opponents but also evoked debate similar to the nineteenth-century quarrel over whose rights should be put first— African Americans' or white women's (Docs. 12–15).

* * *

A. Congressman Andrews of Alabama

Unless this amendment is adopted, the white women of this country would be drastically discriminated against in favor of a Negro woman.

If a white woman and a Negro woman applied for the same job, and each woman had the identical qualifications, the chances are about 99 to 1 that the Negro woman would be given the job because if the employer did not give the job to the Negro woman he could be prosecuted under this bill.

B. Congressman Rivers of South Carolina

It is incredible to me that the authors of this monstrosity . . . would deprive the white woman of mostly Anglo-Saxon or Christian heritage equal opportunity before the employer.

C. Congressman Celler of New York

I heard with a great deal of interest the statement of the gentleman from Virginia that women are in the minority. Not in my house. I can say as a result of 49 years of experience—and I celebrate my 50th wedding anniversary next year—that women, indeed, are not in the minority in my house. As a matter of fact . . . I usually have the last two words, and those words are, "Yes dear." . . .

You know, the French have a phrase. . . . when they speak of women and men . . . they say, "vive la difference."

I think the French are right.

D. Congresswoman St. George of New York

We do not want special privileges. We do not need special privileges. We outlast you—we outlive you—we nag you to death. So why should we want special privileges? . . .

The addition of that little, terrifying word "s-e-x" will not hurt this legislation in any way. . . . It will make it comprehensive. It will make it logical. It will make it right.

E. Congresswoman Griffiths of Michigan

If you do not add sex to this bill . . . you are going to have white men in one bracket, you are going to try to take colored men and colored women and give them equal employment rights, and down at the bottom of the list is going to be a white woman with no rights at all. . . .

It would be incredible to me that white men would be willing to place white women at such a disadvantage except that white men have done this before. . . .

[Y]our great grandfathers were willing as prisoners of their own prejudice to permit ex-slaves to vote, but not their own white wives.

[A] vote against this amendment today by a white man is a vote against his wife, or his widow or his daughter or his sister.

If we are trying to establish equality in jobs, I am for it, but I am for making white women equal also.

F. Congresswoman Green of Oregon

I honestly cannot support the amendment. . . .

For every discrimination that I have suffered, I firmly believe that the Negro woman has suffered 10 times that amount. . . . She has a double discrimination. She was born as a woman and she was born as a Negro. . . . If I have to wait for a few years to end this discrimination against me, and my women friends—then as far as I am concerned I am willing to do that if the rank discrimination against Negroes will be finally ended under the so-called protection of the law.

Source: Congressional Record 110, Pt. 1 (February 8, 1964): 2583, 2577, 2581, 2579–2580, 2581.

In the final House passage of the Civil Rights Act of 1964, including the Smith amendment, all except two of the men who supported that amendment in debate voted against the law.

{r/g}DOCUMENT 124: Title VII, Section (j) of the 1964 Civil Rights Act

During debate in the Senate on Title VII, opponents expressed fear that it would require employers to use some form of quota-hiring. The senior senators from Illinois and North Dakota, Everett Dirksen and Mike Mansfield, respectively, authored provision (j) in an effort to alleviate the possibility of mandated quotas. In later controversies opponents of affirmative action programs repeatedly invoked this provision to support their position.

* * *

Title VII (j)
Nothing contained in this title shall be interpreted to require any employer, employment agency, labor organization or joint labor–management committee subject to this title to grant preferential treatment to any individual or to any group because of the race, color, religion, sex or national origin of such individual or group on account of an imbalance which may exist with respect to the total number or percentage of persons of any race, color, religion, sex or national origin . . . in any community, State, section, or other area, or in the available work force in any community, State, section, or other area.

Source: Laws of 88th Congress, 2nd Session (July 2, 1964): 306.

{r/g}DOCUMENT 125: Comments of Senator Hubert Humphrey, July 2, 1964

In the debate that occasioned section j, Senator Hubert Humphrey of Minnesota adamantly insisted that Title VII "would prohibit preferential treatment for any particular group." In the face of persistent charges to the contrary, he offered a dramatic challenge.

* * *

If the Senator [Robertson from Virginia] can find in Title VII . . . any language which provides that an employer will have to hire on the basis of percentage or quota related to color, race, religion, or national origin, I will start eating the pages one after another, because it is not there.

Source: Congressional Record 110, Pt. 1 (July 2, 1964): 7420.

{r}DOCUMENT 126: Response of Willie King to the Civil Rights Act of 1964

Individuals who identified with the cause of equal rights responded to the passage of the Civil Rights Act in varying ways. Historian Charles Payne has recounted the experience of Silas McGhee, a high school senior in Mississippi and active supporter of the most antiestablishment wing of the civil rights movement, the Student Nonviolent Coordinating Committee. McGhee didn't see how the bill was offering him anything that wasn't already guaranteed in the Constitution and Bill of Rights, but he set about testing it as soon as it was passed. This led to a series of confrontations with segregationists (Payne 1995, 210–218).

In contrast to Silas McGhee, individuals who identified with Martin Luther King Jr. and who viewed the August 1963 March on Washington (and his climactic "I Have a Dream Speech" [Doc. 116]) as the catalyst for the Civil Rights Act greeted its passage with elation. For example, Willie King, who was working for the Southern Christian Leadership Conference, the organization begun by Dr. King, could not contain her joy.

* * *

I think I must have screamed for about five minutes without stopping. We were so elated because a lot of hard work, blood, sweat, and tears had gone into this act. We were extremely happy when the portion about women's rights was included in the act . . . because we thought that it would never pass with that kind of language because people had not taken women's rights seriously.

Source: Making a Right a Reality: An Oral History of the Early Years of the EEOC, 1965–1972 (Washington, DC: EEOC, 1990): 6.

{r}DOCUMENT 127: *Playboy* Interview with Martin Luther King Jr., January 1965

Martin Luther King Jr. was restrained in his assessment of the 1964 law, emphasizing its failure to fully address voting rights, empower the U.S. attorney general to move effectively against civil rights violators, and establish and enforce a national fair housing policy. Moreover, he concurred with other civil rights leaders in calling for the equivalent of a domestic Marshall Plan—the appropriation of $50 billion in federal money over a period of ten years for education, job training, and employment of the ghettoized and impoverished. In January 1965 an interviewer for *Playboy* pressed Dr. King on his views, asking if his criticisms of the Civil Rights Act did not reflect ingratitude and lack of realism. The interviewer also questioned the fairness of proposing to spend $50 billion on one group of citizens. In reply Dr. King stressed that African Americans were "robbed of *any* wages" through two centuries of enslavement and pointed to other instances in American history where preferential programs were carried out without generating resentment—most notably, the GI Bill (Doc. 63).

* * *

King: Why do white people seem to find it so difficult to understand that the Negro is sick and tired of having reluctantly parceled out to him those rights and privileges which all others receive upon birth or entry in America? . . .

All of America's wealth today could not adequately compensate its Negroes for . . . centuries of exploitation and humiliation. . . . [A] program such as I propose would certainly cost far less than any computation of two centuries of unpaid wages plus accumulated interest. In any case, . . . this program of economic aid . . . should benefit the disadvantaged of *all* races.

Source: Playboy (January 1965): 70, 74, 76.

{r}DOCUMENT 128: Lyndon B. Johnson, Special Message to the Congress on Behalf of the Voting Rights Act, March 15, 1965

Lyndon Johnson signed the Civil Rights Act in July 1964, about a month before the Democratic Party nominated him as its candidate for president in the national election. When he emerged as victor in November (over Republican candidate Barry Goldwater), racial tensions were intensifying in every corner of the country. Johnson's responses contrasted sharply with his earlier record. (Between 1937 and 1957 he had consistently voted against civil rights bills.)

Johnson addressed a joint session of Congress in the wake of demonstrations in Selma, Alabama. Events there began and ended with demonstrators being murdered and were punctuated by displays of brutality on the part of Alabama State Police and callousness on the part of Governor George Wallace. In announcing that he was submitting voting rights legislation to Congress, Johnson condemned the racist violence in Selma and appeared to embrace the civil rights movement by invoking the promise of its anthem, "We Shall Overcome."

* * *

Our duty must be clear to all of us. The Constitution says that no person shall be kept from voting because of his race or his color. We have all sworn an oath before God to support and to defend that Constitution. We must now act in obedience to that oath. . . .

But even if we pass [a voting rights bill], the battle will not be over. What happened in Selma is part of a far larger movement which reaches into every section and State of America. It is the effort of American Negroes to secure for themselves the full blessings of American life.

Their cause must be our cause too. Because it is not just Negroes, but really, it is all of us, who must overcome the crippling legacy of bigotry and injustice.

And we shall overcome.

Source: Public Papers of the Presidents. January 1 to May 31, 1965: 283, 284.

{r}DOCUMENT 129: Lyndon B. Johnson, "To Fulfill These Rights," Commencement Address at Howard University, June 4, 1965

At Howard University President Johnson elaborated on his admonition to Congress that passage of the Voting Rights Act would not represent the end of the struggle for justice.

* * *

The voting rights bill will be the latest, and among the most important, in a long series of victories. But this victory—as Winston Churchill said of another triumph for freedom—"is not the end. It is not even the beginning of the end. But it is, perhaps, the end of the beginning."

That beginning is freedom. . . .

But freedom is not enough. . . .

You do not take a person who, for years, has been hobbled by chains and liberate him, bring him up to the starting line of a race and then say, "you are free to compete with all the others," and still justly believe that you have been completely fair. . . .

We seek . . . not just equality as a right and a theory but equality as a fact and equality as a result. . . .

Much of the Negro community is buried under a blanket of history and circumstance. It is not a lasting solution to lift just one corner of that blanket. We must stand on all sides and we must raise the entire cover if we are to liberate our fellow citizens. . . .

Perhaps most important . . . is the breakdown of the Negro family structure. For this, most of all, white America must accept responsibility. It flows from centuries of oppression and persecution of the Negro man. . . .

There is no single easy answer. . . .

Jobs are part of the answer. . . .

Decent homes . . . are part of the answer. . . .

Welfare and social programs better designed to hold families together are part of the answer.

Care for the sick is part of the answer.

An understanding heart by all Americans is another part of the answer.

Source: Public Papers of the Presidents, June 1 to December 31, 1965: 636, 638, 639.

Civil rights leaders, the media, and social analysts recognized the far-reaching implications of the Howard Commencement Address. Those implications were deepened by the fact that Harvard sociologist Daniel Patrick Moynihan, who served as assistant secretary of labor in the Johnson administration, had (with White House aide Richard Goodwin) written Johnson's speech (Steinberg 1997). Moynihan had authored a report on the African American family, where he elaborated on the theme of family breakdown and argued that the remedy for this breakdown would have to extend far beyond existing laws and traditional social programs. The report became public soon after Johnson's speech and while the nation was reeling from an eruption of black rage in the Watts district of Los Angeles. Conservatives warned that in advocating special consideration for African Americans, Moynihan was opening the door to a system of racial preference that would be unacceptable to most whites. Civil rights leaders took Moynihan to task for "blaming the victims" and charged that his recommendations represented a calculated diversion from substantive economic and political reform.

Whatever the import of Moynihan's ideas, the years between their introduction in Johnson's Howard University speech and the end of the Johnson administration in 1968 rank among the most tumultuous periods of American history. Increasingly, nonviolent direct action and community organizing in the service of racial justice gave way to violent eruptions of pent-up anger and demands for Black Power. In 1967 alone, such eruptions shattered the order of 150 cities (including Newark, New Jersey, and Detroit, Michigan, scenes of the most extensive devastation), killing eighty-three people and leaving property damage valued at more than $660 million. When Martin Luther King Jr. was assassinated in the spring of 1968, 110 cities again went up in flames. At the same time, U.S. involvement in the Southeast Asian country of Vietnam was also entering a more bewildering—and progressively tragic—phase. This was the climate in which the Equal Employment Opportunity Commission began its work.

{r/g}DOCUMENT 130: Informational Pamphlet on the Origins and Purpose of the EEOC (Which Officially Opened in 1965)

In the early years one of the main tasks of the Equal Employment Opportunity Commission was to make its presence and mission known. The distribution of literature such as the following pamphlet was one means of doing so.

* * *

On July 2, 1964, Congress passed the Civil Rights Act of 1964. Title VII of the Act, "Equal Employment Opportunity," prohibits discrimination in hiring, upgrading, and all other conditions of employment. It became effective on July 2, 1965.

Title VII established the Employment Opportunity Commission composed of five members appointed by the President and approved by the Senate. The Commission's responsibility is to assure that all Americans will be considered for hiring and promotion on the basis of their ability and qualifications, without regard to race, color, religion, sex or national origin. . . .

The Commission has two basic responsibilities. First, it investigates complaints of discrimination, and if it finds they are justified, seeks a full remedy by the process of conciliation. Second, it promotes programs of voluntary compliance by employers, unions and community organizations to put the idea of equal employment opportunity into actual operation.

If a person believes that he or she is a victim of discrimination by an employer, labor organization, employment agency or joint labor–management program for apprenticeship or training, that person may file a complaint with the Commission.

Source: Facts about Title VII of the Civil Rights Act of 1964 (Washington, DC: EEOC Pamphlet, 1969).

{r/g}DOCUMENT 131: *Wall Street Journal* Report on the Opening of EEOC, May 28, 1965

Initial impressions of the EEOC's prospects for becoming a respected and effective agency were not favorable.

* * *

The agency [EEOC] has not so much as found office space. . . . A handful of transient lawyers, on loan from the Justice and Labor Departments, has churned out some ideas on how to operate, but the five commissioners haven't ploughed through all this paper, much less decided what to adopt. . . .

CORE [Congress of Racial Equality] Director James Farmer . . . is already of the opinion that the commission's operation will be so tangled in red tape that "before an aggrieved person can get a remedy, he may have found another job or starved to death."

Source: James Harwood, "Battling Job Bias," *Wall Street Journal* (May 28, 1965): 1.

{r/g}DOCUMENT 132: Memories of the Early Years of EEOC, 1965–1972

For those who went to work for the new agency, the greatest challenges rose from an overwhelming volume of cases and from the limits that Congress had placed on their authority. The EEOC had no powers of enforcement and a first-year budget allocation based on the expectation of 2,000 complaints, while it actually received 8,856 complaints (Graham 1992, 103). Staff members found these pressures to be intense but exhilarating, as oral history recollections demonstrate.

* * *

A. Ronnie Blumenthal

In the early days I think they thought a few hundred people would come here and file charges of employment discrimination and we would work on it and it would get better. . . . Someone once told me that 4,000 charges were waiting the day they opened the door. So we were always overwhelmed by the numbers, even in the early days.

B. Cora Dixon

The agency was new, there was so much work to be done. We needed more people, more positions, more money. I remember one night leaving around 11:00. When I came in the next morning around 8:30, the staff was there. Some had actually spent the night!

C. Dorothy Howze

Everybody was a little bit crazy. People came to EEOC because they wanted to do good . . . because they cared about civil rights. They'd argue and they'd fight and they'd bitch and scream, but there was always the same direction that everyone was going in. It was an exciting place to work.

Source: Making a Right a Reality: An Oral History of the Early Years of the EEOC, 1965–1972 (Washington, DC: EEOC, 1990): 15, 14, 10–11.

{r}DOCUMENT 133: Executive Order 11246, September 1965

Dedication and noble intentions were not sufficient to meet the demands of civil rights leaders who called attention to the weaknesses of EEOC by orchestrating such a volume of complaints that the agency verged on collapse. Contributing to the disappointment and impatience of activists and reformers was Johnson's decision to decentralize the federal approach to civil rights enforcement. New procedures outlined in the Civil Rights Act of 1964 led to reexamination of the presidential practice of encouraging enforcement through White House committees. The new procedures involved reassignment of many of the responsibilities that had been delegated to such committees (Eisenhower's Government Contract Committee [Doc 86]; Kennedy's Committee on Equal Employment Opportunity [Doc. 102]; and the President's Committee on Equal Employment Opportunity, established by Johnson). By Executive Orders 11246 and 11247 on September 24, 1965, Johnson assigned civil rights enforcement responsibilities to the Civil Service Commission (federal jobs); the EEOC (private sector jobs as covered by Title VII); and various other agencies, according to their stated missions. He placed responsibility for enforcing Title VI of the Civil Rights Act with the attorney general. Of most significance was the assignment of contract compliance in federally funded construction to the Department of Labor, which subsequently created a new committee on contract compliance. This opened the way for a controversial affirmative action initiative that, though beginning in the Johnson era, would come to bear the stamp of Richard Nixon (Doc. 160).

* * *

Part I—NonDiscrimination in Government Employment

Section 101. . . . The policy of equal opportunity applies to every aspect of Federal employment policy and practice.

Section 102. The head of each executive department and agency shall establish and maintain a positive program of equal employment opportunity for all civilian employees and applicants for employment within his jurisdiction in accordance with the policy set forth in Section 101. . . .

Part II—NonDiscrimination in Employment by Government Contractors and Subcontractors

Section 201. The Secretary of Labor shall be responsible for the administration of Parts II and III of this Order and shall adopt such rules and regulations and issue such orders as he deems necessary and appropriate to achieve the purposes thereof.

Source: Federal Register 30 (1965): 12319.

{r/}DOCUMENT 134: Executive Order 11247, September 1965

Executive Order 11247 was administratively efficient but did not promote strong enforcement. As historian Hugh Davis Graham observed, "The major federal departments were called *mission* agencies for good reason. Their ties to client groups and contractual suppliers were governed by a mutual interest in accomplishing the mission. . . . Because most of the federal government's two million annual contracts were of the workaday variety, EEOC enforcement did not rank high in most agency priorities" (Graham 1992, 154).

* * *

Section 1. The Attorney General shall assist Federal departments and agencies to coordinate their programs and activities and adopt consistent and uniform policies, practices, and procedures with respect to the enforcement of Title VI of the Civil Rights Act of 1964.

Source: Federal Register 30 (1965): 12327.

{g}DOCUMENT 135: News Conference of Franklin D. Roosevelt Jr., First Chairman of the Equal Employment Opportunity Commission, July 2, 1965

That Johnson's executive orders failed to include discrimination based on sex was no accident. His vice president, Hubert Humphrey, had advised him to omit references to sex discrimination from the orders. At this time the opinion also prevailed within the EEOC that racism was the commission's central focus, from which complaints of sexism were distractions. This point of view reflected the general state of public opinion which did not take women's issues seriously. Several weeks after the following press conference exchange, the *New York Times* published a sarcastic report followed by a flippant editorial on the alleged dilemma posed by Title VII: what to do if a male applied to become a Playboy Club "bunny" (*New York Times*, August 20, 1965, pp. 1, 33; *New York Times*, August 21, 1965, p. 20).

* * *

"What about sex?" Mr. Roosevelt was asked at the news conference. "Don't get me started," Mr. Roosevelt replied with a laugh. "I'm all for it."
"Seriously," he added, "we can't foretell what problems there will be in this area. We will have to learn as we go along." . . .

Source: New York Times (July 3, 1965).

{r/g}DOCUMENT 136: Excerpts from EEOC Minutes, September 21, 1965

The first EEOC included only one woman among the five appointed commissioners, Aileen Clarke Hernandez. As she later recorded in her memoirs, "The message came through clearly that the Commission's priority was race discrimination, and apparently only as it related to Black *men*." She advocated, with the support of fellow commissioner Richard Graham (known within feminist circles as "a real fighter for women"), for EEOC guidelines against sex discrimination. One of the first issues to occasion internal debate was that of sex-segregated advertisements in the Help Wanted sections of newspapers. According to

Title VII, certain jobs involved gender as a "bona fide occupational qualification for employment"—what quickly came to be known as a BFOQ. Listing such jobs as "Male" or "Female" was therefore permissible. What was not established, however, was a clear definition of BFOQ, a matter of debate among the commissioners.

* * *

A. Aileen Hernandez

It is the advertiser's responsibility to insert in his ad that he does not discriminate and the job is open to males and females. If there is a B.F.O.Q. he should come to the EEOC and get a ruling, not make the determination himself.

B. Tom Powers

If the Commission lets itself get into the position where it has to pass on every single instance in which any covered employer in the United States believes that Sex is a bona fide occupation[al qualification], you are going to load yourself down with so many questions in the Sex area that you are not going to have time to do anything else of significance.

Source: EEOC Minutes, September 21, 1965, quoted in Graham 1992, 110.

{r/g}DOCUMENT 137: EEOC Chairman Franklin Roosevelt Jr. Announces Policy Regarding Sex-Segregated Want Ads, November 1965

On August 18, 1965, the EEOC issued an order ending all separation of Help Wanted advertisements by race and announced the formation of an advisory committee to study the question of separate advertising by sex. Roosevelt announced the findings of the seventeen-member committee (of whom four members were women and ten came from the media or advertising professions) in November 1965.

* * *

Culture and mores, personal inclinations, and physical limitations will operate to make many job categories primarily of interest to men or women. [So the commission would not require unified want ads by gender, as it had done by race.]

Source: Wall Street Journal (November 23, 1965).

{g}DOCUMENT 138: Equal Employment Opportunity Commission Guidelines on Discrimination Because of Sex, December 1965

The other outstanding controversy in regard to sex discrimination revolved around state laws designed to protect women in the workplace. The EEOC assumed an ambivalent stance on this issue and, in effect, passed it back to the Congress and the states.

* * *

The Commission has proceeded with caution in interpreting the scope and application of Title VII's prohibition of discrimination in employment on account of sex. We are mindful that there is little relevant legislative history to serve as a guide to the intent of Congress in this area. Also there is little light in the experience with state statutes. An overly literal interpretation of the prohibition might disrupt long-standing employment practices required by state legislation or collective bargaining agreements without achieving compensating benefits in progress toward equal opportunity. . . .

Probably the most difficult area . . . is the relation of Title VII to state legislation designed originally to protect women workers. The Commission cannot assume that Congress intended to strike down such legislation. . . .

Title VII . . . and state protective legislation . . . cannot easily be harmonized. Clarification and improvements can however be achieved. We believe it desirable—even essential—that Congress and the state legislatures address themselves to this problem.

Source: Federal Register 30, no. 232 (December 2, 1965).

{g}DOCUMENT 139: Statement of Congresswoman Martha Griffiths, June 20, 1966

These EEOC rulings were received within the ranks of the newly emerging woman's rights movement like a lighted match in a bundle of dry kindling. Since the Kennedy Commission in 1963 (Doc. 117), women in politics, reform movements, the professions, and business had been steadily gaining momentum as an organized force, building bridges across old divisions and creating new networks and power bases. In 1966 the momentum rapidly accelerated. Democratic congresswoman Martha Griffiths of Michigan picked up the pace with a scathing attack on the EEOC from the floor of the House of Representatives, June 20, 1966. A national conference of State Commissions on the Status of Women in the same month became the launching pad for what authors Judith Hole and Ellen Levine have called "the first militant feminist group in the twentieth century to combat sex discrimination in all spheres of life"—the National Organization for Women (NOW). Immediately after the formal announcement of its existence in October 1966, NOW began a blitz of petitions, letters, and demonstrations directed against the EEOC's neglect of sex discrimination. Feminists were now applying to their cause the rule long appreciated by civil rights leaders. As historian Charles Payne noted (headnote to Doc. 126), the passage of legislation promised only so much. What counted most was "the willingness of [people] to insist that it be enforced."

* * *

The whole attitude of the EEOC toward discrimination based on sex is specious, negative, and arrogant. The Commission is failing in its duty to educate the public toward compliance with the law, to inform working women of their rights under the law, and to show an affirmative and positive attitude of encouraging employers, employment agencies and unions to comply with the prohibitions against discrimination in employment based on sex. . . .

The whining of Equal Employment Opportunity Commission members and officials has centered around three specific excuses for their attitudes:

First, that the sex provisions of title VII were a "fluke," introduced by Representative Howard Smith, who is no friend of the civil rights movement, and "conceived out of wedlock" and so forth.

I reject that slur on Congress. Congress had enacted the Equal Pay for Women Act in 1963 and was thoroughly familiar with the fact that job discrimination is imposed on women and inflicts severe consequences on their earning capacity. The sex provisions in title VII were supported by the great majority of the House and Senate. . . .

Second. The second excuse used by some EEOC officials is that there is no legislative history on the sex provisions in title VII and that the intent of the Congress is so shrouded in doubt that it is impossible to interpret and administer the law.

The EEOC officials who resort to this excuse just have not made the effort to read the extensive legislative history of the long battle to eliminate sex discrimination in employment. . . .

Third. The third excuse I often hear is that sex discrimination cases take too much time and thus interfere with the EEOC's "main" business of eliminating racial discrimination. This problem, even if it exists, could be substantially reduced if EEOC acted vigorously to enforce the law. . . . Once employers understand that EEOC means to enforce the law, there will be fewer violations.

Source: Congressional Record 112, Pt. 1 (June 20, 1966): 13693–13694.

{g}DOCUMENT 140: Betty Friedan Recalls the Founding of the National Organization for Women (NOW) in 1966

In late June 1966 the third National Conference of the State Commissions on the Status of Women met in Washington, D.C. Copies of Martha Griffiths' speech on the EEOC were circulated among the conferees (Doc. 139). On the second day of the conference Betty Friedan—author of *The Feminine Mystique*, a provocative study of the oppression of women—met with several conference participants in her hotel room, where a debate ensued regarding how best to attack sex discrimination. The next day, as the closing luncheon proceeded along conventional lines, Friedan and like-minded associates were outlining on paper napkins the plans for the National Organization for Women.

* * *

None of us had ever acted on our own behalf as women. There was a *dread*. . . . [W]e knew what had to be done. But why me, why us? Who wants to take the responsibility, to commit oneself to carry it through and risk being laughed at, getting people mad at you, maybe getting fired? . . .

I wonder if Esther Peterson and the other Women's Bureau officials and Cabinet members who talked down to us at lunch knew that those two front tables, so rudely, agitatedly whispering to one another and passing around notes written on paper napkins, were under their very noses organizing NOW. . . .

After . . . lunch . . . we met for an hour before people had to make their planes and agreed we would have a formal organizing conference for NOW in the fall.

Source: Betty Friedan, *It Changed My Life, Writings on the Women's Movement* (New York: Random House, 1963/1976): 75–76, 83.

{g}DOCUMENT 141: Executive Order 11375, October 13, 1967

President Johnson responded to the mounting pressure, replacing his original Executive Order 11246 with a new order that included sex discrimination.

* * *

It is desirable that the equal employment opportunity programs provided for in Executive Order 11246 expressly embrace discrimination on account of sex.

Source: Federal Register 32 (October 17, 1967): 14303.

{d}DOCUMENT 142: Presidential Proclamations on White Cane Safety Day, 1964 and 1965

In the period when NOW was pressing its case against sex discrimination, the blind's eloquent and longtime crusader for his community, Jacobus tenBroek (Docs. 11, 49, 96), was calling attention to the implications of the Civil Rights Act of 1964 for the disabled. tenBroek and the National Federation for the Blind had lobbied for that act to specifically encompass the disabled. While they were unsuccessful in that regard, they did persuade Congress to pass a resolution authorizing the president to designate an annual White Cane Safety Day on October 15. President Johnson followed up with proclamations in 1964 and 1965.

* * *

A. 1964

A white cane in our society has become one of the symbols of a blind person's ability to come and go on his own. Its use has promoted courtesy and special consideration for the blind on our streets and highways. . . .

NOW . . . I, LYNDON B. JOHNSON . . . do hereby proclaim October 15, 1964, as White Cane Safety Day. . . .

I call upon all our citizens to make every effort to promote the safety and welfare of our blind persons on the streets and highways, and thereby to contribute to their independence of spirit and their capability for self-management.

B. 1965

On the streets and highways of our nation, the white cane instantly identifies the blind person, proudly coming and going on his own, but highly dependent for safety upon the courtesy and consideration of others.

Sources: Federal Register 29 (1964): 14051; 30 (1965): 12931.

{d}DOCUMENT 143: Jacobus tenBroek, "The Right to Live in the World: The Disabled in the Law of Torts," 1966

In a learned and densely documented article for the *California Law Review* tenBroek interpreted white cane laws and other legislation regarding the blind in the context of the Civil Rights Act and predicted that the landmark 1964 legislation would eventually include "the disabled within its shelter." When, in the following decade, Section 504 of the 1973 Vocational Rehabilitation Act became law, couched in language lifted directly from the 1964 law (Doc. 242), tenBroek's prediction took on new weight.

* * *

The Civil Rights Act of 1964 does extend to "all persons" and does imply substantive rights. It is therefore possible, if not probable, that when we move away from the moment and the immediate cause of the legislation, the judges will bring the disabled within its shelter.

Source: tenBroek 1966b, 853.

{d}DOCUMENT 144: Jacobus tenBroek, "Are We Equal to the Challenge?" 1967

In 1967 tenBroek delivered one of his last speeches before his death in March 1968. He roused the 1967 convention of the National Federation of the Blind with an address titled "Are We Equal to the Challenge?" Castigating the custodial mentality of social agencies and workplaces that treated the blind "not as workers but as wards," tenBroek reiterated his passionate commitment to freedom and independence.

* * *

The blind have a right to live in the world. That right is as deep as human nature; as pervasive as the need for social existence; as ubiquitous as the human race; as invincible as the human spirit. As their souls are their own, so their destiny must be their own. Their salvation or failure lies within their own choice and responsibility. That choice cannot be precluded or prejudged; those lives cannot be predetermined or controlled. In a democracy the blind have a right to share in the fruits and obligations of the community. They have a right to participate in the decisions that affect their lives and fortunes. And beneath and beyond these democratic rights there is a further one: the right to organize for collective self-expression, and to be represented through their own associations. This, if it does not go without saying, surely goes without disputing.

Source: Quoted in Floyd W. Matson, *Walking Alone and Marching Together* (Baltimore: National Federation of the Blind, 1990): 223.

{g}DOCUMENT 145: EEOC Guidelines on Employment Advertising, August 1968

Meanwhile, the voices raised by women continued to make themselves heard. With NOW picketing its offices (December 1967) and bringing a lawsuit against it (February 1968), the EEOC adopted a firmer stance against sex discrimination. It rescinded its previous position on Help Wanted advertising.

* * *

1604.4 Job Opportunities Advertising

It is a violation of Title VII for a help-wanted advertisement to indicate a preference, limitation, specification, or discrimination based on sex unless sex is a bona fide occupation qualification for the particular job involved. The placement of an advertisement in columns classified by publishers on the basis of sex such as columns headed "Male" or "Female," will be considered an expression of a preference, limitation, specification or discrimination based on sex.

Source: Federal Register 33 (August 14, 1968): 11539.

{g}DOCUMENT 146: EEOC Fourth Annual Report, August 1969

The EEOC also acknowledged that the legal tide had turned against state protective legislation.

* * *

Important legal advances were also recorded in the area of discrimination on the basis of sex. A company's refusal to assign a woman to the position she sought because of her sex was held to be an unlawful employment practice.... [The courts] further ruled that the California hours and weights legislation did not create a bona fide occupation qualification.... In fact it was stated, the legislation was contrary to [Title VII]. Accordingly such statutes are unconstitutional....

[S]imply labeling a job "strenuous" does not meet the burden of proving that the job is within the bona fide occupation qualification exception. ... [T]he employer ... must demonstrate that he has "a factual basis for believing that all or substantially all women would be unable to perform safely and efficiently the duties of the job involved." The employer's reliance upon "stereotyped characterizations" does not satisfy this burden.

Another decision stated that an employer could not justify its refusal to assign a female to a job and its granting of the job to males with less seniority, on the ground that a union contract required that females be granted certain rest periods. As in California, Oregon's weight regulations were nullified.

Source: EEOC *Fourth Annual Report* (Washington, DC: U.S. Government Printing Office, 1970): 15–16.

{r}DOCUMENT 147: *Report of the National Advisory Commission on Civil Disorders*, March 1968

While women's groups were hammering at the EEOC to reshape its policies on sex discrimination, the forces of racial violence were reconfiguring the entire social and political landscape of the United States. With the cities of Detroit and Newark still smoldering after extended rioting in the summer of 1967, President Johnson had appeared on national television to announce the appointment of a Special Advisory Commission on Civil Disorders. The president issued stern warnings against "looting, arson, plunder and pillage," but he also asserted that "the only genuine, long-range solution for what has happened lies in an attack . . . upon the conditions that breed despair and violence." The commission that was to look into those conditions was cochaired by Illinois governor Otto Kerner and New York City mayor John Lindsay. Their report, published in the spring of 1968, held up a mirror to racist America and tallied the inevitable costs of refusing to look into it and failing to reconstruct the distorted and fragmented society that was revealed there. Among the recommendations of the Kerner Commission was a call to expand the authority of the EEOC and to intensify the enforcement by the Department of Labor of federal contracts (Johnson, quoted in *Report of the National Advisory Commission*, 538–541).

* * *

Conclusions

1. The nation is rapidly moving toward two increasingly separate Americas.

Within two decades, this division could be so deep that it would be almost impossible to unite:

• a white society principally located in suburbs, in smaller central cities, and in the peripheral parts of large central cities; and

• a Negro society largely concentrated within large central cities. . . .

2. In the long run, continuation and expansion of such a permanent division threatens us with two perils.

The first is the danger of sustained violence in our cities. . . .

The second is the danger of a conclusive repudiation of the traditional American ideals of individual dignity, freedom, and equality of opportunity. We will not be able to espouse these ideals meaningfully to the rest of the world, to ourselves, to our children. . . .

Objectives for National Action . . .

Opening the Existing Job Structure . . .

Granting to the Equal Employment Opportunity Commission . . . cease and desist power comparable to the enforcement power now held by other federal agencies administering regulatory national policies. . . .

Undertaking, through the Equal Employment Opportunity Commission, an industry and areawide enforcement effort based not only upon individual complaints but upon employer and union reports, showing broad patterns of discrimination in employment and promotion.

Equal opportunity for employment by federal contractors under Executive Order 11246 should be enforced more vigorously against both employers and unions. This is particularly critical in regard to federal construction contracts. Staff and other resources of the Office of Contract Compliance in the Department of Labor should be increased so that withholding federal contracts is made a meaningful sanction.

Source: Report of the National Advisory Commission on Civil Disorders (New York: Bantam Books, 1969): 407, 413, 419.

Within weeks of the commission's warnings about the deep racial divisions in America, the nation's racial wounds were ripped open once again by the assassination of Martin Luther King Jr. on April 4, 1968. Before the country had time to recover from grief, shock, and rage over the murder of Dr. King, another assassination felled Robert Kennedy on June 6, 1968. Against the background of political murders, the repeated shattering of national ideals, and widespread anger and unease, proponents of affirmative action sought to extend and deepen its reach. Increasingly, leaders at all levels concerned themselves with discrimination as a systemic problem, so embedded in national institutions that its effects continued even where the intention to discriminate may no longer have existed.

{d}DOCUMENT 148: Ruth Ellen Ross, Retracing 1960s Advances "Toward a Barrier-Free America"

For numerous disabled groups, the most egregious symbols of systemic discrimination were architectural barriers that impeded their right to traverse public throughways, use public transportation, and enjoy the same public access to buildings that others took for granted. Documents 147 through 153 trace the development of legislation to remove these barriers.

Ruth Ellen Ross, in her account of the evolution of the President's Committee on Employment of the Handicapped, described the origins of architectural barrier laws.

* * *

[T]he first major call to action was inspired by the experience of Hugo Deffner who, as the recipient of the 1956 "Handicapped American of the

Year Award," could not accept his award at the Annual Meeting because he was unable to enter the Department of Labor auditorium. The building had imposing steps rising from the street. . . .

An ad hoc committee was formed, chaired by Leon Chatelain, Jr., former President of the American Institute of Architects, and Professor Timothy J. Nugent who, as an engineer, had led a strong movement to enable students with severe disabilities to attend the University of Illinois. In 1961, after four years of intensive work, the first American Standards Association code for barrier-free construction emerged. Chairman Melvin Maas saw the code as "a declaration of independence for the handicapped." . . . [I]n 1963 the first state law was passed by South Carolina to require public buildings to be barrier-free. Within 10 years every state, through the persuasion of volunteer groups, had passed similar legislation.

Source: Ruth Ellen Ross, *Fifty Years of Progress, the President's Committee on Employment of People with Disabilities* (Washington, DC: President's Committee, June 1997): 11.

{d}DOCUMENT 149: Vocational Rehabilitation Act Amendments of 1965

As part of the Vocational Rehabilitation Amendments of 1965, Congress created a National Commission on Architectural Barriers to Rehabilitation of the Handicapped.

* * *

Section 15. (a) There is hereby established in the Department of Health, Education, and Welfare a National Commission on Architectural Barriers to Rehabilitation of the Handicapped. . . .

(b) The Commission shall (1) determine how and to what extent architectural barriers impede access to or use of facilities in buildings of all types by the handicapped; . . . (3) prepare plans and proposals for such further action as may be necessary to achieve the goal of ready access to and full use of facilities in buildings of all types by the handicapped.

Source: Statutes at Large 79 (November 8, 1965): 1289.

{d}DOCUMENT 150: Kay Arneson, Looking Back on Her Work in the 1960s as First Director of the Architectural Barriers Commission

The first director of the Architectural Barriers Commission was Kay Arneson. In an interview some years later she discussed the objectives of the commission.

* * *

As early as 1965 . . . we said it isn't only the disability of the individual and what the rehab delivery system provides to him that counts, it is what is happening in the environment that affects his capacity to live and work independently; . . . [volunteer organizations and employment agencies] said, "One of the biggest problems is that once you get these people trained, you can't get them into buildings, you can't get them into work, you can't get them to church, you can't get them to shop. So we'd better work on the environment." . . .

[The] National Commission on Architectural Barriers . . . had a three-year mandate and in two years we came up with a proposed law which was the first architectural barriers law.

Source: Quoted in Scotch 1984, 30.

{d}DOCUMENT 151: Report of the National Commission on Architectural Barriers to Rehabilitation of the Handicapped, 1967

The report of the commission became a main source of arguments on behalf of new legislation.

* * *

More than 20 million Americans are built *out* of normal living by unnecessary barriers: a stairway, a too-narrow door, a too-high telephone. At the right moment, their needs were overlooked. . . . [I]n time, the last vestiges of such thoughtlessness will disappear from the American scene.

Source: *Design for All Americans. Report of the National Commission on Architectural Barriers to Rehabilitation of the Handicapped* (Washington, DC: U.S. Department of Health, Education, and Welfare, 1967): 2.

{d}DOCUMENT 152: Ruth Ellen Ross, The Impact of the Vietnam War by 1968

Another source of pressure for legislation came from an increase in the numbers of those disabled by war injuries.

* * *

[T]he Vietnam veterans were beginning to come home, and many of them returned with physical or psychiatric disabilities. The totals were climbing, and by 1968 there would be more amputees from the Vietnam conflict than from World War II and the Korean War combined.

Source: Ruth Ellen Ross, *Fifty Years of Progress, the President's Committee on Employment of People with Disabilities* (Washington, DC: President's Committee, June 1997): 14.

{d}DOCUMENT 153: Federal Architectural Barriers Bill, August 12, 1968

The new legislation emerged in the form of Public Law 90–480, introduced by Alaskan senator E. L. Barrett and approved by Congress on August 12, 1968. Barrett's congressional assistant, Hugh Gallagher, confined to a wheelchair by polio, played a major part in its passage. Exempting privately owned residences and military structures intended "primarily [for] able bodied military personnel," the law required the heads of three federal departments to ensure that buildings within their purview were made accessible to the disabled. A year after the bill became law, regulations for implementing it were published in the *Federal Register*; they differed little from the wording of the bill.

* * *

Section 2. The Administrator of General Services, in consultation with the Secretary of Health, Education and Welfare, is authorized to prescribe such standards for the design, construction, and alteration of buildings . . . as may be necessary to insure that physically handicapped persons will have ready access to, and use of, such buildings.

Section 3. The Secretary of Housing and Urban Development . . . is authorized to prescribe such standards for . . . buildings which are residential structures subject to this Act. . . .

Section 4. The Secretary of Defense . . . is authorized to prescribe such standards for . . . buildings, structures and facilities of the Department of Defense subject to this Act.

Source: Statutes at Large 82 (August 12, 1968): 718–719.

{d}DOCUMENT 154: Berkeley Newspaper Clipping, ca. 1968

As the Architectural Barriers Act was making its way through Congress, another advance for the disabled was under way at several college campuses where "independent living" communities were taking root. For example, at the University of California at Berkeley in 1962 (the same year that James Meredith became the first African American to enroll at the University of Mississippi), Ed Roberts became the first quadriplegic (paralyzed from the neck down) to enroll at the Berkeley campus. Having contracted polio when he was fourteen, Roberts had persisted in completing high school and junior college. He was determined to disprove both the state bureaucrats who initially withheld funding for a university education (declaring it "infeasible" that he could become employable) and the college administrators who told him that they had "tried cripples before and it didn't work." Roberts lived in the campus infirmary, hired attendants to feed and dress him, move him about the campus in a wheelchair, take class notes and— when he became a graduate teaching assistant—transcribe his comments on student papers. When battery-powered wheelchairs came on the market, Roberts learned to operate one and obtained another degree of personal freedom. The following newspaper report described his status and that of two other disabled students who had joined him as they neared graduation. Roberts would soon become the director of rehabilitation for the state of California (Shapiro 1993, Chapter 2).

* * *

In many ways Ed Roberts is a normal graduate student teaching assistant at the University of California at Berkeley.

He carries eight hours of graduate work in political science, teaches two lower-division classes, goes to basketball games and concerts on weekends, and discusses politics and civil rights over an occasional glass of beer. . . .

But Ed Roberts . . . spends 16 hours of every day in an iron lung at the University's Cowell Hospital . . . one of three quadriplegics who live at the hospital under a unique program. . . .

John Hessler, a star athlete in high school whose neck was broken in a diving accident, became the hospital's second student resident.

Then . . . Roberts and Hessler convinced 19 year-old Larry Langdon, who was then completing treatment at the Stanford Rehabilitation Center, that a university education was possible. . . .

By 1969, both Roberts and Hessler will have graduated—Roberts with a Ph.D. and Hessler with a master's degree—and would like to teach on the university level.

"It may be a problem getting a job," Roberts allowed. However, he added, a job and a life in the academic community were certainly within reach. "After all," he said, "we're doing it now. We're proving that we can do it."

Source: Undated/unidentified newspaper clipping from files of Center for Independent Living, Berkeley, CA.

As the disabled attacked architectural barriers and widely held assumptions about their alleged helplessness, African Americans and women pressed courts and lawmakers for more sweeping remedies for the systemic discriminations that unnecessarily limited them. Public discourse incorporated new terminology including "institutional racism" and "disparate impact" (appearing neutral but really affecting one group more than another). The Kerner Commission (Doc. 147) had indicated a need for more vigorous application of Title VII, stronger exercise of federal influence over contractors, and increased authority for the EEOC. Beginning in 1968, federal court rulings strengthened and extended Title VII as a weapon against discrimination. In the same period the Office of Federal Contract Compliance in the Department of Labor launched what came to be called the Philadelphia Plan, a method of requiring federal contractors to set hiring goals for minorities and women, based on the percentage of minority and female workers in each trade in a given geographical area. In the 1972 Equal Employment Opportunity Act Congress expanded the responsibilities and powers of the EEOC.

{r}DOCUMENT 155: *Douglas Quarles and Ephriam Briggs v. Philip Morris Incorporated*, U.S. District Court, Richmond, Virginia, January 4, 1968

When the federal courts first ruled on cases brought under Title VII, the results were startling—greeted with enthusiasm by civil rights advocates and with dismay by conservatives. Setting an early precedent was *Quarles v. Philip Morris*, in which African American workers, whose complaints the EEOC had been unable to resolve, charged that the tobacco plant that employed them practiced discrimination in wages and promotions. The court held that while some of the plaintiffs' charges were not legally supportable, the company was guilty of discrimination with regard to a seniority system that held black workers at a disadvantage. At issue was Section 703(h) of Title VII, which stated that "it shall not be an unlawful employment practice for an employer to apply different standards of compensation or different terms, conditions, or privileges of employment pursuant to a bona fide seniority or merit system." The court ordered the company and the union (Local 203 of Tobacco Workers International Union) to establish a new seniority system "providing equal advancement opportunity."

* * *

Section 703(h) expressly states the seniority system must be *bona fide*. The purpose of the act is to eliminate racial discrimination in covered employment. Obviously one characteristic of a *bona fide* seniority system must be lack of discrimination. Nothing in 703(h), or in the legislative history, suggests that a racially discriminatory seniority system established before the act is a *bona fide* seniority system under the act. . . .

None of the excerpts [of Title VII] upon which the company and the union rely suggests that as a result of past discrimination a Negro is to have employment opportunities inferior to those of a white person who has less employment seniority. . . . The history leads the court to conclude that Congress did not intend to require "reverse discrimination"; that is, the act does not require that Negroes be preferred over white employees who possess employment seniority. It is also apparent that Congress did not intend to freeze an entire generation of Negro employees into discriminatory patterns that existed before the act.

Source: 279 F. Supp. 505 at 517, 516 (1968).

{r}DOCUMENT 156: *Local 189 Papermakers and Paperworkers v. U.S.*, July 1969

Another case revolving around the issue of seniority was brought by African American workers in the Bogalusa, Louisiana, branch of Crown-Zellerbach, a paper manufacturer. Dissatisfied with EEOC rulings on their grievances, the workers brought suit beginning in 1965. The final judgment on their case was issued in July 1969 in the Fifth Circuit Court, where Judge John Minor Wisdom upheld a lower court decision that the company must replace a departmental with a plant-wide system of seniority. The departmental system required black workers who transferred to recently desegregated departments to start at the bottom of the seniority ladder in their new position, losing the seniority that they had acquired in their former departments. A plant-wide system allowed them to carry their seniority from one department to the next. In some cases African American workers with more longevity in the plant moved ahead of white workers with departmental seniority. In reaching their decision the courts applied the concept of "business necessity," determining that in this case departmental seniority was not essential to the operation of the plant and could be easily replaced with a plantwide system.

* * *

Until May 1964, the Company segregated the lines of progression by race, reserving some lines to white employees and others to Negroes. . . . With very few exceptions, the lowliest white jobs paid more and carried greater responsibility than the most exalted Negro jobs. . . .

The Company put new employees on "extra boards" . . . labor pools used to fill temporary vacancies within the lines of progression. . . .

The Company merged the extra boards in May 1964. . . . Merger opened up the lines to Negro entrants, and helped the relatively recent Negro employees on the board. It did not help more senior Negroes already in the lines of progression. . . .

In January 1966 the unions and the Company amended the collective bargaining agreement so as to merge the progression lines within each department. . . . Except for one job in the plant, merger by pay rates merely meant tacking the Negro lines to the bottom of the white lines. . . .

The translation of racial status to job-seniority status cannot obscure the hard, cold fact that Negroes at Crown's mill will lose promotions which, *but* for their race, they would surely have won. Every time a Negro worker hired under the old segregated system bids against a white worker in his job slot, the old racial classification reasserts itself, and the Negro suffers anew for his employer's previous bias.... The crux of the problem is how far the employer must go to undo the effects of past discrimination. . . .

To the extent that Crown and the white union insisted upon carrying forward exclusion of a racially-determined class, *without business necessity*, they committed . . . an unfair employment practice as defined by Title VII.

Source: 416 F. 2d 980 at 983, 984, 988, 997 (1969).

THE ADMINISTRATION OF RICHARD NIXON

{r}DOCUMENT 157: Statement by Richard Nixon on Minority Business Enterprise, March 5, 1969

African American and other minority business owners were also pressing their case for federal support. Response came in the form of an executive order by Richard Nixon establishing the Office of Minority Business Enterprise (OMBE). Authorized in March 1969, the OMBE launched "Project Enterprise" in October, through which funds for capital investment and long-term credit were made available to minority entrepreneurs.

* * *

Blacks, Mexican-Americans, Puerto Ricans, Indians, and others must increasingly be encouraged to enter the field of business . . . not only as workers, but also as managers and owners. . . .

What we are doing is recognizing that in addition to the basic problems of poverty itself, there is an additional need to stimulate those enterprises that can give members of minority groups confidence that . . . Blacks, Mexican-Americans, and others can participate in a growing economy on the basis of equal opportunity at the top of the ladder as well as on its lower rungs.

Source: Public Papers of the Presidents, 1969: 197, 198.

{r}DOCUMENT 158: The Philadelphia Plan, 1969

Another priority of the Nixon administration—this one destined to have major political repercussions—was "the Philadelphia Plan." It originated in the Johnson administration's Department of Labor, headed by Willard Wirtz. To direct the Office of Federal Contract Compliance (OFCC), Wirtz recruited Edward Sylvester, an African American engineer. In a manner reminiscent of New Dealers Harold Ickes and Robert Weaver (Docs. 37–39), Sylvester tied the awarding of federal contracts to requirements that contractors employ acceptable numbers of minority workers. He initiated "manning tables," which employers had to complete, indicating how many minority workers were assigned to every division of the total job crew on a given project. After experimenting with this approach in several cities, he focused in 1968 on Philadelphia, where several hundred million dollars of federal money was earmarked for public construction and where black laborers, excluded by racist union policies, were threatening rebellion. Sylvester teamed up with Warren P. Phelan, the regional representative of the U.S. Department of Housing and Urban Development (HUD). Phelan identified the seven local trade unions that most blatantly discriminated against blacks. The Philadelphia Plan held contractors bidding for federally funded projects responsible for submitting manning tables that included enough minority workers from the seven designated trades to satisfy the OFCC. Sylvester's direction of the plan did not survive the onslaught waged against it by angry contractors in court suits and through appeals to the General Accounting Office. In the same month that Richard Nixon won the presidency, U.S. comptroller general Elmer Staats ruled the Philadelphia Plan to be in violation of federal contract law. Soon after he was settled in the White House, Nixon revived the plan through his secretary of labor, George Schultz, and the African American OFCC director recruited by him, Arthur Fletcher.

* * *

Washington D.C. June 27 1969
Memorandum
To: Heads of all agencies
From: Arthur A. Fletcher, Assistant Secretary for Wage and Labor Standards
Subject: Revised Philadelphia Plan for Compliance with Equal Employ-

ment Opportunity Requirements of Executive Order 11246 [Doc. 133] for Federally-Involved Construction. . . .

Policy: In order to promote the full realization of equal employment opportunity on Federally-assisted projects, it is the policy of the Office of Federal Contract Compliance that no contracts or subcontracts shall be awarded for Federal or Federally-assisted construction in the Philadelphia area on projects whose cost exceeds $500,000 unless the bidder submits an acceptable affirmative action program which shall include specific goals of minority manpower utilization, meeting the standards included in the invitation or other solicitation for bids in trades utilizing the following classifications of employees:

Iron workers.

Plumbers, pipefitters.

Steamfitters.

Sheetmetal workers.

Electrical workers.

Roofers and water proofers.

Elevator construction workers. . . .

Because of the exclusionary practices of labor organizations, there traditionally has been only a small number of Negroes employed in these seven trades. . . . [The Philadelphia Plan] requires that each apparent low bidder to qualify for a construction contract or subcontract must submit a written affirmative action program which would have the results of assuring that there will be minority group representation in these trades. . . .

Acceptability of Affirmative Action Programs: A bidder's affirmative action program will be acceptable if the specific goals set by the bidder meet the definite standards determined in accordance with Section 6 below. . . .

6. *Specific Goal and Definite Standards.* . . .

   c. *Factors Used in Determining Definite Standards.* . . . In determining the range of minority manpower utilization that should result from an effective affirmative action program, the factors to be considered will include, among others, the following:

(1) The current extent of minority group participation in the trade.

(2) The availability of minority group persons for employment in such trade.

(3) The need for training programs in the area and/or the need to assure demand for those in or from existing training programs.

(4) The impact of the program upon the existing labor force.

Source: Department of Labor Memorandum reprinted in *Congressional Record* 112, Pt. 2 (December 18, 1969): 39951.

{r}DOCUMENT 159: Letters from Comptroller General of the United States and Attorney General of the United States Regarding the Philadelphia Plan, 1969

As soon as Fletcher's memo became operative, federal contractors and the comptroller general renewed their attacks on the Philadelphia Plan, supported in Congress by Senator Sam Ervin, who presided over subcommittee hearings on it in December 1969.

* * *

A. *Opinion of Comptroller General* [Elmer B. Staats]

Our interest and authority in the matter exists by virtue of the duty imposed upon our Office by the Congress to audit all expenditures of appropriated funds, which necessarily involves the determination of the legality of such expenditures, including the legality of contracts obligating the Government to payment of such funds. . . .

We have serious doubts covering the main objective of the Plan, which is to require bidders to commit themselves to make every good faith effort to employ specified numbers of minority group tradesmen in the performance of Federal and federally assisted contracts and subcontracts.

The pertinent public policy with respect to employment practices of an employer which may be regarded as constituting unlawful discrimination is set out in Titles VI and VII of the Civil Rights Act. . . .

The legislative history of the Civil Rights Act is replete with statements by sponsors of the legislation that Title VII prohibits the use of race or national origin as a basis for hiring. . . .

If, for example, a contractor requires 20 plumbers and is committed to a goal of employment of at least five from minority groups, every non-minority applicant for employment in excess of 15 would, solely by reason of his race or national origin, be prejudiced in his opportunity for employment, because the contractor is committed to make every effort to employ five applicants from minority groups. . . .

Until the authority for any agency to impose or require conditions . . . which obligate bidders, contractors, or subcontractors to consider the race or national origin of their employees or prospective employees . . . is clearly and firmly established by the weight of judicial precedent or by additional statutes, we must conclude that conditions of the type proposed by the revised Philadelphia Plan are in conflict with the Civil Rights Act of 1964.

B. *Opinion of the Attorney General* [John N. Mitchell]. . . .

The Comptroller General has . . . expressed the opinion that the provision of the Philadelphia Plan for commitment to specific goals for minority group participation is in conflict with Title VII of the Civil Rights Act of 1964. . . .

I have reached a contrary result. . . .

It is not correct to say that Title VII prohibits employers from making race or national origin a factor for consideration at any stage in the process of obtaining employees. The legal definition of discrimination is an evolving one. . . .

The hiring process, viewed realistically, does not begin and end with the employer's choice among competing applicants. The standards he sets for consideration of applicants, the methods he uses to evaluate qualifications, his techniques for communicating information as to vacancies, the audience to which he communicates such information, are all factors likely to have a real and predictable effect on the racial composition of his work force. Title VII does not prohibit some structuring of the hiring process, such as the broadening of the recruitment base, to encourage the employment of members of minority groups. . . .

Title VII is not and was not understood by Congress to be the exclusive remedy for racially discriminatory practices in employment. . . . Nothing in the language or legislative history of that statute suggests that "affirmative action" may not be required of Government contractors under the Executive Order [11246] above and beyond what the statute requires of employers generally.

It is therefore my view that the Revised Philadelphia Plan is legal and that [the Department of Labor] is authorized to require Federal contracting and administering agencies to implement the Plan.

Source: Congressional Record 115, Pt. 1 (December 18, 1969): 40019–40024.

{r}DOCUMENT 160: Senate Debate on the Philadelphia Plan, December 1969

During Senator Ervin's hearing on the Philadelphia Plan, opponents denounced it as a quota system and an unwarranted extension of federal authority, while proponents emphasized the need for bold action against the seemingly intractable forces of discrimination.

* * *

A. Senator John Pastore (Democrat from Rhode Island)

What we are confronted with is the fact that this Nation suffers with a difficult situation, a very distressing one, which erupted in Philadelphia not too long ago. Because the administration has the responsibility of doing something about it before it erupts all over the country, it initiated a plan it thought would solve the problem for the time being.

It is true that, under the civil rights law, the quota system could not be used. . . . So they used the approach of a goal—unless we construe it to be a quota. Here is where the Attorney General and the Comptroller General disagree, and I think reasonable men can disagree.

The fact remains that the administration, in trying to bring about a solution of this tremendous problem, initiated the so-called Philadelphia plan.

In the process of arguing as to who should have jurisdiction, whether it should be the Comptroller General or the Attorney General, we are disrupting that program, which I think is essential for the stabilization of the situation, which has become a quite irritable one and a serious one in the Nation.

B. Senator John McClellan (Democrat from Arkansas)

Mr. President, the Department of Labor on June 27, 1969 issued the revised Philadelphia plan. . . . Despite the fact that the Comptroller General, on August 5, 1969, issued a decision finding that the Philadelphia plan contravened the 1964 Civil Rights Act . . . the Secretary of Labor is continuing to apply and enforce it. . . .

Executive Order [11246] and the Philadelphia plan do not constitute an implementation of the Civil Rights Act [of 1964] or the congressional intent which was enunciated therein. The plan's requirement that certain Government contractors meet prescribed racial employment quotas is simply an example of the overreaching exercise of Executive power.

C. Senator Edward Brooke (Republican from Massachusetts)

[W]e have learned that simple prohibition of discrimination is not enough. Overt acts of discrimination not only are becoming less common; they were never the heart of the problem to begin with.

The real problem of discrimination in America is what the Civil Rights Commission has referred to as "systematic discrimination," but what I prefer to call "systemic" or "intrinsic" discrimination. Discrimination against minorities, particularly in the employment field, is built into the very structure of American society. Three black children in four in America attend an essentially segregated school from the day they enter kindergarten. . . .

Once a black child has left school, he is two and a half times more likely to be unemployed. . . .

Even those blacks who survive the system, however, find obstacles placed in their way which do not confront most other Americans. If a minority applicant seeks employment . . . he will find that employment is often based upon union recommendation. The union passes the word to its members that an employer is looking for men; those members are predominantly white, and the social patterns are such that they will pass the word along to predominantly white friends. . . .

The policy of assigning minority employees to "traditional" jobs or departments is also an informal, systemic barrier to full opportunity in employment. . . .

These are the kinds of situations which the Philadelphia plan . . . [was] designed to overcome.

Source: Congressional Record 115, Pt. 2 (December 18, 1969): 39961, 39964–39965, 39966–39967.

{r}DOCUMENT 161: Department of Labor Order Number 4, February 1970

The Philadelphia Plan created unusual political alliances. Republicans loyal to Richard Nixon joined with liberal Democrats to defend the plan against conservative Democrats. The latter's position was supported by organized labor, whose members traditionally played key roles in liberal Democratic coalitions. More than one political observer suggested that Nixon had deliberately maneuvered a split between civil rights liberals and their union supporters. Whatever the case, the Philadelphia Plan emerged from all of the politicking intact. When enforcement regulations drawn up by the Office of Federal Contract Compliance in November 1969 were revised and officially issued three months later as the Labor Department's Order Number 4, the Philadelphia Plan became the model for affirmative action policy nationwide.

* * *

Subpart A—General

Title, purpose and scope

[W]ithin 120 days from the commencement of a contract each prime contractor or subcontractor with 50 or more employees and a contract of

$50,000 or more [must] develop a written affirmative action compliance program for each of its establishments. . . .

Any contractor . . . who has not complied fully . . . is not in compliance with Executive Order 11246. . . .

If the contractor fails to show good cause for his failure [to comply] or fails to remedy that failure by developing and implementing an acceptable affirmative action program within 30 days [of notice of noncompliance], the compliance agency . . . shall issue a notice of proposed cancellation or termination of existing contracts or subcontracts and debarment from future contracts and subcontracts. . . .

Subpart B—Required Contents of Affirmative Action Programs

Purpose of affirmative action program

An affirmative action program is a set of specific and result-oriented procedures to which a contractor commits himself to apply every good faith effort. . . . Procedures without effort to make them work are meaningless; and effort, undirected by specific and meaningful procedures, is inadequate. . . .

Required utilization analysis and goals

Affirmative action programs must contain . . .

(a) An analysis of all major job categories at the facility, with explanations if minorities are currently being under-utilized in any one or more job categories. . . . In determining whether minorities are being underutilized in any job category the contractor will consider . . . :

(1) The minority population of the labor area surrounding the facility; . . .

(3) The percentage of minority work force as compared with the total work force in the immediate labor area; . . .

(5) The availability of minorities having requisite skills in an area in which the contractor can reasonably recruit. . . .

Goals, timetables and affirmative action commitments must be designed to correct any identifiable deficiencies. . . .

[M]inority groups are most likely to be underutilized in the following six (6) categories . . . : officials and managers, professionals, technicians, sales workers, office and clerical and craftsmen (skilled). Therefore, the contractor shall direct special attention to these categories in his analysis and goal setting. . . .

Establishment of goals and timetables

(a) The goals and timetables developed by the contractor should be attainable in terms of the contractor's analysis of his deficiencies. . . .

(c) Goals should be significant, measurable and attainable.

(d) Goals should be specific for planned results, with timetables for completion.

(e) Goals may not be rigid and inflexible quotas . . . but must be targets reasonably attainable by . . . every good faith effort. . . .

Source: Federal Register 35, no. 5 (February 5, 1970): 2587, 2589.

{g}DOCUMENT 162: "Sex Discrimination Guidelines," U.S. Department of Labor, June 1970

Absent from the list of categories covered by Order Number 4 were women. This omission stemmed, in part, from the tenacity of the traditional protective legislation lobby, which opposed erasing distinctions between male and female workers. But it also reflected a tacit assumption on the part of the authors of the Philadelphia Plan that the construction industry was a male province. The "manning tables" were based on percentages of male workers in the total population as related to males in given industries. The distribution of women in the workforce was so strikingly different that calculating and addressing discrimination against women in industry in the manner adopted for men presented many problems. Instead of tackling those problems, Secretary of Labor George Shultz developed a special set of guidelines on sex discrimination, which President Nixon signed in June 1970. The guidelines omitted references to the goals and timetables that were the main tool for enforcement on behalf of males in Order Number 4.

* * *

Employers engaged in recruiting activity must recruit employees of both sexes for all jobs unless sex is a bona fide occupational qualification. . . .

The employer must not make any distinction based upon sex in employment opportunities, wages, hours, or other conditions of employment. . . .

The employer may not discriminatorily restrict one sex to certain job classifications. . . .

The employer shall take affirmative action to recruit women to apply for those jobs where they have been previously excluded.

Source: Federal Register 35, no. 111 (June 9, 1970): 8888–8889.

{g}DOCUMENT 163: *A Matter of Simple Justice, Report of the President's Task Force on Women's Rights and Responsibilities*, **Officially Released June 9, 1970 (Transmitted to the President December 1969)**

When Richard Nixon announced the new guidelines on sex discrimination, he also officially released a report prepared at his request. The President's Task Force on Women's Rights and Responsibilities was appointed by Nixon in October 1969, in response to growing pressure from women, especially those in his own party who were dissatisfied by his failure to include significant numbers of women among his political appointments and his apparent lack of interest in women's issues. Task force members, headed by drugstore chain executive Virginia Allan, submitted their recommendations in December. The Nixon administration held the report for the next six months, while White House advisers weighed the political benefits and liabilities of the Equal Rights Amendment, a measure that the report strongly advocated.

Task force members directed their most specific recommendations directly to the president, urging him to establish a new office on women, call a White House conference, and exert influence on Congress to pass the ERA and draft new legislation against sex discrimination, including several amendments to the Civil Rights Act of 1964 and expansion of the Equal Pay Act of 1963 (Docs. 118, 113).

* * *

So widespread and pervasive are discriminatory practices against women they have come to be regarded, more often than not, as normal. Unless there is clear indication of Administration concern at the highest level, it is unlikely that significant progress can be made in correcting ancient, entrenched injustices. . . .

[T]his Task Force recommends that the President . . . send a message to the Congress . . . recommend[ing] the following . . . :

Amendment of Title VII of the Civil Rights Act of 1964 to (1) . . . empower . . . the Equal Employment Opportunity Commission to enforce the law, and (2) extend coverage to State and local governments and to teachers.

Amendment of Titles IV and IX of the Civil Rights Act of 1965 to authorize the Attorney General to aid women and parents of minor girls in suits seeking access to public education. . . .

Amendment of Title II of the Civil Rights Act of 1964 to prohibit discrimination because of sex in public accommodations. . . .

Amendment of the Fair Labor Standards Act to extend coverage of its equal pay provisions to executive, administrative and professional employees.

Source: A Matter of Simple Justice, The Report of the President's Task Force on Women's Rights and Responsibilities (December 15, 1969): iii–v.

{d}DOCUMENT 164: Judith E. Heumann Recalling Her Battle for Employment as a Teacher in the 1970s

Just as minority women bore the double burden of sexism and racism, disabled individuals who also belonged to a racial minority and/ or were women faced the possibility of discrimination on more than one front. At the same time, one form of discrimination often turned out to be the more dominant in the lives of such individuals. This was the case with a twenty-two-year-old woman recently graduated from Long Island College who was denied a teaching license in 1970 because she could not walk. In testimony delivered a decade later before the U.S. Civil Rights Commission, Judith Heumann provided details about her experience.

* * *

I decided in college that I wanted to major in education and that was both a statement that I wanted to work with children, and it was also a statement that in the New York City school system with 70,000 people working in it there were no disabled people who had been accepted as teachers, who in fact became teachers and were disabled at the time they were certified. So I took appropriate courses. . . . However, when it was time for me to take my exams, I passed my oral exam and I passed my written exam and I was failed on my medical exam. . . . When I went for my medical exam, I was greeted by a doctor who informed me that she had never had to give someone like me a medical exam. . . .

I had tried to get the ACLU [American Civil Liberties Union] to handle the case. The ACLU informed me that this was a medical decision and therefore, no court would be willing to look at the case. When I tried to explain to them that, in fact, it was a civil rights issue, that it was a denial of a job purely on a medical diagnosis, not based on my ability to perform the job, they didn't even want to interview me.

Some of the relevant questions that the doctor asked me—she wanted me to show her how I went to the bathroom, and I remember telling her that unless it was going to be a requirement for me to teach elementary school children how to go physically to the bathroom, I didn't see any relevance in my showing her how I went to the bathroom. . . .

When I came back for my second medical interview, I came back with an advocate. The advocate was not allowed in the room. . . .

The long and the short of that story was that I was fortunate enough to get Constance Baker Motley as the judge on the case, who was the first black woman judge appointed to the Federal district court, and she basically made it clear that she was going to keep the case and it looked like she was going to rule in our favor. So they settled out of court. . . . Finally I was placed at the school that I had been a student in.

Source: U.S. Commission on Civil Rights 1980, 234–236.

{d}DOCUMENT 165: "Hope for the Crippled," 1969, U.S. Postage Stamp

The rights of the disabled, as represented in Heumann's case, were not yet at the center of national consciousness. Indeed, the disabled were widely perceived as helpless and in need of charity more than as self-defining and entitled to participate in mainstream society. Judith Heumann highlighted this viewpoint in the following comments on a stamp that the U.S. Postal Service issued in 1969 seeking to recognize the handicapped.

* * *

A. 1969 Stamp

HOPE
FOR THE CRIPPLED

U. S. POSTAGE **6** CENTS

Source: Standard Postage Stamp Catalogue, vol. 1 (Sidney, Ohio: Scott, 1997): 35.

B. Judith Heumann Looking Back at the 1969 Postage Stamp Image of Disability

One very interesting scenario that runs through my story and throughout the story of many disabled individuals . . . [is] that one becomes more "normal" (whatever that means) when one is walking. If one is not walking, one is not "normal." I think you only need to look at the . . . stamp that was put out by the United States Government entitled, "Hope for the Crippled," which was a stamp of a person seated in a wheelchair rising to a standing position; that, to me, indicated what people thought of disabled individuals in a wheelchair—which is a more visible thing, which is why I am sure they selected a wheelchair—you are not considered to be a whole person. However, once you are in the standing position, that is normality.

Source: U.S. Commission on Civil Rights 1980, 231.

{d}DOCUMENT 166: Urban Mass Transportation Assistance Act of 1970

The same social assumptions about disability that held disabled individuals back from good jobs also severely limited their opportunities to reach such jobs and simply to move about in their communities. Most means of transportation available to the general public and funded by public moneys were inaccessible to people using wheelchairs or otherwise unable to manage the high steps, narrow doorways, and immovable seating of most public conveyances. Two 1970 acts of Congress (and the lobbying, debates, and publicity surrounding them) raised awareness and created some action on this issue. Responding to pressure from organizations of disabled citizens, Congress amended the Architectural Barriers Act of 1968 (Doc. 153) to have it apply to the Metro Subway System of the nation's capital, which was then under construction. This amendment was buttressed three years later with a $65 million appropriation to underwrite its implementation. While making the District of Columbia subway handicapped-accessible was practically and symbolically very important, the need remained for a policy covering transportation nationwide. A step toward addressing that need was taken via 1970 amendments to the Urban Mass Transportation Act, which, when it was passed in 1964, made no reference to disability. The amendments, sponsored by freshman congressman Mario Biaggi (Democrat from New York), outlined a national policy of accessibility for the disabled on public transportation. The amendments did not, however, provide for the enforcement of that policy.

* * *

It is hereby declared to be the national policy that elderly and handicapped persons have the same right as other persons to utilize mass transportation facilities and services. . . .

[S]pecial efforts shall be made in the planning and design of mass transportation facilities and services so that the availability to elderly and handicapped persons of mass transportation which they can effectively utilize will be assured; and . . . all Federal programs offering assistance in the field of mass transportation should contain provisions implementing that policy.

Source: 49 *U.S. Code*, vol. 49, sec. 1612a (1970).

{r}DOCUMENT 167: *Contractors Association of Eastern Pennsylvania v. Secretary of Labor*, April 22, 1971, U.S. Court of Appeals, Third Circuit

Policies shaped in the White House and the halls of Congress were repeatedly tested in the courts. In 1971 the regulations governing the Philadelphia Plan (Labor Department Order Number 4) (Doc. 161) were ratified in a federal court of appeals. The case at issue was brought by an association of some eighty contractors from five counties in and around Philadelphia. They sought a legal ruling from a federal district court against the requirement that they comply with the Philadelphia Plan in order to bid for work on a federally funded dam construction project in Chester County, Pennsylvania. The district court ruled against them. The Third Circuit Court of Appeals upheld that ruling. By refusing to hear the case, the U.S. Supreme Court determined that the order would stand.

* * *

The complaint challenges the validity of the Philadelphia Plan. . . .

The plaintiffs contend that the Philadelphia Plan is social legislation of local application enacted by the Executive without the benefit of statutory or constitutional authority. . . .

The district court's answer is that the federal government "has the unrestricted power to fix the terms, conditions and those with whom it will deal." . . .

We conclude . . . that the Philadelphia Plan['s] . . . inclusion as a precondition for federal assistance was within the implied authority of the President and his designees. . . .

The federal interest is in maximum availability of construction tradesmen for the projects in which the federal government has a cost and completion interest. . . .

The judgment of the district court will be affirmed.

Source: 442 F. 2d 159 at 162, 166, 171, 177 (1971).

{g}DOCUMENT 168: *Phillips v. Martin-Marietta Corporation,* U.S. Supreme Court, January 25, 1971

The first case to reach the Supreme Court involving a sex discrimination charge brought under Title VII was *Phillips v. Martin-Marietta Corporation.* The plaintiff in this case was Ida Phillips, whose application for a trainee job with Martin-Marietta was denied because she had preschool children. A federal district court in Florida found that she was not a victim of sex discrimination. Invoking what was known as the "sex-plus theory of employment," the court argued that a woman could be denied employment when a factor in addition to her gender was present—in Phillips' case the preschool children. The Supreme Court struck down this ruling and instructed the lower court to reconsider.

* * *

Section 703(a) of the Civil Rights Act of 1964 requires that persons of like qualifications be given employment opportunities irrespective of their sex. The Court of Appeals therefore erred in reading this section as permitting one hiring policy for women and another for men—each having pre-school-age children. . . . Summary judgment was therefore improper and we remand for . . . further consideration.

Source: 400 U.S. 542 at 544 (1971).

{g}DOCUMENT 169: *Reed v. Reed,* U.S. Supreme Court, November 1971

Several months after *Phillips,* the Supreme Court declared unconstitutional an Idaho state law requiring that only men be appointed executors for wills. This was the first time ever that the highest court had ruled against a state on the basis of sex discrimination.

* * *

MR. CHIEF JUSTICE BURGER delivered the opinion of the Court. . . .
[T]he Idaho Supreme Court concluded that its objective was to eliminate one area of controversy when two or more persons equally entitled under [Section 15–314 of the Idaho Code] seek letters of administration

and thereby present the probate court "with the issue of which one should be named." . . .

The crucial question . . . is whether 15–314 advances that objective in a manner consistent with the command of the Equal Protection Clause. We hold that it does not.

Source: 404 U.S. 71 at 76 (1971).

{r/g}DOCUMENT 170: "Revised Order Number 4," December 1971

As a trend favoring women developed in the rulings of federal courts, the Department of Labor quietly revised Order Number 4 one more time, including women among those for whom federal contractors must devise employment goals and timetables.

* * *

Subpart B—Required Contents of Affirmative Action Programs
subsection 60–2.10 Purpose of affirmative action program. . . .

An acceptable affirmative action program must include an analysis of areas within which the contractor is deficient in the utilization of minority groups and women. . . .

subsection 60–2.11 Required utilization analysis

[W]omen are likely to be underutilized in departments and jobs within departments as follows: officials and managers, professionals, technicians, sales workers (except over-the-counter sales in certain retail establishments), craftsmen (skilled and semi-skilled). . . .

"Underutilization" is defined as having fewer minorities or women in a particular job classification than would reasonably be expected by their availability. . . . [T]he contractor shall conduct [a workforce] analysis separately for minorities and women.

Source: Federal Register 36 (December 4, 1971): 17445.

{r/g}DOCUMENT 171: *Griggs et al. v. Duke Power Co.,* U.S. Supreme Court, March 8, 1971

Between *Phillips v. Martin-Marietta* and *Reed v. Reed* (Docs. 168, 169), the Supreme Court had issued another decision with sweeping consequences for women and minorities: *Griggs et al. v. Duke Power Company*. Black employees at the Dan River Steam Station of the power company in Draper, North Carolina, filed suit against a company requirement that, to be hired and to transfer within the company, workers must possess a high school diploma and pass two standardized tests that were said to measure general intelligence and "mechanical comprehension." The high school diploma had been required since 1955. The company added the test requirement when Title VII took effect in 1965. Before passage of Title VII, the plant had been segregated, with African American workers confined to departments where the pay was lowest. When the plant desegregated in compliance with the law, African Americans seeking to transfer to previously "white departments" argued that the transfer requirements were discriminatory, since the only workers exempted from them were whites working in those departments before the requirements were imposed. In addition, a Jim Crow education system resulted in lower graduation rates for African Americans and a much lower pass-rate on the tests. Finally, the plaintiffs were able to prove that the tests themselves did not measure abilities to perform the specific jobs in that plant. After two lower courts ruled against the African American workers, the Supreme Court ruled in their favor, with all the justices except Justice Brennan (who did not take part in the decision) signing on to the ruling. In delivering the opinion, Chief Justice Burger drew upon the language of the Richmond District Court in *Quarles* (Doc. 155). Also as in *Quarles*, Section 703(h) was again at issue, this time in regard to its provision that it would not be "an unlawful employment practice for an employer to give and to act upon the results of any professionally developed ability test provided that such test . . . is not designed . . . to discriminate because of race, color, religion or national origin. . . ."

* * *

The objective of Congress in the enactment of Title VII is plain from the language of the statute. It was to achieve equality of employment opportunities and remove barriers that have operated in the past to favor an identifiable group of white employees over other employees. Under the Act, practices, procedures, or tests neutral on their face, and even neutral in terms of intent, cannot be maintained if they operate to "freeze" the status quo of prior discriminatory employment practices. . . .

If an employment practice which operates to exclude Negroes cannot be shown to be related to job performance, the practice is prohibited. . . .

The Equal Employment Opportunity Commission, having enforcement responsibility, has issued guidelines interpreting 703 (h) to permit only the use of job-related tests. The administrative interpretation of the

Act by the enforcing agency is entitled to great deference. . . . Since the Act and its legislative history support the Commission's construction, this affords good reason to treat the guidelines as expressing the will of Congress. . . .

What Congress has commanded is that any tests used must measure the person for the job and not the person in the abstract.

Source: 401 U.S. 424 at 429–430, 431, 433–434, 436 (1971).

{r/g}DOCUMENT 172: Economist Daniel Seligman Interpreting the 1971 *Griggs* Ruling

The *Griggs* ruling was a pivotal event in the evolution of affirmative action, celebrated by some and lamented by others. All observers, then and since, agree that *Griggs* strongly reinforced the EEOC. While civil rights activists believed that such reinforcement was overdue, their opponents—joined by various academics and social critics—worried that the EEOC had already overstepped the boundaries that Congress intended it to respect and that *Griggs* "represented judicial ratification of this disregard of congressional intent." *Griggs'* import as a precedent was also clear to everyone. Over the next decade courts at every level would invoke *Griggs* to strike down barriers to the advancement of minority workers. From the perspective of those workers and their supporters, this represented a major victory. However, significant numbers of employers, union leaders, and social critics viewed the decision as corrosive—eating away at qualifications and requirements. Economist Daniel Seligman summarized this point of view.

* * *

Companies that have high standards and want to defend them will immediately perceive that the ground rules, which not only place the burden of proof on the employer but require coping with some formidable-looking validation procedures, are not inviting. Many will obviously conclude that it is simpler to abolish their standards than to try justifying them.

Source: Seligman 1973, 166.

In the presidential election year of 1972 the interest of politicians in civil rights and woman's rights intensified. Three issues proved to be of particular interest: the ERA; augmented authority for the EEOC; and discrimination based on sex and race in educational institutions receiving federal funds. Each of these issues generated new legislation—a revived ERA, the Equal Opportunity Act of 1972, and the Higher Education Act of 1972.

{g}DOCUMENT 173: Representatives Griffiths, Celler, and Green Square Off on the ERA, August 1970

A reworded ERA (Doc. 36) had passed the House and died in the Senate in 1970. Reintroduced in 1971, it was approved by both legislative bodies. Opponents Emanuel Celler in the House and Sam Ervin in the Senate attached a time limit for state ratification. Thirty-eight states would have to ratify by March 22, 1979. During the ratification attempt (which was later extended to June 30, 1982), every ramification of the proposed ERA became the subject of public controversy. At the root of that controversy lay conflicting assumptions about appropriate roles for men and women. These assumptions were clearly articulated in the hearings and debates that preceded the House and Senate votes of 1971 and 1972. On August 10, 1970, Representative Martha Griffiths of Michigan introduced the latest version of the ERA onto the floor of the House of Representatives. She was supported by numerous colleagues and with special verve by Representative Edith Green of Oregon. Their most adamant opponent was the congressman from New York, Emanuel Celler.

* * *

Mrs. Griffiths. [F]or 47 consecutive years this amendment has been introduced into the Congress of the United States. . . .

[T]he Supreme Court . . . has on not one single occasion granted to women the basic protection of the fifth or 14th amendment. The only right guaranteed to women today by the Constitution . . . is the right to vote and to hold public office.

It is time . . . that in this battle with the Supreme Court, that this body and the legislatures of the States come to the aid of women by passing this amendment.

Mr. Celler. [W]e are being asked to . . . vote on a constitutional amendment, the consequences of which are unexamined, its meaning non-defined, and its risks uncalculated. . . .

[E]ver since Adam gave up his rib to make a woman, throughout the ages we have learned that physical, emotional, psychological and social differences exist and dare not be disregarded. . . .

[T]here is as much difference between a male and a female as between a horse chestnut and a chestnut horse—and as the French say, Vive la difference.

Any attempt to pass an amendment that promises to wipe out the effects of these differences is about as abortive as trying to fish in a desert—and you cannot do that.

There is not really genuine equality. . . .

[T]here is only one place where there is equality—and that is in the cemetery.

Mrs. Green of Oregon. . . . [I]t actually seems incredible to me that in the last quarter of the 20th century we are still debating whether or not the majority of the American people have equal rights under the Constitution.

It has been said that if this amendment is passed it will create profound social changes. . . . It is high time some profound social changes were made in our society. . . . I hope that the debate today will not be based on "vive la difference" arguments, but rather with the words of Walt Whitman in mind: "That whatever degrades another degrades me, and whatever is said or done returns at last to me." . . .

Women know that there is no such thing as equality per se but only equal opportunity to . . . make the best one can of one's life within one's capability and without fear of injustice or oppression or denial of those opportunities.

Source: Congressional Record 116, Pt. 21 (August 10, 1970): 28000–28001, 28014.

{g}DOCUMENT 174: Testimony of Wilma Scott Heide before the Senate Subcommittee on Constitutional Amendments, May 1970

The Senate Subcommittee on Constitutional Amendments held hearings on the ERA in May and September 1970. Among those giving testimony both times was the outspoken chairman of the Board of Directors of NOW, Wilma Scott Heide. In the May hearings she stressed the pervasiveness of sexism in American society.

* * *

All of my social conditioning teaches me to be grateful for the opportunity to speak in a public forum convened by Senators. Yet I am really outraged to even consider gratitude as an appropriate response for a chance to plead for what is the birthright of every male in the United States. . . .

[T]his Nation is antifemale in its laws, its expressions, its value systems, its language, everything. . . .

We find the ridicule of feminists even by people otherwise liberal. Antifeminism is the last stronghold of sanctioned prejudice. . . .

This women's liberation, actually human liberation, is, I think, the most profound social movement ever. It promises to inject some massive new insights into the bloodstream of our culture, not because women are so different, but because it will bring the life experience of the other half of the population to bear on our common problems and opportunities.

Source: Hearings before the Subcommittee on Constitutional Amendments of the Committee on the Judiciary, U.S. Senate (May 5–7, 1970): 563, 565, 568.

{g}DOCUMENT 175: Wilma Scott Heide's Testimony, September 1970

In the September hearings Heide drew upon her professional standing as a behavioral scientist. She also inserted into the record the history of how the Senate subcommittee had been pressured into holding hearings.

* * *

[S]ocial roles are learned phenomena. Parenthood is a social role after birth, legislator is a social role, teacher is a social role. . . . With several crucial exceptions, all social roles can be fulfilled by some men or some women. Therefore there are only two roles or jobs no man is or could be qualified to perform: Human incubator and wet nurse; likewise, there is only one role or job which no woman is or could be qualified to perform: Sperm donor. . . .

Those hearings in May . . . were only held because 20 of us led by me interrupted the hearings of the Senate Subcommittee on Constitutional Amendments on the issue of the 18 year old vote and demanded some action on the equal rights amendment. The original transcript of May 7, 1970, when I testified for the equal rights amendment, clearly quoted the presiding Senator that it was through our disruptive action on February 17, 1970, and the response of the Senate Constitutional Subcommittee chairman that the earlier May 1970 hearings were held. . . . I want today's record to clearly indicate what was necessary to effect those hearings.

Source: Hearings before the Subcommittee on Constitutional Amendments of the Committee on the Judiciary, U.S. Senate (September 15, 1970): 290, 293.

{g}DOCUMENT 176: Proposed Twenty-seventh Amendment to the U.S. Constitution (the Equal Rights Amendment), March 22, 1972

On March 22, 1972, the Equal Rights Amendment was sent from Congress to the states for ratification.

* * *

Section 1. Equality of rights under the law shall not be denied or abridged by the United States or by any State on account of sex. Congress and the several States shall have power, within their respective jurisdictions, to enforce this article by appropriate legislation.

Source: Congressional Record 116 (August 10, 1970): 28004.

{r}DOCUMENT 177: Testimony of Clarence Mitchell, Hearings of the Senate Committee on Public Welfare, August 11, 1969

From its beginnings the Equal Employment Opportunity Commission had been a disappointment to the civil rights community, repeatedly attacked by feminists, and regarded by legal analysts as enfeebled. By 1972, making the EEOC effective had become a major objective of advocates for racial justice and proponents of gender equality. They pursued this objective through legislative means, lobbying Congress to transform the commission from a merely investigative body whose commissioners could only attempt to negotiate resolutions to complaints of discrimination, to a body with enforcement powers ("cease and desist" authority) and entitled to sue in federal court. The need for such a change was framed by warnings, such as the admonition that NAACP lobbyist Clarence Mitchell had delivered in hearings held in 1969 by the Senate Committee on Public Welfare. Mitchell led into his warning with a story about a young African American friend who had grown a beard in an effort to gain respect from his white associates.

* * *

I am sorry to say that in my opinion, the reason why you see a great many colored people walking around with African robes on that are called Dashikis, many of them wearing these beards, is because that has been the only way that they can get attention. We come in here . . . I and my associates, dressed as normal Americans. We speak in modulated voices. We present you with intelligent information. Some of the best legal brains in this country are here. . . . Against that we have the highest level of our Government coming in and saying that we are all wrong. . . .

The administration . . . says "We don't need this" [cease and desist powers granted to the EEOC]. Now, . . . it is true that the administration . . . has offered something . . . a kind of shifting of the use of legal talent . . . , but what we are in need of is a massive infusion of confidence which will let the country know, and which will let the unhappy people and the dissident elements know that we are really serious about this effort of trying to eliminate job discrimination.

What the administration proposes is going to look to the man in the street like another effort to give him the runaround. . . .

I believe that this is unfair to the people, . . . to the country, and I believe it is unrealistic in the times in which we live. The day will never come . . . when I personally will join the forces of those who believe that by force and violence they can achieve their ends. . . . But I am also a realist and I know that we cannot answer the man about to throw a Molotov cocktail if we say "We are not going to give you cease and desist powers. . . . What we are going to give you is a chance to have a different set of lawyers. . . ."

Source: Senate Committee on Labor and Public Welfare, Hearings on Equal Employment Opportunity Enforcement Act (August 11, 1969): 81.

Legislators wrestled with EEOC reform from 1965 until 1972. Representatives Augustus Hawkins and James Roosevelt introduced a House bill in 1965 that passed April 27, 1966, granting cease and desist authority to the agency. Without Senate action the bill remained a dead letter. In April 1968 Senator Tom Clark laid a similar measure before his colleagues with no result. In November 1970 the Senate approved a measure offered by Senator Harrison Williams; the measure's House counterpart died in that chamber's Rules Committee. The 92d Congress of 1971–1972 reached a compromise between a House bill passed in September 1971 and a measure approved by the Senate in February 1972. The bills were sent to a conference committee, which recommended the Senate version. Both houses accepted that recommendation, and President Nixon signed the resulting Equal Employment Opportunity Act on March 24, 1972.

{r/g}DOCUMENT 178: Consensus on the Need to Strengthen the EEOC, 1972–1973

Observations in the media and legislative conference reports reflect the emergence of a strong consensus by 1971 on three points: that the EEOC was failing in its mission, that the failure could not be tolerated, and that discrimination based on race and sex was more deeply embedded in American society than was previously realized.

* * *

A. *New York Times*, January 27, 1972

The question of giving enforcement teeth to the [Equal Employment Opportunity] commission is one of the last of the pure civil rights issues in Congress that began with the Civil Rights Act of 1964 and continued through the Voting Rights Act of 1965 and the Open Housing Act of 1968.

Source: New York Times (January 27, 1972), 1, 17.

B. Report of the Senate Committee on Labor and Public Welfare, 1973

In a special report released this year by the Bureau of the Census . . . the evidence is clear that while some progress has been made toward bettering the economic position of the Nation's black population, the avowed goal of social and economic equality is not yet anywhere near a reality. For example, the report shows that the median family income for Negroes in 1970 was $6,279, while the median income for whites during the same period was $10,236. This earnings gap shows that Negroes are still far from reaching their rightful place in society. [The report concluded that the major problem with the 1964 act was that the EEOC did not have] the authority to issue judicially enforceable orders to back up its findings of discrimination.

Source: Bureau of National Affairs, *Equal Employment Opportunity Act of 1972, Appendix E* (Washington, DC: Bureau of National Affairs, 1973): 228, 230.

C. House Committee on Education and Labor, 1973

During the preparation and presentation of Title VII of the Civil Rights Act of 1964, employment discrimination tended to be viewed as a series of isolated and distinguishable events, due, for the most part, to the ill-will on the part of some identifiable individual or organization. . . . It was thought that . . . conciliation rather than compulsory processes would be more appropriate for the resolution of this essentially "human" problem. . . . experience, however, has shown this to be an oversimplified expectation. . . .

Employment discrimination as we know it today is a far more complex and pervasive phenomenon. Experts familiar with the subject generally describe the problem in terms of "systems" and "effects" rather than simply intentional wrongs. . . . The forms and incidences of discrimination which the commission is required to treat are increasingly complex [and include pattern or practice discrimination].

Pattern or practice discrimination is a pervasive and deeply imbedded form of discrimination. Specific acts or incidences of discrimination within the commission's jurisdiction are frequently symptomatic of a pattern or practice which Title VII seeks to eradicate. . . . It is imperative that [the commission] be empowered . . . to deal with "pattern or practice" discrimination in order to deal comprehensively with systematic discrimination.

Source: Bureau of National Affairs, *Equal Employment Opportunity Act of 1972, Appendix D* (Washington, DC: Bureau of National Affairs, 1973): 162, 168.

Legislative debate on how to improve the EEOC and eradicate systemic discrimination took many twists and turns, revealing multiple agendas among the legislators. Nixon loyalists, guarding executive control over the administration of contract compliance programs, opposed granting cease and desist powers to the EEOC and advocated judicial action to enforce equal employment policies. When liberal Democrats agreed to judicial enforcement, rivalries among federal agencies sparked disagreements over who should be authorized to pursue litigation. Meanwhile, states' rights diehards tried to obstruct extension of Title VII guarantees to state and local government employees and to dismantle the entire federal antidiscrimination effort. When the smoke cleared, the obstructionists had been marginalized, Title VII coverage was substantially expanded, and both the EEOC and the executive branch of government held new powers of enforcement.

{r/g}DOCUMENT 179: Amendment to the Equal Employment Opportunity Act Proposed by Senator Ervin, January 28, 1972

One of the major obstructionists was Senator Sam Ervin of North Carolina, who attempted to amend the Equal Employment Opportunity Act with wording that would have, in effect, tied the hands of everyone involved in the enforcement of antidiscrimination laws.

* * *

No department, agency, or officer of the United States shall require an employer to practice discrimination in reverse by employing persons of a particular race, or a particular religion, or a particular national origin, or a particular sex in either fixed or variable numbers, proportions, percentages, quotas, goals or ranges. If any department, agency, officer, or employee of the United States violates . . . the provisions of the preceding sentence, the employer or employee aggrieved by the violation . . . may bring a civil action in the United States District Court in the District in which he resides or in which the violation occurred.

Source: Congressional Record 118 (January 28, 1972): 1662.

{r/g}DOCUMENT 180: Senate Debate on the Ervin Amendment

As his colleague from New York, Senator Jacob Javits, pointed out, Ervin's sweeping reference to "officer of the United States" in the proposed amendment would include judges and thereby invalidate court orders against employment discrimination. With his amendment, Ervin set an early example of a practice later adopted by many opponents of civil rights and affirmative action: purporting to be opposed to "discrimination" by using that term to support a status quo that has historically always discriminated against minorities. Ervin's amendment was defeated by a vote of 22 to 44.

* * *

A. Senator Ervin [Democrat from North Carolina]. . . . I urge the Senate to adopt this amendment. . . . [I]t is in perfect harmony with the objective of the bill to forbid discrimination in employment. . . .

I find as I travel to and fro among the people of this land, that people cannot understand why the Federal Government orders employers to practice discrimination in employment while they are supposed to be preventing discrimination in employment. . . .

B. Senator Javits [Democrat from New York]. . . . [T]his amendment . . . would torpedo orders of courts seeking to correct a history of unjust discrimination in employment on racial or color ground, because it would prevent the court from ordering specific measures which could assign specific percentages of minorities that had to be hired, and that could apply to government as well as private employers.

C. The Presiding Officer. All time on this amendment has now expired. . . .
    On this question the yeas and nays have been ordered. . . .
    The result was announced—yeas 22, nays 44. . . .
    So Mr. Ervin's amendment was rejected.

Source: Congressional Record 118 (January 28, 1972): 1663, 1675, 1676.

The significance of the defeat of this and several related amendments offered by Ervin occasioned differences of opinion among scholars and politicians. Those favorably disposed to race-conscious and gender-conscious employment policies read the Senate action as sanctioning such policies within the framework of Title VII. Opponents of affirmative action maintained that in turning back Ervin's amendments, the Senate merely expressed itself on his particular proposals and that the color-blind intent of Title VII as originally affirmed by its sponsors and section j (Doc. 124) remained unchanged.

{r/g}DOCUMENT 181: Summary of the Equal Employment Opportunity Act of 1972

The primary changes and general impact of the Equal Employment Opportunity Act of 1972 were summarized in an operations manual prepared by the Bureau of National Affairs.

* * *

When Congress began to consider amendments to Title VII of the Civil Rights Act of 1964 the primary objective was to give the Equal Employment Opportunity Commission enforcement powers.

The amendments adopted in 1972 went much further. In addition to giving the Commission authority to institute court proceedings to enforce the prohibition against employment discrimination based on race, color, religion, sex, or national origin, the new Act made significant changes relating to coverage and exemptions, record keeping, administration, government contracts and time for filing charges.

THE CHANGES IN COVERAGE

By a series of amendments, the coverage of Title VII is extended to millions of employees and union members. . . .

• Prior to the amendments Title VII applied only to employers with 25 or more employees and unions with 25 or more members. The amendments reduce the number of employees and union members required for coverage to 15. . . .

• Under the original Act, state and local governments and their employees were excluded from coverage. The amendments extend coverage to all state and local governments, governmental agencies, political subdivisions, and departments and agencies of the District of Columbia. . . . There are some exemptions, discussed below. . . .

THE CHANGES IN EXEMPTIONS

Under the 1964 Act, there was an exemption for educational institutions with respect to individuals whose work involved educational activities. The amendments eliminate this exemption.

This change will bring under Title VII an estimated 120,000 educational institutions, with about 2.8 million teachers and professional staff members and another 1.5 million nonprofessional staff members. . . .

The amendment extending coverage to state and local governments and their employees provides an exemption for elected officials, their personal assistants, and their immediate advisers. It was stressed in the legislative history that this exemption "is intended to be construed very narrowly and is in no way intended to establish an over-all narrowing of the expanded coverage of state and local governmental employees."

ENFORCEMENT

The most fundamental changes made by the 1972 amendments relate to enforcement. As part of the compromise that led to the adoption of the 1964 Act the Equal Employment Opportunity Commission was given virtually no enforcement powers. . . .

Under the 1972 amendments, if it is unable to obtain an acceptable conciliation agreement within 30 days after the filing of [a charge of discrimination] . . . the Commission may bring a civil suit in a federal district court for an injunction and other remedies against the charged employer, union, employment agency, or joint labor–management committee. In cases involving a state or local government the Attorney General is authorized to bring the action. . . .

In another enforcement change, the Commission is given concurrent jurisdiction with the Justice Department for a period of two years to bring actions to eliminate patterns or practices of unlawful employment discrimination. At the end of the two years, the Commission will have exclusive jurisdiction over such actions. . . .

ADMINISTRATIVE CHANGES

The broadening of its jurisdiction and enforcement powers poses many problems for the Equal Employment Opportunity Commission. In the current fiscal year . . . the Commission is about 22 months behind in its processing of cases.

With the Commission's new enforcement powers, these problems will be compounded. . . .

As part of the change in the administrative organization, the amendments provide for making the General Counsel of the Commission a Presidential appointee, subject to Senate confirmation. Five regional legal offices were to be established immediately.

During the deliberations of the Conference Committee, there was a significant deletion of a provision included in the House bill. The provision would have made the EEOC the sole federal authority to police employment discrimination of the types forbidden by the Act. The deletion has been construed as permitting an aggrieved individual to seek relief in several forums: the EEOC, OFCC [Office of Federal Contract Compliance], NLRB [National Labor Relations Board], state or local agencies, and arbitration, although there have been court decisions to the contrary. . . .

Another change affecting administration . . . establishes an Equal Employment Opportunity Coordinating Council. Members of the Council will be the Secretary of Labor, the Chairman of the EEOC, the Attorney General, the Chairman of the U.S. Civil Service Commission, and the Chairman of the U.S. Civil Rights Commission or their respective designees. The objective is to coordinate the activities of all branches of the government that have responsibility for equal employment opportunity.

Source: Bureau of National Affairs, *The Equal Employment Opportunity Act of 1972, a BNA Operations Manual* (Washington, DC: Bureau of National Affairs, 1973): 1–4.

The complexities of the federal government's ever-evolving equal opportunities apparatus were matched by contradictions in presidential behavior and rhetoric. Richard Nixon—who had rescued and championed the Philadelphia Plan, promoted the judicial enforcement remedies in the 1972 Equal Employment Opportunity Act, and insisted on keeping a strong executive hand on Title VII implementation—campaigned for reelection by attacking civil rights and denouncing the very kind of race-conscious tactics employed by his own Labor Department. Victorious in the election, Nixon proceeded to direct unprecedented funding to the agencies responsible for enforcing civil rights and at the same time augmented the budget for the Office of Minority Business Enterprise (Doc. 157).

{r/g}DOCUMENT 182: Acceptance Speech of Richard Nixon, August 23, 1972

In the summer of 1972 both major political parties held their national conventions. The Democrats established guidelines for the gender and racial makeup of the delegations to their convention, to ensure diversity. In his acceptance speech at the Republican National Convention, Richard Nixon alluded to those guidelines derisively and—ignoring his own administration's role in establishing preferential hiring policies— denounced them as "quotas."

* * *

Tonight, I again proudly accept your nomination for President of the United States. . . .

[Y]ou have demonstrated to the Nation that we can have an open convention without dividing Americans into quotas.

Let us commit ourselves to rule out every vestige of discrimination in this country of ours. But . . . the way to end discrimination against some is not to begin discrimination against others.

Source: Public Papers of the Presidents (1972): 788.

{r/g}DOCUMENT 183: *Business Week*, March 24, 1973

Once reelected, Nixon provided generously in the national budget for agencies charged with enforcing antidiscrimination laws in business and employment.

* * *

Civil rights forces and their allies have greeted President Nixon's deep budget cuts in social action programs with loud cries of anguish. But almost unnoticed, the current budget also provides substantial increases in some areas vital to the interests of those same forces. . . .

[T]here will be more government lawyers to file cases against companies for race and sex discrimination in employment, more investigators to check on affirmative action hiring and promotion plans . . . and more help for minority entrepreneurs. . . .

With more money available, the EEOC is expected to expand its legal staff to more than 600.

Source: "The Budget Ax Spares Some Minority Programs," *Business Week* (March 24, 1973): 74.

{g}DOCUMENT 184: Overview of 1970 House Committee Hearings on Education and Women

In the struggle for racial justice, education had long been recognized as a major wellspring of discrimination and therefore a critical target for equal opportunity initiatives. Organizations dedicated to eliminating sex and gender discrimination also targeted education with increasing intensity in the 1970s. One result, little remarked at the time but highly significant in the long run, was congressional passage of the Educational Amendments Act of 1972. Considerable ammunition with which to defend this act had been stockpiled in hearings held by Representative Edith Green in the summer of 1970, in support of an earlier bill directed against sex discrimination that had not passed. Historians Judith Hole and Ellen Levine described the seven days of testimony before Green's House Special Subcommittee on Education.

* * *

The 1250 pages of testimony that resulted . . . constitute the most extensive compilation of feminist arguments against the educational system ever gathered in one place. . . . The testimony touched on every aspect of the educational process: picture books for nursery school children; reading books for elementary school children; the effect of sex-segregated classes on high school boys and girls; the status of female students in undergraduate and graduate schools; the status of female teachers in elementary, secondary, undergraduate and graduate schools; the status of females in corresponding administrative ranks; the effect of career counseling on women; the sociology of education; the psychology of education; minority women and education; and the need for strong federal legislation banning sex discrimination from the educational process.

Source: Judith Hole and Ellen Levine, *Rebirth of Feminism* (New York: Quadrangle Books, 1971/1973): 316–317.

The same feminist energy evident in Representative Green's hearings was felt in the simultaneous spread of women's consciousness-raising groups, campaigns for nonsexist textbook reform, a growing women's studies movement, and an explosion of grievances and lawsuits against sex discrimination in manifold areas of employment and in athletics. The next three documents are samples of feminist protest as it was cresting in the 1970s.

{g}DOCUMENT 185: "What Every Young Girl Should Ask," Feminist Questionnaire for High School Women, 1970s

The strategy of "consciousness-raising" became a staple of the women's movement in the 1970s. Throughout the country women gathered in small groups to confront questions that until that time had been treated as taboos. All ages were touched by consciousness-raising. Document 185 presents some of the questions that adult women urged the rising generation to consider.

* * *

• Can you play basketball, soccer, football?
• Did you ever pretend to be dumb?
• Are your brothers asked to help clean house?

* * *

• How are women portrayed in the books you read?

* * *

• In extracurricular coed organizations, do girls make decisions? Or do they take minutes?
• Are girls with boyfriends winners? What do they win?
• Do you ask boys out? If not, why not?
• Do you believe boys get sexually aroused fast, at a younger age, and more often than girls? Who told you *that*? . . .

Source: High School Women's Liberation Coalition Questionnaire, New York City, reprinted in Judith Hole and Ellen Levine, *Rebirth of Feminism* (New York: Quadrangle Books, 1971/1973): 330.

{g}DOCUMENT 186: Donna A. Lopiano, "Growing Up with Gender Discrimination in Sport" in the 1970s

Donna A. Lopiano exemplifies the untold numbers of highly talented women who grew up at midcentury surrounded by reminders that their

talents were not valued and—in many instances—that they were prohibited from exercising them, except within closely guarded limits. Passionately devoted to sports, Lopiano found that "gender discrimination
. . . lurked around every corner of my life." Not only was this true in
childhood, she recalled, but "every job I held in educational sports [in
the early 1970s] . . . paid me less than my male counterparts." When
the women's movement began to launch its frontal attacks on sexism,
Lopiano joined in, at one point risking her job to testify before a congressional committee. As director of women's athletics at the University
of Texas for seventeen years and, in the 1990s, executive director of
the Women's Sports Foundation, Lopiano both helped to shape, and
has benefited from, the changes that began in the 1970s in laws, policies, and attitudes affecting women.

                                    * * *

From the age of five, I dreamed of the day that I would pitch for the
New York Yankees. And I didn't just dream. I practiced and prepared
myself for that career. Every day after school I would throw five hundred
pitches against the side of my parents' garage. By the time I was ten, I
had developed a rising fast ball, an impressive curve that would drop
off the table and was hard at work on a Bob Turley drop. There was no
doubt that I was more than prepared to take the first step in the rites of
passage to becoming a major league ballplayer—Little League.

I can remember the Saturday morning when I and a bunch of the
"guys" on my street went to tryouts. We were nervous, but I knew that
I was good. I remember my intensity. . . .

Imagine my excitement when we were assigned to a team and lined
up for uniforms! My team colors were navy blue and white—Yankee
colors! And we were getting real hats, wool baseball caps for which you
had to know your head size, not those caps with plastic backs. . . . I was
literally trembling with excitement. The moment ranked high as one of
the best feelings of the my life.

I was standing there, punching my hand into my glove, grinning,
when a very tall father came to stand beside me. He held a rulebook
that was open to page 14. On the right-hand side of the page were four
words that would change my life forever. "No girls are allowed." For
the first time in my life, I was told that I couldn't play with my friends.
I was devastated. More disappointed than angry. I cried for three
months. . . .

I didn't really get angry about this terrible occurrence until I was much
older. . . .

My anger is not the volatile kind. It's the long-lasting kind that will
stew under the surface for a long time. And it's not really about not

being able to play for the New York Yankees. It is all about someone telling me that I could not pursue my dream, my most passionate belief about how good I could be and what I wanted to do in life. I am angered about the prospect of any child being told that he or she could not chase a dream—could not even try. I do what I do today because I do not want any little girl to feel the way I felt or to go through life wondering if she could have realized her dream.

Source: Donna A. Lopiano, "Growing Up with Gender Discrimination in Sport," in *The Ethnic Moment, the Search for Equality in the American Experience*, edited by Philip L. Fetzer (New York: M. E. Sharpe, 1997): 98, 99.

{r/g}DOCUMENT 187: Shirley Chisholm, Discrimination from the Perspective of an African American Woman, 1970

Shirley Chisholm became the first African American woman to win election to the House of Representatives and the first African American to represent Brooklyn, New York, in Congress, when she handily bested her opponent, James Farmer, former leader of the Congress of Racial Equality (Doc. 103), in a historic election in 1968. She served in the House for the next fourteen years and was actively involved with NOW (Doc. 140) and an array of women's issues. When Chisholm sought the Democratic nomination for president of the United States in 1972, her candidacy evoked a lukewarm reception from both men and women, a reaction that she attributed to entrenched sexist prejudices. She wrote in her autobiography (*Unbought and Unbossed* [New York: Avon Books, 1970], 12): "Of my two 'handicaps,' being female put many more obstacles in my path than being black." In testimony she delivered on the Equal Rights Amendment two years before her run for the presidential nomination, Chisholm expanded on sexism in American political life.

* * *

[C]olored minority group Americans are not the only second class citizens in this country. The largest single group of second class citizens is the majority of Americans, American women. . . .

More than half of the population of the United States is female, but women occupy only 2 percent of the managerial positions. They have not even reached the level of tokenism yet. No women sit on the AFL–CIO [American Federation of Labor and Congress of Industrial Organizations] Council or the Supreme Court. There have been only two women who have held Cabinet rank and at present there are none. Only two women now hold ambassadorial rank in the diplomatic corps. In Congress we are down to a Senator and 10 Representatives.

Source: "Hearings of the Senate Subcommittee on the Equal Rights Amendment." Reprinted in Catharine Stimpson, *Women and the "Equal Rights" Amendment. Senate Subcommittee Hearings, 91st Congress* (New York: R. R. Bowker, 1972): 24.

While consciousness-raising and challenges to conventional stereotypes by growing numbers of individual women helped push the women's movement forward, movement leaders also campaigned for legislative reforms. Among the experts in marshaling data and arguments for new laws were psychologist Bernice Sandler and lawyer Pauli Murray.

{g}DOCUMENT 188: Bernice Sandler and Legal Reform on Behalf of Women, 1970

As the leading force in class-action suits brought in 1970 by the Women's Equity Action League (WEAL) against over 300 colleges and universities, Sandler was once described as "the scourge of the universities."

* * *

Half of the brightest people in our country . . . are women. Yet these gifted women will find if very difficult to obtain the same kind of quality education that is so readily available to their brothers. These women will encounter discrimination after discrimination—not once, not twice but time after time in the very academic institutions which claim to preach the tenets of democracy and fair play. The women will face discrimination in admission where they will encounter both official and unofficial quotas; they will face discrimination when they apply for scholarships and financial assistance. When they graduate, their own university will discriminate against them in helping them find jobs. They will be discriminated against in hiring for the faculty. . . .

Even when women are hired they generally remain at the bottom of the academic hierarchy. The higher the rank, the lower the percentage of women. . . .

Women are denied admission to graduate and professional training programs because of the rather odd and illogical reasoning on the part of university decisionmakers: if a woman is not married, she'll get married. If she is married, she'll probably have children. If she has children, she can't possibly be committed to a profession. If she has older children, she's too old to begin training. . . . [I]t is true that she may very well marry. Many of her fellow male students will do likewise. She may very well have children. Men also become parents, but we do not as a society punish them by limiting their professional development and professional opportunities.

Essentially our universities punish women for being women. They punish women for not only having children but even for having the potential to bear children. . . .

[B]elieve it or not, it is completely within the law to discriminate against women in universities and colleges. [Title VII exempts education institutions.] . . . Title VI of the same Civil Rights Act . . . only applies to discrimination based on race, religion or national origin. . . . The Equal Pay Act of 1963 specifically excludes "executive, administrative, or professional employees." Even the U.S. Commission on Civil Rights has no jurisdiction whatsoever concerning sex discrimination. . . .

Executive Order 11246 as amended . . . is at best an administrative remedy for [sex] discrimination in academia. . . .

[L]et us not forget that the Executive Order does not have the status of law. . . . There are simply no laws that forbid universities and colleges from continuing their vicious patterns of sex discrimination and their violation of the human rights of women.

Source: "Hearings of the Senate Subcommittee on the Equal Rights Amendment." Reprinted in Catharine Stimpson, *Women and the "Equal Rights" Amendment. Senate Subcommittee Hearings, 91st Congress* (New York: R. R. Bowker, 1972): 247–248, 250, 253.

{r/g}DOCUMENT 189: Pauli Murray and Legal Reform on Behalf of Women, 1971

Murray, a lifelong pathbreaker who had challenged the color line at the University of North Carolina in 1938, been arrested for sit-ins at segregated restaurants in Washington, D.C., in the 1940s, and was a founding member of NOW, held a law degree from Yale University. An article written by her for the Valparaiso University *Law Review* in 1971 was read into the *Congressional Record* by Indiana senator Birch Bayh on the eve of debate over new legislation that would come to be the Educational Amendments of 1972 (Doc. 191).

* * *

Sexual inequality is the oldest and most intransigent form of discrimination in human culture. . . . As in the case of racial bias the individual's status is defined at birth, and legal and social disabilities are imposed by virtue of visible, permanent physical characteristics which identify one's sex. . . . At the same time . . . unlike a racial or ethnic minority, women are distributed evenly with men throughout the entire population and share the class characteristics of the men with whom they are closely associated as wives, mothers or daughters. This duality of status partly obscures the pervasiveness of discriminatory treatment. . . . Notwithstanding a total impact which is far more extensive than other forms of bias, there is a strong tendency to minimize sex discrimination, to avoid the moral implications of so vast a social injustice and to afford it greater immunity from public condemnation. . . .

Sex bias takes a greater economic toll than racial bias [as wage comparisons and comparisons of male and female headed households demonstrate]. . . .

The unemployment rate is higher among women than men, among girls than boys. . . .

Essential justice requires the Federal government to give much greater attention to the elimination of sex discrimination and to the needs of women in poverty.

Source: Congressional Record 118 (February 25, 1972): 5654.

{r/g}DOCUMENT 190: Statistics on Women's Earnings Presented by Pauli Murray, 1971

Dr. Murray supported her assertions with numerous statistics, including the following tables.

* * *

A. Earnings of Full-Time Year-Round Workers by Sex, 1969

Earnings	Women	Men
Total	100.0	100.0
Less than $3,000	14.4	5.7
$3,000–$4,999	36.2	9.8
$5,000–$6,999	29.7	18.2
$7,000–$9,999	14.9	31.2
$10,000–$14,999	4.2	23.9
$15,000 and over	.7	11.1

Source: U.S. Department of Commerce, Bureau of the Census Current Population Reports, P-60, No. 75, Women's Bureau Report, reprinted in *Congressional Record* 118 (February 25, 1972): 5662.

B. Median Wage or Salary Income of Full-Time, Year-Round Workers, by Sex and Selected Major Occupation Group, 1969

Major Occupation Group	Women	Men	Women as percent of men's
Professional and technical workers	$7,309	$11,266	64.9
Nonfarm managers, officials, and proprietors	6,091	11,467	53.1
Clerical workers	5,187	7,966	65.1
Salesworkers	3,704	9,135	40.5
Operatives	4,317	7,307	59.1
Service workers (except private household)	3,755	6,373	58.9

Source: U.S. Department of Commerce, Bureau of the Census Current Population Reports, P-60, No. 75. Women's Bureau Report, reprinted in *Congressional Record* 118 (February 25, 1972): 5662.

{g}DOCUMENT 191: Educational Amendments Act of 1972

In June 1972 Congress passed Public Law 92–318. Also titled the Educational Amendments Act of 1972, the new law took effect on July 1. Title IX of the law—destined to become a magnet for controversy—addressed sex discrimination.

* * *

Title IX—PROHIBITION OF SEX DISCRIMINATION

Sec. 901. (a) No person in the United States shall, on the basis of sex, be excluded from participation in, be denied the benefits of, or be subjected to discrimination under any education program or activity receiving Federal financial assistance. . . .

Source: *Laws of 92nd Congress, 2nd Sess.* (June 23, 1972): 444.

While regulations for the implementation of Title IX would be three years in the making (Doc. 220), the work of Congress in 1972 represented, in the words of historian Hugh Davis Graham, "a consolidation" of a process begun when John F. Kennedy issued Executive Order 10925 in 1961 (Doc. 102).

{d}DOCUMENT 192: Speech of Senator Hubert Humprey on Behalf of Senate Bill 3094, January 1972

Legislative and judicial consolidation of policies directly affecting the disabled was, in 1972, still a matter for the future. However, in Congress a little-noticed initiative by Senator Hubert Humphrey (Minnesota) and Representative Charles Vanik (Ohio) proved to be a portent of actions that, would, over time, attract a great deal of attention. In January 1972 Humphrey and Vanik introduced in their respective houses of Congress amendments to the Civil Rights Act of 1964 that would have included discrimination because of "physical or mental handicap" in the list of prohibited categories of discrimination.

* * *

I am insisting that the civil rights of 40 million Americans now be affirmed and effectively guaranteed by Congress—our several million disabled war veterans, the 22 million people with a severe physically disabling condition, the one in every ten Americans who has a mental condition requiring psychiatric treatment, the six million persons who are mentally retarded, the hundreds of thousands crippled by accidents and destructive forces of poverty, and the 100,000 babies born with defects each year.

These people have the right to live, to work to the best of their ability—to know the dignity to which every human being is entitled. . . .

These are people who can and must be helped to help themselves. That this is their constitutional right is clearly affirmed in a number of recent decisions in various judicial jurisdictions.

Source: Congressional Record 118 (January 1972): 526.

{d}DOCUMENT 193: Historian Richard Scotch on the 1972 Humphrey–Vanik Effort

Congress held no hearings and took no vote on the Humphrey and Vanik bills. Historian Richard Scotch attempted to track the bills' passage into oblivion after each was referred to the judiciary committees of the House and Senate.

* * *

Although there is no record of what happened when the bills were referred to the House and Senate Judiciary Committees, it may be that they were killed by committee liberals. The bills do not appear to have been opposed by conservatives . . . nor by those responding to protests from the recipients of federal funds who would have been required to comply with the proposed amendments. Rather, the opposition apparently came from those who were committed to protecting the groups already covered by Title VI of the Civil Rights Act, notably blacks. . . .

Source: Scotch 1984, 44.

{d}DOCUMENT 194: *Pennsylvania Association for Retarded Children* [PARC] *v. Commonwealth of Pennsylvania*, 1972

Whatever undermined the efforts of Humphrey and Vanik to amend the 1964 Civil Rights Act, other developments were turning out more favorably for the disabled. In particular, two 1972 court cases were considered to be keys to further judicial and legislative recognition of the rights of the disabled. Both were concerned with education for mentally retarded children. The first case (*Pennsylvania Association for Retarded Children v. Commonwealth of Pennsylvania*) was a class-action suit filed in the names of fourteen retarded students and others who shared their handicap. The suit charged the state of Pennsylvania with "arbitrarily and capriciously" denying the students' rights to an education. The case was brought to settlement by a consent decree.

* * *

[I]t is the Commonwealth's obligation to place each mentally retarded child in a free, public program of education and training appropriate to the child's capacity.

Source: 343 F. Supp. 279 at 285 (1972).

{d}DOCUMENT 195: Robert L. Burgdorf on *PARC v. Commonwealth*, 1972

Analyst Robert L. Burgdorf assessed the impact of *PARC v. Commonwealth*.

* * *

As one of the first statewide, federal, class action lawsuits brought on behalf of handicapped persons, it is often considered the cradle of the whole legal rights movement for handicapped people.

Source: Robert L. Burgdorf Jr., *The Legal Rights of Handicapped Persons* (Baltimore: Brookes, 1980): 90.

{d}DOCUMENT 196: *Mills v. Board of Education of the District of Columbia*, 1972

The other case (*Mills v. Board of Education of the District of Columbia*), which concluded shortly after *PARC v. Commonwealth of Pennsylvania*, was also brought on behalf of retarded children and decided in their favor. However, the *Mills* decision encompassed a wider range of disability than was designated in the *Pennsylvania* case.

* * *

[T]he District of Columbia shall provide each child of school age a free and suitable publicly-supported education regardless of the degree of the child's mental, physical, or emotional disability or impairment. Furthermore, defendants shall not exclude any child resident in the District of Columbia from such publicly-supported education on the basis of a claim of insufficient resources.

Source: 348 F. Supp. 866 at 878 (1972).

{d}DOCUMENT 197: Summary of Rehabilitation Act of 1972

As advocates for retarded children united to take common action, so did persons from throughout the ranks of the disabled come together and consolidate their forces. One example of this trend was the "independent living movement." In communities throughout the country— Urbana, Illinois; Columbus, Ohio; Houston, Texas; and, most famously (because of Ed Roberts [Doc. 154]), Berkeley, California—disabled groups established centers that provided information, education, and services to enable their constituents to exercise the maximum degree of control over their own lives. The creation of these independent living programs—which ranged from housing and attendant referrals, to wheelchair repairs, to courses on life skills—was both politicizing and unifying. They established "independent living as the institutional cornerstone of a new generation of disability policy" (Berkowitz 1987, 202).

One of the first manifestations of the "new generation of disability policy" was the Rehabilitation Act of 1972. Sponsored and guided to passage by Senators Jennings Randolph and Alan Cranston, the bill created a new division for Rehabilitation Services within the Department of Health, Education and Welfare (HEW), established the severely disabled as the priority group for such services (a shift of focus from the moderately handicapped), and initiated an independent living services program. This program emphasized quality of life for the severely disabled and did not require that employment result from the services. Following is a summary of the 1972 Rehabilitation Act, taken from *The Congressional Quarterly Almanac.*

* * *

[A]s cleared [the act] would have . . .
• Permitted pursuit of non-vocational goals and provision of goods and services to enable a handicapped individual to live more independently. . . .

Title VII

• Established a new federal interagency committee on handicapped employees to devise an affirmative action plan for the hiring of handicapped persons by the federal government, a national commission on transportation and housing for the handicapped and an architectural and transportation barriers compliance board.

Source: Congressional Quarterly Almanac 28 (1972): 953.

{d}DOCUMENT 198: Richard Nixon's Veto of the 1972 Rehabilitation Act

Richard Nixon included the new law among nine bills that he vetoed in October 1972. He objected especially to the new focus on severe disability and the high cost of service personnel and equipment involved in the independent living program.

* * *

[I]n this memorandum are nine measures which I cannot sign without breaking my promise to the American people that I will do all in my power to avoid the necessity of a tax increase next year. . . .

Rehabilitation Act of 1972 . . .
This measure would seriously jeopardize the goals of the vocational rehabilitation program and is another example of Congressional fiscal irresponsibility. Its provisions would divert this program from its basic vocational objectives into activities that have no vocational element whatsoever or are essentially medical in character. . . .

Source: Public Papers of the Presidents (1972): 1042, 1043.

{d}DOCUMENT 199: Eunice Fiorito Recalls Protest by the Disabled of Nixon's Veto of the 1972 Rehabilitation Act

The disabled community was profoundly angered by Nixon's veto. The President's Committee on Employment of the Handicapped held its annual banquet in Washington shortly after the veto was announced. A segment of the guests went straight from the banquet to a demonstration against the veto staged at the Lincoln Monument. Among the demonstrators was blind activist and organizer Eunice Fiorito.

* * *

We all came out of the President's Committee the night of the big banquet, all of the kids had this march and demonstration and then had this all-night vigil, over at the Lincoln Monument. I went to the banquet in my very formal outfit and then [demonstrated] in the rain for about six hours.

Source: Quoted in Scotch 1984, 56–57.

While Congress failed to override the veto in 1972, supporters of the law were galvanized by defeat to fight another day.

Between 1964 and 1972 traditional initiatives, aimed at establishing nondiscrimination at the present moment and into the future, were superseded more and more by complicated interventions that included the weight of past discrimination in calculating what would constitute fairness and justice for all. By fits and starts—and with minimal coordination—presidents, legislators, agencies, and courts had cobbled together the apparatus by which "affirmative action" would operate in the years ahead. Awkward and disjointed, the mechanism had only begun to touch the lives of disabled citizens, but it was promoting significant changes in the racial and gender makeup of industrial crews, student bodies, faculties and management teams throughout the country. At the same time, it provoked sharp antagonisms and added new, passionately argued cases to federal court dockets.

Part IV

1973–1980: A Time of Testing: Affirmative Action Applied, Challenged, Upheld, and Challenged Again

THE FINAL NIXON YEARS

In the early days of the civil rights movement Martin Luther King Jr. had declared that "we must transform democracy from thin paper to thick action." In subsequent years, courts, Congress, federal agencies, and myriad groups in both the public and private sectors produced a new thickness of paper—decisions, laws, regulations, plans—that, in the decade of the 1970s provoked considerable "thick action" as advocates of affirmative action sought to claim new ground and opponents challenged their claims.

{d}DOCUMENT 200: The Vocational Rehabilitation Act of 1973

The new ground promised to the disabled in the vetoed Rehabilitation Act of 1972 became again contested ground when Congress introduced essentially the same bill, renamed the Rehabilitation Act of 1973. Congress passed it, the president again vetoed it, a vote to override the veto fell short in the Senate by four votes, and the bill was reintroduced for a third time. The final version was less expensive and contained fewer programs than its predecessors. It also placed more limits on the new Rehabilitative Services Administration than had been the case in the earlier versions. With these changes Nixon found it possible to affix his signature, and the bill became law on September 26, 1973. For the first time (in Title V of the bill) the concept of "affirmative action" was formally applied to the disabled (Section 503), and—of particular consequence—their civil rights were formally guaranteed (Section 504).

* * *

Section 7. DEFINITIONS

(6) The term "handicapped individual" means any individual who (A) has a physical or mental disability which for such individual constitutes or results in a substantial handicap to employment and (B) can reasonably be expected to benefit in terms of employability from vocational rehabilitation services. . . .

TITLE V—MISCELLANEOUS

Employment of Handicapped Individuals

Section 501. (a) There is established . . . an Interagency Committee on Handicapped Employees. . . . It shall be the purpose and function of the Committee . . . to review . . . the adequacy of hiring, placement, and advancement practices with respect to handicapped individuals by each department, agency, and instrumentality in the executive branch of Government. . . .

Architectural and Transportation Barriers Compliance Board

Section 502 (a) There is established . . . the Architectural and Transportation Barriers Compliance Board. . . .

(b) It shall be the function of the board to: (1) insure compliance with the standards prescribed by the General Services Administration, the Department of Defense, and the Department of Housing and Urban Development pursuant to the Architectural Barriers Act of 1968 [Doc. 153]. . . .

Employment under Federal Contracts

Section 503. (a) Any contract in excess of $2,500 entered into by any Federal department or agency . . . shall contain a provision requiring that, in employing persons to carry out such contract the party contracting with the United States shall take affirmative action to employ and advance in employment qualified handicapped individuals. . . .

NonDiscrimination under Federal Grants

Section 504. No otherwise qualified handicapped individual in the United States . . . shall, solely by reason of his handicap, be excluded from the participation in, be denied the benefits of, or be subjected to discrimination under any program or activity receiving Federal financial assistance.

Source: U.S. Statutes at Large 87 (September 26, 1973): 357, 361, 390, 391, 392, 393, 394.

{d}DOCUMENT 201: Testimony of John Nagle before the Senate Subcommittee on the Handicapped, January 10, 1973

Section 504 had the potential to become something of an Aladdin's lamp for the disabled, raising thrilling possibilities for better lives and unprecedented opportunities to "live in the world," as Jacobus tenBroek had so often quoted. However, fiscal conservatives and various other critics soon suggested that 504 was a Pandora's box from which flew endless public policy nightmares. To what degree the authors and supporters of the 1973 law understood the implications of 504 is a matter of some debate. What is not disputed is its heavy impact on national public life.

With a few notable exceptions, most sponsors, supporters, and opponents of the Rehabilitation Act ignored Section 504 during congressional hearings and debates on the bill. One of the exceptions was John Nagle, director of the National Federation of the Blind, in whose commentary one might detect echoes of Jacobus tenBroek.

* * *

This civil rights for the handicapped provision . . . brings the disabled within the law when they have been so long outside of the law. It establishes that because a man is blind or deaf or without legs, he is not less a citizen, that his rights of citizenship are not revoked or diminished because he is disabled. But most important of all, the civil rights for the handicapped provision . . . creates a remedy when a disabled man is denied his rightful citizenship rights because of his disability. It gives him a legal basis for recourse to the courts that he may seek to remove needless barriers, unnecessary obstacles and unjustified barricades that impede or prevent him from functioning fully and in full equality with all others.

Source: Hearings before the Subcommittee on the Handicapped of the Committee on Labor and Public Welfare, U.S. Senate (January 10, 1973): 282–283.

{r/g}DOCUMENT 202: Source of the Title *"A Unique Competence"*: *A Study of Equal Employment Opportunity in the Bell System*, 1971

The long shadow of Title VII, especially Senator Howard Smith's "little amendment" (Doc. 122), reached one of the nation's largest corporations, American Telephone and Telegraph (AT&T), in the early 1970s. Sex discrimination proved to be the pivotal issue in the landmark settlement announced on January 18, 1973, between federal authorities and AT&T. When the EEOC initiated legal action against the corporation in December 1970, more than 2,000 charges filed by AT&T employees were pending. Public hearings conducted under the auspices of the Federal Communications Commission (FCC) and out-of-public negotiations between government agents and company management were conducted simultaneously during 1971 and 1972. In September 1972 the Department of Labor entered the negotiations, cementing a federal united front that carried the day. The resulting consent decree was ratified on January 18, 1973, in U.S. District Court by Judge Leon Higginbotham, who called it "the largest and most impressive civil rights settlement in this nation."

EEOC had spelled out the case against AT&T in an eleven-chapter report, augmented by 500 pages of statistical charts and tables. In February 1972 Congresswoman Shirley Chisholm had the entire report read into the *Congressional Record*.

The title of the report, according to EEOC economist Phyllis Wallace, "was culled from a statement by AT&T vice president Walter Straley" (Wallace 1976, 248).

* * *

AT&T Vice President Walter Straley . . . stated . . . in 1968:

"We think our experience as an employer hiring some 200,000 persons each year, provides us with a unique competence to play a leading role in the improvement of employment opportunity."

Therefore, as will be emphasized throughout this report, any substantial underrepresentation of women or minorities in certain job categories manifestly cannot be attributed to [AT&T management's] lack of skill. Absent discrimination, one would expect a nearly random distribution of women and minorities in all jobs.

Source: Congressional Record 118, Pt. 4 (February 17, 1972): 4509.

{g}DOCUMENT 203: The Theme of Sex Discrimination in *"A Unique Competence,"* 1971

Sex discrimination constituted a major theme of the report.

* * *

While the majority of the employees in the Bell System are female, almost all jobs in the company are sex segregated.

The Bell System originated and encourages the common conception of certain jobs as male or female.

The sex segregation is uniform from company to company.

The Operator, Service Representative, and clerical classifications are almost exclusively female and contain 80% of all females in the System.

Nearly all craft jobs and middle and upper level management jobs are held by males.

"Male" jobs invariably pay more, are more rewarding, and provide greater promotional opportunities than "female" jobs. . . .

The Bell monolith is, without doubt, the largest oppressor of women workers in the United States.

Source: Congressional Record 118, Pt. 4 (February 15, 1972): 4512, 4522.

{r}DOCUMENT 204: The Theme of Racial Discrimination in "A Unique Competence," 1971

A second and related theme was racial discrimination.

* * *

Black employment in the Bell System increased steadily from the virtual exclusion of the 1930s and 1940s to an all-time high at the end of the 1960s. . . .

Most of the increase . . . came in a low-paying, dead-end, and otherwise highly undesirable job, that of Operator. . . .

[B]lack females continue to pour *into* and *out of* the job of Operator. . . .

The Operator job is, quite pointedly, a *horrendous* job. . . . [R]ather than restructure the job, improve the wages, and provide important new avenues for promotion and transfer . . . AT&T has decided to keep the wages depressed and simply hire more and more black females.

Source: Congressional Record 118, Pt. 4 (February 17, 1972): 4525, 4529.

{r}DOCUMENT 205: The Status of Hispanic Employees at AT&T according to "A Unique Competence," 1971

The report identified Hispanic employees as "invisible."

* * *

Spanish-surnamed Americans have been described as "the invisible minority," and in the Bell System this is quite literally true. . . .

Every statistical measure points to the exclusion of Spanish-surnamed Americans from the System's work-force, particularly at the higher levels. The same pernicious system which has blocked the progress of blacks also serves as an obstacle to Spanish-surnamed Americans.

Source: Congressional Record 118, Pt. 4 (February 17, 1972): 4530.

{r/g}DOCUMENT 206: Authors of *"A Unique Competence"* on AT&T Management, 1971

The authors of *"A Unique Competence"* laid bare the assumptions guiding the management of AT&T.

* * *

[T]he operating companies force all applicants into one of two stereo-typed molds. For instance . . . Northwestern Bell mapped the entire career of its female and male applicants as follows:

"Men will probably be interested in outside construction, in skilled inside and outside Plant occupations, truck driving, sales and so forth. Most of them will think in terms of starting long range career employment. Women will probably be interested principally in secretarial, stenographic, receptionist, clerical, switchboard operation or in-plant selling types of work. Starting long range careers will probably be secondary. . . ."

A 1971 Southwestern Bell "School Talk" defines the interests of boys and girls as follows:

"Most of our entrance jobs that girls are normally interested in have a starting salary of $67.50 per week. The ones that boys are normally interested in start at $78.50 per week." . . . In October 1969, an extremely important "Report on Force Loss and Urban Labor Market" was presented by AT&T Vice President Walter Straley to the assembled Presidents of all Bell companies. According to the report, "What a telephone company needs to know about its labor market is who is available for work paying as little as $4000 to $5000 a year." According to Straley's remarks, two out of three persons available at that wage were black. . . . The report continues:

"Population and labor force projections are not at all encouraging. The kind of people we need are going to be in very short supply. . . . Most of our new hires go into entry level jobs which means we must have access to an ample supply of people who will work at comparatively low rates of pay. That means city people more so than suburbanites. That means lots of black people. . . .

"It is therefore perfectly plain that we need nonwhite employees, not because we are good citizens. Or because it is the law as well as a national goal to give them employment. We need them because we have so many jobs to fill and they will take them."

Source: Congressional Record 118, Pt. 4 (February 17, 1972): 4517, 4524.

As the report was compiled, various racial, ethnic, and women's groups testified in specially arranged hearings at sites accessible to the witnesses. Chicanos and Asian Americans were heard in Los Angeles and San Francisco. In New York City, representatives of African American, Spanish American, and women's organizations testified. A third set of hearings took place in Washington, D.C., where similar groups, including the National Organization for Women, presented their testimony (Wallace 1976, 249–250).

{r/g}DOCUMENT 207: Testimony of AT&T Vice President, John W. Kingsbury

In August 1972 the FCC hearings turned to testimony on behalf of AT&T. The company's lead witness was John W. Kingsbury, assistant vice president for Human Resource Development.

* * *

[T]he primary reason that the Bell System exists is to provide communications service to the American public, not merely to provide employment to all comers, regardless of ability. . . .

[U]nless we maintain relevant hiring standards our training costs would soar astronomically and these costs would necessarily be passed on to our customers. . . .

In addition, in some of our job categories there are very real obstacles that stand in the way of providing immediate employment to anybody who has not gained necessary experience in entry-level jobs. . . . [U]ntil significant numbers of interested women can be brought into these lower level craft jobs it is not realistic to talk in terms of filling the higher level craft jobs with significant numbers of women immediately.

A significant number of our salaried and management jobs require engineering background. . . . [U]ntil our engineering schools are graduating significantly more minorities and women the relevant labor market for engineers will continue to be almost exclusively white and male.

Source: Testimony of John W. Kingsbury, FCC Docket No. 19143 (August 1, 1972): 3–5, 13, as reprinted in Wallace 1976, 261–262.

{r/g}DOCUMENT 208: The AT&T Affirmative Action Plan, 1973

On January 18, 1973, Judge Higgenbotham "ordered, adjudged and decreed" a settlement between the EEOC and U.S. secretary of labor, on the one hand, and AT&T and twenty-four of its subsidiary companies, on the other. By accepting the settlement, the corporation avoided any admission of guilt. At the same time it bound itself to compliance with the goals and timetables of a far-reaching affirmative action plan, including promotions, transfers, wage adjustments, and back pay totaling $30.9 million, affecting about 40,000 minority and female employees. The thrust of the settlement is evident in the objective stated at the outset of the affirmative action plan.

* * *

The equal employment objective for the Bell System is to achieve within a reasonable period of time . . . full utilization of minorities and women at all levels of management and non-management and by job classification at a pace beyond that which would occur normally; to prohibit discrimination in employment, because of race, color, religion, national origin, sex or age; and to have a work environment free of discrimination.

Source: "A Model Affirmative Action Program for the Bell System," quoted in Wallace 1976, 269.

{g}DOCUMENT 209: *Frontiero v. Richardson*, 1973

The Supreme Court continued to wrestle with discrimination in its multiple forms. On the matter of sex discrimination the justices were pushed by the Women's Rights Project, established by the American Civil Liberties Union after the *Reed v. Reed* decision of 1971 (Doc. 169). The director of the project was Ruth Bader Ginsburg, successful lawyer for the plaintiff in *Reed* and future associate justice of the Supreme Court. In 1973 she argued the case of Sharron A. Frontiero, an officer in the air force. Frontiero brought suit against a policy that denied her husband the dependents' benefits that men in the armed services received for their wives. A majority of the justices found for

Frontiero, but only three of them accepted Ginsburg's contention that the courts should subject all sex discrimination cases to the same strict scrutiny as cases in which racial discrimination was the issue. They maintained that taking such a stance on sex discrimination would pre-empt the legislative process, then under way, for passing the ERA.

* * *

Mr. Justice William J. Brennan, Jr.:

There can be no doubt that our Nation has had a long and unfortunate history of sex discrimination. Traditionally, such discrimination was rationalized by an attitude of "romantic paternalism" which, in practical effect, put women, not on a pedestal, but in a cage. . . .

Congress itself has concluded that classifications based upon sex are inherently invidious. . . .

With these considerations in mind, we can only conclude that classifications based upon sex . . . must . . . be subjected to strict judicial scrutiny. . . .

The sole basis of the classification established in the challenged statutes is the sex of the individuals involved. Thus . . . a female member of the uniformed services seeking to obtain housing and medical benefits for her spouse must prove his dependency in fact, whereas no such burden is imposed upon male members. . . .

Mr. Justice Lewis F. Powell, Jr., with whom the Chief Justice and Mr. Justice Harry A. Blackmun join, concurring in the Opinion:

I agree that the challenged statutes constitute an unconstitutional discrimination against servicewomen . . . but I cannot join the opinion of Mr. Justice Brennan which would hold that all classifications based upon sex . . . are "inherently suspect. . . . " The Equal Rights Amendment, which if adopted will resolve the substance of this precise question, has been approved by the Congress and submitted for ratification by the States. If this Amendment is duly adopted, it will represent the will of the people accomplished in the manner prescribed by the Constitution. . . . It seems to me that this reaching out to pre-empt by judicial action a major political decision which is currently in process of resolution does not reflect appropriate respect for duly prescribed legislative processes.

Source: 411 U.S. 677 at 684, 687, 688, 691, 692 (1973).

{g}DOCUMENT 210: *Torbin H. Brenden v. Independent School District*, U.S. District Court, Minnesota, May 1, 1972

While feminist lawyers pressed the highest court to raise sex discrimination to a fully "suspect category," others, bringing suits in the lower courts, sought to chip away at time-honored assumptions about fundamental differences between the sexes. Nowhere were these assumptions more deeply rooted than in the arena of athletics. When two highly skilled female athletes, Tony St. Pierre and Peggy Brenden, were barred from joining the male tennis and cross-country skiing teams in their Minnesota high school, they took their case to U.S. District Court. The school district argued that physiological considerations required single-sex teams. The District Court disagreed.

* * *

As testified to by defendants' expert witnesses, men are taller than women, stronger than women by reason of a greater muscle mass; have larger hearts than women and a deeper breathing capacity, enabling them to utilize oxygen more efficiently than women, run faster, based upon the construction of the pelvic area, which, when women reach puberty, widens, causing the femur to bend outward, rendering the female incapable of running as efficiently as a male. These physiological differences may, on the average, prevent the great majority of women from competing on an equal level with the great majority of males.

[H]owever, these physiological differences . . . have little relevance to Tony St. Pierre and Peggy Brenden. Because of their level of achievement in competitive sports, Tony and Peggy have overcome these physiological disabilities. There has been no evidence that either Peggy Brenden or Tony St. Pierre, or any other girls, would be in any way damaged from competition in boys' interscholastic athletics, nor is there any credible evidence that the boys would be damaged.

Source: 342 *Federal Supplement* 1224 at 1233 (1972).

{g}DOCUMENT 211: *Torbin H. Brenden v. Independent School District*, U.S. Court of Appeals, 8th Circuit, April 18, 1973

When school officials appealed the District Court ruling, the appeals court upheld the right of St. Pierre and Brenden to compete with boys.

* * *

Essentially the testimony of those witnesses who concluded that females were wholly incapable of competing with men in interscholastic athletics was based on subjective conclusions drawn from the physiological differences between the sexes by individuals who were not themselves familiar with mixed competition. . . .

We note that there is at least one systematic study of mixed competition in non-contact sports [a study in 1969 by the New York State Department of Education]. Discussion [in the course of that study] with various medical personnel elicited a unanimous expression that there are no medical reasons to prohibit girls from competing on boys' teams in selected non-contact sports.

Source: 477 F. 2d 129 at 1300, 1301 (1973).

{r/g}DOCUMENT 212: "Statement of Purpose," National Black Feminist Organization, May 1974

While sex and race remained distinct categories in judicial action, that separation was denounced by women who bore the burden of both kinds of discrimination. In the spring of 1973, thirty African American women, meeting in New York City, formed the National Black Feminist Organization. From their first conference the following November emerged a statement of purpose, which attacked both racism and sexism.

* * *

We must together, as a people, work to eliminate racism from without the Black community which is trying to destroy us as an entire people; but we must remember that sexism is destroying and crippling us from within.

Source: The National Black Feminist Organization, "Statement of Purpose," reprinted in *MS* (May 1974): 99.

Following its successful attack on racism and sexism within AT&T (Docs. 202–208), the EEOC initiated a broad and sweeping campaign directed at scores of other large corporations and unions. The objectives were to institute consent decrees, obtain restitution for employees who were victims of past discrimination, and incorporate into all future practices of hiring, salary, and promotion a version of affirmative action that met EEOC requirements. The companies targeted by EEOC included Ford Motor Company, General Electric, General Motors, the International Union of Electrical Radio and Machine Workers, Sears Roebuck, the United Auto Workers, the United Electrical Workers, the "Big Ten" steel companies, and the United Steelworkers. The steel industry was among the first to yield, signing an industry-wide consent decree in the U.S. District Court of Birmingham, Alabama, in April 1974. Under the decree the steel companies and the steelworkers' union were bound to completely restructure the seniority system and practice affirmative action in hiring women and minorities. The impact of these orders on the lives of the steelworkers can be glimpsed in the next interviews and observations taken from two studies of steelworkers.

{r}DOCUMENT 213: The 1974 Consent Decree through the Eyes of African American Steelworkers

The 1998 Public Television documentary *Struggles in Steel* included a segment on how the implementation of affirmative action plans affected African American steelworkers.

* * *

STEELWORKER CHARLES JAMES: [Some of the other African American workers] said to me "you're going to have all those whites mad." And I said, "hell! *I've* been mad for 25 years!"

STEELWORKER ROBERT J. HUBBARD (A plaintiff in the suit which led to the decree): Here come my black brother . . . [asking], "You gonna take that white man's job?" I said, "If they had put me on the job when I first came here he wouldn't be on the job in the first place."

OLIVER MONTGOMERY (research analyst, United Steelworkers of America): The rank and file black caucus [of the union] wanted a half billion dollars in reparations. That thirty-some million—we thought that was pennies.

The $30.5 million in back pay that the consent decree called for translated into a few hundred dollars for the individual workers.

NARRATOR RAYMOND HENDERSON: I had a lot of black men come to me who just felt so insulted by the fact that [someone was giving them] six hundred dollars for twenty years' worth of discrimination. [They said], "That didn't get my kid through college. That didn't buy me no automobile. That didn't buy me no home. . . ."

STEELWORKER ROBERT DONALDSON (ARMCO Steel, Baltimore): There was a stipulation on the back of the checks. . . . You signed away any future rights to sue the company for discrimination. If you accepted the money you also signed away your rights.

A number of the workers refused to take the money.

STEELWORKER FRANCIS BROWN: They gave me 700 bucks.
NARRATOR HENDERSON: How did you feel?
FRANCIS BROWN: Well, if it was one on one I'd of beat them up. . . .
STEELWORKER JAMES SHARPLEY: They [the corporate managers] did not immediately act on the consent decree. They tried to circumvent the consent decree in a great number of instances.
STEELWORKER CHARLES L. DANZEY: The consent decree was designed to fail. . . . Everything had to go through the implementation committee [comprising representatives of the African American workers, the company, the union and the government]. . . . They had to have a unanimous decision or [the issue] would revert to the judge. . . . They never ruled in favor of the blacks. . . .
STEELWORKER FRANCIS BROWN (who was the only African American on the implementation committee in his company): We didn't ask for a consent decree. We asked for our rights. Every time we ask for our rights they come up with some method that we don't even understand. I was the representative on this consent decree and I ain't understand it. I was the only one. They put one black man in the position to make him look bad. They gave me papers stacked up that high, everyday. . . . And what they did was to say, "we'll break his back and break the back of the movements along with some others." You can't expect a consent decree from the northern district courts of Alabama pushed by Judge Sam Pointer to be placed in the hands of a young black man named Francis Brown and ask him to get the job done. . . . The people from the union that set on the board with me and the people from the company . . . and the government reps all had someone working with them, in terms of attorneys and whatnot. I had no one but myself.
STEELWORKER PRISCILLA BURGESS: It [entering the steel mill under the consent decree] was tough. I would go into the bathroom and pray. . . . I happened to see the white girl's [time card]. We worked on the same job, side by side. . . . She was punched five classes above what I was punched [and therefore was paid at a rank five times higher.]
STEELWORKER LATTIE KING: There was a girl doing the same job I was doing. . . . They were paying her class seven for the same job I was doing. They were paying me "Labor" [the lowest pay level]. I told them, you know you're going to make me hate blond haired females. . . .
NARRATOR HENDERSON: Even though the Consent Decree was not

enforced the way we thought it should be, we were finally getting good paying jobs.

Source: Struggles in Steel, video documentary, produced and directed by Tony Buba and Raymond Henderson (Braddock Films, 1996).

{g}DOCUMENT 214: Post-Consent Decree Experiences of Female Steelworkers in the 1970s

A 1977 doctoral thesis at Ohio State University highlighted the experiences of white and African American women who obtained steel mill jobs as a result of court-mandated affirmative action. As with the workers in the previous document, these women found that the consent decree was not an automatic entrée to equal treatment.

* * *

Initially, management did not believe that women would be interested in jobs as steelworkers. One supervisor remarked, "We never expected them to even apply." Another said, "I was shocked that women would even want to work in the mill. I know this might sound like prejudice, but my idea of a woman is a step above a steelworker. . . ."

During the intake interviews, personnel officials repeatedly emphasized the negative aspects of the job, particularly their perception of potential harassment from male co-workers. Typical were such remarks: "They kept stressing that men didn't want the women in there and they would be rough on me. . . ."

I asked union officials how the men in the mill first responded. . . . One official told me:

You heard things like, we are getting those broads on the gang now; broads are coming to work in the mill and they are going to have preference over us; maybe I can get a good-looking helper.

According to union officials, there was widespread fear that women would not be able to do the job and that the men would have to work twice as hard. Some of the men resented a perceived threat to a territory they had exclusively staked out for themselves. One union official said, "Some of those who are hollering the most about women are the same ones who don't appreciate the blacks and other minorities achieving goals greater than theirs. . . ."

Black workers do not always feel that they can be honest in their social relations with white workers in the mill. Attempting to converse across sex and race lines poses special problems for black women. One woman said:

I prefer to work with another black person 'cause it is hard to talk to a white person all day. . . . Black and white workers get along fine as long as the black person lets a white person feel as though they are still on top. . . .

Sexism took a variety of forms within the plant. . . . One woman believed that the company deliberately tried to ensure the failure of women, by placing unqualified women in difficult positions. . . .

Another woman believed that the testing procedure for apprenticeships was biased and successfully argued the case with her employer. . . .

In addition to the structural features of sexism, there is the tension and psychological strain associated with being the first woman to cross occupational barriers. . . . "You are constantly being watched." Sometimes they feel the pressure to be the standard bearer for the entire population of women. . . .

Sometimes their sexuality is called into question. One woman remarked, "If you are too nice, you are a whore, if you aren't nice enough, you're a bitch." . . .

Despite the hassles, women steelworkers were satisfied with their jobs because the alternatives were less desirable.

Source: Mary Margaret Fonow, "Occupation/Steelworker: Sex/Female," in *Feminist Frontiers III*, edited by Laurel Richardson and Verta Taylor (Hightstown, NJ: McGraw-Hill, 1983): 217–222.

{g}DOCUMENT 215: Girls' Challenge to Little League Baseball in the 1970s

---

Like men in the steel mills, men and boys on athletic playing fields perceived the entry of women onto that "turf" as an invasion. In the same season that the steel industry consent decree was signed, the Superior Court of New Jersey ruled in favor of Frances Pescatore, who demanded the right to play Little League baseball. She presented an affidavit to the court that stated, "I am 11 years old, and therefore three years of my career have been wasted." Reaction to the court ruling was reported in *Sports Illustrated*.

* * *

The New Jersey verdict was that the Little League is a *place* of public accommodation, as much as a train or a carnival is a "place." This decision gives girls everywhere an opening, and suits are popping up all over. . . .

The Little League, which represents two million male players in 31 countries on a tight $800,000 budget, could be emasculated financially by a plethora of court actions, win or lose. . . .

[T]he real dispute is neither physical nor cosmetic nor medical. The real dispute is social: what identity do we perceive for the sexes in America?

Source: Frank De Ford, "Now Georgy-Porgy Runs Away," *Sports Illustrated* (April 24, 1974): 27, 28, 30.

{r}DOCUMENT 216: Racial Stance of the Little League

While Little League maintained barriers against girls, the official policy of the organization opposed discrimination on the basis of race.

* * *

When Little League began a lot of activities in America were segregated. But Little League right off the bat was against any kind of discrimination. I recall in the early 1950s there was a Little League official in Maryland who told me, "These kids don't know the difference between white or black unless we tell them. And we don't tell them!"

Source: John Lindemuth, quoted in Harvey Frommer, *Growing Up at Bat, 50 Years of Little League Baseball* (New York: Pharos Books, 1989): 55.

{g}DOCUMENT 217: The Admission of Girls to Little League Baseball in 1974

Little League's policy of barring girls ended in June 1974.

* * *

June 30, 1974 Little League Baseball announced that because of "the changing social climate" girls would be allowed to play on its teams.

Source: Harvey Frommer, *Growing Up at Bat, 50 Years of Little League Baseball* (New York: Pharos Books, 1989): 55.

Playing fields and factories were not the only places where the admission of women and racial minorities was stirring deep feelings. Tension was increasing over hiring and admissions in universities and professional schools. The charge of "reverse discrimination" received increasing attention as white students challenged admissions policies that counted race as a "plus factor" for minorities, in much the same way that being the child of an alumnus, having athletic talent, or coming from a family that had made generous donations to the applicant's school of choice had always counted as "plus factors."

{r}DOCUMENT 218: *DeFunis et al. v. Odegaard et al.,* April 1974

The case brought by Marco DeFunis Jr. against the University of Washington Law School was a portent of many conflicts to come. In denying DeFunis admission, the law school administration acknowledged that minority applicants who were admitted at the same time would not have been accepted if they had been judged under the same procedures that were applied to DeFunis and other whites. Thirty-six of the thirty-seven minority applicants who were admitted had scores on a "Predicted First Year Average" index lower than DeFunis'. Forty-eight other nonminorities who were admitted also had scores lower than his, including twenty-three veterans; the rest possessed some other characteristic that, as Justice William Douglas observed, "made them attractive . . . despite their relatively low Averages." The state court that first ruled on DeFunis' petition ordered the law school to admit him. The school complied but appealed to the state supreme court, which ruled against DeFunis. However, Justice Douglas issued a "stay" until the U.S. Supreme Court could hear the case. DeFunis proceeded with his studies and was in his final year when the Supreme Court began its review. That review led to a "per curiam" opinion, declaring the case to be "moot" and no longer within the authority of the Court, since DeFunis was on the verge of graduation. Nonetheless, Justice Douglas wrote a lengthy dissent, and Justice Brennan, with his colleagues Douglas, White, and Marshall concurring, also dissented. Douglas argued along lines that opponents of affirmative action would elaborate in the future, implying a "color-blind" Constitution, emphasizing individual merit, and maintaining that persons benefiting from racial preferences would carry a "stigma."

* * *

Mr. Justice Douglas, dissenting. . . .

There is no constitutional right for any race to be preferred. . . . A DeFunis who is white . . . has a constitutional right to have his application considered on its individual merits in a racially neutral manner. . . .

The key to the problem is consideration of such applications *in a racially neutral way.* . . .

The Equal Protection Clause commands the elimination of racial barriers, not their creation in order to satisfy our theory as to how society ought to be organized. The purpose of the University of Washington cannot be to produce black lawyers for blacks, Polish lawyers for Poles, Jewish lawyers for Jews, Irish lawyers for Irish. It should be to produce good lawyers for Americans and not to place First Amendment barriers against anyone.

One other assumption must be clearly disapproved: that blacks or browns cannot make it on their individual merit. That is a stamp of inferiority that a State is not permitted to place on any lawyer.

[The dissent of Justice Brennan included a warning.]

* * *

Mr. Justice Brennan, with whom Mr. Justice Douglas, Mr. Justice White, and Mr. Justice Marshall concur, dissenting. . . .

I can . . . find no justification for the Court's straining to rid itself of this dispute. . . .

The constitutional issues which are avoided today concern vast numbers of people, organizations, and colleges and universities. . . . Few constitutional questions in recent history have stirred as much debate, and they will not disappear.

Source: 416 U.S. 312 at 336, 340, 342, 343, 349, 350 (1974).

THE INTERIM YEARS OF GERALD FORD

{g}DOCUMENT 219: Lower Court Findings in Support of Female Athletes in the 1970s

Although the Supreme Court had ducked the issues raised by *DeFunis*, its call in *Griggs* (Doc. 171) for "great deference" to EEOC regulations guided lower courts in the federal judiciary system. The lower courts also continued to rule in favor of women in cases involving athletics.

* * *

Court Findings in Support of Female Athletes (Mid-1970s)

Case	Court	Nature	Ruling
Gilpin vs. Kansas State High School Act Assoc. Inc., 1974	U.S. District Court, District Kansas	Girl wanted to be on cross-country team	Ruled in favor of girl
Commonwealth of Pennsylvania vs. Pennsylvania Interscholastic Athletic Assoc., 1975	Commonwealth Court of Pennsylvania	Commonwealth filed suit against athletic association, maintaining rule forbidding mixed competition was unconstitutional under the state ERA	Rule declared unconstitutional
Darrin vs. Gould, State of Washington, 1975	Supreme Court, State of Washington	Two Darrin girls wanted to play on the high school football team; class action challenging a state athletic association rule excluding girls.	In favor of girls; said the association rule discriminated on the basis of sex, which was in violation of the state's ERA
Carnes vs. Tenn. Secondary School Athletic Assn. [TSAA], 1976	U.S. District Court, Eastern District Tennessee	Female high school senior seeking preliminary injunction against TSAA prohibiting enforcement of a rule prohibiting mixed participation in contact sports, of which baseball is so named and in which plaintiff seeks participation	Preliminary injunction granted
Cape vs. Tennessee Sec. School Athletic Assn., 1976	U.S. District Court, Eastern District Tennessee	Female high school junior claimed that the application of six-player, half-court basketball rules which allow only forwards to shoot is a deprivation of her right to equal protection of the laws guaranteed by the Fourteenth Amendment; also claimed right to relief under Title IX	Rules declared to be in violation of the Equal Protection Clause of the Fourteenth Amendment

Source: Adapted from "Summary of Court Cases on Sex Discrimination in Athletics," in Geadelmann et al. 1977, 74.

{g}DOCUMENT 220: Congressional Regulations for Implementing Title IX, September 1975

Title IX, passed by Congress in 1972 (Doc. 191), was intended to eradicate sex discrimination in all educational institutions receiving any type of federal support. Because the measure implied far-reaching changes in the allocation of resources to male athletic teams and programs, a battle developed over the wording of the regulations by which Title IX was to be enforced. The battle pitted a strong lobby organized by the National Collegiate Athletics Association and the presidents of universities with major athletic teams, against the Association for Intercollegiate Athletics for Women (formed in 1971) and a coalition of an estimated sixty women's groups that came together in 1974 as the Education Task Force and later changed their name to National Coalition for Women and Girls in Education. In September 1975 Congress passed, and President Gerald Ford signed, an elaborate body of Title IX Regulations that addressed treatment of women students and faculty in all areas of academic life. Since the provisions related to athletics satisfied none of the interest groups, the struggle would continue on that front, as HEW attempted to formulate a "policy interpretation" that would not become final until December 1979 (Doc 266).

* * *

Title IX Regulations

Section 86.3 A recipient [of federal support] found to have discriminated on the basis of sex in an education program or activity *must* take remedial action. In the absence of such a finding, a recipient *may* take affirmative action to overcome the effects of conditions which resulted in limited participation by a particular sex, but the foregoing in no way alters any affirmative action obligation under Executive Order 11246 [Doc. 133]. . . .

Section 86.21 No person shall, on the basis of sex, be denied admission, or be subjected to discrimination in admission. In the admissions process, a recipient must not rank applicants differently, employ quotas, or otherwise treat applicants differently on the basis of sex. . . .

Section 86.31 In providing any aid, benefit, or service to a student, a recipient shall not discriminate on the basis of sex. . . .

Section 86.34 Courses (including health, physical education, industrial, business, vocational, technical, home economics, music, and adult education) and other education programs or activities must not be conducted separately, or participation by students be required or refused, on the basis of sex. . . .

Portions of classes in elementary and secondary schools dealing exclusively with human sexuality may be separate. In voice activities, requirements based on vocal range or quality which may result in choruses of one or predominantly one sex are permitted. . . .

Section 86.37 Athletic scholarships or grants-in-aid must provide reasonable opportunities for each sex in proportion to the students of each sex participating in interscholastic or intercollegiate athletics. However, separate awards for members of each sex may be provided as part of separate athletic teams to the extent consistent with the foregoing and Section 86.41 below. . . .

Section 86.41 No person shall, on the basis of sex, be excluded from or treated differently in any interscholastic, intercollegiate club, or intramural athletics offered by a recipient, and no recipient shall provide any athletics separately on such basis.

Notwithstanding the foregoing, a recipient may operate or sponsor separate teams for each sex where selection is based on *competitive skill* or the *activity involved is a contact sport*. However, where a recipient operates or sponsors a team in a particular sport for only one sex and athletic opportunities for the other sex have previously been limited, members of the excluded sex must be allowed to try out for the team offered *unless the sport involved is a contact sport*. Contact sports include boxing, wrestling, rugby, ice hockey, football, basketball, and other sports mainly involving bodily contact. . . .

Unequal aggregate expenditures for each sex, or unequal expenditures for male and female teams does not constitute noncompliance with this section, but the failure to provide necessary funds for teams for one sex may be considered in assessing equality of athletic opportunity. . . .

Section 86.51 No person shall, on the basis of sex, be subjected to discrimination in any aspect of employment under any education program or activity operated by a recipient which receives or benefits from federal financial assistance. . . .

Source: "Title IX Regulations," reprinted in Education Committee of the States, *A Digest of Federal Laws and Regulations Affecting Equal Rights for Women in Education* (Denver: Education Commission of the States, October 1976): 16–21.

{d}DOCUMENT 221: Public Law 94–142, The Education for All Handicapped Children Act of 1975

While lawmakers and lobbyists wrestled with the implications of Title IX, Congress proceeded with the passage of another major law establishing rights and entitlements for disabled children. The Education for All Handicapped Children Act of 1975 (Public Law 94–142) took its place next to the Architectural Barriers Act (Doc. 153) and the Vocational Rehabilitation Act of 1973 (Doc. 200) to create the foundation of civil rights for the disabled. A unique feature of the 1975 law was the requirement that every child covered by it must have an individual education plan (IEP). For those charged with monitoring and evaluating the implementation of Public Law 94–142, IEPs were highly useful tools.

* * *

Section 3 (c). . . . It is the purpose of this Act to assure that all handicapped children have available to them . . . a free appropriate public education which emphasizes special education and related services designed to meet their unique needs, to assure that the rights of handicapped children and their parents or guardians are protected, to assist States and localities to provide for the education of all handicapped children, and to assess and assure the effectiveness of efforts to educate handicapped children. . . .

Section 4 (a). . . . The term "free appropriate public education" means special education and related service which (A) have been provided at public expense, under public supervision and direction, and without charge, (B) meet the standards of the State educational agency, (C) include an appropriate preschool, elementary, or secondary school education in the State involved, and (D) are provided in conformity with the individualized education program required under section 614(a) (5). . . .

Section 614 (a) (5). . . . [T]he local educational agency . . . will establish . . . an individualized education program for each handicapped child at the beginning of each school year and will then review and, if appropriate revise, its provisions periodically, but not less than annually.

Source: U.S. Statutes at Large 89 (1975): 775, 786.

{r/g}DOCUMENT 222: The Continuing Uncertainty of Title VII Law as of 1977

If lawmakers used unusually specific language in Public Law 94–142 to spell out the requirements for its implementation, the language used by the authors of the 1964 Civil Rights Act continued to evoke varied interpretations, as illustrated in the erratic record of rulings related to Title VII issuing from the U.S. Supreme Court. Legal scholar Kenneth Lopatka commented on this record in a review of Title VII law in 1977. He observed that although Supreme Court rulings were ambiguous, the EEOC and the lower courts acted as though the definition of discrimination adopted in the *Griggs* decision (Doc. 171) was a permanent "given."

* * *

The Meaning of Discrimination

When Congress enacted Title VII of the Civil Rights Act in 1964, it was obvious to all that the Act addressed overt discrimination based on race, color, religion, sex, or national origin. . . .

Not so obvious when Title VII was enacted was the status of facially neutral criteria used in hiring, promoting, or classifying individuals which, though used without any tinge of class-based motive, have a disparate impact on a protected class. . . .

Notably, the Supreme Court has not specifically approved the extension of *Griggs* to these so-called "pure effects" discrimination cases.

Conclusion

Title VII is now almost 13 years old, but a surprising number of fundamental issues are unresolved. . . . That the yarn from which the lower courts have spun an imposing web of Title VII law may be unraveled is . . . disturbing both to those who must plan to comply with Title VII and to those who stand to benefit from it. But the uncertainty is a consequence of the general posture of minimal intervention in Title VII litigation which the Supreme Court has, until recently assumed. . . . [T]he Supreme Court has recently shown that if it is convinced they have misinterpreted the statute or the Constitution, it will not hesitate to overrule the lower courts.

Source: Kenneth T. Lopatka, "Developing Concepts in Title VII Law," in *Equal Rights and Industrial Relations* by Farrell E. Bloch et al. (Madison, WI: Industrial Relations Research Association, 1977): 31–33, 69.

As Lopatka indicated, the Supreme Court delivered mixed messages throughout the 1970s. On the one hand, supporters of affirmative action were heartened by the 1975 decision in *Albemarle Paper Co. v. Moody*, when the Court ruled against the owners of a segregated paper mill and invalidated the aptitude tests that they used in hiring. The decision involved the same "broad exercise" of judicial powers that characterized *Griggs* (Doc. 171) and, as in *Griggs*, granted "great deference" to EEOC guidelines. On the other hand, several notable high court decisions appeared to temper the *Griggs* ruling, including *McDonnell Douglas v. Green* (1973), *Washington v. Davis* (1976), and *International Brotherhood of Teamsters v. U.S.* (1978). In *McDonnell Douglas* the Court affirmed the right of an employer to refuse to rehire an African American employee who had participated in an illegal "stall-in," blocking the entrance to the employer's plant. Although a lower court found the employer's action to have a "disparate racial impact," the Supreme Court supported it as a legitimate business decision. At issue in *Washington v. Davis* was a test used in selecting trainees for the police force of Washington, D.C. The test, which African Americans failed at four times the rate of whites, violated guidelines of the EEOC. The challenge to the test was based on the Fourteenth and Fifteenth Amendments because Title VII had not yet been amended to cover public employees. The Court argued that these constitutional standards were not the same as the standards of Title VII that had applied in *Griggs*, and, therefore, since there was no proof that the police department intended to discriminate, it could continue to use the test. In the 1978 case the Court refused to overturn a seniority system established before Congress passed Title VII.

{r}DOCUMENT 223: *McDonald v. Santa Fe Trail Transportation Company*, 1976

In *McDonald v. Santa Fe Trail Transportation Company*, the Supreme Court rendered a unanimous decision, which would be used as ammunition for "reverse discrimination" claims by the opponents of affirmative action. Three employees of the transport company—L. N. McDonald, Raymond L. Laird (both white), and Charles Jackson (African American)—had been found guilty of stealing sixty gallons of antifreeze from their employer. The company fired McDonald and Laird but retained Jackson. The two white men filed complaints of discrimination, which the EEOC failed to resolve and which were dismissed by two lower courts. Associate Justice Thurgood Marshall delivered the unanimous opinion of the Supreme Court, supporting the white workers' claims.

* * *

Mr. Justice Marshall delivered the opinion of the Court.

Title VII of the Civil Rights Act of 1964 prohibits the discharge of "any individual" because of "such individual's race." Its terms are not limited to discrimination against members of any particular race. . . .

Title VII prohibits racial discrimination against the white petitioners in this case upon the same standards as would be applied were they Negroes and Jackson white.

Source: 427 U.S. 273 at 2578, 2579 (1976).

THE ADMINISTRATION OF JIMMY CARTER

The case of McDonald and Laird occasioned little public comment. But two years later, when lawyers for another white man argued his case before the Supreme Court, again charging "reverse discrimination," racial alarms went off throughout the country—among whites threatened by the recent gains of the civil rights movement and enforcement of affirmative action and among minorities, perceiving that these gains were already about to evaporate. *Regents of the University of California v. Bakke*—prompted by the denial of admission to the university's Medical School at Davis of white applicant Allan Bakke—revealed just how badly the American house was still divided against itself.

{r}DOCUMENT 224: Divided Public Opinion on Helping Minorities, Fall 1977

In the following selection, historian Allan Sindler presents and interprets a *New York Times*/CBS survey in the fall of 1977 indicating the nature of this division.

* * *

Public Opinion on Help for Minorities in Employment and Education

Question	Whites		Blacks	
	Approve	Disapprove	Approve	Disapprove
"How about requiring large companies to set up special training programs for members of minority groups?"	63%	32%	88%	9%
"... would you approve or disapprove of requiring business to hire a certain number of minority workers?"	35%	60%	64%	26%
"What about a college or graduate school giving special consideration to the best minority applicants, to help more of them get admitted than otherwise. Would you approve or disapprove of that?"	59%	36%	83%	16%
"What if a school reserved a certain number of places for qualified minority applicants. Would you approve or disapprove of that even if it meant that some qualified white applicants wouldn't be admitted?"	32%	60%	46%	42%

A clear majority of whites opposed the assigning of a minimum number of jobs or admissions places to minorities, but supported the more moderate means of special job training or the rather ambiguously worded "special consideration to the best minority applicants" to college or graduate school. Among blacks, more approved than disapproved of each item and by margins markedly greater than those of whites. Still, the direction of change in black sentiment on each question paralleled that among whites, which suggested the common tug of shared values. Particularly noteworthy was the last question, dealing with a *Bakke*-like situation, on which blacks were almost evenly split and whites expressed disapproval by an almost two-to-one ratio.

Source: Allan P. Sindler, *Bakke, DeFunis, and Minority Admissions, the Quest for Equal Opportunity* (New York: Longman, 1978): 15–16.

{r}DOCUMENT 225: Admissions Criteria and Minority Students at the Davis Medical School, 1973, 1974

As historian Timothy O'Neill has noted (O'Neill 1985, 26), the special admissions program challenged by Bakke was developed in a climate of racial consciousness and was similar to programs adopted by 100 other medical schools. The impetus at the Davis institution (which opened in 1968) came from faculty who believed that the total absence of African Americans and Chicanos in the first class and the enrollment of only two African Americans and one Chicano in 1969 indicated that "admissions criteria unfairly hindered minority access" to their program. They voted to institute a special program that took into account a variety of factors: grades, letters of recommendation, statements of purpose written by the candidates, test scores, and—for those who made the first cut—interviews. However, the quantifiable factors, particularly test scores, became the focal point of controversy. O'Neill summarized and commented on the differences between the scores of regular and special candidates admitted to Davis in 1973 and 1974.

* * *

Test Score and Grade Comparisons, 1973, 1974

	Regular Admittees (1973)	Task Force Admittees (1973)	Regular Admittees (1974)	Task Force Admittees (1974)
Science GPA	3.51	2.62	3.36	2.42
Range	2.57–4.0	2.11–2.93	2.5–4.0	2.20–3.89
Overall GPA	3.49	2.88	3.29	2.62
Range	2.81–3.99	2.11–3.76	2.79–4.0	2.21–3.45
MCAT Scores (as percentile rank)				
Verbal	81	46	69	34
Quantitative	76	24	67	30
Science	83	35	82	37
General	69	33	72	18

In 1973 and 1974, the lowest-ranking regular candidate's grade point average (GPA) in science courses was three-tenths to five-tenths of a point higher than the lowest-ranking special admittee's. . . . The special admittees fare more poorly when Medical College Admission Test [MCAT] scores are compared.

Source: Timothy J. O'Neill, *Bakke & the Politics of Equality, Friends and Foes in the Classroom of Litigation* (Middletown, CT: Wesleyan University Press, 1985): 27–28.

{r}DOCUMENT 226: The Evolution of Medical School Admissions Policies, 1950s–1970s

As Joel Dreyfuss and Charles Lawrence explain in the following selection, historical and demographic influences had shaped admissions policies and the increasing emphasis placed on standardized tests. Dreyfuss and Lawrence also challenge the reliability of test scores as predictors of performance.

* * *

The Medical College Aptitude Test was introduced in the 1950s to help reduce the attrition rate. . . . The high attrition rate of the time was the result of a basically "open admissions" policy at many medical schools. The mean MCAT science score of accepted students was 516 in 1957 and 615 in 1975. The quantitative score on the test went from 517 to 620 in that period, [a reflection of the impact on admissions of the postwar baby boom]. "Because of the larger pool of academically qualified students," said the AAMC [American Association of Medical Colleges], "medical schools have raised their admissions standards well beyond the minimum level necessary to ensure completion of the course of study leading to the M.D. degree." . . .

[T]he pressure of competition . . . raised the level of academic qualifications far beyond what is needed to succeed. . . . [S]ome of those who complain loudly about lowered standards [in 1974] are complaining about students who match and even surpass the "qualifications" they used to get into professional schools just a generation ago. . . .

[A] 1967 study of 180 physicians working in Public Health Service hospitals . . . showed a *negative* correlation between their MCAT scores and rating of their work by supervisors. "If an admissions committee were to follow literally the implications of studies relating MCAT scores to physician performance," facetiously suggests a brief in support of special admissions, filed in the *Bakke* case by an organization of black law students, "it should prefer candidates with lower scores."

If the evidence is so overwhelming about the irrelevance and racial bias of standardized tests, why do officials continue to use them? Primarily because they are a convenient tool for paring down an overwhelming number of applicants. A semblance of fairness is created by having every applicant take the same examination, although the test itself has virtually no value in predicting what contribution the student will make to the profession he or she is about to enter.

Source: Joel Dreyfuss and Charles Lawrence III, *The Bakke Case, the Politics of Inequality* (New York: Harcourt Brace Jovanovich, 1979): 128, 129, 130–131.

{r}DOCUMENT 227: Bakke's Quest for Admission to Medical School, 1973, 1974

From Allan Bakke's point of view, every applicant taking the same examination should have been evaluated for admissions by the same criteria. Any other approach, he argued, was not only unfair but unconstitutional. While his name would soon become synonymous with "victim of reverse discrimination," he was in several respects an unusual medical school applicant. Over thirty, married with children, and already established in another career, he originally applied to eleven medical schools, knowing that his age would weigh against him. He applied, and was rejected, twice by the University of California Medical School at Davis, in 1973 and 1974.

The outcome of Bakke's two efforts to enter the Davis medical school would later be summarized by Supreme Court Justice Powell when he delivered the decision in Bakke's legal case.

* * *

Allan Bakke is a white male who applied to the Davis Medical School in both 1973 and 1974. In both years Bakke's application was considered under the general admissions program, and he received an interview. His 1973 interview was with Dr. Theodore C. West, who considered Bakke "a very desirable applicant to [the] medical school." ... Despite a strong benchmark score of 468 out of 500 Bakke was rejected. His application had come late in the year, and no applicants in the general admissions process with scores below 470 were accepted after Bakke's application was completed ... After his 1973 rejection, Bakke wrote to Dr. George H. Lowrey, Associate Dean and Chairman of the Admissions

Committee, protesting that the special admissions program operated as a racial and ethnic quota.

Bakke's 1974 application was completed early in the year. . . . His student interviewer gave him an overall rating of 94, finding him "friendly, well tempered, conscientious and delightful to speak with." . . . His faculty interviewer was, by coincidence, the same Dr. Lowrey to whom he had written in protest of the special admissions program. Dr. Lowrey found Bakke "rather limited in his approach" to the problems of the medical profession and found disturbing Bakke's "very definite opinions which were based more on his personal viewpoints than upon a study of the total problem." . . . Dr. Lowrey gave Bakke the lowest of his six ratings, an 86; his total was 549 out of 600. . . . Again Bakke's application was rejected. . . . In both years, applicants were admitted under the special program with grade point averages, MCAT scores, and benchmark scores significantly lower than Bakke's.

After the second rejection, Bakke filed the instant suit in the Superior Court of California.

Source: 438 U.S. 265 at 276–278 (1978).

{r}DOCUMENT 228: The Carter Administration and *Bakke*, 1977

The state court ruled that the Davis Medical School violated federal and state constitutions and Title VI by having a special admissions program and must, therefore, end the program. The court further ruled that Bakke had not proved that the special program was the sole reason for his being denied admission, and, therefore the school did not have to admit him. Bakke appealed to the California Supreme Court, which ignored the issue of whether the school violated the state constitution or Title VI but found that it was violating the Equal Protection Clause of the Fourteenth Amendment and must, therefore, end the special program. The California Supreme Court also ruled that the school could not prove that it denied Bakke admission for reasons other than the special program and thus would have to admit him. The University of California appealed the decision to the Supreme Court.

Lawyers for the university and for Bakke were not alone in preparing arguments to be reviewed by the highest court in the nation. When the case was called, 117 institutions, organizations, and interest groups had filed "friend of the court" (*amicus curia*) briefs.

The Justice Department also submitted a brief on behalf of the administration of President Jimmy Carter, but not before a confrontation between Carter's attorney general, Griffin Bell, and his health, education, and welfare (HEW) secretary, Joseph Califano. Bell and attorneys in the Justice Department initially argued in support of Bakke's admission to the Davis Medical School, calling the school's admissions program unconstitutional. Califano denounced their position as "bad law and pernicious social policy." In his autobiography the HEW secretary described a presidential cabinet meeting at which the issue was broached.

* * *

[Ambassador to the United Nations Andrew Young] commented on the *Bakke* case stingingly. "The *Bakke* case is perceived as a betrayal of the black community by the judicial system. Blacks feel that the University of California does not want to win the case. Bakke has been denied admission by twelve other medical schools, some of which had no blacks or Chicanos, on the basis of his age."

I followed Young. I said the *Bakke* brief would be the most read brief filed by this administration. . . . I urged Carter to "take a strong stand in favor of affirmative action." . . .

Bell was uncomfortable. . . . The President was noncommittal.

[The final version of the brief reflected the point of view of Young and Califano.]

Source: Joseph A. Califano Jr., *Governing America* (New York: Simon and Schuster, 1981): 241.

{r}DOCUMENT 229: Memo from Thurgood Marshall, April 13, 1978

After the Supreme Court heard the case in October 1977, and as the justices deliberated, the only African American member of the Court, Thurgood Marshall, shared his point of view with the other "brethren" of the supreme bench.

* * *

[T]he decision in this case depends on whether you consider the action of the Regents as *admitting* certain students or as *excluding* certain other students. If you view the program as admitting qualified students who, because of this Nation's sorry history of racial discrimination, have academic records that prevent them from effectively competing for medical school, then this is affirmative action to remove the vestiges of slavery and state imposed segregation by "root and branch." If you view the program as excluding students, it is a program of "quotas" which violates the principle that the "Constitution is color-blind.". . . .

[With regard to] the question of whether Negroes have "arrived," . . . just a few examples illustrate that Negroes most certainly have not. . . . In our own Court, we have had only three Negro law clerks, and not so far have we had a Negro Officer of the Court. . . . This week's *U.S. News and World Report* has a story about "Who Runs America." They list some 83 persons—not one Negro, even as a would-be runnerup. And the economic disparity between the races is increasing. . . .

The dream of America as the melting pot has not been realized by Negroes—either the Negro did not get into the pot, or he did not get melted down. . . . [T]he vast gulf between White and Black America . . . was brought about by centuries of slavery and then by another century in which, with the approval of this Court, states were permitted to treat Negroes "specially." . . .

We are not yet all equals, in large part because of the refusal of the *Plessy* Court to adopt the principle of color-blindness. It would be the cruelest irony for this Court to adopt the dissent in *Plessy* [Doc. 25] now and hold that the University must use color-blind admissions.

Source: Thurgood Marshall, "Memo," April 13, 1978, quoted in Schwartz 1988, 127–129.

{r}DOCUMENT 230: Summary of the Split Decision in the Case of Allan Bakke, 1978

The decision of the full Court was awaited with a sharp sense of anticipation. The decision, as delivered by Justice Powell, revealed that the Court was split. In six opinions, the justices concentrated on three basic issues.

* * *

Supreme Court's *Bakke* Rulings (1978)

Issue	Justices Voting "Yes"	Justices Voting "No"	Justices Arguing That the Issue Does Not Apply to This Case
Admission of Allan Bakke to medical school	Powell, Burger, Stevens, Rehnquist, Stewart	Brennan, White, Marshall, Blackmun	
Is the special admissions program used by Davis Medical School valid?	Brennan, White, Marshall, Blackmun	Powell, Burger, Stevens, Rehnquist, Stewart	
Is the consideration of the race of an applicant valid in admissions decisions?	Powell, Brennan, White, Marshall, Blackmun		Burger, Stevens, Rehnquist, Stewart

Source: 438 U.S. 265 (1978).

{r}DOCUMENT 231: *University of California Regents v. Bakke*: Justice Powell

The justices who found against the special admissions program acknowledged the value to the university of selecting a diverse student
body but declared the use of racial classifications to be unlawful.

* * *

[T]he attainment of a diverse student body . . . clearly is a constitutionally
permissible goal for an institution of higher education. . . .

Although a university must have wide discretion in making the sensitive judgments as to who should be admitted, constitutional limitations
protecting individual rights may not be disregarded. . . . As the interest
of diversity is compelling . . . the question remains whether the program's racial classification is necessary to promote this interest. . . .

In summary, it is evident that the Davis special admissions program
involves the use of an explicit racial classification never before counte-
nanced by this Court. It tells applicants who are not Negro, Asian, or

Chicano that they are totally excluded from a specific percentage of the seats in an entering class. . . .

The fatal flaw in petitioner's preferential program is its disregard of individual rights as guaranteed by the Fourteenth Amendment.

Source: 438 U.S. 265 at 311–312, 314–315, and 319–320 (1978).

{r}DOCUMENT 232: *University of California Regents v. Bakke*: Justices Brennan, White, Marshall, Blackmun

---

The justices who upheld the right of an educational institution to take race into account stressed the disadvantaged position of minorities in professions such as medicine.

* * *

Opinion of Mr. Justice Brennan, Mr. Justice White, Mr. Justice Marshall, and Mr. Justice Blackmun, concurring in the judgment [delivered by Mr. Justice Powell] in part and dissenting in part. . . .

The difficulty of the issue presented—whether government may use race-conscious programs to redress the continuing effects of past discrimination—and the mature consideration which each of our Brethren has brought to it have resulted in many opinions, no single one speaking for the Court. But this should not and must not mask the central meaning of today's opinions: Government may take race into account when it acts not to demean or insult any racial group, but to remedy disadvantages cast on minorities by past racial prejudice. . . .

Davis had a sound basis for believing that the problem of underrepresentation of minorities was substantial and chronic and that the problem was attributable to handicaps imposed on minority applicants by past and present racial discrimination. Until at least 1973, the practice of medicine in this country was, in fact, if not in law, largely the prerogative of whites. In 1950, for example, while Negroes constituted 10% of the total population, Negro physicians constituted only 2.2% of the total number of physicians. . . . By 1970, the gap between the proportion of Negroes in medicine and their proportion in the population had widened. . . . The number of Negro admittees to predominantly white medical schools, moreover, had declined in absolute numbers during the years 1955 to 1964. . . .

Davis clearly could conclude that the serious and persistent under-representation of minorities in medicine depicted by these statistics is the result of handicaps under which minority applicants labor as a consequence of a background of deliberate, purposeful discrimination against minorities in education and in society generally, as well as in the medical profession. . . .

Moreover, there is absolutely no basis for concluding that Bakke's rejection as a result of Davis' use of racial preference will affect him throughout his life in the same way as the segregation of the Negro schoolchildren in *Brown I* would have affected them. . . . [T]he use of racial preferences for remedial purposes does not inflict a pervasive injury upon individual whites in the sense that wherever they go or whatever they do there is a significant likelihood that they will be treated as second-class citizens because of their color. . . .

The Davis program . . . compensates applicants, who it is uncontested are fully qualified to study medicine, for educational disadvantages which it was reasonable to conclude were a product of state-fostered discrimination. Once admitted, these students must satisfy the same degree requirements as regularly admitted students; they are taught by the same faculty in the same classes; and their performance is evaluated by the same standards by which regularly admitted students are judged.

Source: 438 U.S. 265 at 324–325, 369–371, 375–376 (1978).

{r}DOCUMENT 233: *University of California Regents v. Bakke*: Justices White and Stevens

After the Supreme Court as a whole agreed to disagree on the case of Allan Bakke, the justices also submitted separate opinions that revealed profound conflict among them on certain points. For example, the opinion of White and that of Stevens (who was joined by four other justices) focused on Title VI, the former arguing that Bakke had no grounds to bring suit under that law and Stevens et al. insisting that he did.

* * *

Mr. Justice White

The role of Title VI was to terminate federal financial support for public and private institutions or programs that discriminated on the basis of race. . . . But there is no express provision for private actions to enforce Title VI, and it would be quite incredible if Congress, after so carefully attending to the matter of private actions in other Titles of the Act, intended silently to create a private cause of action to enforce Title VI.

Mr. Justice Stevens, with whom the Chief Justice, Mr. Justice Stewart, and Mr. Justice Rehnquist join, concurring in the judgment in part and dissenting in part.

To date, the courts, including this Court, have unanimously concluded or assumed that a private action may be maintained under Title VI. The United States has taken the same position. . . . Congress has repeatedly enacted legislation predicated on the assumption that Title VI may be enforced in a private action. The conclusion that an individual may maintain a private cause of action is amply supported in the legislative history of Title VI itself. . . .

Source: 438 U.S. 265 at 381, 408, 419–420 (1978).

{r}DOCUMENT 234: *University of California Regents v. Bakke*: Justice Marshall

In his separate opinion, Marshall delivered a detailed and eloquent treatise on the history of the African American struggle against the savagery of slavery and the corrosive consequences of an enduring racism in American life. He returned to the theme of the "cruel irony" that appeared in the memo that he circulated when his colleagues were still deliberating (Doc. 229), pillorying the notion that the U.S. Constitution had ever been color-blind. Describing congressional initiatives during Reconstruction as "affirmative action programs," Marshall suggested that by striking down the Davis affirmative action program, the Court was repeating the pattern of the post-Reconstruction Civil Rights and *Plessy* cases (Docs. 24, 25).

* * *

While I applaud the judgment of the Court that a university may consider race in its admissions process, it is more than a little ironic that, after several hundred years of class-based discrimination against Negroes, the Court is unwilling to hold that a class-based remedy for that discrimination is permissible. . . . [T]oday's judgment ignores the fact that for several hundred years Negroes have been discriminated against, not as individuals, but rather solely because of the color of their skins. . . . The experience of Negroes in America has been different in kind, not just in degree, from that of other ethnic groups. It is not merely the history of slavery alone but also that a whole people were marked as inferior by the law. And that mark has endured.

It is because of a legacy of unequal treatment that we now must permit the institutions of this society to give consideration to race in making decisions about who will hold the positions of influence, affluence, and prestige in America. . . . I do not believe that anyone can truly look into America's past and still find that a remedy for the effects of that past is impermissible. . . .

I fear that we have come full circle. After the Civil War our Government started several "affirmative action" programs. This Court in the *Civil Rights Cases* and *Plessy v. Ferguson* destroyed the movement toward complete equality. For almost a century no action was taken. . . . Then we had *Brown v. Board of Education* and the Civil Rights Acts of Congress followed by numerous affirmative-action programs. *Now*, we have this Court stepping in, this time to stop affirmative-action programs of the type used by the University of California.

Source: 438 U.S. 265 at 400–402 (1978).

{r}DOCUMENT 235: *University of California Regents v. Bakke*: Justice Blackmun

The separate reflections of Justice Blackmun were an attempt to reach beyond the divisions of the present and affirm the capacity of the United States to mature into a more perfect union.

* * *

I yield to no one in my earnest hope that the time will come when an "affirmative action" program is unnecessary. . . . I would hope that we could reach this stage within a decade at the most. But the story of *Brown v. Board of Education*, decided almost a quarter of a century ago, suggests that that hope is a slim one. At some time, however . . . the United States must and will reach a stage of maturity where action along this line is no longer necessary. . . .

It is worth noting, perhaps, that governmental preference has not been a stranger to our legal life. We see it in veterans' preferences. We see it in the aid-to-the-handicapped programs. We see it in the progressive income tax. We see it in the Indian programs.... [T]hese preferences exist and may not be ignored....

I suspect that it would be impossible to arrange an affirmative action program in a racially neutral way and have it successful. To ask that this be so is to demand the impossible. In order to get beyond racism, we must first take account of race. There is no other way. And in order to treat some persons equally, we must treat them differently. We cannot— we dare not—let the Equal Protection Clause perpetuate racial supremacy.

Source: 438 U.S. 265 at 403, 406, 407 (1978).

{r}DOCUMENT 236: Reaction to *Bakke* by Carter's Assistant Secretary of Education, Mary Frances Berry

Reactions to *Bakke* ranged among uncertainty, confusion, and dissatisfaction. Like many African Americans, President Carter's assistant secretary of education, Mary Frances Berry, would look back on the case as a crushing reversal for equality of opportunity.

* * *

When I went to Washington to run education in the Carter administration in 1977, one of the first things that happened was the head of my statistical agency came in to see me and she said, "Good news. The college-going rate for blacks is equal to the college-going rate for whites for the first time in American history." ... [T]his was just wonderful news. And I thought to myself, "Boy, if we can just keep up this progress for the next few years, just think of how far we will have come."

Little did I know that by 1978, there would be the *Bakke* case, which would have a chilling effect on the affirmative action efforts, and that there would be a redirection of the student aid programs away from the poor. And by 1979, those numbers that I'd been so happy about had started to go down....

One of the things that happened ... was a ... struggle over language. ... [W]hen you start talking about affirmative action as being "preferential treatment" you have already set up a situation where anybody who is the beneficiary of preferential treatment will lose. If you say "reverse discrimination" against somebody, it already sounds like a bad thing is happening, and you don't focus on what the injustice was.

Source: "Mary Frances Berry," in *Voices of Freedom, an Oral History of the Civil Rights Movement from the 1950s through the 1980s*, edited by Henry Hampton and Steve Fayer (New York: Bantam Books, 1990): 641–642, 644.

{r}DOCUMENT 237: Reaction to *Bakke* by Davis Medical School Graduate Toni Johnson-Chavis

From the vantage point of one of the minority students whom the Davis medical faculty admitted when they rejected the application of Allan Bakke, the special admissions program was valid and essential.

* * *

Ten years after *Bakke*, there are only two black pediatricians existing in Compton, California. [It was] considered an all-black city. It's largely Hispanic now. There are a large amount of poor people. The two black pediatricians both came from that period of time. One guy who came out of the inner city, Indianapolis, Indiana, and myself, who came from Compton, California. There is no one else who's made a selection to come in. If the two of us had not been trained in that era and were not here, who would fill the void now?

Source: "Toni Johnson-Chavis," in *Voices of Freedom, an Oral History of the Civil Rights Movement from the 1950s through the 1980s* edited by Henry Hampton and Steve Fayer (New York: Bantam Books, 1990): 645.

{r}DOCUMENT 238: The Medical Career of Allan Bakke from the Perspective of 1995

In 1995 journalist Nicholas Lemann followed up on the career of Allan Bakke.

* * *

Allan Bakke, after graduating from medical school, did his residency at the Mayo Clinic in Minnesota. Today he is an anesthesiologist in Rochester, Minn. Bakke doesn't speak to the press. . . . He does not appear to have set the world on fire as a doctor. He has no private practice and works on an interim basis, rather than as a staff physician, at Olmsted Community Hospital.

Source: Lemann 1995, 62.

{r}DOCUMENT 239: *Newsweek* Report on *Bakke*, July 10, 1978

After so much sound and fury observers were left asking what *Bakke* really signified.

* * *

"This is a landmark case, but we don't know what it marks," said University of Chicago law Prof. Philip B. Kurland. "We know it's terribly important, but we won't know for many years what the impact will be. . . ."

Source: "The Landmark Bakke Ruling," *Newsweek* (July 10, 1978): 31.

{d}DOCUMENT 240: Cartoon by Paine, 1970s

While the case of Allan Bakke was working its way toward the U.S. Supreme Court, disabled activists continued to challenge the policies and stereotypes limiting their full participation in human society. The following cartoon from the mid-1970s offers a commentary on the gulf between standard public perception and the capabilities and aspirations of disabled citizens.

Getting Around

"I suppose the hardest part to accept is
the not being able to get around!"

Source: Raymond Cheever, ed., *Laugh with Accent* (Bloomington, IL: Accept Special Publication, 1975).

{d}DOCUMENT 241: Emergence in the 1970s of the American Coalition of Citizens with Disabilities (ACCD)

A widening coalition was taking shape among disabled organizations. Just as women a decade earlier had formed progressively wider and more coordinated networks, culminating in the National Organization for Women (Doc. 140), disabled groups began to link up with one another. In a manner again reminiscent of NOW's origins—with "radicals" whose first planning sessions took place in the middle of a gathering of the moderate, federally sponsored President's Commission on the Status of Women—the American Coalition of Citizens with Disabilities emerged from caucusing among the more "radical" participants at an annual meeting of the moderate and federally sponsored President's Committee on Employment of the Handicapped. From interviews with the original organizers historian Richard Scotch reconstructed the beginnings of ACCD.

* * *

The annual meetings of the President's Committee on Employment of the Handicapped [PCEH] provided a forum for communication among some of the younger, more militant disability rights activists. Several remained in contact in the times between meetings, and an evolving network helped to organize the demonstrations against the presidential vetoes of the Rehabilitation Act in 1972 and 1973 [Docs. 198, 199].

This loose network was formed into an organization at the 1974 PCEH meeting. Judy Heumann and Eunice Fiorito [Docs. 164, 165, 199] of Disabled in Action of New York, along with others, organized workshop sessions that met in the middle of the lobby of the conference hotel. . . . About 150 people got together to discuss discrimination issues not included in the formal program, and this group organized a cross-disability organization . . . the ACCD.

A steering committee was formed and ACCD held its first formal meeting the following year.

Source: Scotch 1984, 82–83.

{d}DOCUMENT 242: Amendments to the Vocational Rehabilitation Act of 1973, December 7, 1974

High on the agenda of the ACCD was publication of HEW regulations for Section 504 (Docs. 200, 201). The expectation that these regulations were forthcoming had been building since 1974, when the 1973 act was amended. The amendments, revised the definition of "handicapped individual," which had been limited only to persons who were "employable." The amendments also laid the groundwork for a White House Conference on Handicapped Individuals (Doc. 249).

* * *

An Act . . . to make certain technical and clarifying amendments. . . .
Section III (a). . . . ["Handicapped individual"] means any person who (A) has a physical or mental impairment which substantially limits one or more of such person's major life activities, (B) has a record of such an impairment, or (C) is regarded as having such an impairment. . . .

TITLE III. . . .
Section 302 (a) The President is authorized to call a White House Conference on Handicapped Individuals . . . in order to develop recommen-

dations and stimulate a national assessment of problems, and solutions to such problems, facing individuals with handicaps.

Source: U.S. Statutes at Large 88, Pt. 2 (December 7, 1974): 1617, 1619, 1631.

{d}DOCUMENT 243: HEW Secretary Joseph Califano Recalling the Struggle in the 1970s over Section 504

In the summer of 1975 staff members in the Office of Civil Rights submitted a draft version of Section 504 regulations to their boss, HEW director David Mathews. As all interested parties awaited his action, President Gerald Ford issued an executive order (11914) mandating timely publication of the regulations. Also in 1976, a federal district court found in favor of the Action League for Physically Handicapped Adults (ALPHA), which had sued the government for not publishing the 504 guidelines.

Paralleling court action by ALPHA was direct action by ACCD (Doc. 241), which held demonstrations in the office of the HEW director, David Mathews, in the spring of 1976. Those demonstrations, coupled with promises of others to be carried out at the upcoming Republican National Convention, moved Mathews to publish in the *Federal Register* "a notice of intent to publish proposed rules" (Scotch 1984, 93). After the thirty-day comment period required for such a notice, the Office of Civil Rights staff revised the draft regulations in light of public comment and resubmitted them to Mathews in January 1977, just as his term was expiring. The HEW secretary of the new Carter administration, Joseph Califano, inherited the issue of Section 504. Perceptions of what happened next vary according to who is offering the account. Califano included his recollections of the 504 struggle in his autobiography, *Governing America.*

* * *

From the moment I glanced at it [Section 504], I knew we were on the brink of another, though very different, civil rights revolution. . . . I passed the word that I intended to take ample time to review the regulations and restructure them. . . . Meanwhile, handicapped groups printed signs and buttons: "Sign 504!" . . .

The handicapped groups announced that they would demonstrate at each of the ten HEW regional offices. I welcomed the prospect. . . . I hoped the demonstrations would raise the public's awareness of the pending regulations.

Source: Joseph Califano, *Governing America* (New York: Simon and Schuster, 1981): 259, 260.

{d}DOCUMENT 244: The 1977 "504" Struggle as Reported by the National Council on Disability

In early April 1977 the ACCD took their "Sign 504" message directly into Califano's office and ten other regional HEW offices around the country. A retrospective account of this action is included in a history of the Americans with Disabilities Act prepared under the auspices of the National Council on Disability.

* * *

In Washington, . . . [m]ost of the activists . . . remained outside the HEW building to make sure the protest stayed in the eye of the media. A second group of about fifty activists . . . stealthily entered the building in small groups and then gathered in the waiting room outside Califano's office. . . . When the protesters tried to order food around 5:00 P.M. the guards ripped the phones from the wall. Security also shadowed activists to the restrooms to prevent use of public phones. . . . The protesters went without food and stayed over night—sleeping on couches, desks, and the floor. On Wednesday, April 6 Secretary Califano met with the protesters and asked them to leave. But he would not commit to signing the regulations immediately. The demonstrators discussed staying and being forcibly arrested, but voted to end the protest that afternoon instead.

The longest demonstration was in San Francisco, where the group refused to leave the HEW building until the regulations were signed. . . . [L]argely due to the intervention of Governor Jerry Brown, protesters were ultimately allowed to stay in the building and receive outside assistance. Within days, the number of people dwelling inside the building grew to well over 100.

[T]heir actions left Secretary Califano little choice but to sign the regulations without change, which he finally did on April 28.

Source: Equality of Opportunity, the Making of the Americans with Disabilities Act (Washington, DC: National Council on Disability, July 1997): 23, 24.

{d}DOCUMENT 245: Califano Aide Peter Libassi's Recollections of the "504" Confrontations of April 1977

In an interview seven years later, an aide of Califano's, Peter Libassi, indicated that, as interviewer Richard Scotch summarized, "Califano was publicly conciliatory and privately fuming" during the sit-ins, especially the one in his office.

* * *

They stayed in the HEW building . . . and Joe was really upset about that. . . . [His attitude was] . . . It's bad politics. It's bad for the country. It's bad for the causes to think that sit-in demonstrations were the way the government was going to make basic public policy.

[When law enforcement figures recommended evicting the demonstrators, the central issue for Califano was public relations.]

We agreed that evicting the blind and the halt and the lame on TV was not quite what the Carter Administration needed in its first months in office.

Source: Scotch 1984, 113–114.

{d}DOCUMENT 246: Regulations for Section 504 of the Vocational Rehabilitation Act, Published May 1977

Scotch also interviewed sit-in participants who were convinced that without their protest the regulations would have been substantially weakened. The 504 Regulations appeared in the *Federal Register*.

* * *

Nondiscrimination on the Basis of Handicap in Programs and Activities Receiving or Benefiting from Federal Financial Assistance . . . Effective June 3, 1977. . . .

SUPPLEMENTARY INFORMATION

Background. . . .

Section 504 . . . represents the first Federal civil rights law protecting the rights of handicapped persons and reflects a national commitment to end discrimination on the basis of handicap. . . . It establishes a mandate to end discrimination and to bring handicapped persons into the mainstream of American life. The Secretary intends vigorously to implement and enforce that mandate. . . .

Overview of Regulation

The regulation is divided into seven subparts. . . .

Subpart C sets forth the central requirement of the regulation—program accessibility. All new facilities are required to be constructed so as to be readily accessible to and usable by handicapped persons. Every existing facility need not be made physically accessible, but all recipients [of federal funds] must ensure that programs conducted in those facilities are made accessible. . . .

Subpart D is concerned with preschool, elementary, and secondary education. Its provisions have been closely coordinated with those of the Education for All Handicapped Children Act of 1975 [Doc. 221]. . . .

Subpart G [deals with procedures]. The Secretary has adopted the title VI [of the 1964 Civil Rights Act] complaint and enforcement procedures for use in implementing section 504.

Source: Federal Register 42, no. 86 (May 4, 1977): 22676, 22677, 22694.

{d}DOCUMENT 247: *U.S. News & World Report,* ". . . New Rules Stir Turmoil," May 9, 1977

The regulations for Section 504 provoked immediate outcries from those who would be held accountable for meeting them, particularly education systems and institutions. A *U.S. News and World Report* account quoted a representative of the National Association of Secondary School Principals.

* * *

"In our zeal to be more humane to those less fortunate, we sometimes lose our sense of proportion. Some school administrators are literally being pushed to the point of rebellion on the issue of compliance with these sweeping regulations."

Source: "Rights for the Handicapped—New Rules Stir Turmoil," *U.S. News & World Report* (May 9, 1977): 84.

{d}DOCUMENT 248: *Nelda K. Barnes v. Converse College,* July 13, 1977

The first test of the 504 regulations in federal court was not long in coming. A deaf student enrolling in summer school classes at Converse College in Spartanburg, South Carolina, precipitated court action when she requested that the college pay for a sign language interpreter. Although a district court ruled in her favor, the disgruntled judge also issued a sharp critique of HEW.

* * *

Nelda K. Barnes is an English teacher at the Cedar Springs School for the Deaf and Blind, Spartanburg, South Carolina. . . . Plaintiff is periodically required by the State Department of Education to earn additional college credits to maintain her "out-of-field" permit to teach in the public schools of South Carolina. She must earn six hours of graduate English credit in summer school in order to teach in the Fall, and has been accepted academically at Converse College. Plaintiff requires an interpreter to participate in classroom activities. . . .

Defendant, Converse College, would, in this action, be faced with the relatively minor financial damage of an interpreter's fee which has been estimated at somewhat less than $1,000. Defendant's chief concern, however, is not the cost of the interpreter in this particular action . . . [but] with the financial burden which it may ultimately have to bear as a result of compliance . . . in the future. . . . [T]his court is most sympathetic with the plight of . . . a private institution which may well be forced to make substantial expenditures of private monies to accommodate the federal government's generosity. Converse College is subject to regulation . . . because it receives federal financial assistance. None of this . . . assistance, however, was given . . . for the purpose of providing auxiliary aids for the handicapped. . . .

Despite the obvious inequities inherent in the enforcement of this regulation . . . this court is bound by law to give it effect. . . .

Therefore, the defendant . . . will procure and compensate a qualified interpreter of its choosing for the purpose of assisting the plaintiff in her summer school classes.

Source: 436 F. Supp. 635 at 636, 638, 639 (1977).

{d}DOCUMENT 249: Recommendations from the White House Conference on Handicapped Individuals, 1977

In the same month that the controversial 504 regulations became final, the White House sponsored a Conference on Handicapped Individuals. The concept of such a conference was a carryover from the Ford administration, where it had been viewed with distrust in many quarters. In a memorandum to the president, White House staffer Jim Cannon observed that "such conferences tend to produce few substantive results while automatically generating pressures for higher funding regardless of need" (quoted in Berkowitz 1987, 209). Held in the early days of the Carter administration, the conference involved 3,700 participants from every U.S. state and territory. The following summary information, from a member of the Implementation Advisory Committee established to follow up on conference recommendations, indicates the thrust and scope of those recommendations.

* * *

The entire conference record [of the 1977 White House Conference on Handicapped Individuals (WHCHI)] overwhelmingly reflects that formal articulation of a right is one matter; the general enjoyment of that right is quite another. It should not be necessary to vindicate the basic rights of handicapped individuals on a case by case basis in local communities throughout the Nation. Instead, legislation must be restated with greater force and precision. More adequate administrative mechanisms for enforcement are needed. . . .

[T]he various actions voted and recommended as a result of WHCHI were broken down and classified under these major headings:

A. Architectural Accessibility and Safety
B. Attitudes and Awareness
C. Civil Rights
D. Communication
E. Cultural and Leisure Activities
F. Economics
G. Education
H. Government Organizations and Practices
I. Health
J. Housing
K. Services to Disabled Veterans

L. Special Populations—Handicapped Aged Persons, Minority Handicapped Persons

M. Transportation

Source: U.S. Commission on Civil Rights 1980, 33–34.

{r/g}DOCUMENT 250: U.S. Commission on Civil Rights, Evaluation of Federal Civil Rights Enforcement, 1977

As this agenda laid out by the White House conference added to the many pressures forcing HEW to gear up to guarantee implementation of Section 504, pressure was also building for a reorganization of federal civil rights enforcement agencies to improve their efficiency and effectiveness. The U.S. Commission on Civil Rights was one source of this pressure.

* * *

The Equal Employment Opportunity Coordinating Council, created by Congress in 1972 to eliminate conflict, competition, duplication, and inconsistency among the units of Federal Government responsible for implementing equal employment opportunity law, has almost completely failed to achieve its purpose. From July 1975 until it ceased being active in November 1976, it came to an agreement on only one major issue— affirmative action—and even this agreement glossed over areas of dissension, focusing instead on general principles. . . .

This Commission reaffirms its recommendation for the creation of a single agency [to coordinate all civil rights enforcement in the area of employment].

Source: U.S. Commission on Civil Rights, *To Eliminate Employment Discrimination: A Sequel. The Federal Civil Rights Enforcement Effort, 1977* (December 1977): 332, 333.

{r/g}DOCUMENT 251: Additional Criticism of the Federal Agencies Responsible for Civil Rights Enforcement, 1970s

Georgetown University legal expert Theodore V. Purcell urged a two- or three-year study to determine the most rational and promising course of reform.

* * *

In recent years, the EEOC has come under increasingly severe criticism from employers, unions, civil rights groups, the GAO [General Accounting Office], and congressional committees. Long delays in resolving complaints meant injustices to both employers and employees. There have been severe personnel and organizational weaknesses within the EEOC. We can note at least five deficiencies . . . but especially . . . the internal bad management of the EEOC. It had five chairmen in its first ten years, with its last chairman resigning after only eight months.

The OFCCP [the Labor Department's Office of Federal Contract Compliance Programs] has also been criticized by the U.S. Commission on Civil Rights, Urban America, the National Urban Coalition, the Potomac Institute, and the Council on Economic Priorities. . . . Employers criticized its Revised Order Nos. 4 and 14 as intolerably detailed, making for mountains of paper work; they were unhappy with compliance officers as ill-informed about industrial relations matters and excessively rule-conscious. . . .

In my judgment, because of the piecemeal growth of the last 13 years, the entire federal compliance program has become a patchwork apparatus beautiful mainly to some lawyers' eyes. Congress might well set up a bipartisan advisory commission to study the overall simplification and unification of federal equal employment opportunity regulatory agencies, regulations, and practices.

Source: Theodore V. Purcell, "Management and Affirmative Action in the Late Seventies," in *Equal Rights and Industrial Relations*, edited by Farrell E. Bloch et al. (Madison, WI: Industrial Relations Research Association, 1977): 80–81, 83.

{r/g/d}DOCUMENT 252: Executive Order 12067, 1978

President Carter chose to issue an executive order by which he eliminated the Equal Employment Opportunity Coordinating Council, established by Richard Nixon, and consolidated enforcement authority within the EEOC.

* * *

By virtue of the authority vested in me as President of the United States by the Constitution and statutes of the United States . . . it is ordered as follows:

1–1. *Implementation of Reorganization Plan.*

1–101. The transfer to the Equal Employment Opportunity Commission of all the functions of the Equal Employment Opportunity Coordinating

Council, and the termination of that Council. . . .

1–201. The Equal Employment Opportunity Commission shall provide leadership and coordination to the efforts of Federal departments and agencies to enforce all Federal statutes, Executive orders, regulations, and policies which require equal employment opportunity without regard to race, color, religion, sex, national origin, age, or handicap. It shall strive to maximize effort, promote efficiency, and eliminate conflict, competition, duplication and inconsistency among the operations, functions and jurisdictions of the Federal departments and agencies having responsibility for enforcing such statutes, Executive orders, regulations and policies. . . .

Source: Federal Register 43 (June 30, 1978): 28967.

{g}DOCUMENT 253: Author Joan Abramson Questions EEOC Capabilities, 1977

Whether the EEOC would be able to meet the expectations set forth by President Carter was an open question, for reasons spelled out in a 1979 study of sex discrimination by Joan Abramson.

* * *

Eleanor Holmes Norton, Carter's first appointee as EEOC chair, . . . claims that when she took over there was "nothing in the agency" that did not need drastic overhauling. . . .

Perhaps the most persistent criticism of EEOC in the past has been directed at the agency's inability to overcome its case backlog. The backlog grew from over 15,000 cases in 1969 to close to 130,000 cases in 1977. . . . Every effort to bring the backlog under control had ended in failure. . . .

Norton split complaints of discrimination into two categories: backlogged cases and incoming cases. Some investigative units in each district office were assigned exclusively to handle cases already on the books. . . .

According to Peter Robertson, EEOC, who in 1978 served as a director of Program Planning and Review, the new standard for settlement of [backlogged] cases is that both parties are in agreement. . . .

[T]here are thousands of people who have filed charges of discrimination over the years who will get no remedy or who, at best, will gain a few thousand dollars or perhaps a belated promotion for their trouble. There is no guarantee in the system that, once they have settled, they will not immediately experience retaliation. There is no guarantee, and little likelihood, that having filed a complaint, settlement will place them in a nondiscriminatory situation.

Source: Joan Abramson, *Old Boys, New Women, the Politics of Sex Discrimination* (New York: Praeger, 1979): 56, 57, 58–59, 62, 63.

{r/g}DOCUMENT 254: 1978 Uniform Guidelines on Employee Selection Procedures

In this consolidating of its authority, the EEOC finally prevailed in a long struggle over the issue of employment tests. Between 1966 and 1978 a dozen versions of guidelines for the use of such tests by government and employers with government contracts were put forward. They came from various sources: the EEOC (1966, 1970, 1976, 1978), the OFCC (1968, 1971), the Equal Employment Opportunity Coordinating Council (1973, 1974, 1975, 1976), and a cooperative effort by the Department of Labor, the Civil Service Commission, and the Justice Department (1976). The versions promoted by the EEOC required meticulous validation of all tests as predictors of job performance and for assessing the tests' effect on designated racial groups. Other government agencies, business and industrial spokespersons, and industrial psychologists advocated less stringent guidelines. They maintained that the EEOC requirements were unduly—and in many cases impossibly— costly and complicated. Critics accused the EEOC of attempting to eliminate employment tests altogether, which—in the critics' view— meant the end of hiring according to individual merit and the entrenchment of hiring policies designed just to fill racial and gender quotas.

EEOC adopted the stringent version of guidelines for testing in 1978.

* * *

Section 3. Discrimination defined: Relationship between use of selection procedures and discrimination. . . .

A. The use of any selection procedure which has an adverse impact on the hiring, promotion, or other employment or membership opportunities of members of any race, sex or ethnic group will be considered to be discriminatory and inconsistent with these guidelines, unless the procedure has been validated in accordance with these guidelines. . . .

Section 4. Information on impact. . . .

A. Each user should maintain and have available for inspection records or other information which will disclose the impact which its tests and other selection procedures have upon employment opportunities of persons by identifiable race, sex or ethnic groups as set forth in subparagraph B below. . . .

B. The records called for by this section are to be maintained by sex, and the following races and ethnic groups: Blacks (Negroes), American Indians (including Alaskan Natives), Asians (including Pacific Islanders), Hispanic (including persons of Mexican, Puerto Rican, Cuban, Central or South American, or other Spanish origin or culture, regardless of race), whites (Caucasians) other than Hispanic. . . .

Section 5. General standards for validity studies. . . .

B. Evidence of the validity of a test or other selection procedure by a criterion-related validity study should consist of empirical data demonstrating that the selection procedure is predictive of or significantly correlated with important elements of job performance. . . . Evidence of the validity of a test or other selection procedure by a content validity study should consist of data showing that the content of the selection procedure is representative of important aspects of performance on the job for which the candidates are to be evaluated. . . . Evidence of the validity of a test or other selection procedure through a construct validity study should consist of data showing that the procedure measures the degree to which candidates have identifiable characteristics which have been determined to be important in successful performance in the job for which the candidates are to be evaluated. . . .

Section 6. Use of alternate selection procedures . . . to eliminate adverse impact. . . .

A. A user may choose to utilize alternative selection procedures in order to eliminate adverse impact or as part of an affirmative action program. . . .

Section 13. Affirmative Action.

B. These guidelines are also intended to encourage the adoption and implementation of voluntary affirmative action programs by users who have no obligation under Federal law to adopt them; but are not intended to impose any new obligations in that regard.

Source: Federal Register 43 (August 25, 1978): 38297, 38298, 38299, 38300.

{r/g}DOCUMENT 255: "Comments of the Ad Hoc Group on Proposed Uniform Guidelines," 1978

As soon as the "Uniform Guidelines" appeared in the *Federal Register*, an ad hoc group of private businessmen, government personnel officials, and academics offered a critique. Within the group were representatives of such bodies as the National Association of Manufacturers, the Labor Policy Association, the American Iron and Steel Institute, the College and University Placement Association, the U.S. Chamber of Commerce, AT&T, Ford Motor Company, General Electric, IBM, Sears Roebuck, and "a substantial number of prominent industrial and measurement psychologists" associated with the American Psychological Association and its Division of Industrial-Organizational Psychology. Additionally, the group encompassed the National League of Cities, the Conference of Mayors, the Conference of State Legislatures, and the Council of State Governments.

* * *

Section 6A suggests that as part of an affirmative action program or to avoid adverse impact, users "may" consciously select alternatives.... Nothing is said about the job-relatedness of these alternatives or how "general competency" or "qualified" is to be determined....

The concern raised by publication of Section 6A is intensified when one reviews reports ... that EEOC ... may intend to ... discourage validation and encourage invalid race, ethnic and sex-conscious selection decisions. This possibility, perhaps inadvertently, is enhanced by remarks of EEOC Chairman Norton at the December 22, 1977 meeting:

There is not any way in which black people tomorrow as a group are going to, no matter what kind of test you give them, score the same way that white people score.... I can't live with that. I think employers can. And I think test validation gives them an A-1 out ... I sincerely believe that tests do not tell us very much about who is qualified to do the job.... Thus, I think that by giving alternatives, we relieve especially minorities of the frustration they find inevitably in taking validated tests.

While Ms. Norton has consistently supported (in other statements) the right of public and private employers to hire the best qualified individual, this seeming encouragement of alternatives to validation is not easy to reconcile with that commitment.

It is counterproductive, as well as illegal, to say: "you must take a route other than valid selection procedures." It is nearly as dangerous to encourage the use of unvalidated selection procedures on a voluntary basis where the alternatives recommended are of doubtful legality if used other than to remedy proved past discrimination. The least that should be expected from government is to recommend and require only what is lawful.

Source: "Comments of the Ad Hoc Group on the Proposed Uniform Guidelines," February 17, 1978, reprinted in Mary Green Miner and John B. Miner, *Employee*

Selection within the Law (Washington, DC: Bureau of National Affairs, 1978): 471–472.

Advocates of woman's rights remained active during reorganization of federal civil rights enforcement and while the national spotlight had focused on a white male in the *Bakke* case. Feminist legal scholars noted that "not a single opinion in *Bakke* indicated that sex, like race, should be a suspect classification subject to strict scrutiny" (Hoff 1991, 266). What is more, on an issue that was emerging as particularly vital to women—the entitlement of pregnant women to employees' benefits—the Court had come to a very discouraging position, from a woman's rights point of view. The surge of feminist activism and coalition-building around this issue eventually led to passage of the Pregnancy Disability Act, signed by President Carter in October 1978.

Women's organizations had targeted maternity benefits as a critical issue by the time of the EEOC suit against AT&T, which resulted in the first of many consent decrees against major corporations (Documents 202–208). The AT&T decree failed to incorporate guarantees on this issue, but attorneys for AT&T female employees expressed optimism that ongoing court action would soon resolve the issue in their favor (Lisa Cronin Wohl, "Liberating Ma Bell," *MS* [November 1973]: 94). That optimism went unrewarded in two Supreme Court rulings—*Geduldig v. Aiello* (1974) and *General Electric v. Gilbert* (1976)—where the Supreme Court held that employers were not legally bound to provide insurance coverage for disabilities related to maternity in the way that they provided coverage for other disabilities. In a third case, *Nashville Gas Company v. Nora D. Satty* (1978), the Court distinguished between an employer's right to deny a pregnant worker sick pay and the worker's right to retain her seniority while she is absent for maternity reasons.

{g}DOCUMENT 256: *Geduldig, Director, Department of Human Resources Development v. Aeillo et al.,* June 17, 1974

In *Geduldig v. Aiello* four women who worked for the state of California challenged the policy of excluding pregnancy from coverage by the state disability insurance system. A Supreme Court majority ruled that the exclusion was constitutional and that the state had the right to keep the costs of the insurance program down by choosing to not cover pregnancy.

* * *

Mr. JUSTICE STEWART delivered the opinion of the Court.

For almost 30 years California has administered a disability insurance system. . . . The appellees brought this action to challenge the constitutionality of a provision of the program that . . . excludes from coverage certain disabilities resulting from pregnancy. . . .

We cannot agree that the exclusion of this disability from coverage amounts to invidious discrimination under the Equal Protection Clause. . . . Although California has created a program to insure most risks of employment disability, it has not chosen to insure all such risks. . . .

There is nothing in the Constitution . . . that requires the State to subordinate or compromise its legitimate interests solely to create a more comprehensive social insurance program than it already has.

Source: 417 U.S. 484 at 486, 494, 495, 496 (1973).

{g}DOCUMENT 257: Dissenting Opinion in *Geduldig v. Aiello*, 1974

Justices Brennan, Douglas, and Marshall dissented from the majority decision in *Geduldig*.

* * *

Mr. JUSTICE BRENNAN, with whom Mr. JUSTICE DOUGLAS and Mr. JUSTICE MARSHALL join, dissenting.

[In the California disability insurance program] workers are compensated for . . . voluntary disabilities such as cosmetic surgery or sterilization, disabilities unique to sex or race such as prostatectomies or sickle-cell anemia. . . .

[T]he economic effects caused by pregnancy-related disabilities are functionally indistinguishable from the effects caused by any other disability. [B]y singling out for less favorable treatment a gender-linked disability peculiar to women, the State has created a double standard for disability compensation. . . . Such dissimilar treatment of men and women, on the basis of physical characteristics inextricably linked to one sex, inevitably constitutes sex discrimination.

Source: 417 U.S. 484 at 497, 500–501 (1973).

{g}DOCUMENT 258: *General Electric Co. v. Gilbert et al.,* 1976

Two and a half years after the *Geduldig* ruling the Supreme Court responded to a similar case involving women employees of the General Electric Corporation. Two lower courts, finding in favor of the women, had decided that because *Geduldig* had been argued on the basis of the Equal Protection Clause of the Fourteenth Amendment, it was not applicable to *General Electric v. Gilbert*, which relied primarily on Title VII. The Supreme Court majority rejected the lower courts' views and reversed their decisions.

* * *

Mr. JUSTICE REHNQUIST delivered the opinion of the Court.

The Court of Appeals was . . . wrong in concluding that the reasoning of *Geduldig* was not applicable to an action under Title VII. Since . . . a finding of sex-based discrimination . . . must trigger . . . the finding of an unlawful employment practice [under Title VII], *Geduldig* is precisely in point in . . . holding that . . . exclusion of pregnancy from a disability-benefits plan . . . is not a gender-based discrimination. . . .

The Plan . . . is nothing more than an insurance package, which covers some risks, but excludes others . . . [G]ender-based discrimination does not result simply because an employer's disability-benefits plan is less than all-inclusive. . . .

Source: 429 U.S. 125 at 127, 136, 138–139 (1976).

{g}DOCUMENT 259: Dissent of Justices Brennan and Marshall in *General Electric v. Gilbert,* 1976

As in *Geduldig*, Justices Brennan and Marshall dissented.

* * *

[T]he Court's assumption that General Electric engaged in a gender-neutral risk-assignment process is purely fanciful. . . . Surely it offends common sense to suggest . . . that a classification revolving around pregnancy is not, at the minimum, strongly "sex related." . . .

[T]he plan . . . insures risks such as prostatectomies, vasectomies, and circumcisions that are specific to the reproductive system of men and for which there exist no female counterparts covered by the plan. Again, pregnancy affords the only disability, sex-specific or otherwise, that is excluded from coverage.

Source: 429 U.S. 125 at 148, 149, 152 (1976).

{g}DOCUMENT 260: *Nashville Gas Co. v. Satty*, December 6, 1977

While holding fast to their previous rulings that denying disability benefits for pregnancy was constitutional, the Court majority in *Nashville Gas Co. v. Satty* did rule against an employer who denied seniority rights to workers on maternity leave.

* * *

Mr. JUSTICE REHNQUIST delivered the opinion of the Court.

Petitioner requires pregnant employees to take a formal leave of absence. The employee does not receive sick pay while on pregnancy leave. She also loses all accumulated job seniority. . . .

We conclude that petitioner's policy of denying accumulated seniority to female employees returning from pregnancy leave violates . . . Title VII. . . .

[P]etitioner's policy of not awarding sick-leave pay to pregnant employees is legally indistinguishable from the disability-insurance program upheld in *Gilbert* [Doc. 258].

Source: 434 U.S. 136 at 137, 139, 143 (1977).

{g}DOCUMENT 261: Statements of Wendy Williams and Susan Deller Ross before the Subcommittee on Labor of the U.S. Senate Committee on Human Resources, April 16, 1977

Feminists took their case against the Supreme Court rulings directly to Congress in hearings held by subcommittees of the House and the Senate in April 1977. Among those testifying in both hearings were Wendy W. Williams, assistant professor of law at Georgetown University, and Susan Deller Ross, a staff attorney for the American Civil Liberties Union.

* * *

A. Susan Deller Ross

I am appearing today on behalf of the campaign to end discrimination against pregnant workers. The campaign is a broad-based group of women's rights organizations, civil rights groups, labor unions and other public interest groups formed just 1 week after the Supreme Court handed down its decision in *GE* [Doc. 258]. . . .

Employers routinely fire pregnant workers, refuse to hire them, strip them of seniority rights and deny them sick leave and medical benefits given other workers.

Such policies have a lifetime impact on women's careers. . . . Thus, discrimination against women workers cannot be eradicated unless the root discrimination, based on pregnancy and childbirth, is also eliminated.

B. Wendy W. Williams

The starting point for analysis is the fact that around 80 percent of all women become pregnant at some point in their worklives. Moreover, even women who do not actually become pregnant are, until they pass childbearing age, viewed by employers as among the *potentially* pregnant. Thus all women are subject to the effect of the stereotype that women are marginal workers. . . .

The intangible effects of employer pregnancy policies on the women workers' psyche, motivation and commitment are incalculable. At some level, women do understand the treatment of pregnancy as a message to women workers: "You have chosen the woman's role of pregnancy and motherhood and have thereby forfeited your place and rights in the workforce. Go home where you belong." Thus is the prophecy that women are marginal workers with no lasting commitment to the work-force reinforced, and the prophecy becomes self-fulfilling.

Source: Hearings before the Subcommittee on Labor of the Committee on Human Resources, U.S. Senate, Ninety-Fifth Congress, First Session (April 26, 1977): 117–118, 130, 137–138.

HR 6075 and its Senate counterpart, S.995, passed and was signed by President Carter in October 1978. The new legislation extended Title VII of the 1964 Civil Rights Act (Docs. 119, 121, 122) to prohibit all discrimination on the basis of pregnancy.

{r}DOCUMENT 262: *United Steelworkers of America v. Weber,* 1979

Feminists and other advocates of increasing economic and social opportunity did not have a monopoly on persistence. Their opponents also persisted and repeatedly leveled the charge of "reverse discrimination" against race- and gender-conscious policies. That charge worked its way again onto the docket of the U.S. Supreme Court in the 1979 case *United Steelworkers of America, AFL-CIO-CLC v. Weber et al.* Brian Weber was a white laboratory technician in the Kaiser Aluminum plant in Gramercy, Louisiana. The plant was included in a "master collective bargaining agreement" that created a training program for craft workers (of whom there were only 1.83 percent African American workers in a 39 percent African American workforce in the Gramercy area) and stipulated that 50 percent of the trainees were to be African American until the percentage of African American craft workers was "commensurate" with the percentage of African Americans in the workforce. Weber applied for the program and was not accepted. Three of the African American employees who were accepted had less seniority than he did. He sued in Federal District Court and won. The case went to the Federal Court of Appeals, which upheld his victory. A Supreme Court majority of five (Justices Brennan, who wrote the opinion, Stewart, White, Marshall, and Blackmun) overturned the district and appeals courts' decisions. Supporters of affirmative action, while pleased with the outcome, realized how precariously close the Court was to an opposite conclusion. If Justice Powell (who was ill) and Justice Stevens (who excused himself from the case because the law firm for which he once worked had handled legal work for Kaiser) had participated, they might well have sided with Weber. Their positions in the *Bakke* case indicated that this would have been so. Furthermore, friends of affirmative action could not miss the ominous anger with which the dissenters in *Weber*, Justices Burger and Rehnquist, denounced the majority opinion.

* * *

A. Majority Opinion delivered by Justice Brennan

The only question before us is ... whether Title VII *forbids* private employers and Unions from voluntarily agreeing upon bona fide affirmative action plans that accord racial preferences in the manner and for the purpose provided in the Kaiser-USWA plan. . . .

Had Congress meant to prohibit all race-conscious affirmative action ... it easily could have ... by providing that Title VII would not require or *permit* racially preferential integration efforts. But Congress did not choose such a course. . . .

We therefore hold that Title VII's prohibition ... against racial discrimination does not condemn all private, voluntary, race-conscious affirmative action plans. . . .

At the same time, the plan does not unnecessarily trammel the interests of the white employees. The plan does not require the discharge of white workers and their replacement with new black hirees. . . . Nor does the plan create an absolute bar to the advancement of white employees; half of those trained in the program will be white. Moreover, the plan is a temporary measure; it is not intended to maintain racial balance. . . .

We conclude, therefore, that the adoption of the Kaiser-USWA plan for the Gramercy plant falls within the area of discretion left by Title VII to the private sector voluntarily to adopt affirmative action plans designed to eliminate conspicuous racial imbalance in traditionally segregated job categories. Accordingly, the judgment of the Court of Appeals for the Fifth Circuit is *Reversed*.

B. Concurring opinion of Justice Blackmun

In his dissent from the decision of the United States Court of Appeals for the Fifth Circuit, Judge Wisdom pointed out that . . . the broad prohibition against discrimination places the employer and the union on what he accurately described as a "high tightrope without a net beneath them." . . . If Title VII is read literally, on the one hand they face liability for past discrimination against blacks, and on the other they face liability to whites for any voluntary preferences adopted to mitigate the effects of prior discrimination against blacks. . . .

Weber's reading of Title VII . . . places voluntary compliance with Title VII in profound jeopardy. The only way for the employer and the union to keep their footing on the "tightrope" it creates would be to eschew all forms of voluntary affirmative action. Even a whisper of emphasis on minority recruiting would be forbidden. . . . Judge Wisdom concluded that employers and unions who had committed "arguable violations" of Title VII should be free to make reasonable responses without fear of liability to whites. . . . Preferential hiring along the lines of the Kaiser program is a reasonable response for the employer.

C. Dissent from Chief Justice Burger

It is often observed that hard cases make bad law. I suspect there is some truth to that adage, for the "hard" cases always tempt judges to exceed the limits of their authority, as the Court does today by totally rewriting a crucial part of Title VII. . . . [The late Justice Benjamin Cardozo] no doubt had this type of case in mind when he wrote:

The judge . . . is not a knight-errant, roaming at will in pursuit of his own ideal of beauty or of goodness. . . . He is not to yield to spasmodic sentiment, to vague, and unregulated benevolence. . . .

What Cardozo tells us is to beware of the "good result," achieved by judicially unauthorized or intellectually dishonest means on the appealing notion that the desirable ends justify the improper judicial means. For there is always the danger that the seeds of the precedent sown by good men for the best of motives will yield a rich harvest of unprincipled acts of others also aiming at "good ends."

D. Dissent from Justice Rehnquist

The Court's frequent references to the "voluntary" nature of Kaiser's racially discriminatory admission quota bear no relationship to the facts of this case. Kaiser and the Steelworkers acted under pressure from an agency of the Federal Government, the Office of Federal Contract Compliance. . . . Bowing to that pressure, Kaiser instituted an admissions quota preferring blacks over whites. . . .

There is perhaps no device more destructive to the notion of equality than the *numerus clausus*—the quota. Whether described as "benign discrimination" or "affirmative action," the racial quota is nonetheless a creator of casts, a two-edged sword that must demean one in order to prefer another. . . . With today's holding the Court introduces into Title VII a tolerance for the very evil that the law was intended to eradicate. . . . By going not merely *beyond*, but directly *against* Title VII's language and legislative history, the Court has sown the wind. Later courts will face the impossible task of reaping the whirlwind.

Source: 443 U.S. 193 at 200, 205, 208, 209–210, 218–219, 246, 254–255 (1979).

{r}DOCUMENT 263: U.S. Civil Rights Commission Hearings on "Issues of Euro-Ethnic Americans," December 1979

Justice Rehnquist's concern that affirmative action could "demean one group of workers in order to prefer another" echoed the feelings of many white ethnics. In December 1979 the U.S. Commission on Civil Rights held hearings in Chicago on "Issues of Euro-Ethnic Americans in the United States." Among those who testified was Leonard F. Walentynowicz, national executive director of the American Polish Congress. Walentynowicz was an attorney who served during the administration of Gerald Ford in the State Department's Bureau of Security and Consular Affairs.

* * *

The first thought that I'd like to express . . . is the belief that the most important thing the Commission can do . . . is . . . receive inputs from . . . what I call, the new classes of left outs. . . .

Employment and ethnicity can be approached from a number of directions . . . I think it best to start from the viewpoint of data collection and the use such data is put to.

[T]he Federal Government presently collects data regarding employment policies and practices in five categories: black, Hispanic, Native American, Asian American and White other than Hispanic, which categories are repeated for both sexes. . . .

Over the years as efforts to fight discrimination and promote affirmative action developed, there has occurred a belief that persons in the first four categories have been the victims of discrimination and deserve the benefits of affirmative action, regardless of personal circumstances, and that everyone in the last category either was guilty of discrimination or had to suffer the consequences of providing the benefits of affirmative action to the persons in the first four categories. . . .

[S]uch restricted data collection and use and the beliefs and practices resulting therefrom are fundamentally unfair and violate the civil rights of a good many Americans, including a good number of Euro-ethnics, especially those in the last category. . . .

We recognize and believe that America is black and white, male and female, Hispanic and Non-Hispanic, but we also believe that we will never achieve true equality unless we recognize that America is *more* than black and white, male and female and Hispanic and Non-Hispanic. Part of that *more* is *us*.

Source: Leonard F. Walentynowicz, "Employment and Ethnicity," in U.S. Commission on Civil Rights, *Civil Rights Issues of Euro-Ethnic Americans in the United States: Opportunities and Challenges. A Consultation Sponsored by the United States Commission on Civil Rights* (Chicago, December 3, 1979): 379, 397, 399.

{r}DOCUMENT 264: Columnist Meg Greenfield, "Teaching Kids the New Discrimination," *Newsweek*, 1977

From yet another perspective—that of an aunt pondering a conversation between her nine-year-old niece, Robin, and seven-year-old nephew, Adam—*Newsweek* columnist Meg Greenfield also raised questions about new, race-based policies. The conversation that prompted her questions concerned an art class for which only children of color were eligible. She was struck by the easy acceptance on the part of her young relatives that they could not participate in the class and their pleasure that a mutual friend who was "half-Indian" had been able to join it. To Greenfield this was an example of "the weird and alarming side effect of our drive to achieve racial fairness."

* * *

The real issue is . . . [that] by our brazen, clinical insistence on a Nuremberg-like analysis of each child's racial and ethnic background—is he half of this or only a quarter that?—we are giving the young to believe that these distinctions are the proper stuff of official decisions. . . .

Should we not be taking stock of how far we have wandered into a morass of new discriminations, which we are teaching the children of this country to view as the normal democratic landscape?

Source: Meg Greenfield, "Teaching Kids the New Discrimination," *Newsweek* (July 4, 1977): 80.

{g}DOCUMENT 265: Joseph Califano on Enforcing Title IX in the 1970s

"Reverse discrimination" was only one focus of growing unrest over laws and policies designed to attack racism and sexism. Title IX's threat to the male status quo was another. With enforcement of Title IX lagging, the U.S. District Court for Washington, D.C., handed down what came to be known as the *Adams Order* in December 1977. The order approved settlement of three suits brought against HEW, including a suit by the Women's Equity Action League (WEAL). The order, as summarized by the U.S. Civil Rights Commission, established "time frames for processing complaints and eliminating the complaint backlog and specifying the number of sex discrimination complaints to be processed and Title IX compliance reviews to be conducted" the following year. President Carter's first appointee as secretary of HEW, Joseph Califano (named in the WEAL suit and sued a second time by WEAL just before he left his post in the summer of 1979), recalled the problems that he encountered in establishing a policy of Title IX enforcement.

* * *

Women's groups thought we allowed too big an exemption for football, male coaches charged that the guidelines would kill bigtime football. An unexpected source of opposition came quietly, but forcefully, from many blacks, who were concerned that funds which went to women's athletic programs would reduce the number of scholarships available for black male athletes.

Source: Joseph Califano, *Governing America* (New York: Simon and Schuster, 1981): 266.

{g}DOCUMENT 266: "HEW Policy Interpretation Regarding Title IX," December 1979

When Califano let it be known that he was planning to send proposed guidelines to Congress, both sides persuaded him that such a course of action would lead to the law's being either "gutted or repealed." He opted instead for a "policy interpretation," which would not require congressional approval. Women's groups greeted the first version of the policy interpretation with caution. They were relieved that Califano held firm in applying Title IX to revenue-producing sports but worried that the application had too many loopholes and that, overall, the policy was too ambiguous. In the interval given for public comment on the Title IX athletics policy, Congress and HEW received over 800 letters, most opposing the policy. Nonetheless, Joseph Califano's successor at HEW, Patricia Roberts Harris, released a final, official policy interpretation in December 1979, accompanied by a list of sixty-two colleges with athletics programs designated as out of compliance with Title IX.

* * *

The following Policy Interpretation represents the Department of Health, Education, and Welfare's interpretation of the intercollegiate athletic provisions of Title IX of the Education Amendments of 1972 and its implementing regulation. . . .

Athletic Financial Assistance (Scholarships) . . .

The Department will measure compliance . . . by dividing the amounts of aid available for the members of each sex by the numbers of male or female participants in the athletic program and comparing the results. Institutions may be found in compliance if this comparison results in substantially equal amounts or if a resulting disparity can be explained by adjustments to take into account legitimate, nondiscriminatory factors. . . .

This section does not require a proportionate number of scholarships for men and women or individual scholarships of equal dollar value. It does mean that the total amount of scholarship aid made available to men and women must be substantially proportionate to their participation rates. . . .

Equivalence in Other Athletic Benefits and Opportunities. . . .

In determining whether an institution is providing equal opportunity in intercollegiate athletics, the regulation requires the Department to consider, among others, the following factors:

(1) accommodation of student interests and abilities;
(2) provision and maintenance of equipment and supplies;
(3) scheduling of games and practice times;
(4) travel and per diem expenses;
(5) opportunity to receive coaching and academic tutoring;
(6) assignment and compensation of coaches and tutors;
(7) provision of locker rooms, practice and competitive facilities;
(8) provision of medical and training services and facilities;
(9) provision of housing and dining services and facilities; and
(10) publicity.

Accommodation of Student Interests and Abilities . . .

Selection of Sports

In the selection of sports, the regulation does not require institutions to integrate their teams nor to provide exactly the same choice of sports to men and women. However, where an institution sponsors a team in a particular sport for members of one sex, it may be required either to permit the excluded sex to try out for the team or to sponsor a separate team for the previously excluded sex. . . .

The Enforcement Process . . .

. . . . [T]here are two ways in which enforcement is initiated: Compliance Reviews . . . [and] Complaints. . . .

The Department has 90 days to conduct an investigation and inform the recipient of its findings, and an additional 90 days to resolve violations by obtaining a voluntary compliance agreement from the recipient. . . .

When a recipient is found in noncompliance and voluntary compliance attempts are unsuccessful, the formal process leading to termination of Federal assistance will be begun.

Source: Reprinted in Appenzeller and Appenzeller 1980, 359, 367–370, 380–381, 384–385.

{g}DOCUMENT 267: Executive Order 12135, May 9, 1979

While women athletes and their supporters concentrated on Title IX, a renewed and reorganized presidential advisory body was at work assessing the status of women in all areas of national life. The group took its direction from an executive order issued by Jimmy Carter in May 1979. He appointed Linda Robb, the daughter of former President Lyndon Johnson, to chair the committee.

* * *

The National Advisory Committee for Women is continued and redesignated the President's Advisory Committee for Women.

The President shall appoint not more than thirty individuals to serve on the Committee. The President shall designate one member to chair the Committee and may designate two members as vice-chairs.

Source: Executive Order 12135, reprinted in *Voices for Women, 1980 Report of the President's Advisory Committee for Women* (Washington, DC: U.S. Government Printing Office, 1980): 141.

Among the questions occupying disabled activists and advocates in the spring of 1979 were two of particular concern: whether the U.S. Department of Transportation (DOT) would establish viable regulations for implementing and enforcing accessibility in public transportation and how the Supreme Court would rule in the pending case of a woman barred from a nursing program because she was deaf. From the point of view of organizations of the disabled the DOT regulations proved acceptable, but the Supreme Court decision in *Southeastern Community College v. Davis* was controversial.

{d}DOCUMENT 268: Department of Transportation "Final Rule," May 1979

The transportation regulations evolved from a lengthy and complicated process begun in the early 1970s, when the Urban Mass Transit Administration of the federal transportation department (DOT) was pressured by court action (initiated by the organization Disabled in Action of Baltimore) to formulate rules for making public transportation facilities accessible to all citizens. The final version of those rules, published in 1976, had barely begun to be implemented when the HEW regulations for Section 504 (Doc. 246) took effect, forcing federal transportation officials back to the drawing board to bring DOT rules into line with the HEW guidelines. The end result contrasted significantly with previous versions by eliminating opportunities for local decision makers to exercise their discretion. No longer could they choose to have a separate transportation system for disabled consumers, such as the "Dial-a-Ride" approach used in some communities, whereby consumers could arrange to be picked up by a van or bus reserved just for their use. The new regulations, published in May 1979, required full accessibility for disabled users of all public conveyances.

* * *

Briefly the new rule requires that:

1. *Public transit buses* . . . must be wheelchair accessible. . . . Within ten years, half the buses used in peak hour service must be wheelchair accessible, and these buses must be utilized before inaccessible buses during off-peak hours. . . .

2. The rule adopts a system-wide approach to rapid rail and mandates that key stations must be made accessible in 30 years if station accessibility involves extraordinary costs, with less costly changes in three years. . . . We expect that at least one-third of the key stations should be made accessible within 12 years. . . .

3. *Commuter rail systems* must be made accessible. . . .

4. *Light rail* (trolley and streetcar) systems must be made accessible. . . .

5. For Federally-assisted urban mass transportation systems that will not be accessible within three years . . . *interim accessible transportation* must be provided. . . .

6. *New airport terminals* must be accessible with respect to general passenger flow, ticketing areas, baggage check-in and retrieval, aircraft boarding and exiting, telephones, vehicular loading and unloading, parking, waiting areas, and public services. Existing air carrier airport terminals must be made accessible within three years.

7. New rest area facilities along federally assisted *highways* must be made accessible. Existing rest area facilities on Interstate highways must be made accessible within three years. . . .

8. Every new *railroad* station constructed with Federal financial assistance must be accessible. . . . Existing stations must be made accessible within five years for certain stations, and within 10 years for all stations. . . .

9. The rule prohibits *employment discrimination* against the handicapped in relation to programs that receive or benefit from Federal financial assistance from DOT.

Source: Federal Register 44, no. 106 (May 31, 1979): 31442, 31443.

Greeted by disabled citizens with general satisfaction, the new regulations raised a tempest among local transportation officials and the private sector operators of transportation services whose complaints were expressed in a *New York Times* editorial against "making every bus kneel to pick up a few passengers" (quoted in Eisenberg 1982).

{d}DOCUMENT 269: *Southeastern Community College v. Davis,* June 11, 1979

If public opinion was not ready to support transportation accessibility as a civil right, neither was the Supreme Court ready to interpret Section 504 in terms broad enough to accommodate the needs of a deaf student seeking to enter the nursing program at Southeastern Community College in North Carolina. Frances B. Davis, who was hearing-impaired, filed suit in a federal district court when she was denied admission to the nursing program of Southeastern Community College. When that court found in favor of the college, she appealed. The Fourth Circuit Court of Appeals reversed the district court decision. In the interval between the two rulings the HEW regulations for Section 504 had been published, and the appeals judge found in them grounds for requiring Southeastern Community College to accommodate Davis. The college sought a ruling from the Supreme Court, presenting that body with its first opportunity to interpret Section 504 (Doc. 200). The high court justices agreed with the original district court ruling and upheld the college's right to bar her from the nursing program.

* * *

[N]either the language, purpose, nor history of section 504 reveals an intent to impose an affirmative-action obligation on all recipients of federal funds. . . .

It is possible to envision situations where . . . a refusal to modify an existing program might become unreasonable and discriminatory. . . .

In this case, however, . . . Southeastern's unwillingness to make major adjustments in its nursing program does not constitute such discrimination. . . . It is undisputed that the respondent could not participate in Southeastern's nursing program unless the standards were substantially lowered. Section 504 imposes no requirement upon an educational institution to lower or to effect substantial modifications of standards to accommodate a handicapped person.

Source: 442 U.S. 397 at 411, 412–413 (1979).

{d}DOCUMENT 270: Leslie B. Milk, Testimony at U.S. Civil Rights Commission Hearings, May 1980

The *Southeastern* case put disabled observers and their supporters on edge as they debated what its impact would be. At a Civil Rights Commission hearing a year after the decision, the director of Mainstream Inc., an organization concerned with employment issues for the disabled, commented on the case.

* * *

The emotionally charged image of a registered nurse [Frances Davis] unable to hear and heed a patient's cry for help is not likely to produce a sober-minded analysis of accommodation of employment standards for disabled people. The High Court ruling [*Southeastern College v. Davis*] did set limits on the rights of handicapped people and did uphold the right to establish "necessary physical requirements." But handicapped people cannot any longer be denied access to jobs and job training based on broad exclusionary standards.

Source: U.S. Commission on Civil Rights 1980, 119.

{d}DOCUMENT 271: Leslie B. Milk Calls for the Disabled to Be Included in the Civil Rights Act of 1964, May 1980

The May 1980 Civil Rights Commission hearings brought into focus the objectives of the increasingly well organized community of disabled citizens. Testimony at these hearings emphasized the overall objectives of assuming their rightful place within the civil rights movement and establishing their right to participate fully in mainstream society. Employment specialist Leslie Milk was among those who called for Title VII of the 1964 Civil Rights Act to be amended to include the rights of disabled citizens, an action that Senator Hubert Humphrey and others had sought to place on the legislative agenda nearly a decade earlier (Docs. 192, 193).

* * *

If all the workers [in any given workplace] are white, someone will report that something is amiss. Depending on the part of the country, someone will ask, Where are the Hispanics, the Asian Americans, the Native Americans? But no matter where the workplace, no matter what the work, we know that no one will ask, Where are the people in wheelchairs? . . .

Decades after it became unacceptable to say all black people have rhythm, it is still perfectly acceptable to state, "the deaf are good workers in print shops," or "epileptics cannot operate machinery," "diabetics shouldn't drive," or "people in wheelchairs should not have to travel." . . .

There are a number of steps that can and should be taken by the United States Commission on Civil Rights. . . . The first is to accept responsibility for dealing with the concerns of handicapped Americans as part of the civil rights agenda of the Nation. . . .

Another important step is to support the passage of legislation to include people with disabilities in the protection of Title VII of the 1964 Civil Rights Act. This would achieve three important goals: expansion of employment rights, clarification of judicial rights, and recognition of the human rights of handicapped people.

Source: U.S. Commission on Civil Rights 1980, 112, 117, 124.

{d}DOCUMENT 272: Goals of the Disability Rights Movement Stated by Judith E. Heumann, 1980

Activist and organizer Judith E. Heumann (Docs. 164, 165) summarized the vision of the movement in which she was one of the pioneers.

* * *

The reality of the situation is that disabled individuals want to be able to use everything that exists within communities, that we want to be able to be mainstreamed, that we want to be able to become an integral part of this country, that the charitable approach, which has long existed in this country and around the world, which basically allows the Jerry Lewis telethon to go on, allows the Easter Seal telethons to go on . . . telethons which in fact do not allow for pride within disabled people; but rather continue to prey on the fears of nondisabled people . . . — "give money so that you don't have one of us." The government really has allowed these kinds of programs . . . to continue, because of its failure to provide appropriate services.

Source: U.S. Commission on Civil Rights 1980, 237–238.

{d}DOCUMENT 273: Attorney Deborah Kaplan on the Absence of the Disabled among Decision Makers, 1980

Among the political barriers identified by the disabled as standing in their way was the absence of people like themselves in decision-making positions. Deborah Kaplan (founder of the Disability Rights Center of Oakland, California) and Heumann were among those who stressed this point in their testimony. Kaplan linked the inadequacy of affirmative action in the employment of disabled individuals with the failure to involve the disabled in policy making and implementation.

* * *

Clearly, affirmative action in hiring disabled people should be more than filing papers, putting up a poster or two during "National Employ the Handicapped Week" (should affirmative action be reduced during the rest of the year?), and printing pictures of disabled employees in the agency newsletter. . . .

Many agencies have yet to establish working advisory groups of disabled employees, as previously required, to provide their expertise on such issues as outreach and recruiting, removing barriers, making accommodations, and much more. Disabled people are one of the most knowledgeable resources available, yet many agencies overlook them.

Source: U.S. Commission on Civil Rights 1980, 50, 51.

{d}DOCUMENT 274: Judith E. Heumann on Decision Making for the Disabled, 1980

Heumann carried the argument one step further, directly questioning the ability of able-bodied decision makers to act effectively on behalf of disabled persons.

* * *

All the systems . . . education, welfare, health, rehabilitation, have one thing in common that severely affects disabled people. These agencies are staffed, with few exceptions, by able-bodied persons. All the good intentions and charitable feelings in the world will not provide these professionals with the knowledge of what it feels like to grow up disabled in a white male-dominated, able-bodied society. . . . [A]n obvious remedy is an affirmative action hiring policy of disabled professionals for these agencies.

Source: U.S. Commission on Civil Rights 1980, 225.

{d}DOCUMENT 275: Ronald L. Mace of Barrier Free Environments, Inc., 1980

In further testimony at the hearings of May 1980, Ronald Mace described the personal struggle that is part of the disabled person's "normal" routine.

* * *

[T]he problem of physical accessibility goes beyond architectural issues. . . .

The barriers . . . are inherent in everything we have, everything that we live with: our parks, our streets, our building sites, the products our manufacturers make, the vehicles that we try to ride on. . . .

I think I might go back for a minute and tell you what happened to me this morning. . . . To come to this meeting—I am housed in a hotel about 20 miles away because it is the only one that was available with a so-called accessible room. It is in a location where there is no transportation whatsoever to get me here. A van service was to be there at 8 o'clock. . . . It doesn't arrive at 8 o'clock. . . . So I left with a cab after the hour they were to arrive. The cab driver drops me off three blocks from here and tells me that is the correct hotel. So I am in the wrong hotel three blocks away.

You should try to get a cab driver to pick you up in a wheelchair and drive you only three blocks. It is hard enough to get one when you are walking. Since I couldn't get a cab . . . I tried to make it over here on my own. It took me almost an hour to get here, crossing curbs and getting people to help me at every curb.

This is not an unusual experience. This is an everyday occurrence for someone with a rather severe mobility impairment.

Source: U.S. Commission on Civil Rights 1980, 276, 277.

{d}DOCUMENT 276: Peter D. Rosenstein on the Cost of Providing Accessibility, 1980

A dominant theme in the 1980 hearings on civil rights of the disabled was, inevitably, cost. The disabled individuals and activists who took up the cost issue in their testimony emphasized the concept of long-term social investment and the urgency of replacing programs that foster dependence with facilities that enable independence for Americans with physical handicaps. Peter Rosenstein was among those who forcefully argued this point of view.

* * *

[When critics] talk about the $6 billion cost of making our systems accessible, they usually neglect to add that that is over a 30-year span. They try to make people think that that is a cost outlay tomorrow; it is going to end up on the Federal Government's tax budget this year. It is not. It is a long-term proposition. It is an investment . . . in our entire society to allow people to become independent and functioning, people that we now, and over those 30 years, will spend probably a lot more than $6 billion on if we continue to force them to be dependent on our social service system.

Source: U.S. Commission on Civil Rights, 1980, 345.

{d}DOCUMENT 277: Additional Thoughts on the Cost Issue from Paul G. Hearne, 1980

Disabled organizer Paul G. Hearne also addressed the issue of cost.

* * *

I would like to turn the financial argument around for a moment. I would like to propose that it is not more costly to provide for reasonable accommodations . . . that in fact it costs more with the present situation that exists right now. . . .

[T]here are primarily three different types of disabled persons . . . the disabled person who is not employed, not in school and on public benefits. That . . . is the largest portion of the disabled population. There is, number two, the disabled person who is . . . younger . . . who may be . . . in secondary education and still on public benefits. And, number three, there is the disabled person that is employed, which is probably the smallest portion of disabled persons. . . .

In 1974 the . . . public benefit programs [which support disabled individuals] amounted to a total of $8.3 billion. In the same year payments . . . to State agencies that provide . . . those support services which pay for disabled individuals attaining employment, was about $500 million, and with that $500 million roughly 150,000 disabled people were employed. . . .

If . . . billions of dollars are . . . not spent by Congress . . . on access to employment, on transportation, on the real issues that affect disabled people, it is far more costly. . . . If . . . money is turned into vocational rehabilitation funds and individuals are placed in jobs, they become taxpayers. So that there is a twofold benefit . . . they are taken off the public assistance rolls; and . . . they are also paying taxes and broadening the tax base.

Source: U.S. Commission on Civil Rights, 1980, 200, 201.

{d}DOCUMENT 278: The Issue of Handicapped-Accessibility Standards, 1980

As the civil rights commissioners took up the question of implementation of policies to foster the independence of disabled persons, they came to the matter of the standards that each federal agency was required by the Architectural Barriers Act of 1968 (Doc. 153) to develop and apply in making public structures handicapped-accessible. These standards became very specific, stipulating the measurements of doorways, rest room stalls, and so on. Ronald Mace spoke to the question of whether having more than one set of standards was effective.

* * *

Vice Chairman Horn. Mention has been made of the competing standards which we have from Federal agencies. We have GSA [General Services Administration], HEW, Postal Service. We have the new standard by a voluntary group. . . .

Is it saving money for government to have these specialized agency standards . . . or do we really know?

Mr. Mace. No, it is not saving anybody money for these agencies to have different standards. I can give you . . . a specific example. . . . We are talking about inches, fractions of inches in the technical specifications. . . .

Take, for example, the requirement for a simple lavatory in a toilet room. If one agency says it has to have 29 inches clearance underneath and that the rim height above the floor has to be 34 [inches]. . . .

Then somebody in one of the agencies in their divine wisdom decides that they are going to make it 30 inches and 33 inches because they think that might be better. What they have done is eliminate . . . products that are on the market that fit within the [original specifications].

So then a manufacturer, in order to furnish a fixture that will be acceptable within that agency's facilities, has to manufacture an element that is special . . . and that is an extra cost item. The industry will respond to that. They will put it on the market at extra cost. And, yes, it costs the taxpayers extra money. . . .

And then the other cost issue . . . is . . . the different standards and delays that it causes. . . . I think those affect disabled people in a very important way. . . .

[It] generates the complaints [from contractors] of, "My God, look at the cost you're giving me. . . . This agency is saying I have to do this, but my local building code is saying that I have to do this. . . ." So they say, "Look at those handicapped people that are out there demanding these regulations. I'm overregulated. I'm up to my neck in regulations." . . .

Source: U.S. Commission on Civil Rights 1980, 296, 297, 298.

{d}DOCUMENT 279: Testimony on Coordination of Laws and Programs for the Disabled, 1980

Ronald Mace's testimony on the issue of standards was reinforced by Peter Rosenstein, who had originally directed the implementation effort for the White House Conference on the Handicapped. Rosenstein stressed the critical matter of coordination and, in the process, expressed considerable impatience with the federal government's approach to ensuring the rights of the disabled.

* * *

It took us less than 10 years to walk on the moon. It has taken us 10 years to do even a demonstration project on how to get people from one place to another in an accessible bus. There is something wrong with that. . . .

I have just spent 15 months doing a survey and analysis of what has happened since the White House Conference on the Handicapped . . . in May 1977. . . .

There is no real focus. The White House Conference requested that a person in the Executive Office of the President be designated as a coordinator for the concerns of disabled Americans. We have a coordinator for women's concerns, for minority concerns, and it was stated that there be a coordinator for the concerns of disabled Americans. That is pretty simple. . . . That wasn't done. Therefore, we have four different accessibility guides or standards being developed. . . . we have HEW developing 504 guidelines and most other agencies still not having developed them; we have agencies that are making excuses why they can't be developed; we have agencies spending money on duplication of services. . . . We have a glut, approximately 330 Federal programs dealing in the area of disability. Rarely do they talk to each other.

Source: U.S. Commission on Civil Rights 1980, 345, 346, 347.

{r}DOCUMENT 280: The Public Works Employment Act of 1977

While the disability rights movement faced the threat of being swallowed up in the federal bureaucratic maze, the civil rights movement for African Americans confronted another "reverse discrimination" challenge from a white male. In the summer of 1980 the Supreme Court ruled on charges brought by H. Earl Fullilove against federal affirmative action on behalf of minority contractors. While *Bakke* had dealt with the right of a state institution to use race in admissions criteria (Doc. 230), and *Weber* had addressed whether the private sector (a corporation and a union) could employ race in selecting trainees for an apprentice program (Doc. 262), the case of *H. Earl Fullilove et al. v. Phillip M. Klutznick* called into question the right of Congress to pass laws that included racial preferences. Fullilove was one of a number of contractors and subcontractors who challenged the Public Works Employment Act of 1977, specifically, the provision of that act that 10 percent of the federal funds granted to public works projects must be paid to contractors belonging to any of six minority groups. Maryland representative Parren J. Mitchell had authored the provision and successfully guided it through the House. Senator Brooke of Massachusetts had sponsored a similar provision when the act reached the Senate. The conference committee that drafted the final version of the bill had kept the provision intact.

* * *

Except to the extent that the Secretary [of Commerce] determines otherwise, no grant shall be made under this Act for any local public works project unless the applicant gives satisfactory assurance to the Secretary that at least 10 per centum of the amount of each grant shall be expended for minority business enterprises. For purposes of this paragraph, the term "minority business enterprise" means a business at least 50 per centum of which is owned by minority group members or, in case of a publicly owned business, at least 51 per centum of the stock of which is owned by minority group members. For the purposes of the preceding sentence minority group members are citizens of the United States who are Negroes, Spanish-speaking, Orientals, Indians, Eskimos, and Aleuts.

Source: Quoted in 448 U.S. 448 at 451 (1980).

{r}DOCUMENT 281: Parren J. Mitchell, Author of the Public Works Employment Act of 1977

In a 1993 interview Congressman Mitchell recalled the thinking behind the set-aside amendment and the strategy employed in securing its passage.

* * *

[T]he time was ripe. . . . My experience with the [contract compliance and civil rights enforcement] agencies had been that they would come in and I'd ask them what are they doing on minority business and they'd say, "we're making an effort." What percent? "Oh, it's three-tenths of one percent." And they kept telling me, "look, Mr. Congressman just have faith in us, we'll do better." They didn't do better all those years. And I knew they had to have a law and that law [the Public Works bill] was the first real shot I had of putting that amendment through. It was the ideal one because everybody wanted public works. . . . the way I counted it, it would pass overwhelmingly. So I said whooosh! There goes my amendment!

Source: Parren Mitchell, quoted in Thomas J. McNeill/Ajani Osei Osaze, "Parren J. Mitchell: Trailblazer from Black Baltimore" (M.A. thesis, Department of History Morgan State University, 1994): 138–139.

{r}DOCUMENT 282: Congressman Mitchell's Advocacy for the Public Works Employment Act of 1977

Mitchell reminded his fellow congressmen of the extreme disparity in contract receipts between majority and minority recipients of federal public works dollars, and he couched his argument in the language of economic growth.

* * *

In the process to parity, the minority business sector should receive from 15 to 18 percent of the contract receipts; however, in fiscal year 1976 the minority business sector received less than 1 percent of the contract receipts of the Federal Government. . . . As the Public Works and Transportation Committee utilizes targeting to emphasize the value of domestic economic growth through the use of a "buy America provision," I am emphasizing the value of minority business development by targeting and adopting the provision that 10 percent of the articles, materials, and supplies which will be used in any accelerated public works project must be procured from minority business enterprises. My amendment ensures domestic growth. . . .

Source: Congressional Record 123, Pt. 4 (February 23, 1977): 5097, 5098.

{r}DOCUMENT 283: *Fullilove v. Klutznik*, July 2, 1980

Unlike other civil rights measures that had occasioned lengthy debate, Mitchell's amendment passed almost without comment. However, in December 1977 H. Earl Fullilove and others challenged the set-aside law in federal district court, where it was upheld. The case proceeded to the U.S. Court of Appeals (Second Circuit), where the law again was upheld. It was argued before the Supreme Court in November 1979. The following summer Chief Justice Burger delivered the majority opinion affirming the prior court rulings. While six justices agreed that the law was constitutional, their individual reasons differed, producing, in addition to the Burger opinion, concurring opinions presented by Justices Marshall and Powell. Three members of the Court filed dissenting opinions.

* * *

A. Majority opinion delivered by Justice Burger

Petitioners are several associations of construction contractors and subcontractors, and a firm engaged in heating, ventilation, and air conditioning work. Their complaint alleged that they had sustained economic injury due to enforcement of the 10% MBE [minority business enterprise] requirement and that the MBE provision on its face violated the Equal Protection Clause of the Fourteenth Amendment, the equal protection component of the Due Process Clause of the Fifth Amendment, and various statutory antidiscrimination provisions. . . .

[W]e are satisfied that Congress had abundant historical basis from which it could conclude that traditional procurement practices, when applied to minority business, could perpetuate the effects of prior discrimination. Accordingly, Congress reasonably determined that the prospective elimination of these barriers . . . was appropriate to ensure that those businesses were not denied equal opportunity to participate in federal grants to state and local governments which is one aspect of the equal protection of the laws. . . .

It is not a constitutional defect in this program that it may disappoint the expectations of nonminority firms. When effectuating a limited and properly tailored remedy to cure the effects of prior discrimination, such "a sharing of the burden" by innocent parties is not impermissible. . . .

The MBE provision of the Public Works Employment Act of 1977 does not violate the Constitution.

B. Concurring Opinion by Justice Powell

I . . . write separately to apply the analysis set forth by my opinion in *University of California Regents v. Bakke* . . . [Doc. 231].

[A] race-conscious remedy is not compelling] unless . . . two requirements [are] met. First, the governmental body that attempts to impose a race-conscious remedy must have the authority to act in response to identified discrimination. . . . Second, the governmental body must make findings that demonstrate the existence of illegal discrimination. In *Bakke*, the Regents failed both requirements. They were entrusted only with educational functions and they made no findings of past discrimination. . . .

Unlike the Regents of the University of California, . . . Congress has the authority to identify unlawful discriminatory practices, to prohibit those practices, and to prescribe remedies to eradicate their continuing effects. . . .

[T]he petitioners contend with some force that they have been asked to bear the burden of the set-aside even though they are innocent of wrongdoing. I do not believe, however, that their burden is so great that the set-aside must be disapproved. . . . the Court of Appeals calculated that the set-aside would reserve about 0.25% of all the funds expended yearly on construction work in the United States for approximately 4% of the Nation's contractors who are members of minority groups. . . . The set-aside would have no effect on the ability of the remaining 96% of contractors to compete for 99.75% of construction funds.

C. Concurring Opinion by Justice Marshall [joined by Justices Brennan and Blackmun]

As my Brother Blackmun observed in *Bakke*: "In order to get beyond racism, we must first take account of race. There is no other way." . . .

Congress recognized these realities when it enacted the minority set-aside provision at issue in this case. Today, by upholding this race-conscious remedy, the Court accords Congress the authority necessary to undertake the task of moving our society toward a state of meaningful equality of opportunity, not an abstract version of equality in which the effects of past discrimination would be forever frozen into our social fabric. I applaud this result.

D. Dissent of Justice Stewart

I think today's decision is wrong for the same reason that *Plessy v. Ferguson* [Doc. 25] was wrong. . . .

Under our Constitution, the government may never act to the detriment of a person solely because of that person's race. . . .

The rule cannot be any different when the persons injured by a racially biased law are not members of a racial minority. . . .

On its face, the minority business enterprise (MBE) provision at issue in this case denies the equal protection of the law. . . . The statute . . . bars a class to which the petitioners belong from having the opportunity to receive a government benefit. . . .

[T]here are indications that the MBE provision may have been enacted to compensate for the effects of social, educational, and economic "disadvantage." No race, however, has a monopoly on social, educational, or economic disadvantage, and any law that indulges in such a presumption clearly violates the constitutional guarantee of equal protection.

E. Dissent of Justice Stevens

The statutory definition of the preferred class includes "citizens of the United States who are Negroes, Spanish-speaking, Orientals, Indians, Eskimos, and Aleuts." . . .

There is not one word in the remainder of the Act or in the legislative history that explains why any Congressman or Senator favored this par-

ticular definition over any other or that identifies the common characteristics that every member of the preferred class was believed to share.
Nor does the Act or its history explain why 10% of the total appropriation was the proper amount to set aside for investors in each of the six
racial subclasses. . . .

Quite obviously, the history of discrimination against black citizens in
America cannot justify a grant of privileges to Eskimos or Indians.

Even if we assume that each of the six racial subclasses has suffered
its own special injury at some time in our history, surely it does not
necessarily follow that each of those subclasses suffered harm of identical
magnitude. . . .

[I]f . . . history can justify such a random distribution of benefits on
racial lines as that embodied in this statutory scheme it will serve not
merely as a basis of remedial legislation, but rather as a permanent
source of justification for grants of special privileges . . . [by] almost any
ethnic, religious, or racial group with the political strength to negotiate
"a piece of the action" for its members. . . .

I cannot accept this slapdash statute as a legitimate method of providing classwide relief.

Source: 448 U.S. 448 at 455, 478, 484, 492, 496, 498, 504, 514–515, 517, 522, 523,
525–526, 527, 529–530, 535, 536, 537–538, 539 (1980).

{g}DOCUMENT 284: *Voices for Women, 1980 Report of the President's Advisory Committee for Women*, December 1980

In the final weeks of 1980 President Carter's Advisory Committee for
Women (Doc. 267) submitted a report. Distinguishing it from the first
presidential commission document, generated in the Kennedy administration (Doc. 117), were an unequivocal stance in favor of the ERA,
adoption of affirmative action as a necessary mechanism, and an emphasis on diversity.

* * *

The Equal Rights Amendment is the single most critical step necessary
to accelerate progress for women and to guarantee that the institutions
of American government will truly provide equal justice for all. It must
be ratified. . . .

[Every issue examined in the report was related to the specific circumstances of specific groups of women, designated as "target populations."]

[EDUCATION] ISSUES AFFECTING TARGET POPULATIONS

American Indian/Alaska Native Women. . . .

subject to a wide range of cumulative educational disadvantages from past and present inequities. . . .

Asian/Pacific American Women. . . .

including Indo-Chinese refugees . . . are isolated and denied full access to educational opportunities. . . .

Black Women. . . .

continue to face barriers that are rooted in the social and political fabric of this Nation. . . .

Hispanic Women. . . .

[are underrepresented] in educational institutions and in the labor force. . . .

Migrant Women. . . .

[are] the most educationally disenfranchised. . . .

Adolescent Parents. . . .

are denied access at a stage in life when intellectual development is crucial to long-term educational and economic development. . . .

Disabled Women. . . .

suffer from multiple discrimination which profoundly influences their capacity to function effectively in a society that reinforces traditional sex roles and lacks understanding of handicapping conditions.

Elderly Women. . . .

Few Federal policies and programs adequately serve [their] needs. . . .

Incarcerated Women. . . .

represent the totality of an abused and neglected population. . . .

Rural Women. . . .

are often isolated and economically unable to take advantage of educational opportunities comparable to their male and urban female counterparts. . . .

Single Parents. . . .

dominate the bottom of the continuum of social and economic indices in this country. . . .

Affirmative Action . . . should be a priority program in every administration with focus on strict and effective enforcement and implementation.

Source: Voices for Women, 1980 Report of the President's Advisory Committee for Women (Washington, DC: U.S. Government Printing Office, December 1980): 21, 44–47, 124, 125.

{r/g/d}DOCUMENT 285: Barnhill–Hayes Survey of Employers' Attitudes toward Affirmative Action, April 1979

As the decade of the 1980s began, anyone contemplating the status of affirmative action and related issues could consult a survey released in April 1980. The survey reported on the views of affirmative action held by 286 corporate executives. Those views were gathered by the international research organization McBain Research. The survey was commissioned by the management consulting firm of Barnhill–Hayes, Inc. The U.S. Civil Rights Commission included it in the published findings of its May 1980 hearings. The concluding document of Section IV of this documentary history of affirmative action consists of several questions from that survey and tabulations of the executives' responses.

* * *

Question: **Would you say that as a result of affirmative action, your company's employee productivity has been diminished in recent years?**

Has been diminished because of affirmative action	15%
Has not been diminished	72%
Has been diminished, but for reasons other than affirmative action	12%
No opinion	1%

Question: **How likely do you think it is that a woman will become the chief executive officer of your company within the next 10 to 15 years?**

Very likely	1%
Likely	5%
Not very likely	91%
No answer	3%

Question: **How likely do you think it is that a black will become the chief executive officer of your company within the next 10 to 15 years?**

Very likely	—
Likely	2%
Not very likely	69%
No chance at all	27%
No answer	2%

Question: Thinking for a moment about the different minority groups affected by affirmative action, which of the groups below would you say stands the best chance of making significant employment strides over the next five years?

Women	51%
Blacks	21%
Hispanics	8%
Vietnam veterans	10%
Handicapped	10%

Question: And which group would you say stands the least chance of making significant employment strides over the next five years?

Women	3%
Blacks	13%
Hispanics	16%
Vietnam veterans	20%
Handicapped	47%
Don't know	1%

Question: Thinking about the accomplishments of affirmative action to date, to what extent do you feel affirmative action has helped to advance the cause of women and minorities in employment in the private sector?

A great deal	52%
Somewhat	42%
Hardly at all	5%
Not sure	—
No answer	1%

Question: To what extent do you agree or disagree with the following statements?

Statement	Agree Strongly	Agree Somewhat	Disagree Somewhat	Disagree Strongly
Affirmative action as an issue of concern to top management is on the decline.	8%	36%	29%	25%
With the Bakke decision, affirmative action takes on new importance for our company.	1%	19%	42%	36%

Statement	Agree Strongly	Agree Somewhat	Disagree Somewhat	Disagree Strongly
If the courts rule in favor of Weber (in *Weber vs. Kaiser Aluminum*), it would "destroy affirmative action as it is currently practiced—on a voluntary basis."	9%	26%	36%	24%
The Equal Employment Opportunity Commission should be more concerned with the overall results of a company's affirmative action program than with outlining the measures a company should take to achieve equal employment opportunity.	63%	25%	7%	5%
The EEOC should require that companies justify on a job-related basis using hiring and promotion tests that by their nature discriminate against women, the handicapped, racial minorities, and others.	35%	32%	13%	10%

Source: Barnhill–Hayes, "Employer Attitudes toward Affirmative Action," April 1979, reprinted in *Civil Rights Issues of Handicapped Americans: Public Policy Implications* (Washington, DC, 1980): 507, 511, 532, 535, 536, 539, 548, 551–552.

Part V

1981–2000: Affirmative Action Entrenched and Embattled

In the final decades of the twentieth century opposition to affirmative action grew in numbers, political muscle, financial support, and tactical sophistication. Backed in the 1980s by the Reagan–Bush White House, this opposition won striking victories. However, advocates of affirmative action did not stand still. They successfully countered some attacks and responded to adverse developments with alternative approaches to creating and maintaining campus and workforce diversity. Of the three movements represented in this documentary history, the disability rights movement made the greatest advance in these decades, with passage of the Americans with Disabilities Act (Doc. 333). As the twentieth century ended, the fate of affirmative action was unclear. Some critics confidently predicted that it was in its final days; some advocates insisted that it must and would be preserved. The most accurate observation may well have been that of historian Herman Belz. Although he was speaking specifically of the Reagan years, his words still applied in the era of President Clinton: "Affirmative action was probably too deeply entrenched to be radically eliminated . . . as some thought could be done" (Belz 1994, 207).

THE REAGAN–BUSH YEARS

"The Reagan Revolution"—launched with the victory of conservative Republican Ronald Reagan over Jimmy Carter in the presidential election of 1980—dominated the 1980s. Reagan appointed to key posts outspoken critics of affirmative action. These individuals, called "Reaganauts" in opposition quarters, included as chairman of the U.S. Civil Rights Commission Clarence Pendleton. An African American Republican who had switched parties, Pendleton termed affirmative action "bankrupt." Clarence Thomas, who denounced affirmative action as "a narcotic of dependency," replaced Eleanor Holmes Norton as the head of the EEOC. As U.S. attorney general Reagan first selected William French Smith, who was later succeeded by Edward Meese, both opponents of affirmative action. Of most importance in the Justice Department was William Bradford Reynolds, assistant attorney general for civil rights, who "quickly acquired the reputation of being a reactionary ideologue intent on rolling back the civil rights revolution" (Belz 1994, 184).

{r/g/d}DOCUMENT 286: Position of U.S. Commission on Civil Rights on Affirmative Action in the 1980s, January 1981

In the same month as Ronald Reagan's inauguration, the Civil Rights Commission (whose moderate Republican leader, Arthur Flemming, had not yet been replaced) published a position statement on "Affirmative Action in the 1980's." With the Reaganite forces poised to charge, the commission's unabashed assertion that systemic discrimination required race- and gender-conscious remedies had the ring of a brave "last stand."

* * *

[W]e maintain our unwavering support for affirmative action plans and the full range of affirmative measures necessary to make equal opportunity a reality of historically excluded groups. . . .

A steady flow of data shows unmistakably that most of the historic victims of discrimination are still being victimized and that more recently arrived groups have also become victims of ongoing discriminatory attitudes and processes. Social indicators reveal persistent and widespread gaps throughout our society between the status of white males and the rest of the population. . . .

[D]iscrimination has become a process that builds the discriminatory attitudes and actions of individuals into the operations of organizations and social structures. . . . Perpetuating past injustices into the present . . . this discriminatory process produces unequal results along the lines of race, sex, and national origin, which in turn reinforce existing practices

and breed damaging stereotypes which then promote the existing inequalities that set the process in motion in the first place. . . .

[W]hen such a process is at work, antidiscrimination efforts to eliminate prejudice by insisting on "color-blindness" and "gender-neutrality"
are insufficient remedies.

Source: "Affirmative Action in the 1980's: Dismantling the Process of Discrimination: A Proposed Statement of the U.S. Commission on Civil Rights" (January
1981): 3, 4, 5.

{r}DOCUMENT 287: Senator Orrin Hatch on a Proposed Constitutional Amendment, Spring 1981

In the spring and summer of 1981 Republican senator Orrin Hatch
used his position as chairman of the Senate Judiciary Committee to
promote a proposed constitutional amendment prohibiting any federal
government action based on "distinctions on account of race, color or
national origin." The thrust of the Hatch amendment and of the Judiciary Committee hearings on it contrasted harshly with the assumptions
and tone of the Civil Rights Commission (CRC) hearings two months
earlier.

* * *

[T]he longer we continue to distribute benefits and privileges on the
basis of such factors as race or ethnicity, the more such protected groups
come to view such benefits and privileges as entitlements.

The more affirmative action is viewed as an entitlement by its supposed beneficiaries, the more difficult it will be to reverse this policy
short of enormous social divisions and tensions.

Affirmative action, in other words, is not an issue that is gently going
to go away.

Source: Hearings before the Subcommittee on the Constitution of the Committee
on the Judiciary, U.S. Senate (May 4, June 11, 18, July 16, 1981): 474.

{r}DOCUMENT 288: Lyrics by Ian Mackaye of Minor Threat, 1981

The Reagan backlash was not confined to government circles and
did not occur in a vacuum. Such forces as the splintering of social

movements into factions (including those calling for armed revolution and Black Power) and the divisive and violent turmoil generated by the war in Vietnam had changed American society and altered race relations. Some sense of this alteration may be glimpsed in the evolution of the music associated with the white youth culture. Through the folk and rock music that had popular appeal in the 1960s ran themes of peace and justice as common causes for "black and white together." The heavy metal, punk rock, and hard-core sounds that were popular with many young whites in the 1980s conveyed little evidence of such common ground. For example, the following lyrics were written by Ian Mackaye for the punk rock/hard-core group Minor Threat. He later recalled "many experiences in the d.c. [Washington, D.C.] public school system that made me feel as though i was being judged on my skin color and harassed (and occasionally assaulted) for being white. . . . at the time it was my reality and that was what i was singing about." Mackaye's purpose was "to say that racism exists in many levels . . . of our society, and that it is wrong," but the song "Guilty of Being White" also suggests the racially charged climate of the times—a climate becoming increasingly hostile to remedies such as affirmative action (Letter from Ian Mackaye to Jo Ann Robinson, April 5, 2000).

* * *

I'm sorry
For something I didn't do
Lynched somebody
But I don't know who
You blame me for slavery
A hundred years before I was born
Guilty of being white

Source: Minor Threat, "Out of Step," Washington, DC: Dischord Label, 1981.

{r/g}DOCUMENT 289: *New York Times* Commentary by Nell Irvin Painter, December 1981

The Reagan Revolution dismayed proponents of affirmative action but did not dissuade them from continuing to defend it. In a *New York Times* commentary historian Nell Irvin Painter reflected on conversations that she had experienced recently. One was with a white male who lamented his failure to find a university teaching position and who envied Painter for being "black and female, because of affirmative action." He told her, "You count twice." The other was with a group of young African American women, college undergraduates who considered affirmative action a stigma.

* * *

To hear people talk, affirmative action exists only to employ and promote the otherwise unqualified, but I don't see it that way at all. I'm black and female, yet I was hired by two history departments that had no black members before the late 60's, never mind females. Affirmative action cleared the way. . . .

I wish I could take [the white man and the college undergraduates] back to the early 60's and let them see that they're reciting the same old white-male-superiority line, fixed up to fit conditions that include a policy called affirmative action. Actually, I will not have to take those people back in time at all, for the Reagan Administration's proposed dismantling of affirmative action fuses the future and the past.

Source: Nell Irvin Painter, "Hers," *New York Times* (December 10, 1981): C2.

{g}DOCUMENT 290: Historian Elizabeth Pleck and Political Leader Frances Farenthold on the Defeat of the ERA, August 1982

The feminist movement praised by Painter had breathed new life into the oft-rejected Equal Rights Amendment, securing congressional passage for it in March 1972 (Doc. 176). The process of state ratification proceeded rapidly at first but was stalled by 1976. Although they were able to persuade Congress to extend the ratification deadline to June 30, 1982, ERA supporters failed to obtain the requisite approval of thirty-eight states by that time. In the August 1982 issue of its *Newsletter*, the Organization of American Historians published commentaries on the causes and consequences of the ERA's defeat.

* * *

A. Elizabeth Pleck
The urgency of ERA was . . . undermined by the superficial appearance of equality created by the passage of so much federal legislation in the 1960s and 1970s. Women had already been granted equal rights, the "antis" claimed. . . .

B. Frances Farenthold
[T]he passage of ERA would have provided a uniform approach to sex discrimination public laws. . . .

Because ERA was not ratified at this time, the process of changing discriminatory laws will be much slower and will involve litigation of many individual cases. . . . Without ERA, women will be left to rely on suits under Title VII of the Civil Rights Act of 1964 (which covers employment discrimination only). . . .

Women's legal rights are still vague and have no solid constitutional base which could withstand changes in mores and political climates.

Sources: Elizabeth Pleck, "The ERA Defeat: An Historian's Perspective," and Frances Farenthold, "Some Legal Ramifications of the Failure to Ratify ERA," in *The OAH Newsletter* (August 1982): 3, 11.

{r/g}DOCUMENT 291: *Dale H. Jurgens v. Clarence Thomas and Equal Employment Opportunity Commission*, September 9, 1982

Since the EEOC opened in 1965, both feminist and civil rights activists had lobbied for it to take on increased authority and enforcement powers. EEOC leadership had at the same time worked toward shaping the agency into an exemplary model of affirmative action by developing ambitious annual affirmative action plans and aggressively implementing them. In 1978 white male employees sued the EEOC, claiming that the annual plans were biased in favor of women and Hispanics and violated Title VII. They won their case in federal district court in September 1982. Ironically, by then Clarence Thomas was the defendant for policy decisions that contradicted his own beliefs, and Leon Higginbotham—whose judgments historically were supportive of the EEOC—was the judge who rendered the ruling against the agency and against its effort to invoke the *Weber* case (Doc. 262).

* * *

The issue before the court is whether Title VII prohibits the EEOC from adopting its hiring scheme favoring minorities and women, a scheme referred to as "affirmative action," when no statistical disparity exists between the number of those employees in its workforce and the labor force and there is no history of discrimination against those employees by the agency. . . .

The plan in *Weber* was approved because it would "end as soon as the percentage of black skilled craftworkers in the Gramercy plant approximated the percentage of blacks in the local labor force." . . . The plan was not "intended to maintain racial balance, but simply to eliminate a manifest racial imbalance." . . .

The [EEOC] plans were not remedial because jobs were not tradition-ally closed to women and minorities. Nor were they temporary. . . .

The EEOC claims to have been determined to build an agency that exemplified its congressionally imposed duty to attack discrimination. That determination can hardly be faulted. In its execution, however, the EEOC fell into a . . . trap of believing that matches [*sic*] of employee pro-file and workforce makeup is the legal command. No law known to this court so requires. . . . I do not intend to demean the high-mindedness of the EEOC, despite the close kinship of that quality with high-handedness. Nor is it my purpose to mask the deep complexity of the concerns addressed by Weber by neat turns of words. In plain language, this is a case of the cow stepping into the bucket.

Source: Federal Equal Opportunity Reporter (September 9, 1982): 257, 259.

{g}DOCUMENT 292: House Resolution 190, November 16, 1983

On top of defeat of the ERA, advocates of woman's rights found other hard-won gains being called into question. District court rulings in 1982 and 1983 left the enforcement of Title IX surrounded in ambi-guity. In *University of Richmond v. Bell* a panel of judges absolved that university of compliance with Title IX because it did not receive "di-rect" federal funding (only federal money for student financial aid). In *Hillsdale College v. HEW* another court limited that college's compli-ance to the one department receiving federal funds and rejected HEW's claim that the entire college was subject to Title IX regulation. In con-trast, two separate judicial panels ruled in *Haffer v. Temple University* and *Grove City College v. Bell* that Title IX covers both direct and indirect federal aid and can be enforced against the entire institution receiving that aid. Legislators, not only anxious about Title IX enforce-ment but fearing that assaults on one instrument of affirmative action portended attacks on all affirmative action statutes, took immedi-ate action in the form of a resolution on behalf of broad application of Title IX.

* * *

Resolved, That it is the sense of the House of Representatives that title IX of the Education Amendments of 1972 and regulations issued pursuant to such title should not be amended or altered in any manner which will lessen the comprehensive coverage of such statute in eliminating gender discrimination throughout the American educational system.

Source: Congressional Record 129 (November 16, 1983): 33104.

{r/g/d}DOCUMENT 293: Remarks of Representative Paul Simon on HR 190, November 1983

During debate on House Resolution 190 its supporters made clear its intended application to other fundamental civil rights laws. Among these supporters was Representative Paul Simon of Illinois, cosponsor of HR 190.

* * *

Mr. SIMON. . . . Because title IX, title VI and section 504 are so closely linked, House Resolution 190 also signals clearly to the administration that the House also believes that title VI of the Civil Rights Act of 1964, which restricts discrimination on the basis of race, and section 504 of the Rehabilitation Act of 1973, which prohibits institutions from discriminating against the handicapped also must be extended as broadly as possible.

Source: Congressional Record 129 (November 16, 1983): 33105.

{g}DOCUMENT 294: *Grove City College et al. v. Bell, Secretary of Education, et al.,* February 1984

Maintaining that the receipt of federal funds only in the form of student financial aid entailed no Title IX compliance, Grove City College petitioned the Supreme Court. A court majority ruled in February 1984 that Title IX applied exclusively to the student aid program. Justices Brennan and Marshall concurred in requiring Title IX compliance, but dissented from limiting it to a single progam. By this time the Justice Department's position had shifted—from insisting that Grove City sign a blanket "assurance of Compliance" to agreeing with the Court majority.

* * *

Justice WHITE delivered the opinion of the Court.
We conclude that the receipt of BEOG's [basic educational opportunity grants from the federal government] by some of the Grove City's stu-

dents does not trigger institution-wide coverage under Title IX. In purpose and effect, BEOG's represent federal financial assistance to the College's own financial aid program, and it is that program that may properly be regulated under Title IX. . . .

JUSTICE BRENNAN, with whom JUSTICE MARSHALL joins, concurring in part and dissenting in part. . . .
[T]he Court completely disregards the broad remedial purposes of Title IX that consistently have controlled our prior interpretations of this civil rights statute. . . .
The absurdity of the Court's decision is . . . demonstrated by examining its practical effect. According to the Court, the "financial aid program" at Grove City College may not discriminate on the basis of sex because it is covered by Title IX, but the College is not prohibited from discriminating in its admissions, its athletic programs, or even its various academic departments. The Court thus sanctions practices that Congress clearly could not have intended.

Source: 465 U.S. 555 at 557, 573–574, 581, 583, 601 (1984).

{r}DOCUMENT 295: *Firefighters Local Union No. 1784 v. Stotts*, June 12, 1984

If the Grove City decision pleased the Reagan Justice Department, another Supreme Court ruling in the summer of 1984 positively delighted Assistant Attorney General Reynolds. The case originated with a class-action suit filed by African American firefighters against the city of Memphis. Although the suit was settled by a consent decree approved by a federal district court, city employee layoffs due to a budget shortfall reopened the issue. Under the consent decree the city was committed to a goal of bringing the proportion of African Americans in the Fire Department up to their proportion in the local labor force. Under the prevailing seniority system African Americans would bear the brunt of the layoffs, virtually negating the goal set by the consent decree. Consequently, the District Court issued an injunction against laying off African American firefighters. White firefighters who were laid off despite their seniority appealed the injunction. They lost the appeal but gained a hearing before the Supreme Court, where they won. William Bradford Reynolds declared *Stotts* to be "an exhilarating decision."

* * *

Justice WHITE delivered the opinion of the Court.

The issue at the heart of this case is whether the District Court exceeded its powers in entering an injunction requiring white employees to be laid off, when the otherwise applicable seniority system would have called for the layoff of black employees with less seniority. We are convinced that the Court of Appeals erred in resolving this issue and in affirming the District Court. . . .

[T]here is no mention of layoffs or demotions within . . . the [consent] decree; nor is there any suggestion of an intention to depart from the existing seniority system or from the City's arrangement with the Union. . . .

Title VII protects bona fide seniority systems. . . .

[T]here was no finding that any of the blacks protected from layoff had been a victim of discrimination and no award of competitive seniority to any of them. . . .

[T]he judgment of the Court of Appeals is reversed.

Justice Blackmun, writing for the Court members who dissented from the majority, argued that the Court should never have taken this case in the first place, since the layoffs had ended and those affected by them had been returned to their jobs within a month. He termed the majority decision "an improper exercise of judicial power" and then addressed the arguments with which the majority supported their decision.

Justice BLACKMUN, with whom Justice BRENNAN and Justice MARSHALL join, dissenting.

[T]he Court . . . focuses on an issue that is not in these cases. It begins its analysis by stating that the "issue . . ." is the District Court's power to "enter an injunction requiring white employees to be laid off." That statement, with all respect, is simply incorrect. . . . The preliminary injunction did not require the city to lay off any white employees at all. In fact, several parties interested in the suit, including the union, attempted to persuade the city to avoid layoffs entirely by reducing the working hours of all Fire Department employees. . . .

[T]he . . . request for a preliminary injunction did not include a request for individual awards of retroactive seniority—and contrary to the implication of the Court's opinion, the District Court did not make any such awards. Rather, the District Court order required the city to conduct its layoffs in a race-conscious manner. . . . The city remained free to lay off any individual black so long as the percentage of black representation was maintained. . . .

[I]t is improper and unfair to fault respondents for failing to show

"that any of the blacks protected from layoff had been a victim of discrimination." . . . for the simple reasons that the claims on which such a
showing would have been made never went to trial. The whole point of
the consent decree in these cases . . . is for both parties to avoid the time
and expense of litigating the question of liability and identifying the
victims of discrimination.

Source: 467 U.S. 561 at 572–573, 574, 579, 583, 593, 605, 613–614, 615–616 (1984).

{r}DOCUMENT 296: Cartoon by Mike Lane, June 6, 1985

The zeal with which William Bradford Reynolds seized upon *Stotts*,
using it as a legal pry bar to reopen and readjudicate fifty-one consent
decrees involving urban fire and police departments, contributed to a
popular image of him as arrogant and callous. That image was reflected
in the following editorial cartoon created by Mike Lane of the *Baltimore
Evening Sun*.

* * *

Source: Mike Lane, *Baltimore Evening Sun* (June 6, 1985).

The Justice Department was not the only federal agency to welcome the *Stotts* decision. By 1984 President Reagan, despite spirited counterefforts in Congress, had managed to appoint to the Civil Rights Commission a majority of commissioners who shared his stance against affirmative action and to top off that majority with an aggressive new staff director, Linda Chavez, who also enthusiastically opposed the concept. In January 1985 Chavez joined Chairman Pendleton and Vice-Chairman Morris Abrams in a press conference, where they celebrated the *Stotts* decision as "a milestone in civil rights law [that] will have a profound impact in limiting the use of so-called remedies such as quotas and similar devices" (quoted by Weiss 1997, 176). Two months later the commission scheduled hearings on "Selected Affirmative Action Topics in Employment and Business Set-Asides." The day before the hearings Pendleton spoke to the National Press Club, where he denounced "preferential treatment" and referred to civil rights leaders as "new racists," expecting "results to be guaranteed without competition" (Weiss 1997, 177). Angered and offended, supporters of affirmative action who had been invited to send representatives to the hearings declined to participate. Overall, the hearings, resonant with hostility toward affirmative action, were a kind of overture to the work of undoing set-asides that would culminate in the 1989 Supreme Court decision of *Richmond v. Croson* (Doc. 312).

{r}DOCUMENT 297: Statement to the Civil Rights Commission by Parren J. Mitchell, March 1985

Maryland congressman Parren Mitchell, the author of the first set-aside legislation (Docs. 280–282), made a brief appearance at the CRC hearings, submitted a strong written statement, and expressed his opinion that Pendleton's Press Club comments were "repugnant." Mitchell's statement and the testimony of others made reference to the Small Business Act, which originated in the 1950s, authorized set-asides for small businesses, and more recently had been amended to authorize programs—designated 8(a) and 8(d)—specifically for minority business set-asides.

* * *

The incessant attacks on affirmative action over recent years cause those of us who believe in equity to defend constantly that which should need no defending. . . .

[T]he Congress routinely uses a system of both preferences and sanctions in order to achieve desired economic results. The Buy American Act often requires that American business firms be given a bid preference . . . over foreign firms when competing for Federal contracts. Public Law 85–804 authorizes the military to pay extraordinary contractual relief to essential defense contractors. . . . The tax laws allow our largest defense contractors to postpone the payment of Federal income taxes pending the total completion of a defense system. . . .

Although only 1 percent of the firms in the United States are large business concerns, they are receiving over 80 percent of the Federal purchase dollar. Of the less than 20 percent received by small business, more than one-half of that meager amount comes through the small business-set-aside program. . . .

A *particular* contractor fails to obtain a Federal contract because it was awarded to an 8(a) firm. Our innocent contractor claims to be a victim. . . . But is this contractor really a victim? . . . Did our disappointed contractor have a right to this contract or merely an expectation that the system would continue as it has in the past, that it would benefit from the preservation of the results of past discrimination?

Source: "Selected Affirmative Action Topics in Employment and Business Set-Asides," Consultation/Hearing of the U.S. Commission on Civil Rights (March 6–7, 1985): 67, 69, 70.

{r}DOCUMENT 298: Statement of the Associated Specialty Contractors, Inc., to the U.S. Commission on Civil Rights, March 1985

The CRC hearings on set-asides attracted spokesmen for large contractors' associations. The president of the Associated Specialty Contractors, Inc., Kurt A. J. Monier, described his association as an umbrella organization for eight national associations of construction specialty contractors.

* * *

Virtually all contractors have gone through the same growing pains to get where they are. This assures that the survivors are competent contractors. . . . There is not enough work to keep everyone in business who wants to be a subcontractor, and many fail in the process. There is no reason why minority-controlled firms should not have the same right to succeed *or* fail as nonminority firms, and it does not behoove the government to use set-asides, quotas, and subsidies as a temporary economic prop for firms that would not otherwise succeed. . . .

In one of a series of articles . . . the *Washington Post* . . . reported that increasingly examples had become known of SBA [Small Business Administration] contracts going to unqualified companies, among them organizations headed by wealthy white businessmen who used poor blacks and other minority persons as fronts.

Source: Kurt A. J. Monier, Statement of the Associated Specialty Contractors, Inc., "Selected Affirmative Action Topics in Employment and Business Set-Asides," a Consultation/Hearing of the U.S. Commission on Civil Rights (March 6–7, 1985): 243–244, 245.

{r/g}DOCUMENT 299: Testimony of Minority Entrepreneurs Presented to the U.S. Commission on Civil Rights, March 1985

The final portion of the CRC hearings involved a panel of four minority business executives, each of whom was asked to address the questions, "Is there a buddy system out there and if so, does it work to the disadvantage of minority business enterprises?" and "What other barriers do you see to the success of your firms?" Responses ranged from the outspoken denunciations of racism on the part of Toni Y. Luck, president of a food manufacturing company, to the cautious reflections of construction company executive Roger R. Blunt. Chairman Pendleton reserved the last word of the hearings for himself.

* * *

Ms. Luck. There are organizations of folk who get together—and it's basically an old boy network and it shuts out women; it shuts out blacks; it shuts out Hispanics. . . .

Mr. Blunt. I rather suspect our problem is one of credibility and performance and getting on the inside to demonstrate that we can deliver. . . .

I would say in construction . . . one of the real barriers is access to surety support, bonding. . . .

In talking with majority firms . . . I repeatedly get the answer, "You give me a minority firm or any firm that can give me a bond and I'd be happy to deal with that firm. . . ."

Ms. Luck. [W]e cannot get bonds; we have problems with access to capital; we have problems with access to knowledge; and all that comes out of the public perception of being a minority and also the public perception that the government is standing around handing out to minorities all these wonderful deals. . . .

CHAIRMAN PENDLETON. [O]ne has to look at whether the government brings you together or does it do things . . . that divide you? I think a lot of these preferences are a result of doing things to people, not really helping people to get along.

Source: "Selected Affirmative Action Topics in Employment and Business Set-Asides," Consultation/Hearing of the U.S. Commission on Civil Rights (March 6–7, 1985): 168, 169, 171–172, 176.

{r}DOCUMENT 300: *Wygant et al. v. Jackson Board of Education et al.*, May 19, 1986

The Supreme Court ruling in *Stotts* (Doc. 295) and its judgment in a school system employment policy case in May 1986 were noted by many commentators as evidence of a hardening of the highest court against civil rights and affirmative action initiatives. The school system case began in 1972, when the Teachers Union and School Board of Jackson, Michigan, negotiated a collective bargaining agreement that included a provision (designated "Article XII") that in the event of layoffs, the percentage of minority teachers laid off would never exceed the percentage of minority teachers employed at the time of the layoff. The agreement was ratified by a majority vote of the membership (which was 80 percent white) and renewed by the same means in six successive contract renegotiations. When layoffs occurred in 1974, the School Board ignored Article XII, retaining white tenured teachers and laying off African American probationary teachers. The union and two African American teachers sued and lost in federal district court, then filed a new suit in state court, which found in their favor. As a result of the state court finding, when layoffs occurred in 1976–1977 and 1981–1982, the School Board let go some whites with seniority and retained some African Americans still on probation. This prompted the laid-off whites to sue in federal district court. That court justified Article XII of the collective bargaining agreement as an appropriate means of providing "role models for minority school children." The white petitioners then took their case to the Supreme Court, where a majority of justices—Powell, Burger, Rehnquist, O'Connor, and White—reversed the previous decision and declared the layoff policy to be unconstitutional. Justice Marshall submitted a dissent joined by Brennan and Blackmun. In a separate statement, Justice Stevens also dissented.

* * *

JUSTICE POWELL announced the judgment of the Court. . . .

This Court never has held that societal discrimination alone is sufficient to justify a racial classification. Rather, the Court has insisted upon
some showing of prior discrimination by the governmental unit involved
before allowing limited use of racial classifications. . . .

[T]he role model theory employed by the District Court has no logical
stopping point.

Carried to its logical extreme, the idea that black students are better
off with black teachers could lead to the very system the Court rejected
in *Brown v. Board of Education*. . . .

We have previously expressed concern over the burden that a
preferential-layoffs scheme imposes on innocent parties. . . . In cases involving valid *hiring* goals, the burden to be borne by innocent individuals is diffused to a considerable extent among society generally.
Though hiring goals may burden some innocent individuals, they simply
do not impose the same kind of injury that layoffs impose. Denial of a
future employment is not as intrusive as loss of an existing job. . . .

We therefore hold that, as a means of accomplishing purposes that
otherwise may be legitimate, the Board's layoff plan is not sufficiently
narrowly tailored. Other, less intrusive means of accomplishing similar
purposes—such as the adoption of hiring goals—are available. . . .

We . . . reverse the judgment of the Court of Appeals for the Sixth Circuit.

JUSTICE MARSHALL, with whom JUSTICE BRENNAN and JUSTICE
BLACKMUN join, dissenting.

When an elected school board and a teachers' union collectively bar-
gain a layoff provision designed to preserve the effects of a valid minority recruitment plan by apportioning layoffs between two racial
groups, as a result of a settlement achieved under the auspices of a su-
pervisory state agency charged with protecting the civil rights of all citizens, that provision should not be upset by this Court on constitutional
grounds.

In his separate dissent Justice Stevens responded to Justice Powell's
critique of the position that African American teachers are needed as
"role models."

JUSTICE STEVENS, dissenting

In the context of public education, it is quite obvious that a school
board may reasonably conclude that an integrated faculty will be able
to provide benefits to the student body that could not be provided by

an all-white, or nearly all-white, faculty. . . . It is one thing for a white child to be taught by a white teacher that color, like beauty, is only "skin deep"; it is far more convincing to experience that truth on a day-to-day basis during the routine, ongoing learning process. . . .

Source: 476 U.S. 267 at 269, 274, 275, 276, 282–284, 295, 312, 313, 315 (1986).

{r}DOCUMENT 301: *Local 28 of the Sheet Metal Workers' International Association et al. v. Equal Employment Opportunity Commission et al.*, July 2, 1986

Just as the Reagan Justice Department had executed a 180-degree turn of policy in regard to Title IX (Doc. 191), the Reagan EEOC made a similar turnabout in a case started in the 1970s by New York minority sheet metal workers against their union. By the time the case reached the Supreme Court in 1986, the agency (led by Clarence Thomas) reversed its position and supported the union against the claims of the minority workers. Although Supreme Court majorities had recently disappointed civil rights advocates, in this instance the Court upheld affirmative action on behalf of the minority workers.

Beginning in 1975, Local 28 of the Sheet Metal Workers union and its apprenticeship committee in the New York City area were repeatedly found guilty by lower courts of violating Title VII. When they failed to comply with district court orders in 1982 and again in 1983, that court found them guilty of contempt and levied a fine of $150,000. This amount was to be placed in a fund for the employment, training, education, and recruitment of minorities, and a goal was set to increase nonwhite union membership by 29.23 percent by August 1987. With EEOC backing, the union and apprenticeship committee appealed to the Supreme Court on the grounds—among other arguments—that the lower court order violated Title VII, especially Section 706g, by requiring hiring quotas and establishing a discriminatory fund. The Supreme Court upheld the lower court order, but the justices differed on specific points. Six justices—Brennan (who wrote the majority opinion), Marshall, Blackmun, Stevens, Powell, and White—agreed that the District Court had not overstepped its authority in the specific requirements to which it held the union. Five justices—those just listed minus White—agreed that the "membership goal" (called a "quota" by the union) and the fund order did not violate Title VII and were constitutional. Justices O'Connor, Rehnquist, and Burger dissented.

* * *

JUSTICE BRENNAN announced the judgment of the Court.

In this case, several factors lead us to conclude that the relief ordered by the District Court was proper.

First, both the District Court and the Court of Appeals agreed that the membership goal and Fund order were necessary to remedy petitioners' pervasive and egregious discrimination. . . .

Second, the District Court's flexible application of the membership goal gives strong indication that it is not being used simply to achieve and maintain racial balance, but rather as a benchmark against which the court could gauge petitioners' efforts to remedy past discrimination. . . .

Third, both the membership goal and Fund order are temporary measures . . . [which] did not require any member of the union to be laid off, and did not discriminate against *existing* union members. . . .

The judgment of the Court of Appeals is hereby *Affirmed*. . . .

JUSTICE WHITE, dissenting.

I am convinced . . . that holding the union in contempt for failing to attain the membership quota during a time of economic doldrums in the construction industry and a declining demand for the union skills involved in this case was for all practical purposes equivalent to a judicial insistence that the union comply even if it required the displacement of nonminority workers by members of the plaintiff class. The remedy is inequitable . . . and . . . I dissent.

Source: 478 U.S. 421 at 426, 476, 477–478, 479, 483, 499–500 (1986).

{r}DOCUMENT 302: *Local Number 93, International Association of Firefighters, AFL-CIO v. City of Cleveland,* July 2, 1986

On the same day that the Supreme Court ruled on Local 28, the same five justices who formed the majority on that decision (Brennan, Marshall, Blackmun, Powell, and Stevens) were joined by O'Connor in another decision that lifted the spirits of affirmative action advocates and blunted the force of the campaign by the Department of Justice against consent decrees on behalf of minorities and women in various cities. In *Local Number 93, International Association of Firefighters, AFL-CIO v. City of Cleveland* the Supreme Court upheld lower court rulings favoring affirmative action measures to increase the numbers of African American and Hispanic firefighters hired and promoted in the Cleveland Fire Department. After this decision the Justice Department—which had sided with the white firefighters' union—began backing away from the position it took after *Stotts* (Doc. 295) and ceased pressuring other cities to abandon their affirmative action plans. With regard to *Stotts*, the Court majority agreed with a Court of Appeals conclusion that "this case involves a consent decree and not an injunction [which] makes the legal basis of the *Stotts* decision inapplicable" (478 U.S. at 513). In dissenting from this position, Justices White and Rehnquist set forth points of view that would emerge in the not-distant future as the majority opinion of the highest court.

* * *

Justice BRENNAN delivered the opinion of the Court.

The question presented in this case is whether . . . Title VII of the Civil Rights Act of 1964 . . . precludes the entry of a consent decree which provides relief that may benefit individuals who were not the actual victims of the defendant's discriminatory practices. . . .

The Court holds today in *Sheet Metal Workers v. EEOC* . . . [Doc. 301] that courts may, in appropriate cases, provide relief under Title VII that benefits individuals who were not the actual victims of a defendant's discriminatory practices. We need not decide whether this is one of those cases, however. For we hold that whether or not subsection 706g [of Title VII] precludes a court from imposing certain forms of race-conscious relief after the trial, that provision does not apply to relief awarded in a consent decree. We therefore affirm the judgment of the Court of Appeals.

Justice WHITE dissenting.

[L]eapfrogging minorities over senior and better qualified whites is an impermissible remedy under Title VII. . . .

None of the racially preferred blacks in the present case was shown to have been a victim of discriminatory promotion practices; and none of the whites denied promotion was shown to have been responsible or in any way implicated in the discriminatory practices recited in the decree.

Source: 478 U.S. 501 at 504, 515, 534–535 (1986).

{r}DOCUMENT 303: *United States v. Paradise*, February 25, 1987

In the early months of 1987 the Supreme Court continued to rule favorably on antidiscrimination and affirmative action cases. In February the Court decided *U.S. v. Paradise*, affirming lower court orders on behalf of the employment and promotion of qualified African Americans by the Alabama Department of Public Safety as state troopers. Roots of the *Paradise* case reached back to 1972, when the NAACP brought a class-action suit against the Alabama Department, charging that it systematically excluded African Americans from being hired as other than menial workers. After nearly twelve years, three federal district court orders (one upheld on appeal), and two consent decrees, the District Court judge in 1983 found an "intolerable scenario" in which discrimination in the department was "pervasive and conspicuous at all ranks above entry-level positions." Observing that the consequences of past discrimination would not "wither away of their own accord," he ordered that "for a period of time" 50 percent of promotions in the upper ranks must go to African Americans, so long as qualified black candidates were available and if a given rank was less than 25 percent black at the time of the promotions. The Reagan Justice Department then appealed the District Court order of 1983, claiming that it violated the Fourteenth Amendment. When the appeals court upheld the order, the attorney general turned to the Supreme Court, which affirmed the decisions of the lower courts. Justices Brennan, Marshall, Blackmun, and Powell, with Stevens concurring in a separate opinion, formed the court majority. White, O'Connor, and Scalia dissented.

* * *

JUSTICE BRENNAN announced the judgment of the Court. . . .

The remedy imposed here is an effective, temporary, and flexible measure. It applies only if qualified blacks are available, only if the Department has an objective need to make promotions, and only if the Department fails to implement a promotion procedure that does not have an adverse impact on blacks. . . .

The race-conscious relief imposed here was amply justified and narrowly tailored to serve the legitimate and laudable purposes of the District Court. . . .

In a footnote Justice Brennan took issue with fellow justice O'Connor.

n. 28   JUSTICE O'CONNOR'S dissent states that [other remedies could have been attempted]. . . . [W]e note that these "alternatives" were never proposed to the court. [W]e think JUSTICE O'CONNOR'S dissent overlooks the District Judge's patient accommodation of the Department's asserted needs and the long history of recalcitrance that preceded the race conscious order.

JUSTICE O'CONNOR . . . dissenting. . . .

The District Court had available several alternatives that would have achieved full compliance with the consent decrees without trammeling on the rights of nonminority troopers. The court, for example, could have appointed a trustee to develop a promotion procedure. . . . Alternatively, the District Court could have found the recalcitrant Department in contempt of court.

Source: 480 U.S. 149 at 152, 185–186, 177, 196, 199–200 (1987).

{g}DOCUMENT 304: *Paul E. Johnson v. Transportation Agency, Santa Clara County, California,* March 25, 1987

In March 1987 the Supreme Court affirmed for the first time that women as a group were entitled to affirmative action; however, the Court still refrained from placing gender discrimination on the same legal plane as race discrimination. The case at issue—*Johnson v. Santa Clara County*—arose from a dispute between a man and woman over the job of dispatcher in the Transportation Agency of Santa Clara County, California. The director of the agency was authorized to select any of seven applicants who qualified for what had always been a male position. Following the guidelines of an agency affirmative action plan, the director selected Diane Joyce for the job. During the initial interviews, where candidates were scored and where a mark of 70 was required for eligibility, Joyce had received 73 points. Another applicant, Paul Johnson, had received 75 points. He filed a complaint with the EEOC charging that he had been denied the dispatcher's job because of his sex. The EEOC ruled that he had grounds for a lawsuit, which he filed and won in a U.S. district court. Diane Joyce succeeded in having the district court decision overturned by a federal appeals court, whereupon Johnson carried the case to the Supreme Court and lost. The majority decision was delivered by Justice Brennan on behalf of himself and Associate Justices Marshall, Blackmun, Powell, and Stevens, with concurring opinions filed by Stevens and O'Connor. Dissents were filed by Scalia, Rehnquist, and White.

* * *

It is clear that the decision to hire Joyce was made pursuant to an Agency plan that directed that sex or race be taken into account for the purpose of remedying underrepresentation. The Agency Plan acknowledged the "limited opportunities that have existed in the past" . . . for women to find employment in certain job classifications. . . . [W]omen were only 2 of the 28 Officials and Administrators, 5 of the 58 Professionals, 12 of the 124 Technicians, none of the Skilled Craft Workers, and 1—who was Joyce—of the Road Maintenance Workers. . . .

Given the obvious imbalance in the Skilled Craft category, and given the Agency's commitment to eliminating such imbalances, it was plainly not unreasonable for the Agency to determine that it was appropriate to consider as one factor the sex of Ms. Joyce in making its decision. . . .

[P]etitioner [Johnson] had no absolute entitlement to the road dispatcher position. Seven of the applicants were classified as qualified and eligible, and the Agency Director was authorized to promote any of the seven. . . . [W]hile the petitioner in this case was denied a promotion, he retained his employment with the Agency, at the same salary and with the same seniority, and remained eligible for other promotions. . . .

The Agency earmarks no positions for anyone; sex is but one of several factors that may be taken into account in evaluating qualified applicants for a position. . . .

We therefore hold that the Agency appropriately took into account as one factor the sex of Diane Joyce in determining that she should be promoted to the road dispatcher position.

Justice Scalia's dissent (joined by Chief Justice Rehnquist and joined in part by Justice White) depicted Paul Johnson as a victim of an inverted interpretation of Title VII and as one of innumerable citizens rendered vulnerable by the majority decision to preferential employment policies based on race and gender.

Justice Scalia . . . dissenting.

The Court today completes the process of converting [Title VII] from a guarantee that race or sex will *not* be the basis for employment determination, to a guarantee that it often *will*. . . . [W]e effectively replace the goal of a discrimination-free society with the quite incompatible goal of proportionate representation by race and by sex in the workplace. . . .

It is unlikely that today's result will be displeasing to politically elected officials, to whom it provides the means of quickly accommodating the demands of organized groups to achieve concrete, numerical improvement in the economic status of particular constituencies. Nor will it displease the world of corporate and governmental employers . . . for whom the cost of hiring less qualified workers is often substantially less . . . than the cost of litigating Title VII cases. . . . In fact, the only losers in the process are the Johnsons of the country, for whom Title VII has been not

merely repealed but actually inverted. The irony is that these individuals—predominantly unknown, unaffluent, unorganized—suffer this injustice at the hands of a Court fond of thinking itself the champion of
the politically impotent. I dissent.

Source: 480 U.S. 616 at 634, 637, 638, 641–642, 658, 677 (1987).

{r}DOCUMENT 305: *New York Times*, December 15, 1986

While Justice Scalia expressed animosity against the affirmative action program upheld in the Johnson case, white supremacist factions
began to rise on college campuses, using physical and verbal violence
against African Americans and targeting affirmative action for special
vilification. In December 1986 the *New York Times* reported "a growing pattern of bigotry" on predominantly white campuses, including a
cross burning at the University of Alabama.

* * *

"We have seen resentment on the part of white students who perceive
that black students have been given a 'free ride' so to speak," said Dennis
Wynn of the Community Relations Service, a Justice Department agency.

Source: Lena Williams, "Officials Voice Growing Concern over Racial Incidents
on U.S. Campuses," *New York Times* (December 15, 1996): A18.

{r/g/d}DOCUMENT 306: Civil Rights Restoration Act of 1988

As 1987 gave way to 1988, affirmative action appeared to be holding
its own with the Supreme Court, at least for the time being. Meanwhile,
its supporters in Congress continued to battle the implications of the
Grove City decision (Doc. 294) by launching the Civil Rights Restoration Act, which both houses had passed by March 1988, only to have
President Reagan veto it. Riled lawmakers swiftly overrode the veto,
and the act was signed into law. Like House Resolution 190 in 1983
(Doc. 292), it left no doubt as to congressional intent regarding not
only Title IX (the focus of Grove City) but other major statutes designed
to prohibit discrimination based on race, gender, disability, national
origin, and age. The definition of "Program or Activity" specified for
Title IX in the following excerpt was repeated with regard to the other
statutes in the remainder of the act.

* * *

Section 2. The Congress finds that—

(1) certain aspects of recent decisions and opinions of the Supreme Court have unduly narrowed or cast doubt upon the broad application of title IX of the education Amendments of 1972, section 504 of the Rehabilitation Act of 1973, the Age Discrimination Act of 1975, and title VI of the Civil Rights Act of 1964; and

(2) legislative action is necessary to restore the prior consistent and long-standing executive branch interpretation and broad, institution-wide application of those laws as previously administered.

Section 3. (a) Title IX of the Education Amendments of 1972 is amended by adding . . . the following . . .

the term "program or activity" and "program" mean all of the operations of—

(1) (A) a department, agency, special purpose district or other instrumentality of a State or of a local government. . . .

(2) (A) a college, university, or other postsecondary institution, or a public system of education. . . .

(3) (A) an entire corporation, partnership or other private organization, or an entire sole proprietorship.

Source: U.S. Statutes at Large 102, Pt. 1 (1990): 28–29.

{d}DOCUMENT 307: Announcement of a Student Rally at Gallaudet University, March 1, 1988

During the campaign for the Civil Rights Restoration Act disabled activists worked closely with civil rights organizations to encourage and bolster congressional resistance to the Reagan Revolution. Soon, disabled activism, calling on ideals and strategies reminiscent of the civil rights movement, created a compelling drama at Gallaudet University in 1988 that attracted the attention of the world. In February 1988 students at Gallaudet—a highly respected center of higher education serving deaf students for 124 years—insisted that the next president of their institution must be deaf. When the governing board announced three finalists for the position, including two deaf candidates, student expectations soared. When the board selected the only hearing candidate (Dr. Elizabeth Ann Zinser), students erupted with outrage. They not only mobilized by shutting down and occupying the campus but reached out to Congress as well as family, friends, and supporters throughout the country. After a week of dramatic student resistance against her appointment, broadcast around the world by the media, the new president withdrew, and Gallaudet alumnus and former dean (Dr. I. King Jordan) became the first deaf president. The students' victory was understood as an advance for all disabled people.

Students demonstrated their strong feelings about the selection of the seventh president of their university by staging a rally during the selection process. At the same time they wrote to every member of the House and Senate of the United States requesting support for a deaf president.

* * *

It's time! In 1842, a Roman Catholic became president of the University of Notre Dame. In 1875, a woman became president of Wellesley College. In 1886, a Jew became president of Yeshiva University. In 1926, a Black person became president of Howard University.

AND in 1988, the Gallaudet University presidency belongs to a DEAF person. To show OUR solidarity behind OUR mandate for a deaf president of OUR university, you are invited to participate in a historical RALLY!

Source: Quoted in Gannon 1989, 20.

{d}DOCUMENT 308: Cartoon by Mike Keefe, 1988

Television, radio, and print media both covered and learned from the Gallaudet student movement. Having to adapt interview methods to communicate with the deaf participants (e.g., remembering to hand the microphone to the interpreter rather than the deaf interviewee) and moved by the self-determination of the young people, reporters became their advocates. For some media veterans who had covered the civil rights movement two decades earlier, there were striking similarities between that movement and Gallaudet, except, noted one reporter, for the "eerie quiet" of the deaf campaign. Both the tendency to draw a connection to civil rights and the respect of the media for the Gallaudet students emerge in Mike Keefe's editorial cartoon, which appeared in the *Denver Post*.

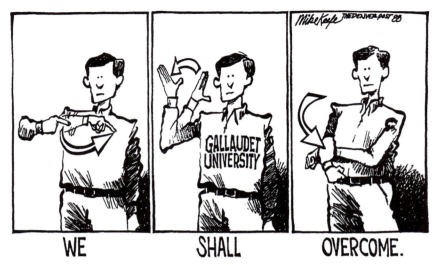

WE   SHALL   OVERCOME.

Source: Mike Keefe, *Denver Post* (March 1988), in Gannon 1989, 69.

{d}DOCUMENT 309: I. King Jordan on the Gallaudet Protests of 1988

A year after assuming the presidency of Gallaudet, I. King Jordan reflected on the significance of the events that brought him to that post.

* * *

People who before March 1988 knew little or nothing about deafness are now advocates for our rights. More people realize now that deafness is a difference, not a deficiency. . . . All of us who have an interest in the rights and empowerment of disabled or minority people have benefited from the events of that week in March. The ramifications of what the students and their supporters achieved during the week will continue for years.

Source: I. King Jordan, "Epilogue," in Gannon 1989, 173, 175.

{g}DOCUMENT 310: *"Hard-Hatted Women"* and Affirmative Action, 1988

The policy debates that occupied Congress and the courts and large-scale public campaigns that made headlines reveal much about the

politics of affirmative action, but it is necessary to turn to the life experiences of individuals to glean information about the effect of policy
on ordinary people. In *Hard-Hatted Women*, a book about women
workers who entered traditionally male jobs, editor Molly Martin presented the personal stories of women who made use of affirmative
action.

* * *

A. Interview with Rose Melendez, Latina Police Officer

The process of entering the San Francisco Police Department . . .
started for me in 1973 . . . when community groups got together and filed
a suit to open up the job to women and minorities. . . .

The first two classes of sixty recruits, in July and November of 1975,
included about thirty women each. The instructors let us know right
away they didn't want us, saying, "We'd like to welcome you all here,
even though we know a lot of you shouldn't be here." They weren't
prepared for women. There were no locker room facilities. They put us
in men's uniforms. At one point they tried making us shower with the
men, then they split us up because it was worse for the men—they were
shyer than we were. . . .

I'm a training officer now. It's only been in the last several years that
women have started to train new recruits in the field. . . . I'm doing just
what I want. . . . I like feeling that I'm changing things from within, and
having the satisfaction of seeing young women come into a better working situation.

B. Lucy Lim, the Daughter of an Asian Father and a Mexican Mother,
Interviewed by Shelley D. Coleman

My first nontraditional job was in an open-pit copper mine in Arizona.
. . . The company was pushing affirmative action, because it had a class-
action suit brought against it by a group of women in the mines in
1973. . . .

Now I work in San Francisco for Pacific Gas and Electric . . . [as] a
systems operator, or switch operator. We work in the electrical substa-
tions, where we do high voltage electrical switching and operate circuit
breaker disconnects. . . .

From doing nontraditional work, I've definitely become more confi-
dent—partly because I've topped out; I'm now journey level. I feel like
I've really achieved something. . . . I feel fortunate to be working with a
great group of guys now. Maybe it's just the times. It's the way it should
be, that women are now less a novelty. But it hasn't always been easy
dealing with the men. . . .

Sometimes I wonder how I have survived working with men. On a
one-to-one basis, it's okay, but when they're in a pack, watch out. Some

of them tell me that I was hired because of affirmative action, that I am a token. I just say I don't care, it has to start somewhere, and there are going to be lots of other women after me!

C. Susan Eisenberg, Electrician, 1988
Like many of the first women in their locals . . . I started in 1978, when affirmative action guidelines were mandated. . . .

I had both my children after I became a journeyman. As the second woman in my local to give birth, I found I had to do a lot of ground-breaking. Our union's disability and health and welfare policies were written only for the pregnancies of a member's wife. A group of women in the local . . . wrote a pamphlet explaining how these benefits applied to a pregnant union member. . . . [T]he pamphlet was only in circulation as long as the women members passed it around themselves. . . .

Driving around Boston, I love pointing out to my daughter and son "the jobs we worked together." It brings back the times when I felt like I carried a delicious secret: lying on a plank across an open airshaft on the roof of a building, tying in a fan motor, talking to the baby-in-utero. It gave me a powerful appreciation for the changes we have brought about. "We built that, Susie?" my daughter asks as we drive by a big hotel. "You bet!" I tell her.

For me, one of the biggest rewards of a high-paying construction job has been to feel less trapped by traditional gender roles at home. My husband and I have been able to switch back and forth between being the primary income-earner and being the primary home- and child-care person.

Source: Molly Martin, ed., *Hard-Hatted Women, Life on the Job* (Seattle: Seal Press, 1988, 1997): 71, 72, 79, 80, 150, 152, 153, 154, 216, 219, 221–222.

{r/g}DOCUMENT 311: "The Business Response to Affirmative Action," 1989

If affirmative action produced glimmers of satisfaction and optimism among women who used that tool to enter nontraditional jobs, it appeared also, by the end of the 1980s, to have secured a permanent hold on at least some sectors of the American business community. The following article from the *Harvard Law Review*, documented by numerous studies, describes a marked shift in attitude on the part of business leaders.

* * *

[I]n the 1970s business attitudes . . . began to change. . . . Businesses began to view affirmative action as a means not only of complying with federal remedial policies, but also of achieving independent nonremedial benefits. . . .

Businesses pursuing progressive social policies, including affirmative action plans, have been shown to outperform their competitors in rates of profitability and growth. When an affirmative action program yields such benefits, they do not accrue to the company alone. . . . All employees benefit. . . . even whites and males benefit from affirmative action to the extent that the program leads to their company's success.

Source: "Rethinking *Weber*: The Business Response to Affirmative Action," *Harvard Law Review* 102, no. 3 (January 1989): 661, 670.

{r}DOCUMENT 312: *City of Richmond v. J. A. Croson Company*, January 23, 1989

Signs of approval for affirmative action among some segments of society did not deter Reaganites from their active opposition to it. As the president's second term neared its end, the collective influence of conservative appointments to the Supreme Court became increasingly obvious. The makeup of the Court had been undergoing gradual change since the Nixon and Ford era. Although Blackmun and Powell (appointed by Nixon) and Stevens (appointed by Ford) proved to be more moderate than doctrinaire on civil rights and affirmative action issues, Nixon's third appointment, Rehnquist, added a strong, conservative voice, which became more influential when Reagan appointed him as chief justice at the 1986 retirement of Warren Burger. In addition, Reagan had the opportunity for three other appointments— O'Connor, often moderate but somewhat unpredictable, and two staunchly conservative individuals, Scalia and Kennedy. The effect of these changes was apparent in the January 1989 ruling in *City of Richmond v. J. A. Croson Company*.

The object of contention in the Richmond case was a set-aside law approved by the local City Council. It was patterned after an affirmative action program pioneered by Mayor Maynard Jackson in Atlanta in 1975 and closely followed the language of Parren Mitchell's set-aside amendment to the 1977 Public Works Employment Act as upheld by the Supreme Court in *Fullilove v. Klutznik* (Docs. 280, 283). The Richmond law required that 10 percent of any federal money allocated to the city or state for public works projects be used to purchase goods and services from minority-owned businesses. After losing a bid to in-stall plumbing fixtures in the Richmond City jail because of a failure to obtain the services of a minority contractor, the J. A. Croson Company filed a suit challenging the law. Historians of the case have noted that Croson's suit was "part of a more general series of challenges to set-aside policies that were being brought to various courts of the nation under the auspices of the Association of General Contractors" (Drake and Holsworth 1996, 142).

In the early stages of the suit a federal district court and an appeals court upheld the set-aside law. However, a strongly argued dissent by one judge at the appeals level (a Reagan appointee) provided incentive and arguments for Croson's appeal to the Supreme Court. That Court at first sent the case back to the appeals court with instructions to reconsider, in light of the high court's recent ruling on *Wygant*, which had raised the standards for scrutinizing race-conscious programs (Doc. 300). In its second look at the *Croson* case the court of appeals reversed itself, ruling against Richmond and the set-aside. It was then the city fathers' turn to appeal to the Supreme Court. This time the Court accepted the case and ruled against the Richmond law. A court majority (O'Connor, Rehnquist, White, Stevens, and Kennedy, with Scalia concurring), for the first time since the Court began ruling on affirmative action cases, demanded strict scrutiny of race-based measures aimed at the effects of past discrimination. The majority found that the Richmond set-aside did not pass such scrutiny and expressed solicitude for the rights of the white contractors who were "disadvantaged" by the law. Disregarding the federal statute from which Richmond had borrowed the language for its set-aside, the majority also impugned the motives of the City Council in including such minorities as Eskimos and Aleuts in their program. In vigorous dissents, Justices Marshall, Brennan, and Blackmun decried the majority's "full-scale retreat" from *Fullilove* and other past decisions upholding race-conscious remedies targeting historically embedded discrimination.

* * *

The Richmond Plan denies certain citizens the opportunity to compete for a fixed percentage of public contracts based solely upon their race. To whatever racial group these citizens belong, their "personal rights" to be treated with equal dignity and respect are implicated by a rigid rule erecting race as the sole criterion in an aspect of public decision making. . . .

To a large extent, the set-aside of subcontracting dollars seems to rest on the unsupported assumption that white prime contractors simply will not hire minority firms. . . .

The city and the District Court also relied on evidence that MBE [minority business enterprise] membership in local contractors' associations was extremely low.... There are numerous explanations for this dearth of minority participation, including past societal discrimination in education and economic opportunities as well as both black and white career and entrepreneurial choices. Blacks may be disproportionately attracted to industries other than construction.... The mere fact that black membership in these trade organizations is low, standing alone, cannot establish a prima facie case of discrimination....

There is *absolutely no evidence* of past discrimination against Spanish-speaking, Oriental, Indian, Eskimo, or Aleut persons in any aspect of the Richmond construction industry.... The random inclusion of racial groups that, as a practical matter, may never have suffered from discrimination in the construction industry in Richmond suggests that perhaps the city's purpose was not in fact to remedy past discrimination....

Justice STEVENS concurring in part and concurring in the judgement....

The ordinance is equally vulnerable because of its failure to identify the characteristics of the disadvantaged class of white contractors that justify the disparate treatment.... The composition of the disadvantaged class of white contractors presumably includes some who have been guilty of unlawful discrimination, some who practiced discrimination before it was forbidden by law, and some who have never discriminated against anyone on the basis of race. Imposing a common burden on such a disparate class merely because each member of the class is of the same race stems from reliance on a stereotype rather than fact or reason....

Justice SCALIA concurring in the judgement....

[I]n Richmond ... the enactment of a set-aside [was] clearly and directly beneficial to the dominant political group, which happens also to be the dominant racial group. The same thing has no doubt happened before in other cities ... and blacks have often been on the receiving end of the injustices. Where injustice is the game, however, turnabout is not fair play....

[T]hose who believe that racial preferences can help to "even the score" display, and reinforce, a manner of thinking by race that was the source of the injustice and that will, if it endures within our society, be the source of more injustice still....

Justice MARSHALL, with whom Justice BRENNAN and Justice BLACK-MUN join, dissenting....

Today, for the first time, a majority of this Court has adopted strict scrutiny as its standard of Equal Protection Clause review of race-conscious remedial measures.... This is an unwelcome development....

The majority's view that remedial measures undertaken by municipalities with black leadership must face a stiffer test of Equal Protection

Clause scrutiny than remedial measures undertaken by municipalities with white leadership implies a lack of political maturity on the part of the Nation's elected minority officials that is totally unwarranted. Such insulting judgments have no place in constitutional jurisprudence. . . .

Justice BLACKMUN, with whom Justice BRENNAN joins, dissenting. . . .

I never thought that I would live to see the day when the city of Richmond, Virginia, the cradle of the Old Confederacy, sought on its own, within a narrow confine, to lessen the stark impact of persistent discrimination. But Richmond, to its great credit, acted. Yet this Court, the supposed bastion of equality, strikes down Richmond's efforts as though discrimination had never existed or was not demonstrated in this particular litigation.

Source: 488 U.S. 469, 502–503, 506, 511, 516, 520, 524, 527–528, 551–552, 555, 561 (1989).

{r}DOCUMENT 313: "The Sunset of Affirmative Action?," *National Black Law Journal*, Spring 1990

The Croson decision greatly alarmed civil rights advocates, many of whom saw in it the seeds of the destruction of affirmative action. This response was summarized in the *National Black Law Journal* about a year after the decision was rendered.

* * *

Opponents of affirmative action approvingly see the *Croson* decision as a virtual death sentence for set-aside programs at the state and local level because it will make it difficult for cities to establish the increased proof required. Ironically, proponents of affirmative action see the ruling as having the same effect. Such supporters will now wonder about the extreme requirements state and local governments must follow to design and implement policies to help minority groups gain an opportunity to overcome the barriers of discrimination.

Source: Christopher H. Davis and Darrell D. Jackson, "The Sunset of Affirmative Action?: *City of Richmond v. J. A. Croson Co.*," *National Black Law Journal* 12, no. 1. (Spring 1990): 86.

{r}DOCUMENT 314: Examining Set-Asides in Richmond, Virginia, in the 1980s

Two African American political scientists at Virginia Commonwealth University provided a different perspective when, in *Croson's* aftermath, they set out to examine the impact of the Richmond set-aside law on the local economy. They concluded that the law was more significant as a political tool wielded by the relatively new African American governing majority than as a source of economic opportunity for the businesses and working classes of Richmond's African American community. The two scholars—W. Avon Drake and Robert D. Holsworth—described a process in which African American politicians consolidated their influence and negotiated an alliance of sorts with the traditional white elite to further an ambitious urban renewal project that included the set-aside program. As this process went forward, according to Drake and Holsworth, grassroots involvement in the civic life of Richmond withered. Of most import to the issue of affirmative action: minority businesses reportedly benefited relatively little from the set-aside program.

* * *

Forty-seven [minority] companies received construction monies . . . in the two-year period [1985–1987]—but these funds were not evenly distributed. . . . [T]wo contractors received a majority of the money. . . .

The dominance of these two companies . . . could be attributed to three factors. First, both businesses were uniquely situated to take advantage of the set-aside opportunity. Dwight Snead had been operating his own company in Richmond for a number of years. . . . he had already developed the name recognition and business reputation that made him a logical choice for nonminority firms looking to comply with the ordinance. . . .

The Quail Oak Company, operated by Curtis Harris and his brother, was also well situated. . . .

A second feature . . . was the nature of the local construction industry. . . . heavily dependent on reputation and skillful networking. . . . Once the Snead and Harris companies were perceived as competent and reliable, white contractors approached them with increasing frequency. . . .

Third, both . . . used the set-aside program as an instrument for diversifying and expanding their companies. . . . [They] are exemplars of what the defenders of affirmative action said should happen. . . . By 1987, when the program was eliminated by the circuit court's decision, both firms had become less dependent on the set-asides for business and more competitive in private bidding for prime contractor jobs. . . . Speaking in 1989 . . . both Snead and Harris suggested that [profits] had not been significantly diminished since the end of the program. But they also mentioned that they are called much less frequently by white contractors and that they would have never reached their current level without the opportunity furnished by the set-aside ordinance.

Source: Drake and Holsworth 1996, 83–85.

{r}DOCUMENT 315: The Detroit Symphony and Affirmative Action in the 1980s

The attack on set-asides carried the same innuendo addressed by Nell Painter (Doc. 289)—that recipients of affirmative action were deficient in training, abilities, and/or qualifications. The innuendo appeared full-blown in the world of classical music when two African Americans in the Michigan state legislature imposed affirmative action demands on the Detroit Symphony Orchestra (DSO). In an effort to remove race or gender from consideration in auditions, the American Federation of Musicians had, since the 1970s, required "blind auditions" (performing behind a screen) for all symphony orchestra contracts. A violinist who had twice auditioned unsuccessfully for the DSO sent a letter of protest in 1984 to the orchestra director, with copies to the legislature. She charged that "the selection procedure did not encourage the identification and selection of qualified black applicants" (quoted in Blanton 1989, 29). African American lawmakers Morris Hood and David Holmes—both members of the state appropriations committee—threatened to withhold symphony funding if the orchestra did not "maximize its affirmative action efforts." Then the governor appointed a panel to make recommendations, which were for "new audition procedures that will . . . assure . . . the hiring of [minority] musicians." The upshot of these developments was a " 'one-time-only' affirmative action hire" in the person of Richard Robinson, a bass player who accepted the position with ambivalence. Other African American musicians, not to mention the majority music establishment, responded negatively. Typical of this response were the following observations in *Commentary*, written by a professional musician using a pen name.

* * *

Everyone in a position to know agrees that Richard Robinson is a fine bass player. . . . But . . . should the Detroit Symphony now begin systematically to lower its musical standards by abandoning blind auditions, it is safe to assume that . . . he will become the unwilling portent of the decline and fall of what once was a very good orchestra. That is a hard load to carry. But it is a load already carried by tens of thousands of talented middle-class blacks who have been hired in the era of mandated equality of outcome and who spend each day having to prove their worth again and again in the eyes of skeptical colleagues.

Source: Blanton 1989, 32.

{r}DOCUMENT 316: *Wards Cove Packing Co., Inc. v. Atonio,* June 5, 1989

Five months after ruling on the *Croson* case (Doc. 312) the Supreme Court announced its decision on *Wards Cove Packing Co., Inc. v. Atonio*. Again a court majority (including all of the majority in *Croson* except Stevens) retreated from precedent and appeared to negate the pivotal 1971 *Griggs* decision (Doc. 171). The Wards Cove Packing Company was a salmon cannery in Alaska. Eskimo, Filipino, and other minority employees sued the company for denying them access to skilled jobs carrying salaries higher than their cannery-line jobs. The workers had persisted since 1974 through various district and appeals court proceedings, finally winning an appeals court judgment in 1987. The cannery then carried the case to the Supreme Court, which overturned the ruling of the appeals court, arguing that the statistical evidence of discrimination provided by the workers was inadequate and increasing the burden of proof to be borne by those alleging discrimination. As Justice Stevens observed in his dissent, the majority was thus "tipping the scales in favor of employers."

* * *

Justice White delivered the opinion of the Court. . . .

Measuring alleged discrimination in the selection of accountants, managers, boat captains, electricians, doctors, and engineers . . . by comparing the number of nonwhites occupying these jobs to the number of nonwhites filling cannery worker positions is nonsensical. . . .

Respondents [the minority workers] will . . . have to demonstrate that the disparity they complain of is the result of one or more of the employment practices that they are attacking . . . showing that each challenged practice has a significantly disparate impact on employment opportunities for whites and nonwhites. . . .

If . . . respondents meet the proof burdens outlined above . . . the case will shift to any business justification petitioners offer for their use of these practices. . . .

[T]here is no requirement that the challenged practice be "essential" or "indispensable" to the employer's business for it to pass muster. . . .

JUSTICE BLACKMUN, with whom JUSTICE BRENNAN AND JUSTICE MARSHALL join, dissenting. . . .

One wonders whether the majority still believes that race discrimination—or more accurately, race discrimination against nonwhites—is a problem in our society, or even remembers that it ever was. . . .

JUSTICE STEVENS, with whom JUSTICE BRENNAN, JUSTICE MARSHALL, AND JUSTICE BLACKMUN join, dissenting. . . .

[The Court majority] made no findings regarding the extent to which the cannery workers already are qualified for at-issue jobs: individual plaintiffs testified persuasively that they were fully-qualified for such jobs. . . .

The majority's opinion . . . departs from the body of law engendered by . . . disparate-impact theory, reformulating the order of proof and the weight of the parties' burdens. Why the Court undertakes these unwise changes in elementary and eminently fair rules is a mystery to me.

Source: 490 U.S. 642 at 651, 657, 658, 659, 661, 662, 675, 678–679 (1989).

{r}DOCUMENT 317: *Martin v. Wilks*, June 12, 1989

A week later the Court, voting in the exact same pattern as their vote in *Wards Cove*, permitted the negation of court-approved affirmative action plans. In *Martin v. Wilks* white firefighters in Birmingham, Alabama, sought the right to open negotiations with the city to overturn a consent decree agreed to by the city and black firefighters in 1981. The district court that had approved the decree found that it was legal, that personnel decisions resulting in promotions of African American firefighters conformed to it, and that, therefore, the whites had no grounds for charging the city with violating Title VII. When an appeals court reversed the district court, city leaders turned to the Supreme Court, where the decision of the appeals court was upheld on behalf of the white firefighters. Legal observers worried that *Martin v. Wilks* could reverse the progress in employment made by racial minorities and women through such measures as consent decrees mandating affirmative action. In fact, within a year at least thirteen cases involving consent decrees were reopened, dating back as far as 1973.

* * *

CHIEF JUSTICE REHNQUIST delivered the opinion of the Court. . . .
A voluntary settlement in the form of a consent decree between one group of employees and their employer cannot possibly "settle," voluntarily or otherwise, the conflicting claims of another group of employees who do not join in the agreement. . . .

The dissenting justices—Stevens, Brennan, Marshall, and Blackmun—took issue with the contention that the legal rights of the white firemen had been violated. Their opinion, written by Stevens, rested on a concept that would increasingly gain currency among supporters of affirmative action—that racism has conferred unearned advantages on whites.

JUSTICE STEVENS, with whom JUSTICE BRENNAN, JUSTICE MARSHALL, and JUSTICE BLACKMUN join, dissenting. . . .
The fact that one of the effects of a decree is to curtail the job opportunities of nonparties does not mean that the nonparties have been deprived of legal rights or that they have standing to appeal from that decree without becoming parties. . . .
The predecessor to this litigation was brought to change a pattern of hiring and promotion practices that had discriminated against black citizens in Birmingham for decades. The white respondents in these cases are not responsible for that history of discrimination, but they are nevertheless beneficiaries of the discriminatory practices that the litigation was designed to correct. . . . Just as white employees in the past were innocent beneficiaries of illegal discriminatory practices, so it is inevitable that some of the same white employees will be innocent victims who must share some of the burdens resulting from the redress of the past wrongs.

Source: 490 U.S. 755 at 758, 768, 769, 771, 791–792 (1989).

{r}DOCUMENT 318: The Impact of Affirmative Action in the 1980s on Birmingham Firefighters James Henson and Carl Cook

Cases such as *Martin v. Wilks* brought into sharp relief the perceptual and experiential divide between white and African American workers, as the following comments from Birmingham firefighters James Henson (white) and Carl Cook (African American) illustrate. Under the (soon to be disputed) consent decree of 1981 Cook was promoted to the position of lieutenant, while Henson, who had scored seventy points higher than Cook on the promotion test, was not advanced.

* * *

James Henson: I can understand that blacks had been historically discriminated against. I can also understand why people would want to be punitive in correcting it. Somebody needs to pay for this. But they want me to pay for it, and I didn't have anything to do with it. I was a kid when all this went on.

Carl Cook: Say your father robs a bank, takes the money and buys his daughter a Mercedes, and then buys his son a Porsche and his wife a home in the high-rent district. Then they discover he has embezzled the money. He has to give the cars and house back. And the family starts to cry: "We didn't do anything." The same thing applies to what the whites have to say. The fact is, sometimes you have to pay up. If a wrong has been committed, you have to right that wrong.

Source: Quoted in Thomas Byrne Edsall and Mary D. Edsall, "Race," *The Atlantic Monthly* (May 1991): 70.

{r/g/d}DOCUMENT 319: R. Roosevelt Thomas Jr., "Affirming Diversity," Spring 1990

As the decade of the 1980s gave way to the 1990s, and Reagan was succeeded in the presidency by his vice president, George Bush, public discourse on affirmative action evolved toward an emphasis on "diversity." R. Roosevelt Thomas, director of the Morehouse College American Institute for Managing Diversity, explained this evolution in relation to the corporate world in the *Harvard Business Review* in the spring of 1990.

* * *

Affirmative action gets . . . new people through the front door. Something else will have to get them into the driver's seat. . . .

The objective is not to assimilate minorities and women into a dominant white male culture but to create a dominant heterogeneous culture. . . .

The reason you want . . . to move beyond affirmative action . . . is because affirmative action fails to . . . develop the full potential of every man and woman. . . . [T]he goal of managing diversity is to . . . empower the diverse human talents of the most diverse nation on earth. It's our reality. We need to make it our strength.

Source: Thomas 1990, 109, 114, 117.

{r}DOCUMENT 320: "Bigots in the Ivory Tower," *Time Magazine*, May 1990

While business leaders explored "diversity" as an extension of affirmative action, college and university administrators continued to grope for the words and strategies with which to acclimate their students to what *Time Magazine* described as the "grand social experiment" that had followed from civil rights and affirmative action laws. *Time* reported that in the period 1986–1990 racist incidents had occurred on over 250 U.S. campuses. The report recorded several examples of vicious bigotry.

* * *

At Bryn Mawr, freshman Christine Rivera found an anonymous note slipped under her door. "Hey Spic," it said, "if you and your kind can't handle the work here, don't blame it on the racial thing. . . . why don't you just get out. We'd all be a lot happier." . . .

"Affirmative action is organized governmental racism against white people," charges Temple University student Michael Spletzer, cofounder of the White Student Union.

Source: Nancy Gibbs, "Bigots in the Ivory Tower," *Time* (May 7, 1990): 104.

{r}DOCUMENT 321: Race Relations Study at University of California at Berkeley, 1990

A two-year study of race relations on the campus of the University of California at Berkeley found pervasive confusion about affirmative action.

* * *

If there is a single pattern emerging from the study, it is that the students are deeply conflicted, disturbed, divided and confused about Affirmative Action as a policy, yet support the idea of diversity.

Source: Troy Duster, *The Diversity Project*, quoted in Takagi 1992, 145.

{r}DOCUMENT 322: *Metro Broadcasting, Inc. v. Federal Communications Commission et al.*, June 27, 1990

In June 1990 a Supreme Court majority affirmed "diversity" on the nation's airwaves in their ruling on *Metro Broadcasting, Inc. v. Federal Communications Commission*. The case stemmed from legal challenges by Metro and Shurberg Broadcasting of Hartford to two policies of the Federal Communications Commission (FCC), including minority ownership as a factor when ruling on applications for new broadcast stations and allowing a broadcaster whose license is designated for a revocation hearing to transfer it without a hearing to an FCC-approved minority buyer. These policies were part of an official position on "Minority Ownership of Broadcasting Facilities" adopted by the FCC in 1978 with congressional approval. At that time minority owners held less than 1 percent of all U.S. radio and television stations. In upholding the FCC policies, the Supreme Court judges placed their 1989 *Croson* decision (Doc. 312) in a perspective that seemed to limit its attack on affirmative action to programs adopted by local governments, while setting forth a two-part "test" for "race-conscious" policies adopted by the U.S. Congress. The decision came from Justices Brennan, White, Marshall, Blackmun, and Stevens, with O'Connor, Rehnquist, Scalia, and Kennedy dissenting.

* * *

JUSTICE BRENNAN delivered the opinion of the Court. . . .

Our decision last Term in *Richmond v. J. A. Croson Co.* . . . does not prescribe the level of scrutiny to be applied to a benign racial classification employed by Congress. . . .

We hold that the FCC minority ownership policies pass muster under the test we announce today. First, we find that they serve the important governmental objective of broadcast diversity. Second, we conclude that they are substantially related to the achievement of that objective. . . .

Just as a "diverse student body" contributing to a "robust exchange of ideas" is a "constitutionally permissible goal" on which a race-conscious university admissions program may be predicated [quoting *Bakke*, Doc. 231] . . . the diversity of views and information on the airwaves serves important First Amendment values. . . . the benefits redound to all members of the viewing and listening audience. . . .

[T]he Commission established minority ownership preferences only after long experience demonstrated that race-neutral means could not produce adequate broadcasting diversity. . . .

Finally, we do not believe that the minority ownership policies at issue impose impermissible burdens on nonminorities. . . . [J]ust as we have determined that "[a]s part of this Nation's dedication to eradicating racial discrimination, innocent persons may be called upon to bear some of the burden of the remedy" [quoting *Wygant*, Doc. 300], we similarly find that a congressionally mandated, benign, race-conscious program that is substantially related to the achievement of an important governmental interest is consistent with equal protection principles. . . .

JUSTICE KENNEDY, with whom JUSTICE SCALIA joins, dissenting. . . .

I cannot agree with the Court that the Constitution permits the Government to discriminate among its citizens on the basis of race in order to serve interests so trivial as "broadcast diversity."

Source: 497 U.S. 547 at 552, 565, 566, 568, 589, 596–597, 631, 633 (1990).

{r}DOCUMENT 323: "A Case for Race Consciousness," 1991

However "trivial" the concept of media diversity may have appeared to the dissenters in the *Metro Broadcasting* case, to the promoters of the "dominant heterogeneous culture" to which R. R. Thomas had referred (Doc. 319) broadcast diversity was critically important. Major articles in leading law journals highlighted that importance. For example, in the *Columbia Law Review* Professor T. Alexander Aleinikoff from the University of Michigan singled out the *Metro Broadcasting* decision as a promising example of how American society might move beyond "race neutral strategies."

* * *

[A]ltering the image of blacks in the white mind requires paying attention to, and crediting, black voices, and to refashioning institutions in ways that will allow those voices to be heard. Here race-conscious programs may be crucial, and the FCC's policies upheld in *Metro Broadcasting* provide an important example.

Source: Aleinikoff 1991, 1116–1117.

{d}DOCUMENT 324: George Bush's Promise to the Disabled at the Republican National Convention, August 1988

Members of the vast and increasingly well organized community of disabled persons were also determined to be heard, to have their voices credited, and to participate in fashioning a definition of national diversity that encompassed their rights, talents, and aspirations. The best hope for reaching such a definition seemed to many to lie in a civil rights law that would specifically address discrimination based on disability. Such a law emerged within the National Council on the Handicapped, an agency that the 1984 Rehabilitation Amendments Act had transformed from an advisory group within the Department of Education to an independent council appointed by the president of the United States. In 1986 the council had recommended "the enactment of a comprehensive law requiring equal opportunity for individuals with disabilities, with broad coverage and setting clear, consistent, and enforceable standards" (National Council on the Handicapped, "Toward Independence: An Assessment of Federal Laws and Programs Affecting Persons with Disabilities—with Legislative Recommendations," February 1986). In 1988 two council members, Robert L. Burgdorf Jr. and Justin Dart Jr., drafted a law that was sponsored by Representative Tony Coelho and Senator Lowell Weicker in their respective bodies of Congress but was "lost in the shuffle" of the final phase of the Reagan administration. During the 1988 presidential election campaign disabled advocates actively lobbied the candidates on behalf of their cause and found Republican George Bush not only receptive but willing to publicly acknowledge the disabled and pledge support for their goals. Some observers believed this receptivity arose from the candidate's personal experiences—the death of a child from leukemia, the learning disability of his son Neil, the disease that forced his son Marvin to undergo surgery to remove a part of his colon, and the polio of a favorite uncle.

By making inclusion of the disabled in the national "mainstream" part of his campaign "mission," George Bush became the first presidential candidate to recognize the disabled as being politically significant (Shapiro 1993, 124–125).

* * *

Let me . . . just tell you more about the mission. . . .

I'm going to do whatever it takes to make sure the disabled are included in the mainstream. For too long they've been left out. But they're not going to be left out anymore.

Source: "Transcript of Bush Speech Accepting Presidential Nomination," *New York Times* (August 19, 1988): A14.

{d}DOCUMENT 325: State of the Union Message of President George Bush, February 9, 1989

Analysts found that the disabled played a significant role in Bush's victory over Democrat Michael Dukakis that November, accounting for at least one and possibly as many as three percentage points in his seven-point margin over his opponent (Shapiro 1993, 125). Once in the White House, Bush maintained his support for the disabled. In his State of the Union Message in February 1989 the president again spoke directly to the disabled. He indicated that they numbered 37 million. In Congress Americans with Disabilities Act (ADA) advocates such as Tom Harkin (Doc. 326) spoke of 43 million disabled Americans. Author Joseph Shapiro has observed that "there are some 35 million to 43 million disabled Americans, depending on who does the counting and what disabilities are included" (Shapiro 1993, 8).

* * *

To those 37 million Americans with some form of disability, you belong in the economic mainstream. We need your talents in America's work force. Disabled Americans must become full partners in America's opportunity society.

Source: Public Papers of the Presidents (1989): 80.

{d}DOCUMENT 326: Senator Tom Harkin on the Americans with Disabilities Act (ADA), September 7, 1989

With the White House on their side, disabled advocates renewed their efforts on behalf of a new law. Senators Tom Harkin and Edward Kennedy reworked the bill that had died in 1988, taking special care to place limits on the costs to be incurred by small businesses and to build in reasonable timetables by which employers would be required to comply with the law.

Like the president, Senators Harkin and Kennedy—and numerous colleagues in both houses of Congress and in both political parties— had relatives and other cherished associates who had been victimized by discrimination because of some disability. The impact of these first-hand experiences was evident in congressional testimony on the bill that would become the Americans with Disabilities Act (ADA). For Senator Harkin the personal connection was with his deaf brother.

* * *

Who are these 43 million Americans with disabilities, one out of every six of our citizenry? . . .

It could be my brother, deaf from birth who has spent a lifetime of work and service proving that the only thing deaf persons cannot do in the words of Dr. I. King Jordan, president of Gallaudet University [Doc. 309], is hear. . . .

We have a vision . . . of an America where persons are judged by their abilities and not on the basis of their disabilities.

Source: Congressional Record 135 (September 7, 1989): 10711.

{d}DOCUMENT 327: Remarks of Senator Orrin Hatch on the ADA, September 7, 1989

Although the primary sponsors of the ADA were Democrats, they were joined by such influential Republicans as Orrin Hatch of Utah, who cried as he spoke on the Senate floor of his late brother-in-law.

* * *

I am a cosponsor of this legislation because I firmly believe in its objective. . . . I had a brother-in-law who contracted both types of polio. He became a paraplegic. . . . I felt deeply toward him. I love him.

I can transfer the love and affection that I have to all persons with disabilities. . . .

This is an emotional thing but I am not doing this just because of the emotions. I think it is the right thing to do.

Source: Congressional Record 135 (September 7, 1989): 10714, 10716.

{d}DOCUMENT 328: Senator Edward Kennedy's Remarks on the ADA, September 7, 1989

Senator Edward Kennedy also brought family experiences to his advocacy of the ADA (including the mental disabilities of his sister and having his son lose a leg to cancer). Additionally, he read into the *Congressional Record* recent reports of cruel discrimination.

* * *

In March 1988 the Washington Post reported the story of a New Jersey zoo keeper who refused to admit children with Downs syndrome because he feared they would upset the chimpanzees.

In its 1985 decision in Alexander versus Choate, the Supreme Court described an example of discrimination in which "a court ruled that a child with cerebral palsy, who was not a physical threat and was academically competitive, was excluded from public school, because his teacher claimed his physical appearance 'produced a nauseating effect' on his classmates. . . ."

[O]ur society is still infected by the ancient, now almost subconscious assumption that people with disabilities are less than fully human and therefore are not fully eligible for the opportunities, services, and support systems which are available to other people as a matter of right. The result is massive society-wide discrimination. . . .

Americans with disabilities deserve to participate in the promise of America.

Source: Congressional Record 135 (September 7, 1989): 10718.

{d}DOCUMENT 329: Disabled Activist Mike Auberger, March 1990

Early the next month (March 1990) disabled citizens arrived in Washington, D.C., to register their demands for swift congressional passage of an effective ADA. Professional health-care workers attending a conference of the National Rehabilitation Association and representatives of the confrontational American Disabled for Accessible Public Transit (ADAPT) were among those who joined forces in a "Wheels for Justice March," sponsored by ADAPT. When the "marchers," numbering between 600 and 800, completed their route from the White House to the capital, they were addressed by several members of Congress and leading disabled figures in the Establishment. In contrast to these traditional advocates was the catalyst for the next stage of the protest—the national director of ADAPT, Mike Auberger. In T-shirt and jeans with long, braided hair he not only spoke from a wheelchair but, at the end of his remarks, led numerous other of the paralyzed protesters in throwing themselves out of their chairs and engaging in a "crawl-up" of the Capitol steps. At the top of the eighty-three steps they dragged themselves inside the building. Each carried a scroll with the first sentences of the Declaration of Independence printed on it. The next day 150 members of ADAPT returned with the purpose of refusing to leave the Capitol Rotunda until representatives of Congress spoke with them. When a brief exchange with three congressmen proved unsatisfactory 104 of the protesters were forcibly removed and arrested. In court the next day an unsympathetic judge dispensed heavy fines and put Auberger and three others on probation for a year. However, when they obeyed the judge's order to appear the following day at the parole office, they could not get in, because the building had no wheelchair ramp (Shapiro 1993, 127–139).

In his "Wheels for Justice" speech Auberger remembered visiting the Capitol when he was nine years old, before he became paralyzed.

* * *

Twenty years ago, I walked up these steps a wholly equal American citizen. Today I sit here with you as less than second-class citizens who are still legally discriminated against daily.... The steps we sit before represent a long history of discrimination and indignities heaped upon disabled Americans.... We will not permit these steps to continue to be a barrier to prevent us from the equality that is rightfully ours. The preamble to the Constitution does not say "We the able-bodied people." It says, "We the People."

Source: Quoted in Shapiro 1993, 132–133.

{d}DOCUMENT 330: Congressman Tom DeLay on the Costs of the ADA, May 15, 1990

Supported by 180 national organizations representing a vast range of disabilities and endorsed also by civil rights and labor groups, the ADA attracted most opposition from the small business and construction industries and private bus companies. As congressional passage of the ADA approached certainty, concern lingered about the cost to both public and private employers involved in providing the accommodations required by the bill. Texas representative Tom DeLay emphasized this concern as the House prepared to approve the law.

* * *

[T]his is a piece of legislation that has the best of intentions. . . . [However], it has been proven time and time again the incredible costs the Rehabilitation Act has had on our Government. Now we are taking that deep pocket theory and applying it to the private sector.

Source: Congressional Record 136 (May 15, 1990): 2316.

{d}DOCUMENT 331: Representative Ron Dellums Celebrates Passage of the ADA, May 22, 1990

The House of Representatives passed the ADA by a vote of 377 to 28 on May 15, 1990, and the following day the bill passed the Senate by a vote of 91 to 6. In the House, following the vote, California congressman Ron Dellums reflected on the historical significance of the act.

* * *

As a black American, I am especially proud to stand here as part of the coalition that has brought equal standing for the disabled in the eyes of the law.

The significance, historic and legal, of our decision to establish disability as a basis for civil rights protection cannot be overstated. We have been moved by the continuing destructive effect of segregation, and we are acting now to reverse those practices, root and branch, and to eliminate their legacy.

Source: Congressional Record 136 (May 22, 1990): 2639.

{d}DOCUMENT 332: President George Bush's Signing of the ADA, July 26, 1990

Before signing the ADA on July 26, 1990, George Bush addressed the largest crowd ever to gather on the south lawn of the White House—some 3,000 disabled citizens and their families and associates.

* * *

This historic act is the world's first comprehensive declaration of equality for people with disabilities—the first. Its passage has made the United States the international leader on this human rights issue. . . .

Last year . . . we rejoiced when the [Berlin Wall] fell.

And now I sign legislation which takes a sledgehammer to another wall, one which has for too many generations separated Americans with disabilities from the freedom they could glimpse but not grasp. . . .

I now lift my pen to sign this Americans with Disabilities Act and say: Let the shameful wall of exclusion finally come tumbling down. God bless you all.

Source: Public Papers of the Presidents (1990): 1068, 1069, 1070.

{d}DOCUMENT 333: Summary of the Americans with Disabilities Act of 1990

Although the phrase "affirmative action" does not appear in the ADA and is largely absent from subsequent regulations and interpretations governing its enforcement, law professors Charles Lawrence III and Mari Masuda have called it "the most radical affirmative action program in the nation's history." They explain that "it goes well beyond the principle of nondiscrimination [to] . . . an affirmative command:

change business as usual, alter old concepts of merit . . . include and welcome those who were previously kept out" (Lawrence and Matsuda 1997, 108).

The text of the ADA includes a statement of purpose ("to provide clear, strong, consistent, enforceable standards addressing discrimination against individuals with disabilities") and a definition of disability ("a physical or mental impairment that substantially limits one or more of the major life activities of [an] individual; a record of such an impairment; or being regarded as having such an impairment"). The law is divided into five titles. These have been summarized in a Justice Department pamphlet.

* * *

I. Employment
- Employers with 15 or more employees may not discriminate against qualified individuals with disabilities. . . .
- Employers must reasonably accommodate the disabilities of qualified applicants or employees, unless undue hardship would result.
- Employers may reject applicants or fire employees who pose a direct threat to the health or safety of other individuals in the workplace. . . .

II. Public Accommodations
- Public accommodations such as restaurants, hotels, theaters, doctors' offices, pharmacies, retail stores, museums, libraries, parks, private schools, and day care centers, may not discriminate on the basis of disability. . . . Private clubs and religious organizations are exempt. . . .
- Auxiliary aids and services must be provided to individuals with vision or hearing impairments or other individuals with disabilities so that they can have an equal opportunity to participate or benefit, unless an undue burden would result.
- Physical barriers in existing facilities must be removed if removal is readily achievable. . . . If not, alternative methods of providing the services must be offered, if those methods are readily achievable.
- All new construction in public accommodations, as well as in "commercial facilities" such as office buildings, must be accessible. . . .

III. Transportation
Public bus systems
- New buses . . . must be accessible to individuals with disabilities.
- Transit authorities must provide comparable paratransit or other special transportation services to individuals with disabilities who cannot use fixed route bus services, unless an undue burden would result.
- New bus stations must be accessible. . . .

Public rail systems

- New rail vehicles . . . must be accessible.
- Existing rail systems must have one accessible car per train. . . .
- New rail stations must be accessible. . . .

IV. State and local government operations

- State or local governments may not discriminate against qualified individuals with disabilities. . . .

V. Telecommunications Relay Services

- Companies offering telephone service to the general public must offer telephone relay services to individuals who use telecommunications devices for the deaf (TDD's) or similar devices. . . .

This document is available in the following accessible formats:

—Braille

—Large Print

—Audiotape

—Electronic file on computer disk and electronic bulletin board. . . .

Source: "The Americans with Disabilities Act," U.S. Department of Justice, Civil Rights Division, Coordination and Review Section (September 1990): 1–6.

{r/g}DOCUMENT 334: Senator Dale Bumpers on the Civil Rights Act of 1991

No sooner had goodwill and increasing respect for the disabled appeared to triumph in the ADA than the mean-spiritedness of racism reasserted itself with a presidential veto of a civil rights bill and a senatorial election campaign conducted with old-style demagoguery. The bill, authored by California representative Augustus Hawkins and Massachusetts senator Edward Kennedy, was meant to counteract Supreme Court rulings (such as *Martin v. Wilks* [Doc. 317]) that had continued after the Civil Rights Restoration Act of 1988 (Doc. 306) to weaken civil rights and affirmative action programs. In refusing to sign it, George Bush denounced "the destructive force of quotas" in employment. This was the same theme on which the incumbent senator from North Carolina, Jesse Helms, played in defeating his opponent, Harvey Gantt. Gantt had made a strong start on becoming the first African American Democratic senator since Reconstruction when the Republican Helms captured the winning votes with the help of a television advertisement. The ad dramatized a disappointed white job-seeker crumpling a rejection letter while a voice-over intoned, "You needed that job, and you were the best qualified. But it had to go to a minority because of a racial quota" (quoted in Takagi 1992, 182).

Having failed by one Senate vote to override Bush's veto of the 1990 civil rights bill, congressional supporters of that bill redoubled their efforts and passed a new version—the Civil Rights Act of 1991—in November of that year. The bill overturned nine recent Supreme Court rulings, including *Martin v. Wilks* (Doc. 317), and reaffirmed the interpretation of Title VII of the 1964 Civil Rights Act, which had governed the *Griggs* Supreme Court ruling in 1971. In that ruling the Court had established that "if an employment practice which operated to exclude Negroes cannot be shown to be related to job performance, the practice is prohibited" (Doc. 171).

Congressional intent in passing the 1991 Civil Rights Act was succinctly put by Senator Dale Bumpers, Democrat from Arkansas.

* * *

Here is a way we can remind ourselves where we have been coming from in the last 30 years and saying we are not going to turn back.

Source: Quoted in *Congressional Quarterly Almanac* 47 (1991): 257.

{r/g}DOCUMENT 335: Provisions of 1991 Civil Rights Act

Compilers of the *Congressional Quarterly Almanac* summarized the main elements of the bill in lay language.

* * *

Purposes. Stated that the legislation's purpose was:

- to provide appropriate remedies for discrimination;
- to codify the concepts of "business necessity" and "job related" offered by the Supreme Court in *Griggs v. Duke Power Co.* in 1971, and in related Supreme Court decisions before *Wards Cove Packing Co. v. Atonio*;
- to provide statutory guidelines for disparate-impact lawsuits under Title VII of the Civil Rights Act of 1964; and
- to respond to recent court decisions by expanding the scope of relevant civil rights statutes to provide adequate protection to victims of discrimination. . . .

Wards Cove cannery workers. Exempted the Wards Cove Packing Co. and workers who had sued the company from these provisions. . . .

Consent Judgments

The court settlements involved in this provision . . . [included the challenge to the consent decree in *Martin v. Wilks*]. . . .

Bar to most challenges. Stated that an employment practice arising from a consent judgment could not be challenged by a person who had actual notice of the proposed judgment or order sufficient to apprise him that the order might adversely affect his interests. . . .

Discriminatory Use of Test Scores

"Race-norming." Barred employers from adjusting the scores of, using different cutoff scores for, or otherwise altering the results of employment-related tests on the basis of race, color, religion, sex or national origin. This provision stemmed from concern among lawmakers in both parties that "race norming" was leading to discrimination against qualified white applicants.

Glass Ceiling Commission

Findings. Stated that, despite a growing presence in the workplace:

- women and minorities remained underrepresented in management and decision-making positions. . . .

Purpose. Established a Glass Ceiling Commission to study how business filled management and decision-making positions, the developmental and skill-enhancing practices used to foster qualifications of advancement, and the pay and reward structures used in the workplace.

Source: Congressional Quarterly Almanac 47 (1991): 258, 259.

{r/g}DOCUMENT 336: President George Bush's Comments on Signing the 1991 Civil Rights Act

Divisions over the 1991 Civil Rights Act were rife not only between political parties and between Congress and the White House but within the Bush administration. Presidential counsel C. Boyden Gray, who wrote a first draft of the speech that Bush would make when he signed the act, clearly had no sympathy for the new law. The remarks that Bush actually read at the signing ceremony had been substantially revised.

* * *

A. First Draft of Presidential Remarks (Prepared by Presidential Counsel Gray)

[The original remarks ordered the heads of all federal departments to review immediately their equal opportunity programs. . . .]

Any regulation, rule, enforcement practice or other aspect of these programs that mandates, encourages or otherwise involves the use of quotas, preferences, set-asides or other similar devices on the basis of race, color, religion, sex or national origin is to be terminated as soon as legally feasible.

B. Remarks Delivered by President Bush, November 21, 1991

This Act promotes the goals of ridding the workplace of discrimination on the basis of race, color, sex, religion, national origin, and disability; ensuring that employers can hire on the basis of merit and ability without the fear of unwarranted litigation; and ensuring that aggrieved parties have effective remedies. This law will not lead to quotas.

Sources: Congressional Quarterly Almanac 47 (1991): 261; *Public Papers of the Presidents* (1992): 1504.

The 1991 Civil Rights Act was a compromise measure, and, as the *Congressional Quarterly Almanac* observed, "most of the compromising was done by Bush." Gaining exemption for the Alaskan cannery (Wards Cove Packing Company) from the provisions of the act was the major concession that his administration managed to obtain. His general acceptance of the bill indicated the sensitive position in which he found himself at the end of 1991. He had to back away from the issue of "quotas" when Louisiana Republican David Duke, who publicly acknowledged past membership in the Ku Klux Klan, incorporated the quota issue into his campaign for governor. While taking care to avoid association with the Klan image, Bush was also occupied with a hornet's nest of race and gender-related controversies created by his nomination of Clarence Thomas to replace Thurgood Marshall on the Supreme Court. For champions of social justice, allegations of sexual harassment brought against Clarence Thomas by a former associate, Anita Hill, only compounded the impression that this appointment represented another setback for civil rights and affirmative action.

{r/g}DOCUMENT 337: "Affirmative Action Is Deeply Ingrained in Corporate Culture," *Business Week*, Summer 1991

The wrangling of political leaders over the civil rights bill and the appointment of Thomas to the Supreme Court appeared to have a relatively minor effect on the realm of big business. Reporters for *Business Week* opined that the civil rights law, whatever its provisions, would matter little "because affirmative action is now so deeply ingrained in American corporate culture that changes at the margin of the law won't have much impact." Acknowledging that there was still ample evidence of resistance to race- and gender-conscious employment policies and that some of those policies were flawed by "tokenism and purely mechanistic compliance," the journalists concluded nonetheless that continuing affirmative action was essential as "an important symbol of America's commitment to civil rights . . . an effective club . . . [and] an economic necessity."

Among the companies examined in the *Business Week* overview of affirmative action in 1991 was AT&T. Noting that minority workers were rapidly increasing in number and represented a resource that employers must tap, AT&T chairman Robert E. Allen told the journal that "affirmative action is not just the right thing to do. It's a business necessity." *Business Week* provided an update on AT&T since the consent decree of the 1970s (Doc. 208).

* * *

The court order expired in 1979, but with CEO [chief executive officer] Allen pushing hard, the company continues its aggressive recruiting of blacks. Today, minorities make up nearly 21% of AT&T's work force. And 17% of the company's managers are minorities, up from 12% in 1984.

AT&T also encourages its minority workers' participation in race-based support groups. These forums, which often have branches at every work site around the country, offer black managers a chance to share ideas, solve problems, and develop the networks white men have long relied on. . . . Such race-based advocacy networks are increasingly common among progressive companies.

Source: "Race in the Work Place, Is Affirmative Action Working?" 1991, 53, 56, 58, 62.

{r}DOCUMENT 338: Ruling of U.S. District Court Judge J. F. Motz on *Podberesky v. Kirwan*, May 15, 1991

While *Business Week* highlighted examples of affirmative action having taken root in corporate America, court action by a college freshman at the University of Maryland threatened to uproot race-conscious programs in higher education. Daniel J. Podberesky, claiming a Hispanic identity from his Costa Rican mother, sued the university when his applications for two scholarships were both rejected. Denied a Francis Scott Key award because his standing based on Scholastic Aptitude Test (SAT) scores and high school grades fell below the eligibility standards, Podberesky argued for special consideration as a Hispanic. At the same time he challenged the special consideration characterizing the Benjamin Banneker Scholarship Program, which existed exclusively for African Americans. He lost his case in Maryland District Court in 1991 but won the following year in the Fourth Circuit Court of Appeals. The Fourth Circuit opinion was upheld when the U.S. Supreme Court refused to entertain a subsequent appeal by the university.

In the 1991 ruling Judge J. Frederick Motz found that the Banneker Scholarship served a "compelling government interest" in helping to address the long history of racial discrimination at the University of Maryland. He reviewed the repeated failures of the university to satisfactorily comply with Title VI of the 1964 Civil Rights Act and identified the Banneker program as a voluntary initiative by the current administration in support of such compliance.

* * *

[T]he effects of long-standing discrimination are pervasive, and there is ample evidence in the record before me to support the view of UMCP [University of Maryland at College Park] officials that it is premature to find that there are no present effects of past discrimination at the institution.

Thus, declaring that the Banneker program is no longer necessary may have the ironic result of awakening the now-dormant specter of past discrimination. . . .

Podberesky decries UMCP's failure to give Hispanics any special consideration for Key scholarships. This contention is baffling and, in light of his principal contention [that special consideration based on race is unconstitutional] at best paradoxical.

Source: 764 F. Supp. 364 at 375, 378 (1991).

THE ADMINISTRATION OF WILLIAM JEFFERSON CLINTON

{r}DOCUMENT 339: Fourth Circuit Court of Appeals Decision on *Podberesky v. Kirwan*, January 31, 1992

The panel of circuit court judges who heard Podberesky's appeal dismissed Judge Motz's assertions regarding the lingering effects of past discrimination.

* * *

It may very well be ... that information exists which provides evidence of present effects of past discrimination at UMCP, but no such evidence was brought to our attention nor is it part of the record. . . .

Judgment for appellees must be based on facts which show that vestiges of past discrimination existed, which made the 1988–90 form of the Banneker Program a legitimate constitutional remedy on or about the time appellant was denied the opportunity to compete for the scholarship. Accordingly, we hereby reverse the grant of summary judgment.

Source: 956 F. 2d 52 at 57 (4th Cir., 1992).

{r}DOCUMENT 340: Asian Americans and Affirmative Action Ruling in Connecticut, May 1993

With affirmative action in financial aid effectively outlawed, University of Maryland officials combined the Banneker and Key scholarships into a new program open to white students but required that all applicants demonstrate a commitment to an improved racial climate through community service, such as having tutored in inner-city schools (*Baltimore Sun*, August 9, 1998). Meanwhile, other cases arose in which minority groups other than African Americans pressed for inclusion in affirmative action programs. For example, in 1993 the Office of Civil Rights (OCR) of the U.S. Department of Education ruled that the state of Connecticut must expand its Minority Advancement Plan, limited to African Americans and Hispanics, to include Asian Americans and American Indians. Connecticut officials had excluded the latter groups from affirmative action consideration because statewide their presence in institutions of higher education was proportionate to the size of their populations. However, on many individual campuses neither group was present. The OCR forced the state to focus not on Asian and American Indian populations generally but on the "available student and faculty pool" within those groups and not on the higher education system as a whole but on the discrete makeup of each campus population. Reactions to the order indicated growing tension among minorities.

In his report on the Connecticut case for *The Chronicle of Higher Education* journalist Scott Jaschik presented varying minority perspectives, including the two examples that follow.

* * *

Karen K. Narasaki, Washington representative of the Japanese American Citizens League, said she hoped the Connecticut decision would give pause to colleges thinking of excluding Asian Americans from affirmative action. . . .

Myron Apilado, vice-president for minority affairs at [the University of] Washington, said . . . minority groups that most need affirmative action . . . lose out if Asian Americans remain in programs, regardless of need. . . .

Source: Scott Jaschik, "Affirmative-Action Ruling on Connecticut Called a 'Big Step' for Asian Americans," *Chronicle of Higher Education* (May 19, 1993): A19, A22.

{r}DOCUMENT 341: Asian Americans and Affirmative Action in the 1990s

As the foregoing suggests, the inclusion of Asian Americans not only complicated public debate on affirmative action but, in the words of sociologist Dana Y. Takagi, "reconstructed" that debate. Before the 1990s, discrimination against Asians was generally perceived by those who opposed it as a variety of racism on the part of whites. In the 1990s charges of discrimination against Asians were recast by opponents of affirmative action to support their view that preferential treatment of African Americans and Hispanics hurt not only whites but also Asians, who were portrayed as an exemplary, high-achieving minority. Although this view ignored the broad spectrum of nationalities and economic backgrounds encompassed by the "Asian" category and inaccurately implied that all Asians opposed affirmative action, it gained credibility, helped along by the media.

In the following extract from her study of racial politics Dana Takagi illustrated the role of the media in promoting the view that affirmative action was antithetical to the interests of Asian Americans.

* * *

In late July 1989 . . . an NBC Nightly News clip on Asian admissions featured an Asian applicant to Berkeley, Hong Jim, a Taiwanese "A" student. . . . He told the NBC correspondent that although two of his black friends with lower grades were accepted at Berkeley, he was rejected. Said Hong Jim, "I don't hold it against them, they're my friends. I want to tell them I still love them, but . . . it's not justice for me. I mean, I think I'm more qualified." The NBC correspondent concluded, "Many Asian Americans are beginning to feel that affirmative action, while a worthy goal, is hurting them."

Source: Takagi 1992, 135.

{r}DOCUMENT 342: Journalist Ruben Navarrette Jr., "New Victims?," Spring 1993

Affirmative action as an instrument of injustice became an increasingly common refrain in high schools when college admissions decisions were announced. Journalist Ruben Navarrette Jr., a Hispanic, remembered the behavior of his classmates in the town of Sanger, California, when he was accepted by Harvard.

* * *

Many [of] my white classmates . . . had grades not as good as mine and were reeling from rejection by the same schools that were admitting me. . . .

"Now, you know, if you hadn't been Mexican . . . ," someone said. "It's not fair!" someone else said. "They turned me down because I'm white. This is reverse discrimination. . . ."

[M]y . . . experience getting into and staying at Harvard . . . taught me that . . . affirmative action is mostly posturing and piecemeal . . . I half-expected to find huge clusters of Mexican-American students in front of Johnston Gate welcoming me to Harvard: Mariachis, nachos, and piñatas at the president's welcoming luncheon. Instead, in a freshman class of over 1,600 students from throughout the country and world, I found myself as one of only 35 Mexican-Americans—each of us with outstanding high school records. . . .

[I]t is against a . . . backdrop of the continued economic disempowerment and educational neglect of the nation's Latino population, along with tragically similar statistics for African Americans, that charges of reverse discrimination are best and most honestly considered.

Source: Navarrette 1993, 9, 52, 53.

{r/d}DOCUMENT 343: Report of National Council on Disability on "Meeting the Unique Needs of Minorities with Disabilities," April 26, 1993

Another issue related to casting the net of affirmative action more widely was raised by the National Council on Disability—the issue of minority persons with disabilities. In a report issued in April 1993 the council explored this subject in relation to African Americans, Hispanic and Latino Americans, Asian Americans, Pacific Islanders, Native Americans, Native Alaskans, and other disabled minorities.

* * *

As a result of factors such as poverty, unemployment, and poor health status, persons of minority backgrounds are at high risk of disability. Based largely on population projections and substantial anecdotal evidence, it is clear that the number of persons from these minority populations who have disabilities is increasing. . . .

These data, or lack thereof, suggest the need for much more research on minority populations with disabilities. . . .

Even the passage of the ADA [Doc. 333] may not, by itself, have a substantial impact on minorities unless both the minority and majority communities become much more aware of, and sensitive to, the needs of minorities with disabilities.

Source: National Council on Disability, *Meeting the Unique Needs of Minorities with Disabilities* (April 26, 1993): 13–14.

{d}DOCUMENT 344: Progress Report on the ADA, 1995

Consistent monitoring of the ADA by the National Council on Disability led to periodic progress reports. Five years after the law's passage, the council issued its second general report. The tone was both optimistic and cautionary; the message emphasized "a need for improved public relations and education regarding the ADA," particularly with regard to the matter of the costs entailed in its implementation.

* * *

The goals of the ADA—for equality of opportunity, full participation, independent living, and economic self-sufficiency—are beginning to shape our national culture. . . .

However . . . accompanying this initial general success [is] . . . a . . . "backlash." . . . The principal expression of this backlash has been found in the charge of some opponents of the ADA that the Act constitutes an "unfunded mandate." This . . . reveals a fundamental misunderstanding of the nature of the ADA [which is] . . . at its core a civil rights law. . . . As such, the rights and freedoms codified in the ADA should not be subject to a debate on their cost, any more than the rights of women, minorities, or religious groups. . . .

Perhaps the greatest single area of misunderstanding regarding the ADA is in the area of cost. . . . [T]here is no concrete requirement that covered entities must absolutely make every accommodation requested by every individual with a disability. Furthermore, it has been found that reasonable accommodations often do not require a great deal of expense. For example . . . a recent study based on the experience of Sears Roebuck, and Company . . . reported that the average accommodation cost the company $121.00 The study also reported that 69% of accommodations cost nothing, 28% cost less than $1000, and only 3% exceeded $1,000. These data are in general agreement with the overall data reported by the President's Committee on Employment of People with Disabilities.

Source: National Council on Disability, "The Americans with Disabilities Act: Ensuring Equal Access to the American Dream" (January 26, 1995): 29, 11, 12–13.

{r/g}DOCUMENT 345: March 1995 Report of the Federal Glass Ceiling Commission

While the National Council on Disability called attention to barriers preventing the disabled from entering fully into the American workplace, the federal Glass Ceiling Commission (established by the Civil Rights Act of 1991 [Doc. 335]) issued its first report documenting impediments still in the way of minority men and all women seeking to advance in the private sector of that workplace. The commission identified three kinds of impediments: "societal barriers" (including prejudice and stereotyping); "internal structural barriers" (including recruitment, placement, and promotional practices favoring white males); and "governmental barriers" (including weak monitoring and enforcement of employment laws).

* * *

The term glass ceiling was popularized in a 1986 *Wall Street Journal* article describing the invisible barriers that women confront as they approach the top of the corporate hierarchy. . . .

The data show that minorities and white women are increasingly earning the credentials that business needs. However, data also show that . . . equally qualified and similarly situated citizens are being denied equal access to advancement into senior-level management on the basis of gender, race or ethnicity. . . . Furthermore, it is against the best interests of business to exclude those Americans who constitute two-thirds of the total population, two-thirds of the consumer markets, and more than half of the workforce (approximately 57 percent).

Composition of the U.S. Workforce (% by Gender, Race, and Ethnicity, 1990)

Race/Ethnicity	Male	Female
White	43.21	35.61
African-American	4.73	5.28
American Indian	0.31	0.31
Asian/Pacific Islander	1.47	1.32
Hispanic	4.58	3.18

- Black men and women with college degrees are more likely to be in executive, managerial, and administrative positions than are Black men and women without degrees. That is not surprising. What is surprising is that the pattern for white women indicates a nearly equal proportion of white women with only high school educations in the same top positions as are Black men and women with college degrees. This suggests that equal educational attainment does not level the playing field for Black men and women.

- Black women are underrepresented in private sector administrative, executive and managerial positions for each educational level. Black and white women continue to be underrepresented in these positions despite their college degrees. White men are overrepresented in top positions regardless of educational level. . . .

The [following] table illustrates the educational attainment level for African Americans and whites. Even when one secures an executive, administrative, or managerial occupation, black men, white women and black women in these positions earn substantially less than do white men.

Executive, Administrative, and Managerial Occupations by Race, Education Attainment, Income, and Gender (Private Sector Only)

	Doctoral Degree	Professional Degree	Master's Degree	Bachelor's Degree	4 or More Years of College	1–3 Years of College	4 Years of High School	Less Than High School	Less Than Bachelor's Degree
Black Female	44,230	54,171	34,006	30,584	32,452	24,262	22,732	18,629	23,291
Black Male	54,741	71,114	47,234	32,001	40,939	26,027	25,534	7,203	23,947
White Female	47,876	61,995	38,391	31,338	32,332	25,195	22,015	20,876	23,230
White Male	70,414	90,610	57,371	47,181	50,052	38,588	33,074	30,275	34,862

Note: Private sector refers to business services, communications, construction, entertainment, manufacturing, public administration, and utilities industries.

Source: Federal Glass Ceiling Commission 1995, 3, 10–11, 74, 81.

{r}DOCUMENT 346: *Adarand Constructors, Inc. v. Pena,* June 12, 1995

Three months after the Glass Ceiling Commission issued its initial report, the Supreme Court launched a frontal attack on the concept of "benign racial classifications," which had governed the race-conscious policies of the FCC upheld in the 1990 *Metro Broadcasting* case and the federal set-aside legislation supported in the *Fullilove* decision of 1980 (Docs. 322, 283). The attack was delivered by Justice O'Connor with the approval of Justices Scalia, Kennedy, and Thomas and Chief Justice Rehnquist. It centered on the case *Adarand Constructors, Inc. v. Pena.* At issue in this case was the federal Small Business Act (SBA), which provided financial incentives to contractors to hire subcontractors who were certified by the government as "disadvantaged." Included in the "disadvantaged" category were African Americans, Latinos, Asians, and Native Americans. Adarand Constructors went to court when their bid for the guardrail portion of a Colorado highway construction project was rejected in favor of the bid submitted by the minority firm of Gonzales Construction. Adarand's claim was that the SBA violated the equal protection clause of the Fifth Amendment. Adarand lost in the federal district court and the circuit court of appeals, where the *Fullilove* and *Metro* decisions (Docs. 283, 322) were cited in favor of Gonzales. The Supreme Court heard the case in January 1995. O'Connor delivered the opinion in June, sending the case back to the lower courts to be reconsidered in light of O'Connor's review of past Court decisions. That review took the form of an interpretation of Court rulings from *Bakke* (Doc. 230) through *Metro* (Doc. 322). According to this interpretation, until the *Metro* ruling, the Court had held that anyone affected by a race-conscious policy had the right to demand "the strictest judicial scrutiny" of that policy (*Adarand v. Pena,* Doc. 346). Justices Scalia and Thomas appended concurring opinions that brought into sharp focus the implications of the O'Connor opinion. The dissenting justices—Stevens, Ginsburg, Breyer, and Souter—objected vigorously to O'Connor's interpretation while emphasizing that, despite that interpretation, the majority had not entirely dispensed with race-conscious remedies for discrimination.

* * *

JUSTICE O'CONNOR announced the judgment of the Court. . . .

Metro Broadcasting departed from prior cases. . . .

[W]e hold today that all racial classifications, imposed by whatever federal, state, or local governmental actor must be analyzed by a reviewing court under strict scrutiny. . . . To the extent that *Metro Broadcasting* is inconsistent with that holding, it is overruled. . . .

Finally, we wish to dispel the notion that strict scrutiny is "strict in theory but fatal in fact" [quoting Justice Marshall in *Fullilove*, Doc. 286]. . . . The unhappy persistence of both the practice and the lingering effects of racial discrimination against minority groups in this country is an unfortunate reality, and government is not disqualified from acting in response to it.

JUSTICE SCALIA, concurring. . . .

In my view, government can never have a "compelling interest" in discriminating on the basis of race in order to "make up" for past racial discrimination in the opposite direction. . . . In the eyes of the government, we are just one race here. It is American. . . .

JUSTICE THOMAS, concurring. . . .

So-called "benign" discrimination teaches many that because of chronic and apparently immutable handicaps, minorities cannot compete . . . without . . . patronizing indulgence. Inevitably, such programs engender attitudes of superiority or, alternatively, provoke resentment among those who believe that they have been wronged by the government's use of race. These programs stamp minorities with a badge of inferiority and may cause them to develop dependencies or to adopt an attitude that they are "entitled" to preferences. . . .

In my mind, government-sponsored racial discrimination based on benign prejudice is just as noxious as discrimination inspired by malicious prejudice. In each instance, it is racial discrimination, plain and simple.

JUSTICE STEVENS with whom JUSTICE GINSBURG joins, dissenting.

There is no moral or constitutional equivalence between a policy that is designed to perpetuate a caste system and one that seeks to eradicate racial subordination. Invidious discrimination is an engine of oppression subjugating a disfavored group to enhance or maintain the power of the majority. Remedial race-based preferences reflect the opposite impulse: a desire to foster equality in society. . . .

JUSTICE SOUTER, with whom JUSTICE GINSBURG and JUSTICE BREYER join, dissenting. . . .

I do not understand that today's decision will necessarily have any effect on the resolution of an issue that was just as pertinent under *Fullilove*'s unlabeled standard as it is under the standard of strict scrutiny now adopted by the Court. The Court has long accepted the view that constitutional authority to remedy past discrimination is not limited to the power to forbid its continuation, but extends to eliminating those effects that would otherwise persist. . . . Indeed, a majority of the Court today reiterates that there are circumstances in which Government may, consistently with the Constitution, adopt programs aimed at remedying the effects of past invidious discrimination. . . .

JUSTICE GINSBURG, with whom JUSTICE BREYER joins, dissenting. . . .

The United States suffers from [the] . . . lingering effects [of racial discrimination] because for most of our Nation's history, the idea that "we are just one race" [quoting Scalia earlier] was not embraced. For generations, our lawmakers and judges were unprepared to say that there is in this land no superior race, no race inferior to any other.

Source: 515 U.S. 200 at 204, 226, 227, 237, 239, 241, 242, 243, 264, 269, 270, 271, 272 (1995).

{r}DOCUMENT 347: Attorney Patricia Williams on "The Infinite Convertibility of Terms," 1995

The *Adarand* decision was symptomatic of not only continuing ambivalence about affirmative action but also a tendency for terms once clearly defined to become increasingly blurred. Lawyer Patricia Williams commented on this development in her 1995 book, *The Rooster's Egg*.

* * *

The focused and meaningful inquiry of strict scrutiny has become a needle's eye through which minority interests are too inherently suspect to pass. Racial and ethnic identification as that against which one ought not discriminate has been twisted; now those very same racial and ethnic classifications are what discriminate. The infinite convertibility of terms is, I suppose, what makes the commerce of American rhetoric so very fascinating. But these linguistic flip-flops disguise an immense stasis of power and derail the will to undo it.

Source: Patricia Williams, *The Rooster's Egg* (Cambridge: Harvard University Press, 1995): 107.

{r/g}DOCUMENT 348: Cartoon by Clay Bennett, 1995

That "the infinite convertibility of terms" could be used by proponents as well as opponents of affirmative action was pointed up in the following cartoon by Clay Bennett.

* * *

Source: Clay Bennett, Editorial Cartoonist, *Christian Science Monitor* (1999).

What meaning could be extracted from the juxtaposition of the Glass Ceiling Commission report with its fulsome documentation of the durability of white male control over American society and the *Adarand* decision with its insistence that rarely, if ever, was the government justified in applying race-conscious remedies to counter the inequities caused by that control? In seeking to answer this question, political leaders, legal experts, and other observers weighed the costs and benefits of some thirty years of affirmative action.

{r/g}DOCUMENT 349: Senator Robert Dole's Call to End Affirmative Action, March 1995

While the *Adarand* case was still under deliberation and on the very day when the *Glass Ceiling Report* was publicly issued, Senator Robert Dole called for the end of affirmative action. What made his call particularly interesting was that he had sponsored the amendment to the legislation that created the Glass Ceiling Commission and his wife, Elizabeth Dole, chaired that commission.

* * *

After nearly thirty years of Government-sanctioned quotas, timetables, set-asides and other racial preferences, the American people sense all too clearly that the race-counting game has gone too far. . . .

Discrimination continues to be an undeniable part of American life.

But fighting discrimination should never become an excuse for abandoning the color-blind ideal. Expanding opportunity should never be used to justify dividing Americans by race, by gender, by ethnic background.

Source: Congressional Record 141, Pt. 6 (March 15, 1995): 7883–7884.

{r/g}DOCUMENT 350: Support for Affirmative Action from Senator Barbara Mikulski of Maryland, June 1995

Robert Dole's Senate colleague, Barbara Mikulski, came to a different conclusion when she assessed the *Glass Ceiling Report* and the *Adarand* ruling. In hearings held by the Senate Committee on Labor and Human Resources, Mikulski addressed her remarks to the chairperson of the committee, Nancy L. Kassenbaum. While stressing the persistence of race and gender bias, she also noted the impact of economic downturns on public thought about affirmative action.

* * *

[By the *Adarand* decision the Supreme] Court made it tougher to keep affirmative action programs in place. . . . It said that race-specific affirmative action programs CAN be administered to correct *"specific provable cases of discrimination."* But it cannot be applied broadly. . . .

Madame Chair, statistics prove that persistent bias exists. The Glass Ceiling [commission] just issued its report which shows the disparity against minorities and women. . . .

It's not *just* about race, it's also about gender too.

Exactly how far have women come? Only 5 percent of senior managers in Fortune 2000 industrial and service companies are women.

Women are over 99.3 percent of dental hygienists, but are only 10.5 percent of dentists. Women are 48 percent of journalists, but hold only 6 percent of the top jobs in journalism. And it's 1995.

Madam Chair, until 1992 you and I were the only female Senators in the entire United States Senate. Now, we have the company of 6 more women. But it took us almost to the year 2000. . . .

Throughout America growing and pervasive economic insecurity has created immense anger and anxiety. . . .

Everyone is afraid of losing their job, being downsized or being left behind.

Blacks and whites, men and women are being pitted against each other. . . . But . . . scapegoating takes us nowhere. . . .

[A]ffirmative action is not a guarantee for those who could not otherwise succeed. It's simply an opportunity to compete. I support giving everyone that opportunity.

Source: Hearing of the Committee on Labor and Human Resources, U.S. Senate (June 15, 1995): 32–33.

{r/g/d}DOCUMENT 351: Speech on Affirmative Action by President Bill Clinton, July 19, 1995

As legislators made their assessments of affirmative action, a White House review of the subject was also under way. Directed by special counsel to the president Christopher Edley Jr., a team of presidential advisers worked over a six-month period to provide President Bill Clinton with a "document that set the record straight about what affirmative action is and isn't, separating myth and polemic from fact and law" (Edley 1996, 16). Guided by the team report as well as the recent *Adarand* ruling by the Supreme Court, Clinton delivered a policy statement on July 19, 1995. The president acknowledged the flawed aspects of affirmative action and gave credence to the notion of "reverse discrimination" while at the same time investing the concept of affirmative action with moral importance. Clinton also linked opposition to affirmative action with changes in the national and world economies.

* * *

When affirmative action is done right, it is flexible, it is fair, and it works....

I know there are times when some employers don't use it in the right way.... They may ... allow a different kind of discrimination. When that happens, it is also wrong. But it isn't affirmative action, and it is not legal ...

Affirmative action did not cause the great economic problems of the American middle class. And because most minorities or women are either members of that middle class or people who are poor who are struggling to get into it, we must also admit that affirmative action alone won't solve the problems of minorities and women who seek to be a part of the American dream. To do that, we have to have an economic strategy that reverses the decline in wages and the growth of poverty among working people....

Today, I am directing all our agencies to comply with the Supreme Court's *Adarand* decision [Doc. 346], and also to apply ... four standards of fairness to all our affirmative action programs.... No quotas in theory or practice; no illegal discrimination of any kind, including reverse discrimination; no preference for people who are not qualified for any job or other opportunity; and as soon as a program has succeeded, it must be retired. Any program that doesn't meet these four principles must be eliminated or reformed to meet them.

But let me be clear: Affirmative action has always been good for America....

The job of ending discrimination in this country is not over....

We should reaffirm the principle of affirmative action and fix the practices. We should have a simple slogan: Mend it, but don't end it.

Source: Public Papers of the Presidents (July 19, 1995): 1108, 1110, 1113.

{r/g}DOCUMENT 352: Affirmative Action on View in the Murder Trial of O. J. Simpson, 1995

For attorney-author Patricia Williams, evaluating affirmative action required an appreciation of the changes that it had wrought, balanced by remembrance of the price entailed in reaching those changes. Recalling the climate of the first courtroom that she had entered twenty years earlier as a law student, where the judge singled her out to express his astonishment that she was becoming a lawyer and to ask if she was related to an "Ella Williams" who had worked for his family as a maid, Williams reflected on the contrast between that courtroom and the one in 1995 where football superstar O. J. Simpson was on trial for allegedly murdering his estranged wife.

* * *

The courtroom [in the O. J. Simpson trial] is filled with a dazzling array of affirmative action babies, from the integrated jury box . . . to the integrated, mixed-gender lawyer lineup . . . to the football hero . . . turned movie star . . . , to Judge Lance Ito . . . ; with Charlayne Hunter-Gault . . . , Bryant Gumbel, Oprah Winfrey, Connie Chung, Nina Totenberg and Katie Couric (affirmative action babies all) dutifully churning it into news. . . .

We have accomplished much in the last twenty or thirty years that is too easily forgotten. As the reality of Asian-American police officers, women firefighters, close-captioned TV and a Caribbean-American general named Colin Powell fade into the backdrop of the "normal," we lose sight of how recent, costly, and precarious this much inclusion has really been.

Source: Patricia Williams, *The Rooster's Egg* (Cambridge: Harvard University Press, 1995): 94–95, 96.

{r/g}DOCUMENT 353: *Cheryl J. Hopwood v. State of Texas,* U.S. Court of Appeals, Fifth Circuit, March 18, 1996

In the spring of 1996 the Fifth Circuit Court of Appeals struck another blow against affirmative action in higher education. In a three-person panel decision on *Cheryl J. Hopwood v. State of Texas,* the appeals court found that admissions procedures at the University of Texas Law School at Austin gave unjustifiable preference to African American and Mexican American applicants. Four white plaintiffs—Cheryl Hopwood, Kenneth Elliot, Douglas Carvell, and David Rogers—were refused admission in 1992. Admissions decisions were based upon the "Texas index," a combination of a student's undergraduate grade average and score on the Law School Aptitude Test (LSAT). University officials also took other factors into account, such as the reputation of the undergraduate school, the student's undergraduate major, and any "special life experiences." Applicants were divided into three categories, those to be rejected at the outset, those to be accepted right away, and a "discretionary" category to be examined more thoroughly. The Texas index cutoff scores for placing nonminority students in these categories were higher than those used for categorizing African American and Mexican American applicants. The District Court for Western Texas found that the law school's procedures violated the plaintiff's rights to equal protection and were not "narrowly tailored" enough to serve the state's purposes in attempting to remedy lingering effects of past discrimination and maintain a diverse student body. When the university appealed this ruling, the Fifth Circuit Court upheld the district court position that the plaintiffs must be admitted and the admissions procedures overhauled. At the same time, two members of the Fifth Circuit panel of three judges also ruled that the state had failed to prove the existence of present evidence of past discrimination and that the state's interest in having a diverse student body was not a legitimate reason for practicing race-conscious admissions. The judges discounted the infamous history of the University of Texas Law School, stretching back to the case of Herman Sweatt (Doc. 82) and continuing into at least the 1970s, when there were still no African Americans enrolled there (Garcia 1997, 233). The Supreme Court, by refusing to review the case, allowed the Fifth Circuit ruling to stand. Taken together with the *Podberesky* decision (Doc. 339), the *Hopwood* judgment strengthened the hand of organized opposition to affirmative action in college, university, and professional school admissions.

* * *

The law school has presented no compelling justification . . . that allows it to continue to elevate some races over others, even for the wholesome purpose of correcting perceived racial imbalances in the student body. . . .

[T]here has been no indication from the Supreme Court, other than Justice Powell's lonely opinion in *Bakke* [Doc. 231], that the state's interest in diversity constitutes a compelling justification for governmental race-based discrimination. Subsequent Supreme Court caselaw strongly suggests, in fact, that it is not. . . .

[K]nowledge of historical fact simply cannot justify current racial classifications. . . . The vast majority of the faculty, staff and students at the law school had absolutely nothing to do with any discrimination that the law school practiced in the past. . . .

In summary, we hold that the University of Texas School of Law may not use race as a factor in deciding which applicants to admit in order to achieve a diverse student body, to combat the perceived effects of a hostile environment at the law school, to alleviate the law school's poor reputation in the minority community, or to eliminate any present effects of past discrimination by actors other than the law school.

Source: 78 F. 3d 932 at 934, 945, 953, 962 (5th Cir. 1996).

{r/g}DOCUMENT 354: Judge Wiener Specially Concurring in *Hopwood v. Texas*, March 1996

Fifth Circuit Judge Wiener departed in a special concurrence from his fellow judges' opinions on diversity and expanded upon the finding that the Texas law school had failed to narrowly tailor its admissions process.

* * *

I respectfully disagree with the panel opinion's conclusion that diversity can never be a compelling governmental interest in a public graduate school. . . . [D]iversity can be a compelling interest . . . [however] the admissions process here under scrutiny was not narrowly tailored to achieve diversity. . . .

[I]f Bakke [Doc. 230] is to be declared dead, the Supreme Court, not a three-judge panel of a circuit court, should make that pronouncement. . . .

[B]lacks and Mexican Americans are but two among any number of racial or ethnic groups that could and presumably should contribute to genuine diversity. . . .

In this light, the limited racial effects of the law school's preferential admissions process . . . more closely resembles a set-aside or quota system for those two disadvantaged minorities than it does an academic admissions program narrowly tailored to achieve true diversity.

Source: 78 F. 3d 932 at 962, 963, 966 (5th Cir. 1996).

Critics of the *Hopwood* ruling decried the judges' failure to look at the issue within a historical context and to take into account other available evidence, including critiques of the Texas index as an accurate predictor of performance and the fact that "109 nonminority residents [of Texas] with numerical scores lower than Cheryl Hopwood were offered admission, and 67 nonminority residents with numerical scores lower than the three other plaintiffs were admitted" to the law school the year they were turned down. Admissions records indicate that Hopwood provided no letters of recommendation and her undergraduate education, acquired mostly at a junior college, was judged to be weak. Nor were the applications of her fellow plaintiffs particularly strong (Garcia, 234–235).

{r}DOCUMENT 355: A "Percentage Plan" as an Alternative to Affirmative Action, 1997

The response of Latino and African American legislators in Texas to the *Hopwood* ruling was a "Ten Percent Plan." Noting that racial segregation had created mostly one-race high schools, the authors of the plan reasoned that offering tuition-free college admission to the top 10 percent of each senior class in every high school would ensure some diversity in every college. The emphasis on economic class rather than race attracted bipartisan support, and the plan was passed by the majority-Republican Texas legislature. Supporters of the plan elaborated on its rationale in a report in *The Nation*.

* * *

The Ten Percent plan puts test scores to one side, but unlike affirmative action, it does so for everyone, and it does so in the name of a standard of merit . . . working hard, getting good grades and doing very well at what's expected of you.

Source: William E. Forbath and Gerald Torres, "The Talented Tenth in Texas," *The Nation* (December 15, 1997): 21.

{r}DOCUMENT 356: Cartoon by "Kal," 1996

The *Hopwood* ruling came at a time of resurgent racism, aspects of which were highlighted in July 1996 by cartoonist Kevin "Kal" Kallaugher.

* * *

Source: Cartoonists and Writers Syndicate, July 2, 1996 (New York).

{r}DOCUMENT 357: Sociologist William Julius Wilson's Call for "Broader Solutions" than Affirmative Action, 1996

The notion of class-based affirmative action was attracting increasing interest and support by the mid-1990s. Among those who found considerable merit in it was sociologist William Julius Wilson. The eminent African American scholar wrote in his 1996 study, *When Work Disappears, the World of the New Urban Poor*, that "we need broader solutions than those we have employed in the past" (p. 199).

* * *

Minority individuals from the most advantaged families tend to be disproportionately represented among those of their racial group most qualified for preferred status, such as college admissions, higher-paying jobs, and promotions. Thus, policies of affirmative action are likely to enhance opportunities for the more advantaged without adequately remedying the problems of the disadvantaged. . . .

The major distinguishing characteristic of affirmative action based on need is the recognition that the problems of the disadvantaged—low income, crime-ridden neighborhoods, broken homes, inadequate housing, poor education, cultural and linguistic differences—are not always clearly related to previous racial discrimination. Children who grow up in homes plagued by these disadvantages are more likely to be denied an equal chance in life because the development of their aspirations and talents is hindered by their environment, regardless of race. Minorities would benefit disproportionately from affirmative opportunity programs designed to address these disadvantages because they suffer disproportionately from the effects of such environments, *but the problems of disadvantaged whites would be addressed as well.*

Source: William Julius Wilson, *When Work Disappears, the World of the New Urban Poor* (New York: Alfred A. Knopf, 1996): 197, 198.

{r}DOCUMENT 358: Richard Kahlenberg, "Class Not Race," April 1995

Author Richard Kahlenberg devoted an entire book to promoting class-based affirmative action. In a preview article for *The New Republic* in April 1995 Kahlenberg argued that changing from race to class was pragmatic with regard to both the politics of liberal reform and the mechanics of implementation.

* * *

The priority given to race over class has inevitably exacerbated white racism. . . .

Class . . . is not one of the suspect categories under the Fourteenth Amendment, which leaves class-based remedies much less assailable. . . .

[I]t is possible to devise an enforceable set of objective standards for deprivation. . . .

It's just not true that a system of class preferences is inherently harder to administer than a system based on race. Race only seems simpler because we have ignored the ambiguities.

Source: Kahlenberg 1995, 24, 25.

{r/g}DOCUMENT 359: Law Professor Deborah C. Malamud Assesses "Class Based Affirmative Action," 1996

Deborah C. Malamud, assistant professor of law at the University of Michigan, raised questions about the viability of basing affirmative action on a measurement of economic need. Although in the interest of "systematic experimentation" in policy making Malamud cautiously supported efforts to fashion a legal definition of class-based affirmative action, she spelled out in detail the myriad complications that such a definition must take into account.

* * *

[A] number of factors . . . shape the economic situations of individuals and families: occupation, income, education, orientation toward educational attainment, and numerous extra-economic characteristics (including race and gender). . . .

[T]he relationships among the elements of economic privilege are not simply additive or multiplicative. They are structural. The factors contributing to relative economic advantage exist in a delicate balance and interact in space and time. . . . No easily administered, quantitative, composite index of the elements of economic inequality can capture their complex interrelationships. . . .

[T]here is ample evidence that the interactions among economic factors differ for men and women, that women are less able than men to take personal advantage of inherited and earned economic and social capital, and that occupation schemes developed for men are less accurate for women.

Theorizing and measuring the economic status of members of racial and ethnic minority groups pose problems of equal magnitude. . . .

[B]lacks and whites who appear to have the same occupation, education, or residential situation when a simple metric is used may well not occupy the same status in reality. . . .

And skin color remains a powerful obstacle. . . .

[I]f an overly simplistic measurement of class is used, systematic differences in the present and historical economic condition of blacks will be ignored, and the socioeconomic privilege of middle class blacks will be overstated. It is highly likely, given the complexity of the phenomenon, that even the most earnest efforts at designing an adequate metric will fail.

Source: Malamud 1996, 1870, 1889, 1891, 1892, 1893, 1894.

While lawyers, scholars, and politicians argued among themselves over the merits and demerits of affirmative action in all its variety, ordinary citizens relied on personal experience and the media to make their judgments on the subject. As to the results produced by affirmative action, the anecdotal evidence was bewildering. Clearly, race-and gender-sensitive policies and recent mandates on behalf of the disabled had reached into places of learning, work, recreation, competitive sports, and many other aspects of daily life across the nation. The extent to which they were perceived and accepted as indicators of national strength and progress and the extent to which they were resented and resisted were hard to measure.

{g}DOCUMENT 360: *U.S. News & World Report* Notes Title IX Results in National and World Sports, July 1996

The impact of Title IX (Doc. 191) on women in sports was hailed in the Summer Olympics of 1996 as—in the words of *Newsweek*—"nothing short of revolutionary." Anticipating that the U.S. women's teams would outperform the men's in the international competitions, the magazine marveled at the dramatic increase in the number of women competitors, from a ratio of six men to one woman in the 1976 Olympics to a ratio of four men to three women twenty years later (*Newsweek*, June 10, 1996, 64, 66). The same refrain ran throughout the sports reporting world. The write-up in *U.S. News & World Report* was typical.

* * *

[I]t is a virtual certainty that the nation's female Olympians will do better overall in their competitions than will U.S. men. Women are now beating world records held by men 10 and 15 years ago. . . .

The impetus for such explosive growth was Title IX of the Education Amendments. . . . It demolished the traditional myth that women aren't interested in sports.

Source: Mike Tharp with Josh Chetwynd and Shannon Brownlee, "Sports Crazy," *U.S. News & World Report* (July 15/July 22, 1996): 33.

America's female athletes rewarded the expectations held for them in the 1996 Olympics, garnering gold medals in women's soccer, softball, basketball, swimming, and track and field.

{r/g}DOCUMENT 361: Author Barbara R. Bergmann Laments Weak Enforcement of Affirmative Action, 1996

If the Olympics symbolized the effectiveness of one affirmative action law, other evidence indicated how useless race and gender laws and policies could be. Author Barbara Bergmann called attention to "continuing high levels of discriminatory segregation in the nation's workplaces" in her 1996 book, *In Defense of Affirmative Action*. She found the cause for the persistence of discrimination in the failure of the federal government, especially the Office of Federal Contract Compliance Programs (OFCCP), to enforce its own policies.

* * *

Unfortunately, the OFCCP, the main government agency pushing affirmative action in the workplace, is understaffed, has few effective ways of encouraging compliance, lacks vigor, and has probably been poorly managed. . . .

Its main sanction is the debarment of a corporation from the approved list of federal contractors. Only forty-one firms have been debarred since 1972, out of thousands whose long-term performance has been unsatisfactory. . . . [D]ebarment virtually ceased during the Reagan-Bush era. . . .

Of the companies debarred since 1972, only four have been large corporations: Prudential Insurance, Firestone, Uniroyal and Timkin Roller Bearing. All were debarred during the Democratic administration of Jimmy Carter. None of those debarments lasted very long; all four companies were reinstated within three months. . . .

[T]he federal government . . . has concentrated on ensuring that each federal contractor has an affirmative action plan somewhere in its files and a poster announcing its nondiscrimination policy on an employee bulletin board somewhere on its premises. . . . Some firms have pushed affirmative action, but many firms have not yet changed their hiring and promotion practices to any significant degree.

Source: Bergmann 1996, 53, 54, 60.

{r/g}DOCUMENT 362: Practice versus Policy at Texaco Corporation, 1996

A dramatic example of the situation described by Bergmann became headline news in November 1996, when secretly recorded conversations on the part of senior executives of the Texaco Corporation were made public by African American employees who sued the company for violating their civil rights. According to the *New York Times*, Texaco was the fourteenth largest corporation in the United States and part of an industry (petroleum) considered to be far behind most other industries in addressing issues of discrimination and diversity. Within that industry Texaco held the worst record for recruiting and promoting minorities and women (*New York Times*, November 10, 1996). As syndicated columnist Clarence Page noted, Texaco also published a mission statement declaring its commitment to equal opportunity. Page juxtaposed that statement with excerpts from the senior executives' conversation.

* * *

A. Executive Meeting August 1994

"It's this diversity thing," grumbles Robert W. Ulrich, then treasurer of Texaco, Inc. "You know how black jelly beans agree."

"That's funny," says Richard Lundwall, then human-resources assistant at the company. "All the black jelly beans seem to be glued to the bottom of the bag."

B. Texaco Annual Report, 1995

"Our commitment to diversity is an inclusive process, grounded in our core value of respect for the individual and in our long-standing policies of equal opportunity for all employees."

Source: Quoted in Clarence Page, "Texaco Tapes: The Case for Affirmative Action" (*Baltimore Sun*, November 8, 1996): 25A.

{r/g}DOCUMENT 363: California's Proposition 209, as Approved by Voters, November 1996

The various forces antagonistic to affirmative action coalesced in California in 1995 and 1996. Although often characterized as a campaign of "Angry White Males," the California attack on affirmative action was led by an African American male, Wardell Anthony Connerly. A conservative Republican businessman, Connerly had been appointed in 1994 by his close friend Republican governor Pete Wilson to the Board of Regents of the University of California. Asserting that race- and gender-sensitive admissions and hiring policies stigmatized the groups that they were intended to uplift and that such policies also discriminated against Asians and whites, Connerly persuaded his fellow Regents to end (effective 1998) the affirmative action policies followed by the university for the past twenty-nine years. Buoyed by this victory, Connerly, with the continuing support of Wilson, went on to promote the "California Civil Rights Initiative," the centerpiece of which was "Proposition 209," a referendum to prohibit the state and local governments from practicing affirmative action in public education, employment, and the letting of contracts. In November 1996 voters approved Proposition 209—54 percent for and 46 percent against.

Once officially approved, Proposition 209 became Article 1, Section 31, of the California Constitution.

* * *

The state shall not discriminate against, or grant preferential treatment to, any individual or group on the basis of race, sex, color, ethnicity, or national origin in the operation of public employment, public education or public contracting.

Source: Quoted in 946 F. Supp. 1480 at 1488 N.D. Cal. (1996).

{r/g}DOCUMENT 364: *Coalition for Economic Equality v. Pete Wilson*, Ninth Circuit Court of Appeals, April 8, 1997

The vote on Proposition 209 was challenged in court by opponents organized as the Coalition for Economic Equity. Thelton H. Henderson, chief judge of the district court, granted them an injunction and placed a temporary restraining order against the implementation of 209. His action provided the opponents with only a short-lived respite. In April of the following year the Ninth Circuit Court of Appeals denied their claim to, and invalidated, the district court injunction.

* * *

A system which permits one judge to block with the stroke of a pen what 4,736,180 state residents voted to enact as law tests the integrity of our constitutional democracy. . . .

That the Constitution *permits* the rare race-based or gender-based preference hardly implies that the state cannot ban them altogether. . . .

To hold that a democratically enacted affirmative action program is constitutionally permissible because the people have demonstrated a compelling state interest is hardly to hold that the program is constitutionally required. The Fourteenth Amendment . . . does not require what it barely permits. . . .

[P]laintiffs are not entitled to a preliminary injunction.

Source: 110 F. 3d 1431 at 1437, 1446, 1448 (9th Cir. 1997).

{r/g}DOCUMENT 365: Critique of Proposition 209 Campaign, 1998

In Proposition 209 observers saw a drastic setback for affirmative action, with representation of minorities and women in all fields placed in jeopardy. After the appeals court invalidated the injunction against the new measure, thousands of protesters marched across the Golden Gate Bridge and rallied in San Francisco, where civil rights leader Jesse Jackson labeled proponents of 209 "dream breakers" and encouraged opponents not to give up (*Baltimore Sun*, August 29, 1997). The Supreme Court, in the first week of November 1997, refused to review the appeals court decision and thereby left Proposition 209 in the California Constitution.

Supporters of affirmative action questioned the validity of the California referendum, citing polling data.

* * *

Harris polls in mid-1996 found that nearly 60% [of the respondents in California] didn't believe that 209 would end affirmative action. Confusion on this simple issue proved to be the most important factor in determining the outcome, since, according to exit polls by the *Los Angeles Times*, when voters were asked whether they supported affirmative action "to help women and minorities get better jobs and educations" 54% said yes, while 46% said no, exactly the opposite results on 209 that day. . . . Other polls indicated that nearly 30% of those voting for 209 thought they had cast a vote *in favor* of affirmative action.

Source: Tim Wise, "Is Sisterhood Conditional?" *NWSA Journal* [National Women's Studies Association] (Fall 1998): 22, note 11.

{r}DOCUMENT 366: "A Return to Segregation?" Asks
The National Jurist, September 1997

Predictions of drastic declines in minority representation in education proved valid in the wake of Proposition 209, particularly in professional schools. In November 1997 the Association of American
Medical Colleges published a study showing an 11 percent decline in
minority enrollments in the nation's accredited medical schools. The
report attributed the decline to a combination of the effects of Proposition 209 and the *Hopwood* decision (Doc. 353) (*Baltimore Sun*, November 2, 1997, p. 13A). Similarly, *The National Jurist* reported in
September 1997 that law schools in Texas and California had become
"ghostly white" and asked if the country was on the verge of returning
to segregation. Faculty and administrators from the University of Texas
School of Law at Austin who were quoted in *The National Jurist* revealed a wide range of opinion about current trends.

* * *

This year Bolt Hall [the law school at the University of California] will
host the same number of black first-year students as the University of
Mississippi School of Law graduated in 1967: one. . . .
    "The effect [of the demise of affirmative action] is so dramatic that it
is hard to argue that it is not segregation," said Juan Zabala, associate
dean for business affairs at University of Texas School of Law in Austin,
where just four black students are expected to attend in the 1997–98
academic year. . . .
    "The only reason you have racial preference is because the preferred
groups do not meet the ordinary standards . . . ," said Lino A. Graglia, a
professor at the University of Texas School of Law.

Source: Anna Marie Stolley, "A Return to Segregation?," *The National Jurist* (September 1997): 34, 38.

{r}DOCUMENT 367: Commencement Address by President
Bill Clinton at the University of California, San Diego,
June 14, 1997

Two months after the durability of Proposition 209 was tested in the
courts and upheld by the Supreme's Court's silence, President Bill Clin-

ton traveled to California as commencement speaker at the University of California, San Diego. Having sidestepped 209 during his reelection campaign—as did his opponent, Robert Dole (Chavez, pp. 248–249)—the president now made direct reference to it and its deleterious effect on progress toward equal opportunity for all citizens.

* * *

I know that the people of California voted to repeal affirmative action without any ill motive. The vast majority of them simply did it with a conviction that discrimination and isolation are no longer barriers to achievement. But consider the results. Minority enrollments in law school and other graduate programs are plummeting for the first time in decades. Soon the same will likely happen in undergraduate education. . . . At the very time when we need to do a better job of living and learning together, we should not stop trying to equalize economic opportunity.

To those who oppose affirmative action, I ask you to come up with an alternative. I would embrace it if I could find a better way.

Source: Public Papers of the Presidents (June 14, 1997): 739.

{r}DOCUMENT 368: Ward Connerly Quoted in the *Baltimore Sun*, June 1997

Sitting on the platform as President Clinton delivered the commencement address was Ward Connerly, who did not take kindly to the president's comments.

* * *

Where [Clinton is] coming into the debate, we've been there, done that. . . . I don't think he should involve himself in second-guessing the people of California and tell us we did something wrong. We've had the debate. We voted. We won. Leave us alone.

Source: "President Urges 'One America,' " *Baltimore Sun* (June 15, 1997): 1A.

{g}DOCUMENT 369: *Cohen v. Brown University*, U.S. Court of Appeals, First Circuit, November 1996 (Supreme Court Refused to Hear It, April 1997)

The same Supreme Court justices who allowed their silence to ratify Proposition 209 and the *Hopwood* ruling (Doc. 353) also chose to remain silent on a major Title IX case, *Cohen v. Brown University*. In this instance the results benefited women athletes. Cohen, a junior at Brown and a champion gymnast, filed suit in 1991 on behalf of all present, future, and potential women students at Brown, alleging violations of their rights under Title IX. The suit was triggered when university officials downgraded four sports—two each for women and men—from varsity to donor-supported. The administration contended that this was an evenhanded action. The women protested that it represented increasing discrimination in an athletic program that already disadvantaged them. A federal district court agreed with them and granted a preliminary injunction against Brown. This ruling was upheld by a circuit court panel, and the case returned to district court for a trial. Again the court found for the women and instructed university officials to develop a plan for achieving compliance with Title IX. The university appealed and lost in the First Circuit Court of Appeals and then requested Supreme Court review. That review was denied in April 1997, forcing Brown authorities to alter its athletics program. That this outcome held implications for all institutions of higher education was evinced by the fact that sixty colleges and universities had joined Brown in its unsuccessful attempt to persuade the Supreme Court to overturn the decision of the appeals court.

The final ruling in *Cohen v. Brown University* was based on the interpretations by the First Circuit Court of Appeals of a three-part "test" established by the civil rights division of the Department of Education for determining Title IX compliance. According to this test, an institution must demonstrate either that the numbers of students of each sex participating in athletic programs are proportionate to enrollment or that there is a continuing expansion of women's athletic programs in the institution or that the "interests and abilities of the underrepresented sex have been fully accommodated." Brown officials claimed to have met the third part (only one part was required). The court did not agree. In addition, lawyers for Brown argued that the *Adarand* case (Doc. 346) brought Title IX under "strict scrutiny." Again the court disagreed and, in the process of doing so, denied that Title IX was an affirmative action statute. The nature of Title IX also figured prominently as an issue in the one dissenting opinion delivered by the chief justice of the circuit court. Finally, the impact on the judges of the 1996 Summer Olympics was evident in their ruling.

* * *

[T]he district court found that . . . "although the number of varsity sports offered to men and women are equal, the selection of sports offered to each gender generates far more individual positions for male athletes than for female athletes. . . ."

[N]ot withstanding Brown's persistent invocation of the inflammatory terms "affirmative action," "preference," and "quota," this is not an affirmative action case. . . ."

Title IX is not an affirmative action statute; it is an anti-discrimination statute. . . .

Like other anti-discrimination statutory schemes, the Title IX regime *permits* affirmative action. . . .

We view Brown's argument that women are less interested than men in participating in intercollegiate athletics . . . with great suspicion. . . .

Interest and ability rarely develop in a vacuum; they evolve as a function of opportunity and experience. . . .

Brown's implicit reliance on *Adarand* . . . is misplaced. . . . [W]hile *Adarand* does make new law, the law it makes is wholly irrelevant to the disposition of this appeal, and even if *Adarand* did apply, it does not mandate the level of scrutiny to be applied to gender-conscious government action. . . .

One need look no further than the impressive performances of our country's women athletes in the 1996 Olympic Summer Games to see that Title IX has had a dramatic and positive impact on the capabilities of our women athletes. . . . What stimulated this remarkable change in the quality of women's athletic competition was not a sudden, anomalous upsurge in women's interest in sports, but the enforcement of Title IX's mandate of gender equity in sports.

TORRUELLA, Chief Judge (dissenting). . . .

It is not necessary to equate race and gender to see that the logic of *Adarand* . . . applies in the context of gender. . . .

I believe that the three prong test, as the district court interprets it, is a quota. . . . I agree that "Title IX is not an affirmative action statute," . . . but I believe that is exactly what the district court has made of it. . . .

[T]he majority has put the power to control athletics and the provision of athletic resources in the hands of the under-represented gender . . .

[and has] failed to give Brown University freedom to craft its own athletic program.

Source: 101 F. 3d 155 at 163–164, 169, 170, 178, 179, 181, 188, 190, 195, 198, 199 (1st Cir. 1996).

{g}DOCUMENT 370 *Education Week* on Women and Sports, June 1997

As they welcomed the outcome of *Cohen v. Brown University*, women's sports advocates reflected on what Donna Lopiano of the Women's Sports Foundation (Doc. 186) called a "half-full, half-empty situation," with equal opportunity for girls and women in athletics still unrealized, not only in higher education but also in elementary and secondary schools. Among the causes of this situation, writers for articles in *Education Week* in June 1997 emphasized two factors—continuing male control of sports and poor federal enforcement.

* * *

A. "25 Years after Title IX . . ."
[W]omen's sports advocates contend that a male-dominated upper-tier of school administrators, athletic directors and coaches—men reared largely in the pre-feminist, pre-Title IX era—are responsible for stunting girls' gains in sports. . . .

But critics of Title IX insist that they are not against the idea of expanding girls' opportunities to play sports. Instead, they say problems arise when that expansion comes at the expense of already established boys' sports.

B. "Absence of Federal Enforcement"
Although 25 years have passed since Title IX was signed into law, advocates for girls' sports say that thousands of elementary and secondary schools have managed to ignore it. . . .

The OCR [Office of Civil Rights] has no routine policy for checking if schools comply with [Title IX]. . . .

OCR can withhold federal funds from schools that are not in compliance with Title IX, but never has.

Sources: Kerry A. White, "25 Years after Title IX, Sexual Bias in K–12 Sports Still Sidelines Girl"; "States Step Up Push for Equity in Absence of Federal Enforcement," *Education Week* (June 18, 1997): 1, 20, 21.

{r/g}DOCUMENT 371: Policy Adopted in 1983 by the Board of Education of Piscataway, NJ (Subject of Legal Proceedings from 1989 to 1997)

Agreement by the Supreme Court in June 1997 to rule on a dispute between the Piscataway, New Jersey, board of education and a teacher, Sharon Taxman, put advocates on both sides of the debate over affirmative action on tenterhooks. As *Education Week* described it, "the case presents a near-textbook scenario for the high court to rule on the boundaries of affirmative action in employment" (Mark Walsh, "Supreme Court Case Plays Out in N.J. School Every Day," *Education Week*, October 8, 1997, 20). The roots of the case went back to a 1975 mandate by the New Jersey Board of Education requiring every school district in the state to adopt affirmative action plans for students and employees. The Piscataway school district complied in 1976 and prepared a revised plan seven years later. According to statistical reviews, throughout this period the number of African Americans employed as teachers in the school district exceeded their numbers in the local labor pool.

* * *

This policy ensures equal employment opportunity for all persons and prohibits discrimination in employment because of sex, race, color, creed, religion, handicap, domicile, marital status, or national origin. In all cases, the most qualified candidate will be recommended for appointment. However, when candidates appear to be of equal qualification, candidates meeting the criteria of the affirmative action program will be recommended.

Source: Quoted in 832 F. Supp. 836 at 839 (D.N.J. 1993).

{r/g}DOCUMENT 372: 1989 Letter That Sparked the *Taxman v. Piscataway* Legal Proceedings, 1989–1997

The board invoked the policy of the preceding document in 1989, when the superintendent of schools recommended a staff reduction in the Business Education Department of the district high school. Based on seniority, there were two candidates for the layoff—Debra Williams, the only African American in the department, and Sharon Taxman, who was white. In qualifications the women were basically equals, and in years of service the women were "tied." The School Board explained in a letter to Taxman on May 22, 1989, how they broke the tie and decided to dismiss her.

* * *

[T]he board of education has decided to rely on its commitment to affirmative action as a means of breaking the tie in seniority entitlement in the secretarial studies category. As a result, the board at its regular meeting on the evening of May 22, 1989, acted to abolish one teaching position and to terminate your employment as a teaching staff member effective June 30, 1989.

Source: Quoted in 832 F. Supp. 836 at 840 (D.N.J. 1993).

{r/g}DOCUMENT 373: *Sharon Taxman v. Board of Education of the Township of Piscataway,* **U.S. Court of Appeals, Third Circuit, August 8, 1996 (Supreme Court Agreed to Hear, June 1997; Out of Court Settlement, November 1997)**

Sharon Taxman filed complaints with both federal and state governments, charging that her rights under Title VII and the New Jersey Law against Discrimination had been violated. The Justice Department during the administration of George Bush sued the school board on Taxman's behalf. When the board tried to have the case thrown out under a statute of limitations argument in federal district court in 1992, the court ruled for Taxman, as it did in 1993 when both sides presented full arguments. Taxman prevailed again in federal appeals court in 1996. By then Clinton occupied the White House, and his Justice Department took the opposite position from that of the Bush years and supported the Piscataway School Board.

Throughout this succession of court appearances, the Board of Education tried to employ language from previous Supreme Court rulings in the *Weber, Johnson, Bakke,* and *Metro Broadcasting* cases (Docs. 262, 304, 230, 322).

A main theme in its reasoning was the importance of diversity in the school setting and the value of role models for minority students. The lower federal courts would have none of the board's arguments.

* * *

We hold that Piscataway's affirmative action policy is unlawful. . . .

The affirmative action plans at issue in *Weber* and *Johnson* were sustained only because the Supreme Court . . . found a secondary congressional objective in Title VII that had to be accommodated—i.e., the elimination of the effects of past discrimination in the workplace. Here, there is no congressional recognition of diversity as a Title VII objective requiring accommodation. . . .

Bakke's factual and legal setting, as well as the diversity that universities aspire to in their student bodies, are, in our view, so different from the facts, relevant law and the racial diversity purpose involved in this case that we find little in *Bakke* to guide us.

Likewise, statements regarding the value of programming diversity made by the Court in *Metro Broadcasting* . . . have no application here. . . .

Moreover, both *Weber* and *Johnson* unequivocally provide that valid affirmative action plans are "temporary" measures that seek to "attain," . . . not "maintain" a "permanent racial . . . balance" [quoting *Johnson*]. . . . The Board's policy, adopted in 1975, is an established fixture of unlimited duration, to be resurrected from time to time whenever the Board believes that the ratio between Blacks and Whites in any Piscataway School is skewed. On this basis alone, the policy contravenes *Weber*'s teaching. . . .

Finally, we are convinced that the harm imposed upon a nonminority employee by the loss of his or her job is so substantial and the cost so severe that the Board's goal of racial diversity, even if legitimate under Title VII, may not be pursued in this particular fashion. This is especially true where, as here, the nonminority employee is tenured.

Source: 91 F. 3d 1547 at 1550, 1558, 1561, 1562–1563, 1564 (1996).

{r/g}DOCUMENT 374: Dissenting Judges in *Taxman v. Piscataway Board of Education*, August 1996

While the Appeals Court majority was unequivocal in rejecting the policy followed by the Piscataway Board of Education, a court minority dissented. Chief Judge Sloviter began his dissent with the observation that "it is often how the question is framed that determines the answer that is received."

* * *

[T]he narrow question posed by this appeal can be restated as whether Title VII *requires* a New Jersey school or school board . . . to make its decision [regarding layoffs] through a coin toss or lottery . . . or whether Title VII *permits* the school board to factor into the decision its bona fide belief . . . that students derive educational benefit by having a Black faculty member in an otherwise all White department. . . .

The majority presents *Weber* and *Johnson* as if their significance lies in the obstacle course they purportedly establish for any employer adopting an affirmative action program. But . . . the significance of each of those cases is that the Supreme Court *sustained* the affirmative action plans presented, and in doing so deviated from the literal interpretation of Title VII. . . .

Judge Sloviter joined with other dissenting judges in their separate opinions. Judges Sirica, Lewis, and McKee each wrote dissents. McKee elaborated on what he saw as unfortunate implications of the ruling against the Piscataway school board.

MCKEE . . . dissenting, with whom SLOVITER . . . and LEWIS join.

We have now come full circle. A law enacted by Congress in 1964 to move this country closer to an integrated society and away from the legacy of "separate but equal" is being interpreted as outlawing this Board of Education's good faith effort to teach students the value of diversity. . . . I cannot believe that Title VII was intended to strike down such an action.

Source: 91 F. 3d 1547 at 1567, 1570, 1578, 1579 (3rd Cir. 1996).

{r/g}DOCUMENT 375: "Key Affirmative Action Case Settled," *Baltimore Sun*, November 22, 1997

The Piscataway Board of Education challenged the appeals court's decision by going to the Supreme Court, which agreed to hear the case. At this point the Justice Department (still under the aegis of the Clinton administration) shifted its position again. First it had requested the Supreme Court to reject the case, because it was untypical. Then after the Court had taken it, the department submitted a brief supporting the concept of a school district's right to use affirmative action on behalf of diversity in hiring and promotions but rarely, if ever, when layoffs are involved. This essentially ended the administration's support of the Piscataway school district (*Education Week*, September 3, 1997). Before the Supreme Court had a chance to reach a decision on the case, the Black Leadership Forum—a coalition of twenty-one civil rights and other social action groups—negotiated an out-of-court settlement with Sharon Taxman. The Court's recent actions, especially letting Proposition 209 stand (Docs. 363, 364), gave affirmative action advocates reason to fear that the conservative majority now directing the Court would use the Piscataway case to render a sweeping judgment against all affirmative action remedies. The terms of the settlement and the thinking on both sides of the issue were reported in the media, including the following article in the *Baltimore Sun*.

* * *

The Rev. Jesse Jackson . . . said, "This case was riddled with problems," and a ruling in it would have been "a distortion of the issues." Jackson said civil rights groups had "outflanked" opponents of affirmative action "because we took this whole thing out of court."

Clint Bolick, litigation director of the Institute for Justice, which opposes affirmative action, said "the defenders of racial preferences are running for the hills."

Source: Baltimore Sun (November 22, 1997): 1A.

{r/g}DOCUMENT 376: Ballot Question Rejected by Houston Voters, November 1997

While resolution of the *Taxman* case was unfolding, voters in Houston, Texas, had responded to a ballot measure akin to California's Proposition 209 (Doc. 363). The outcome of the Houston referendum lent credence to those who claimed that the wording of 209 had misled voters in California. Originally, the Houston antiaffirmative action initiative was a verbatim copy of the California referendum, except that it did not encompass public education. However, the City Council intervened and insisted on wording it in the form of a question, which made the purpose of the measure explicit. The voters rejected it. "What all this demonstrates," opined the Citizens Commission on Civil Rights, "is that voters can be misled by disingenuous political rhetoric" (Citizens' Commission on Civil Rights 1999, 182).

* * *

Shall the charter of the City of Houston be amended to end the use of Affirmative Action for women and minorities in the operation of City of Houston employment and contracting including ending the current program and any similar programs in the future?

Source: Quoted in Citizens' Commission on Civil Rights 1999, 182.

{r}DOCUMENT 377: Nomination Battle over Bill Lann Lee for Assistant Attorney General for Civil Rights, 1997

Along with hotly contested state referenda and portentous court battles, the 1997 nominee of President Clinton for assistant attorney general for civil rights became a storm center because of affirmative action. Bill Lann Lee was Clinton's second nominee for the post. The president had withdrawn the previous nomination of Lani Guinier when her ideas for implementing voting rights through a system of "proportional representation" provoked an extreme reaction from conservatives. The new nominee was an Asian American who had worked for fifteen years for the NAACP Defense Fund. He had opposed Proposition 209 (Doc. 363). His reception by the Senate Judiciary Committee was described in the *Baltimore Sun*.

* * *

[Bill Lan Lee's] appointment has turned into the latest national battleground over affirmative action. . . .

"It's time to take a stand against policies that are ripping America apart," said Sen. Orrin G. Hatch. . . .

To Sen. Mitch McConnell, a Kentucky Republican, Lee's testimony showed an "alarming allegiance to racial preferences and disturbing disregard for the Constitution."

Source: Baltimore Sun (November 7, 1997): 1A, 13A.

When the Senate committee rejected the nomination, Clinton appointed Lee as acting assistant attorney general, a position that he could keep as long as the president chose not to nominate a successor.

{r/g/d}DOCUMENT 378: Scholar Lawrence H. Fuchs Envisions the End of Affirmative Action, 1997

While foes and proponents of affirmative action repeatedly faced off in the political arena, scholars debated the wisdom and constitutionality of promoting opportunity on a group by group basis, as opposed to legislating universal rights applicable to all groups. In the proceedings of a civil rights symposium held at the Balch Institute for Ethnic Studies in Philadelphia in October 1994 (and published in 1997), Brandeis Professor of American Civilization and Politics, Lawrence H. Fuchs, charged that affirmative action advocates had come to the point of treating temporary remedies against discrimination as permanent rights. Stressing the divisive effects of preferential programs, Fuchs recommended first limiting the coverage of affirmative action and then, within twenty-five years, ending it entirely.

* * *

The decision . . . to go beyond antidiscrimination law—intended to cover everyone—to affirmative action was aimed specifically at redressing the grievances of African Americans. There never was a comparable historical justification for including others as designated beneficiary groups. . . . If possible, we should phase out proportionality-based affirmative action remedies for all groups except American-born African Americans by the year 2000.

It would be wise to set a date by which to eliminate all counting-by-race remedies, perhaps by the year 2010. Most Americans want to be assured that the idea of group rights based on color or ethnicity has not become entrenched in the American political system.

Source: Higham 1997/1999, 82, 85.

{r/g}DOCUMENT 379: "Resounding Defeat for Affirmative Action Foes in Georgia," Spring 1998

As the new year of 1998 began, U.S. Court of Appeals chief judge emeritus, A. Leon Higginbotham Jr., reflected on rulings by federal court appointees of Bush and Reagan and particularly on the *Hopwood* case (Doc. 353). "I sometimes feel as if I am watching justice die," he wrote (*New York Times Magazine*, January 18, 1998: 28–29). His words conveyed the gloom settling over civil rights and affirmative action supporters at that point. However, in the next few months a few rays of hope penetrated that gloom, beginning with the defeat of legislation intended to kill affirmative action in the state of Georgia. Details of the defeat were reported by the journal of the Southern Regional Council, *Southern Changes*. In the same issue *Southern Changes* writer Amy Wood exulted that "during 1996 and 1997 only thirteen states actually introduced such legislation, and none of these bills was successful" (Amy Wood, "Going Nowhere Fast," *Southern Changes* [Spring 1998]: 3).

* * *

Opponents of affirmative action suffered a resounding defeat in the Georgia legislature during the 1998 session, when amendments banning affirmative action in the state were killed. . . .

The multi-sided attack on the modest programs in Georgia was met with coordinated action by an unprecedented coalition of civil rights organizations, women's groups, minority business leaders, legal experts, labor unions, equal employment opportunity officers, and representatives of local jurisdictions seeking to maintain voluntary programs.

Source: Ellen Spears and Sarah Torian, "Republican Effort Backfires: Resounding Defeat for Affirmative Action Foes in Georgia," *Southern Changes* (Spring 1998): 20, 21.

{r/g}DOCUMENT 380: Congressional Debate on the McConnell Amendment, 1998

While at least some of the barricades erected to protect affirmative action were holding, opposing forces were also on the rise in Congress. In December 1997 Republican representative Charles Canaday of Florida attempted to revive the bill promoted by him and Senator Dole in the previous congressional session. The bill was designed to eradicate all federal affirmative action programs. Named the "Civil Rights Act of 1997," it was killed by the House Judiciary Committee. Early in the next session foes of affirmative action, led by Republican senator Mitch McConnell of Kentucky, concentrated their attention on the Disadvantaged Business Enterprise Program (DBE) of the federal Department of Transportation. Under the program a minimum of 10 percent of the money allocated for federal transportation projects and federal aid to state and local projects should be paid to firms controlled by minorities and women. McConnell proposed to replace the DBE with a "small business development program." Unlike the earlier "civil rights" bill, McConnell's DBE proposal, in the form of an amendment to the program, would be debated by the full Senate. The Citizens' Commission on Civil Rights summarized the import and outcome of this debate.

* * *

For the first time since the conservatives had begun to attack affirmative action in earnest, there would be a vote by the full Congress on a specific affirmative action program. Everyone involved understood how critical that vote would be. If the DBE program was lost, there would be a virtual avalanche of attacks on affirmative action programs and the momentum would be against affirmative action. If the DBE program was maintained, though the attacks would certainly continue, the momentum would be on the side of the affirmative action advocates. . . .

[T]he McConnell Amendment was defeated by a strong vote of 58 to 37. Several mainstream Republicans joined the vast majority of Democrats in defeating [it]. . . .

When the debate moved to the House it was announced that Congresswoman Marge Roukema (R-NJ) would spearhead an effort the kill the DBE program. . . . [T]he Roukema Amendment was defeated by a vote of 225 to 194.

Source: Corrine M. Yu and William L. Taylor, eds., *The Test of Our Progress: The Clinton Record on Civil Rights* (Washington, DC: Citizens' Commission on Civil Rights, 1999): 175, 177.

{r/g}DOCUMENT 381: Amendment of the Higher Education Act Proposed by Congressman Riggs, 1998

As soon as the McConnell and Roukema amendments were disposed of, congressional opponents of affirmative action launched a new attack. California Republican representative Frank Riggs sought to amend the Higher Education Act, using Proposition 209 (Doc. 363) as the model for the amendment.

* * *

No public institution of higher education that participates in any program authorized under the Higher Education Act of 1965 . . . shall, in connection with admission to such institution, discriminate against, or grant preferential treatment to, any person or group based in whole or in part on the race, sex, color, ethnicity, or national origin of such person or group.

Source: *Congressional Record* 144 (May 6, 1998): 2892.

{r/g}DOCUMENT 382: House Debate on the Riggs Amendment, May 1998

> During House debate on the Riggs amendment, the sponsor of the measure invoked the name of Martin Luther King Jr., arousing the ire of civil rights veteran Congressman John Lewis (Doc. 115).

* * *

A. Congressman Riggs from California

I want to quote . . . [Congressman Goodling of Pennsylvania], from the statement he sent out. He said that he supports my amendment. . . .

He goes on to say that my amendment embodies the idea of a color-blind society. Well, I am not the one that advanced the idea of a color-blind society. In modern times, that vision is the vision of Dr. Martin Luther King, Jr. I think everybody knows that. He was the one that talked about a day when someone would be judged by the content of their character, not the color of their skin.

B. Congressman Lewis of Georgia

I knew Martin Luther King Jr., very well. . . . If he was standing here tonight . . . he would say he believes in a color-blind society, but he would tell us that we are not there yet, and he would not be supporting the Riggs amendment. . . .

[W]e have fought too long and too hard. . . . People have gone to jail. People have been beaten. People have lost their lives. Now we must fight one more time against those who wave the banner of fairness but really want to slam the door of opportunity in the face of young people across our Nation.

Source: Congressional Record—House 144 (May 6, 1988): 2894, 2895.

{r/g}DOCUMENT 383: William G. Bowen and Derek Bok Examine the Effects of Affirmative Action on College Admissions, 1998

The public debate on affirmative action produced an ever-increasing amount of opinion, commentary, contention, and anecdotal information, as well as a mounting number of chart and table-studded surveys, reports, and reviews. From this welter of material one could draw just about any conclusion, depending on the sources that one chose to credit. In the fall of 1998 yet another study appeared. The credentials of the authors, the extensiveness of their data, and the systematic methods of their research and reporting set *The Shape of the River: Long-Term Consequences of Considering Race in College and University Admissions* apart from the general run of writings on affirmative action. The authors were a former president of Princeton University, William G. Bowen, and a former president of Harvard University who had also served as dean of the Harvard Law School—Derek Bok. They grounded their work on a database created by the Andrew W. Mellon Foundation known as College and Beyond (C&B). It consisted of detailed records of more than 80,000 undergraduates who had entered twenty-eight highly selective colleges and universities in 1951, 1976, and 1989. In addition to intensively examining these records, Bowen and Bok carefully described the procedures followed by admissions personnel at the twenty-eight institutions of higher learning. The following passages from their work indicate the nature of their conclusions.

* * *

Looking back over the whole period from the beginning of the civil rights movement to the present day, we see that the percentage of black students graduating from colleges and professional schools has grown enormously. . . .

[T]he number of blacks scoring in the higher SAT ranges nationwide has increased substantially. Still progress has been painfully slow, and the remaining gaps are very large. . . .

There is no reason to suppose that any set of policies is likely to eliminate this gap in pre-collegiate preparation during our lifetimes. Differences between blacks and whites in resources, environments, and inherited intellectual capital (the educational attainment of parents and grandparents) have been long in the making. It would be amazing if they could be eradicated quickly. As a result, it is all but certain that the issue of race-sensitive admissions will continue to be relevant for the foreseeable future. . . .

[A]dmissions officers in virtually all selective colleges and professional schools look well beyond grades and test scores. . . .

Even in law schools, which place the greatest weight on the traditional measures of academic achievement, other factors matter; a recent study estimates that of the 42,287 whites accepted by accredited schools in 1990–91, 6,321 would have been excluded if admissions officers had looked only at grades and test scores. . . .

The myth of pure merit, held and celebrated by many, would have us believe that these [C&B] institutions want only the "book smart, test smart" students, and that racial preferences are interfering with the precise science such a criterion implies. But the truth is that admitting students is far more an eclectic and interpretive art . . . than a series of formulaic calculations. . . .

The high graduation rates of minority students from the twenty-eight selective colleges in our universe demonstrate how well admissions officers in these institutions have succeeded in fulfilling their first responsibility: to choose students capable of completing their academic work successfully. . . .

At the same time, the data reveal a pervasive problem. At almost every college in our sample, black students are not only performing less well academically than whites but also performing below the levels predicted by their SAT scores. . . . Although the reasons for underperformance are not entirely clear, successful programs initiated by several colleges suggest that the problem can be addressed effectively. . . .

At the same time that we encourage efforts to improve academic performance, we should recognize that the great majority of these black students persevered and . . . graduated. . . .

Black college students have a remarkably strong interest in advanced training. . . .

Percentage of Graduates Attaining Advanced Degrees, by Combined SAT Score and Race, 1976 Entering Cohort (*Source*: College and Beyond)

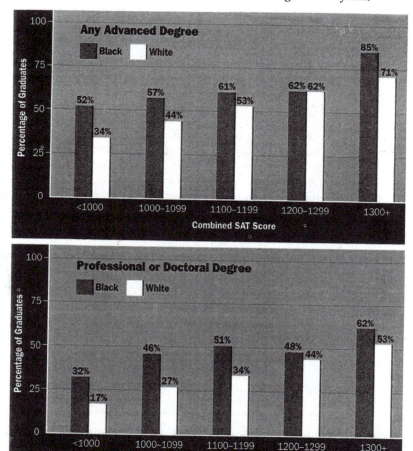

Note: The "Professional or Doctoral Degree" category includes law, medical, business and other professional and doctoral degrees.

The C&B minority graduates with advanced degrees are the backbone of the emergent black and Hispanic middle class. Their presence has brought greater diversity to the emergency clinics and surgery rooms of leading hospitals, to government offices and law firms, to corporate hierarchies, and to the practice of entrepreneurship. They have also gained the training that will allow them to offer medical services to traditionally underserved communities and give political leadership to struggling urban constituencies. . . .

Successful black and Hispanic professionals serve as role models for nephews and nieces and ... provide "networks" similar to those that have benefited the majority white community for many generations. ...

A major purpose of higher education is to build intellectual capital. ...

Having started out with comparatively lower test scores and less family affluence, the black students who entered the C&B schools in 1976 have successfully converted the "capital" provided by academically selective schools into high-paying and satisfying careers—and at young ages. This finding stands out even though we also recognize that there are surprisingly persistent black-white earnings gaps among men, for which we have no convincing explanation. ...

Particularly striking is the high degree of commitment to community and social service organizations by those African Americans with advanced degrees. Of the black C&B respondents with doctorates, one-third (33 percent) were leaders of organizations such as community centers, neighborhood improvement associations, civil rights groups, and hospital planning boards; in contrast, only 6 percent of white holders of doctorates served in such capacities. ...

Many who agree with Justice Blackmun's aphorism, "To get beyond racism, we must first take account of race," would be comforted if it were possible to predict ... when that will no longer be necessary. But we do not know how to make such a prediction, and we would caution against adopting arbitrary timetables that fail to take into account how deep-rooted are the problems associated with race in America.

Source: Bowen and Bok 1998, 9, 22, 23, 25, 51–52, 88, 89, 93, 107, 116, 117, 153, 167, 289.

{r/g}DOCUMENT 384: *Wessmann v. Gittens*, First Circuit Court of Appeals, November 3, 1998

Challenges to race- and-gender-conscious admissions programs were not confined to higher education, as the court case of *Wessmann v. Gittens* illustrates. The father of a white ninth grader, Sarah Wessmann, sued the Boston public school system when his daughter's application to Boston Latin School (BLS) was rejected. BLS was one of three public "examination schools" with entrance requirements. During battles in the 1970s over desegregation a federal district court mandated that BLS maintain a minority representation of 35 percent in every entering class. After the mandate was lifted in 1987, BLS continued to meet the 35 percent goal voluntarily. When this practice was challenged in 1996 by a white applicant, Julia McLaughlin, the court ordered that she be admitted and encouraged BLS to look for a "less racially preferential" alternative to the minority set-aside (160 F. 3d at 813).

The school subsequently adopted a policy by which the applicant pool was selected and ranked based on test scores and grade point averages. Half of the entering class comprised those who ranked highest in the applicant pool. The other half was taken from those who remained in the pool, selected not strictly according to rank but according to "flexible racial/ethnic guidelines." The final selection had to mirror the proportion of white, African American, Hispanic, Asian, and Native American students in the remaining pool. The year that Wessmann applied, ninety slots were available. "The Policy required school officials to allocate the final 45 . . . to 13 blacks, 18 whites, 9 Asians, and 5 Hispanics." Wessmann and ten other white students were rejected in favor of African American and Hispanic students with rankings lower than the whites' (160 F. 3d at 793).

When Wessmann sued, a federal district court upheld the admission policy. On appeal, however, Wessmann prevailed, and BLS was ordered to admit Sarah "without delay" (160 F. 3d at 809). In reaching this conclusion, the appeals court majority discredited virtually all of the evidence presented by school officials regarding the lingering effects of past discrimination. The one dissenter, Judge Lipez, complained that the majority set "the bar of proof . . . unrealistically high" and that they read into certain Supreme Court rulings requirements that were not there (160 F. 3d at 826).

* * *

The court below . . . reasoned that once there has been a past judicial finding of institutional discrimination, no more evidence is needed to justify a policy that employs racial classifications. . . . The lower court was wrong. . . .

We do not write on a pristine page. The Supreme Court's decisions in *Croson* and *Adarand* [Docs. 315, 349] indicate quite plainly that a majority of the Justices are highly skeptical of racial preferences and believe that the Constitution imposes a heavy burden of justification on their use. . . .

[U]nless and until the Justices reconfigure their present doctrine, it is the job of judges in courts such as this to respect the letter and spirit of the Supreme Court's pronouncements. . . .

The judgement of the district court must therefore be reversed. . . .

LIPEZ, Circuit Judge, dissenting. . . .

The majority goes awry because it reads *Wygant*'s [Doc. 300] requirement of a "strong basis in evidence" for an affirmative action program and *Croson*'s [Doc. 312] reference to a "searching judicial inquiry" into the justification for an affirmative action program as demands for evidence grounded in quantifiable social science data rather than human judgments. There is no such demand in *Wygant, Croson* or any other Supreme Court precedent. . . . In this case, the extensive observations of experienced administrators in the Boston public schools, supplemented by the testimony of a highly qualified expert . . . were as probative as the statistical surveys and regression analyses demanded by the majority.

Source: 160 F. 3d 801 at 801–802, 808, 809, 810, 833 (1998).

{r/g}DOCUMENT 385: Initiative 200, Approved by Voters of Washington State, November 3, 1998

How the concept of taking race into account was presented to the public continued to be a major factor in how the public responded. This was demonstrated once again in the state of Washington in November 1998, when voters approved another local initiative put forward by opponents of affirmative action inspired by Ward Connerly and his activities in California (Docs. 363–365).

* * *

BE IT ENACTED BY THE PEOPLE OF THE STATE OF WASHINGTON:
. . .
The state shall not discriminate against, or grant preferential treatment to, any individual or group on the basis of race, sex, color, ethnicity, or national origin in the operation of public employment, public education or public contracting.

Source: Quoted in Citizens' Commission on Civil Rights 1999, 182.

{r/g}DOCUMENT 386: Critique of Initiative 200 Campaign of 1998

Analysts found that the terminology of "preferential treatment" determined the outcome of the Washington vote. Amy Wood reported these findings in the summer 1999 issue of *Southern Changes*.

* * *

Buzz words like "discriminate" and "preferential treatment" conceal the true intent of the initiative. Because discrimination and preferential treatment have historically been used against women and minorities, the language sounds as if the initiative is championing the progressive goals of the Civil Rights Movement. As state Senator Darryl Jones, chair of Florida's Black Leadership Conference says, the language is so "massively misleading, it's so benign that most of us would vote for it if we didn't know what it really meant."

Indeed, the NAACP discovered that during the Washington campaign, the ACRC [Ward Connerly's American Civil Rights Coalition] had duped some of their African-American volunteers into thinking they were working for a progressive civil rights cause.

Source: Amy Wood, "Affirmative Action Foes: Chasing the Initiative," *Southern Changes* (Summer 1999): 5–6.

{r/g}DOCUMENT 387: Advertising against Affirmative Action, January 1999

Another example of opponents of affirmative action couching their opposition in the traditional language of civil rights was the Center for Individual Rights (CIR), self-described as a "public-interest law firm," based in Washington, D.C., and perhaps best known for its role on behalf of the plaintiffs in *Hopwood v. University of Texas* (Doc. 353). CIR placed ads in the student newspapers of fourteen U.S. colleges in January 1999.

* * *

GUILTY BY ADMISSION

Nearly every elite college in America violates the Law. Does yours?

The lingering presence of unlawful racial preferences makes applying to college or professional school all the more difficult and admissions decisions all the more arbitrary. Students need to know whether they are being treated in accordance with the law.

Source: "Paid Advertisement," *Pitt News* (January 26, 1999): 19.

The advertisement invited students to contact CIR for a free copy of a handbook, *Racial Preferences in Higher Education: The Rights of College Students*. The handbook provided detailed instructions for unearthing and "confronting racial preferences" in college or university admissions policies.

{d}DOCUMENT 388: Work Incentives Improvement Act of 1999

While groups such as CIR and Connerly's ACRC sought the end of race- and gender-conscious public policies, continuing congressional support for affirmative action included renewed efforts to include disabled citizens in the workforce. Although architects of the Americans with Disabilities Act had identified employment as a major goal of the law, they had not fully addressed the crucially related issue of health care benefits. Either unable to obtain the kinds of benefits that would enable them to work or finding that once they took a job, they ceased to be eligible for such benefits as Social Security, Medicare, and Medicaid, many willing workers remained unemployed. Congress sought to remedy this dilemma with the Work Incentives Improvement Act, labeled by President Clinton as "the most significant milestone for the disabled since the . . . Americans With Disabilities Act" (*Baltimore Sun*, November 21, 1999). An estimated 2 million individuals stood to become employed with the support of the various benefit and incentive programs and changes in regulations enacted by the bill. As part of the oversight of its implementation, the bill established a citizens' advisory panel, half of whom were to be disabled.

* * *

FINDINGS AND PURPOSES.

(a) FINDINGS—Congress makes the following findings: . . .

(4) For individuals with disabilities, the fear of losing health care and related services is one of the greatest barriers keeping the individuals from maximizing their employment, earning potential, and independence. . . .

(b) PURPOSES—The purposes of this Act are as follows:

(1) To provide health care and employment preparation and placement services to individuals with disabilities that will enable those individuals to reduce their dependency on cash benefit programs.

Source: S. 331, Work Incentive Improvement Act of 1999. http://thomas.loc gov.

{d}DOCUMENT 389: New Frontiers for the Disabled in Sports and Recreation by 1999

While Congress pursued a remedy for the health care and insurance dilemmas faced by disabled workers, various constituencies within the disability rights movement continued their quests for accessibility, filing lawsuits to force restaurants, hotels, banks, and other public accommodations, as well as public transportation systems, to meet ADA standards ("Restaurants among Businesses Targeted . . . ," *Baltimore Sun*: July 31, 1999). At the same time, advances in technology were opening experiences previously unimagined to the disabled in sports and recreation. Among "disabled thrill seekers" featured in a *Baltimore Sun* article were those who kayaked on white water, raced special chairs on bike trails, played rugged versions of rugby, "sled hockey," and wheelchair soccer, and—in chairs adapted for skiing—sailed down snow slopes and across water. The *Sun* quoted the director of a Baltimore-based sports program for disabled youth, Gerry Herman.

* * *

"Now the choices are limitless," [Herman] says. "The barriers are being trampled down. If someone has an interest in it, there's someone who will help you find a way to do it."

Source: Jay Aperson, "Disabled Athletes Play Hard," *Baltimore Sun* (December 14, 1999): 1A, 18A.

{d}DOCUMENT 390: Microsoft Accessibility Policy and "Assistive Technology" for the Disabled, 1999

Another frontier opening to the disabled—the Internet—offered liberating possibilities, but only to the degree that software manufacturers and service providers were responsive to the needs and rights of the disabled. In November 1999 the National Federation of the Blind took America OnLine (AOL) to court, charging that since AOL software was incompatible with technology that converts text to braille, the Internet provider was violating the Americans with Disabilities Act (Doc. 333) (*Baltimore Sun*, January 3, 2000). Meanwhile, another magnate of the computer industry, Microsoft, publicized on-line its commitment to accessibility and the means by which it sought to honor that commitment.

* * *

Microsoft Accessibility Policy

Microsoft Corporation recognizes its responsibility to develop products and information technologies that are accessible and useable by all people, including those with disabilities. . . .

Microsoft is taking a four-pronged approach to making computers more accessible.

1. Making our products accessible. . . .
2. Building relationships with the disability community. . . .
3. Equipping the development community. . . .
4. Empowering customers with information. . . .

Assistive Technology for Computers

Assistive technology, also called accessibility aids, are added to computers by people who use them to make computers more accessible. Some common aids include:

- **Screen enlargers** help people with low vision. . . .
- **Screen reviewers** are for people who are blind. These aids make on-screen information available as synthesized speech or a refreshable Braille display. . . .
- **Voice input aids** assist people with mobility impairments. . . . these enable people to control computers with their voice instead of a mouse or keyboard.
- **On-screen keyboards** are used by people who are unable to use a standard keyboard. . . . [They] let people select keys using a pointing method such as pointing devices, switches, or Morse-code input systems.
- **Keyboard filters** are used by people who have trouble typing. . . . [They] compensate somewhat for erratic motion, tremors, slow response time, and similar conditions. . . .
- **Alternative input devices** allow individuals to control their computers through means other than a standard keyboard or pointing device. Examples include . . . eye-gaze pointing devices, and sip-and-puff systems controlled by breathing.

Sources: http://www.microsoft.com/enable/microsoft/policy.htm and http://www.microsoft.com/enable/microsoft/technology.htm.

{r/g}DOCUMENT 391: Ford Foundation Report, Winter 1999

As the 1990s drew to a close, some evidence pointed to growing public acceptance of diversity and opportunity resulting from successful affirmative action programs. This evidence included two national surveys—a poll conducted by the *Seattle Times* in the summer of 1999 and another under the auspices of the Ford Foundation that fall. The newspaper poll found that "about half the whites . . . say affirmative action is needed. . . . 75 percent of minority respondents say it is. Most whites and minorities are united in wanting to mend, not end affirmative action" ("Discrimination Fight Goes On," *Baltimore Sun*: August 1, 1999).

Results of the Ford Foundation survey were announced in October. Carried out by pollsters of the Daniel Yankelovitch Group, the survey targeted 2,011 registered voters who were asked about diversity in institutions of higher education. Over half of the respondents described themselves as "conservative."

* * *

A new national poll has found widespread support for efforts by colleges and universities to insure a diverse student body and to teach about different cultures. . . .

"Many people thought a poll like this would come out very differently," said Lee C. Bollinger, president of the University of Michigan [the target of a suit by white students against race-conscious admissions]. "This is great news because it shows that we may have misled ourselves about what people really think." . . .

The findings show strong support for efforts to recruit students from a variety of backgrounds. Three out of four of those polled think campus diversity benefits all students, and 66 percent said colleges and universities should take steps to insure this diversity.

Source: Theodora Lurie, Ford Foundation Report, Winter 1999. http://www.fordfound.org/publications.

{r/g}DOCUMENT 392: Florida Governor Jeb Bush's Executive Order 99–281, November 9, 1999

Positive poll results notwithstanding, affirmative action was still embattled, and its intended results were far from complete. In November 1999 Florida governor Jeb Bush short-circuited a voter referendum on affirmative action that had been instigated by Ward Connerly and would have been on the ballot in November 2000. In the face of vehement protest the governor issued an executive order abolishing affirmative action in state employment, contracting, and higher education admissions.

* * *

Section 1: Non-Discrimination in Government Employment. . . .

Unless otherwise affirmatively required by law or administrative rule, neither the Office of the Governor nor any Executive Agency may utilize racial or gender set-asides, preferences or quotas when making decisions regarding the hiring, retention or promotion of a state employee. . . .

Section 2: Non-Discrimination in State Contracting

[N]either the Office of the Governor nor any Executive Agency may utilize racial or gender set-asides, preferences or quotas when making state contracting decisions. . . .

Section 3: Non-Discrimination in Higher Education. . . .

I hereby request that the Board of Regents implement a policy prohibiting the use of racial or gender set-asides, preferences or quotas in admissions to all Florida institutions of Higher Education, effective immediately.

Source: Executive Order 99–281. http://sun6.dms.state.fl.us/eog_new/eog/orders/1999/november/eo99–281.html, November 1999.

{r}DOCUMENT 393: "Toward an Understanding of Percentage Plans in Higher Education" (U.S. Civil Rights Commission Statement, April 2000)

The Florida governor replaced race-conscious student admissions programs with a plan allowing the admission of 20 percent of high school seniors to state universities. These developments prompted an assessment of "percentage plans in higher education" by the U.S. Commission on Civil Rights (CRC). The CRC examined enrollment patterns in California and Texas, where such plans had been in place since 1995 and 1996, respectively.

* * *

[T]he Texas Plan creates an ineffective replacement program when compared with the university's previous affirmative action policy. . . .

[In California] the prestigious campuses of Berkeley and UCLA [University of California at Los Angeles] have yet to reverse the declines in enrollment of black and Hispanic students that occurred following the Regents policy that excluded affirmative action as a race-conscious remedy for the class beginning in 1998 at the undergraduate level and in 1997 at the graduate level. . . .

The major problem with the percentage plans is their inattention to law schools, medical schools, and other graduate and professional schools, where ending affirmative action is devastating. At the law schools of the University of Texas at Austin, the University of California at Berkeley, and the University of California at Los Angeles, African American and Latino enrollment remain well below 1996 figures, which needed increasing, not decreasing. Florida is proposing to voluntarily inflict this harm by ending affirmative action. . . .

The percentage plans are experimental responses to the attacks on affirmative action. But they are no substitute for strong race-conscious affirmative action in higher education. What is required is a Supreme Court decision reaffirming *Bakke* [Doc. 232] and making affirmative action an imperative.

Source: U.S. Commission on Civil Rights, "Toward an Understanding of Percentage Plans in Higher Education: Are They Effective Substitutes for Affirmative Action?" http://www.usccr.gov/percent/stmnt.htm, April 2000.

{d}DOCUMENT 394: The Americans with Disabilities Act after Ten Years, June 2000

In June 2000 ten years had passed since the Americans with Disabilities Act (ADA) became law. To mark this anniversary the National Council on Disability issued an exhaustive assessment of the law's effectiveness. Authors of the report, "Promises to Keep," credited the ADA with permanent changes in the "architectural and telecommunications landscape of the United States," and with raising awareness of the discrimination faced by the disabled. However, they indicated disappointment with federal enforcement of the law and called for a closer partnership between the enforcement agencies (the Justice Department, the EEOC, the FCC, and the Department of Transportation) and the disabled community.

* * *

[T]he federal agencies charged with enforcement and policy development under ADA . . . have been overly cautious, reactive, and lacking any coherent and unifying national strategy. . . . [M]any of the shortcomings of federal enforcement of ADA . . . are inexorably tied to chronic underfunding and understaffing of the responsible agencies. . . . Despite the fact that ADA requires existing agencies to take on new tasks and activities, the budgets and approved staffing levels of these agencies have not changed in a commensurate manner. . . .

[T]here are few opportunities for appropriate input from people with disabilities on setting overall priorities for policy development and litigation, developing appropriate strategies for mitigating the impact of negative court decisions, determining appropriate and feasible accommodations, and advising on the design and dissemination of public education materials . . . [for] people from diverse cultures, people with limited or no English proficiency, those living in institutions, those with cognitive disabilities, and those labeled with psychiatric disabilities.

Input from the disability community is especially important in verifying that covered entities have taken action to correct ADA violations. . . .

[A]s we stand at the dawn of a new century, let us recommit to the vision of an America that keeps its promise of "liberty and justice for all."

Source: National Council on Disability, *Promises to Keep: A Decade of Federal Enforcement of the Americans with Disabilities Act*, June 2000, pp. 8, 9, 13–14, 15, 20.

{g}DOCUMENT 395: Court Challenges to the Constitutionality of the Americans with Disabilities Act, 2000

The disabled community had to grapple not only with poor enforcement of the ADA but also court challenges to its constitutionality. One such challenge reached the Supreme Court in the fall of 2000. Actually two cases originating in Alabama and consolidated by the federal district court, *Patricia Garrett v. the University of Alabama* and *Milton Ash v. Alabama Department of Youth Services* involved state employees who sued Alabama for allegedly violating their rights as guaranteed by the ADA and Section 504 of the Rehabilitation Act of 1973 (Doc. 200). Garrett also invoked the Family Medical Leave Act of 1993 (FMLA). The district court ruled against her and Ash, arguing that the Eleventh Amendment to the U.S. Constitution protected the state from being sued by an individual citizen. This ruling, with regard to the ADA and Section 504, was overturned by a three-judge panel of the Eleventh Circuit Court of Appeals. A majority of the panel upheld the ruling with regard to the FMLA; the third judge dissented on that point. The panel found that the ADA and Section 504 effectively nullified the state's Eleventh Amendment immunity. It based this conclusion on a 1996 Supreme Court ruling (*Seminole Tribe of Florida v. Florida*) that established guidelines for determining when a congressional law can override the Eleventh Amendment. Alabama appealed the finding in favor of Garrett and Ash to the Supreme Court, whose members accepted the case and heard arguments in October 2000. While awaiting their decision the chairperson of the National Council on Disability asked, "Why, before we realize the full potential of the law, are we debating its constitutionality?" ("Statement by National Council on Disability Chairperson Marca Bristo on the U.S. Supreme Court Case—*University of Alabama v. Garrett*," National Council on Disability, October 11, 2000. http://www.ncd.gov/newsroom/news/r01-314.html).

* * *

These two consolidated cases . . . raise the question that is being litigated in various jurisdictions of whether a state is immune from suits by state employees asserting rights under certain federal laws. . . .

It has long been recognized that each state is a sovereign entity in our federal system and is not amenable to suit by an individual without its consent. . . . Under certain circumstances, however, the United States Congress can pass laws which give individual citizens a right of action in federal court against an unconsenting state. Those circumstances require first, that "Congress has 'unequivocally express[ed] its intent to abrogate the immunity,' " which "must be obvious from 'a clear legislative statement,' " and second, that Congress has acted "pursuant to a valid exercise of power." [Quoted from *Seminole Tribe of Florida v. Florida*]. . . .

Congress . . . unequivocally express[ed] its intent for the ADA to abrogate sovereign immunity. [Quoting the ADA:] ("A State shall not be immune under the eleventh amendment to the Constitution of the

United States from an action in Federal or State court of competent jurisdiction for a violation of [the ADA].") . . .

We, therefore, reverse the summary judgment[s] entered . . . against
Patricia Garrett on her ADA claim . . . and against Milton Ash on his
ADA claim. . . .

The language of the Rehabilitation Act as to congressional intent to
abrogate a state's immunity from suit in federal court is as clear as it
was under the ADA. [Quoting the Rehabilitation Act:] ("A State shall
not be immune under the Eleventh Amendment of the Constitution of
the United States from suit in Federal court for a violation of Section 504
of the Rehabilitation Act of 1973 . . .") . . .

We, therefore, reverse the summary judgment[s] entered . . . against
Patricia Garrett on her Rehabilitation Act claim . . . and against Milton
Ash on his Rehabilitation Act claim.

Source: 193 F. 3d 1214 (1999), findlaw.com/case&no.=986069OPN, 2–3, 4–5.

{d}DOCUMENT 396: Report on Congress's Provisions for Disabled Members, November 2000

The impact of the ADA fell not only on the states and the private
sector but also on the federal government, including the authors of the
legislation—the U.S. Congress. In 1996 Max Cleland, a triple-amputee,
was elected to the Senate from Georgia. In the election of 2000 quadriplegic James Langevin from Rhode Island won a seat in the House.
Both chambers had to make adjustments for these members. In Langevin's case this meant providing a ground-floor office, creating sufficient space for his wheelchair in the House chamber, and installing a
special voting machine at his seat. The press reported that these
changes—"the first of their kind made for a House member"—were
made without a stir.

* * *

The House architect has met with Langevin, and the congressman-elect's
staff expects his needs to be met by the time he's sworn in to office in
January.

Source: "First Quadriplegic to Serve in House Joins Fellow Freshmen in Learning
Capitol Ropes," *Baltimore Sun* (November 14, 2000), p. 23A.

{g}DOCUMENT 397: Associated Press Release on the Glass Ceiling, April 24, 2000

While the disabled fought court battles, entered Congress, and continued their quest for accessibility and independence, women and minorities continued to press against "the glass ceiling" (Doc. 345). By 2000 studies based on census figures indicated that increasing numbers of women were breaking through that barrier. However, close reading of the media reports on this "breakthrough" revealed that it was far from complete.

* * *

According to government estimates, more than 7.1 million women held full-time executive, administrative or managerial positions in 1998—a 29 percent jump from 1993. . . .

Men still hold 93 percent of . . . high-profile jobs . . . that often lead to the top spots. . . . [M]any women who achieve executive or management level are shuffled into "staff" positions such as human resources or public relations.

Source: "Census Figures Show That More Women Are Breaking through the Glass Ceiling," *Baltimore Sun* (April 24, 2000).

{r/g}DOCUMENT 398: Women and Minorities at General Electric in the Year 2000

General Electric Corporation (GE) was an example of a company where the glass ceiling remained firmly in place. Although in the 1970s GE had adopted affirmative action guidelines and had begun to place women and minorities in jobs as foremen and managers, in the next decade—when a new chief executive, John F. Welch, took over—the focus shifted to restructuring the company. Massive layoffs and elimination of many middle-level managers fostered a survivalist mentality among the white males who remained in the ranks of management. That mentality neither welcomed nor supported recently hired female and minority additions to those ranks. While other major corporations such as American Express, Maytag, and Hewlett Packard came to be headed by women and minorities, GE maintained a leadership corps that was entirely male and (with a single exception) entirely white. When Welch turned his attention to this situation in the 1990s, he declared that the new global economy made a diverse workforce a "business necessity" for GE. He mandated problem-solving deliberations among the company's top leaders. The plan of action that came from those deliberations was primarily shaped by African American and women employees themselves who took a markedly conservative approach. Instead of challenging the corporate environment they sought to make themselves more valuable within it. They adopted a self-help strategy, avoiding goals, timetables, and other controversial aspects of affirmative action. Some observers saw in this approach a new trend that melded the traditional values of "meritocracy" with new demands for diversity.

* * *

[B]lack managers studied glass-ceiling issues and minority retention at other corporations. . . . In the end they settled on an in-house self-help network, called the African American Forum. Started in 1992 its mandate is narrow: to demystify G.E.'s personnel policies, to provide a setting where G.E. blacks can meet one another and to develop a formal mentor program, in which G.E.'s [white] senior executives are required to participate. G.E. says it's keeping track of which mentors' trainees receive promotions and is rating the mentors accordingly. . . .

As the African American Forum began receiving plaudits . . . managerial women started planning their own self-help network in 1997. . . . [They] focused on coaching women in public speaking, in making effective presentations and in exuding leadership qualities. It also links participants with senior-executive mentors.

Source: Mary Williams Walsh, "Where G.E. Falls Short: Diversity at the Top," *New York Times* (September 3, 2000): sec. 3, pp. 1, 13.

{r/g}DOCUMENT 399: "Showdown in Atlanta" over Affirmative Action Set-Asides, Fall 1999

While women and minorities at General Electric sought to improve their position by self-help and gradualism, female and minority contractors in numerous cities were fighting back against continuing attacks on the set-aside programs from which they stood to gain. The president of the Southeastern Legal Foundation, one of the twenty-two groups leading such attacks, announced with pleasure that "there is not one racial preference program in America that has survived a court challenge since 1989" (quoted in the *Baltimore Sun*, January 30, 2000).

In some cities such as Atlanta, Detroit, and Madison, set-aside criteria were revamped, replacing race and gender with considerations of the size of a company's assets or its urban location. Meanwhile, urban mayors marshaled their resources to turn back unfavorable court rulings. Atlanta mayor Bill Campbell appeared on the cover of *Emerge* magazine in November 1999 wearing boxing trunks and gloves to underscore his determination to save the affirmative action program in his city.

* * *

Overall, more than 1,000 firms are certified by [Atlanta] as minority and women contractors, receiving more than $409 million worth of city work in 1997.

Now . . . the Southeastern Legal Foundation (SLF) . . . has sued Atlanta's program. . . .

"There've only been two issues in my life that I was willing to die for, and that was our fight for equality in the '60s and this struggle for equality in the 90s," [Mayor] Campbell says. "They are all inextricably tied. This is a struggle for economic freedom." . . .

One of the ironies about the increase in Black economic might in Atlanta brought about in part by affirmative action, former Mayor Andrew Young observes, is that it "also generated a growth economy, which has ultimately benefited the White business establishment the most." . . .

Source: Vern E. Smith, "Showdown in Atlanta," *Emerge* (November 1999): 49, 51, 55.

{r/g}DOCUMENT 400: Poet June Jordan's Historical Review of Affirmative Action

Thus, just as "affirmative action was forged in the fire of urban rebellion" in the 1960s and 1970s (Lawrence and Matsuda 1997, 18), so the gathering of forces to preserve, improve, and extend affirmative action was occurring in the nation's cities as the 1990s gave way to 2000. At the same time, these forces were the heirs of a struggle reaching back to the country's origins. Poet and essayist June Jordan angrily called attention to this struggle when Ward Connerly's attack on affirmative action was under way in California (Docs. 363–365). Jordan's recapitulation in free verse provides a fitting conclusion to this documentary history.

* * *

Dedicated to Negro U.C. Regent, Ward Connerly. . . .

We didn't always need affirmative action

. . .

when slavery defined our days and our prayers and our
   nighttimes of no rest

. . .

we did not need affirmative action. No! We needed overthrow
   and a holy fire to purify
  the air.
And so we finally got freedom on a piece of paper.
But. . . . in this crazy land the law and the
   bullets behind the law
continued to affirm. . . .
the gospel of God-given white
   supremacy God-give male
white supremacy. . . .

And neither the Emancipation Proclamation nor the Civil War nor
one constitutional amendment after another one nor one civil rights
legislation after another could bring about a yielding of the followers
of that gospel to the beauty of our human face. Justice don't mean
nothin' to a hateful heart!
And so we needed affirmative action

. . .

And so thirty years ago we agitated
and we agitated until the President declared,
"I now decree our federal commitment
to equality not
just as a right
but to equality
in fact"
and a great rejoicing rose like a spirit
dancing
fresh and happy on the soon-to-be-integrated
and-most-uppity ballroom floor
of these United States.

. . .

But (three decades later) and come to find out

. . .

we never got no kind of affirmative action worth
more than spit in the wind
     . . .
and yesterday
the new man in the White House
the new President
he said, "What we have done for women and minorities is a
     very good thing, but we
must respond to those who feel discriminated against. . . .
     This is a psychologically difficult
time for the so-called angry white man."

Well, I am here to tell the world that 46 percent of my
     children living in poverty
don't feel good to me
and more Black men in prison cells than college
don't feel good to me
psychologically
or otherwise!
     . . .
White men constitute 44 percent of the American labor force
     but white men occupy 95 percent
of all senior management positions!

And 80 percent of the congress, four fifths of tenured
     university faculty, nine tenths of the United States
Senate—and 92 percent of the Forbes 400!
     . . .
I say the problem with affirmative action seems to me like
way too much affirmative talk
but way too little action!

Source: June Jordan, "An Angry Black Woman on the Subject of an Angry White Man," *Affirmative Acts, Political Essays* (New York: Anchor Books, 1998): 100–104.

Selected Bibliography

BOOKS

Appenzeller, Herb, and Thomas Appenzeller. *Sports and the Courts*. Charlottesville, VA: Michie, 1980.

Belz, Herman. *Equality Transformed: A Quarter Century of Affirmative Action*. New Brunswick, NJ, and London: Transaction, 1994.

Bergmann, Barbara R. *In Defense of Affirmative Action*. New York: Basic Books, 1996.

Berkowitz, Edward. *Disabled Policy. America's Programs for the Handicapped*. New York: Cambridge University Press, 1987.

Blum, John, et al. *The National Experience*. New York: Harcourt Brace Jovanovich, 1977.

Bowen, William G., and Derek Bok. *The Shape of the River: Long-Term Consequences of Considering Race in College and University Admissions*. Princeton, NJ: Princeton University Press, 1998.

Carson, Clayborne, ed. *The Papers of Martin Luther King, Jr.: Vol. III*. Berkeley: University of California Press, 1997.

Chavez, Lydia. *The Color Bind: California's Battle to End Affirmative Action*. Berkeley: University of California, 1998.

Citizens' Commission on Civil Rights. *The Test of Our Progress: The Clinton Record on Civil Rights*. Washington, DC: Citizen's Commission on Civil Rights, 1999.

Cose, Ellis. *Color Blind*. New York: HarperCollins, 1997.

Drake, W. Avon, and Robert D. Hollsworth. *Affirmative Action and the Stalled Quest for Black Progress*. Urbana and Chicago: University of Illinois Press, 1996.

Edley, Christopher, Jr. *Not All Black and White. Affirmative Action and American Values*. New York: Hill and Wang, 1996.

Eisenberg, Myron G., et al. *Disabled People as Second Class Citizens*. New York: Springer, 1982.

Flexner, Eleanor. *Century of Struggle*. New York: Atheneum, 1970.

Franklin, John Hope. *From Slavery to Freedom*. New York: Alfred A. Knopf, 1980.

Gallagher, Hugh Gregory. *FDR's Splendid Deception*. New York: Dodd, Mead, 1985.

Gannon, Jack R. *The Week the World Heard Gallaudet*. Washington, DC: Gallaudet University Press, 1989.

Garcia, Mildred, ed. *Affirmative Action's Testimony of Hope*. Albany: State University of New York Press, 1997.

Geadelmann, Christine, et al. *Equality in Sport for Women*. Washington, DC: American Alliance for Health, Physical Education, and Recreation, 1977.

Graham, Hugh Davis. *Civil Rights and the Presidency*. New York: Oxford University Press, 1992.

Greene, Kathanne W. *Affirmative Action and Principles of Justice*. Westport, CT: Greenwood Press, 1989.

Hartman, Chester, ed. *Double Exposure: Poverty and Race in America*. Armonk, NY: M. E. Sharpe, 1997.

Higginbotham, A. Leon, Jr. *In the Matter of Color*. New York: Oxford University Press, 1978.

———. *Shades of Freedom*. New York: Oxford University Press, 1996.

Higham, John, ed. *Civil Rights and Civil Wrongs: Black-White Relations Since World War II*. University Park: Pennsylvania State University Press, 1997/1999.

Hoff, Joan. *Law, Gender and Injustice, a Legal History of U.S. Women*. New York: New York University Press, 1991.

Jordan, Winthrop. *White over Black*. Baltimore: Penguin Books, 1968.

Lawrence, Charles R., III, and Mari J. Matsuda. *We Won't Go Back. Making the Case for Affirmative Action*. New York: Houghton Mifflin, 1997.

Lowery, Charles D., and John F. Marszalek, eds. *Encyclopedia of African American Civil Rights*. Westport, CT: Greenwood Press, 1992.

Maguire, Daniel C. *A New American Justice*. New York: Doubleday, 1980.

Moreno, Paul D. *From Direct Action to Affirmative Action. Fair Employment Law and Policy in America, 1933–1972*. Baton Rouge and London: Louisiana Sate University Press, 1997.

Norris, Kathleen. *Cloister Walk*. New York: Riverhead Books, 1996.

Payne, Charles M. *I've Got the Light of Freedom, the Organizing Tradition and the Mississippi Freedom Struggle*. Berkeley: University of California Press, 1995.

Robinson, Randall. *The Debt: What America Owes to Blacks*. New York: Dutton, 2000.

Schwartz, Bernard. *Behind Bakke, Affirmative Action and the Supreme Court*. New York: New York University Press, 1988.

Scotch, Richard K. *From Good Will to Civil Rights, Transforming Disability Policy*. Philadelphia: Temple University Press, 1984.

Shapiro, Joseph P. *No Pity, People with Disabilities Forging a New Civil Rights Movement*. New York and Toronto: Random House, 1993.

Sochen, June. *Herstory*. New York: Alfred, 1974.

Stern, Mark. *Calculating Visions: Kennedy, Johnson and Civil Rights*. New Brunswick: Rutgers University Press, 1992.

Takagi, Dana Y. *The Retreat from Race. Asian Americans and Racial Politics*. New Brunswick, NJ: Rutgers University Press, 1992.

Terborg-Penn, Rosalyn. *African American Women in the Struggle for the Vote*. Bloomington: Indiana University Press, 1998.

Urofsky, Melvin I. *Affirmative Action on Trial. Sex Discrimination in Johnson v. Santa Clara.* Lawrence: University Press of Kansas, 1997.

Wallace, Phyllis A., ed. *Equal Employment Opportunity and the AT&T Case.* Cambridge, MA: MIT Press, 1976.

Weiss, Robert John. *We Want Jobs: A History of Affirmative Action.* New York: Garland, 1997.

ARTICLES

Aleinikoff, T. Alexander. "A Case for Race Consciousness." *Columbia Law Review* 91, no. 5 (June 1991): 1060–1125.

Berkowitz, Edward. "Strachan and the Limits of the Federal Government." *International Review of History and Political Science* (February 1980): 65–81.

Blanton, James. "A Limit to Affirmative Action." *Commentary* 82, no. 6 (June 1989): 31–32.

Burgdorf, Marcia P., and Robert Burgdorf Jr. "A History of Unequal Treatment: The Qualifications of Handicapped Persons as a 'Suspect Class' under the Equal Protection Clause." *Santa Clara Lawyer* 15 (1975): 855–910.

"Consultation on the Affirmative Action Statement of the U.S. Commission on Civil Rights." *Proceedings* 2 (February 10, 1981): 51.

Kahlenberg, Richard. "Class Not Race." *The New Republic* (April 3, 1995): 24–25.

Knight, W. H., and Adrien Wing. "Weep Not, Little Ones: An Essay to Our Children." In *African Americans and the Living Constitution*, ed. John Hope Franklin and Genna Rae McNeil. 208–234. Washington, DC: Smithsonian Institution Press, 1995.

Lemann, Nicholas. "Taking Affirmative Action Apart." *New York Times Magazine* (June 11, 1995): 36–43, 52–54, 62, 66.

Lenihan, John. Untitled History of Disability. *Performance* 27, nos. 5–7 (November 1976/January 1977): 1–72.

Longmore, Paul K., and David Goldberger. "The League of the Physically Handicapped and the Great Depression: A Case Study in the New Disability History." *The Journal of American History* (December 2000): 888–922.

Malamud, Deborah C. "Class Based Affirmative Action: Lessons and Caveats." *Texas Law Review* 74 (1996): 1847–1900.

McFadden, Margaret, ed. "Affirmative Action Reconsidered." *NWSA Journal* 10, no. 3 (Fall 1998): 1–240.

Murphy, Charles J. V. "G.I.'s at Harvard. They Are the Best Students in the College's History." *Life* (June 17, 1946): 16–18, 21–22.

Navarrette, Ruben, Jr. "New Victims? Weighing the Charges of Reverse Discrimination." *Change* (March/April 1993): 9, 52–53.

"Race in the Work Place. Is Affirmative Action Working?" *Business Week* (July 8, 1991): 53–56.

Schnapper, Eric. "Affirmative Action and the Legislative History of the Fourteenth Amendment." *Virginia Law Review* 71 (1985): 753–790.

Seligman, Daniel. "How 'Equal Opportunity' Turned into Employment Quotas." *Fortune* (March 1973): 165, 166.

Steinberg, Stephen. "The Liberal Retreat From Race During the Post-Civil Rights Era." In *The House That Race Built*, ed. Wahneema Lubiano. 13–47. New York: Pantheon Books, 1997.

Sugrue, Thomas J. "The Tangled Roots of Affirmative Action." *American Behavioral Scientist* 4, no. 7 (April 1998): 886–897.

tenBroek, Jacobus. "The Disabled and the Law of Welfare." *California Law Review* 54 (1966a): 809–839.

———. "The Right to Live in the World: The Disabled in the Law of Torts." *California Law Review* 54 (1966b): 841–920.

Thomas, R. Roosevelt, Jr. "From Affirmative Action to Affirming Diversity." *Harvard Business Review* (March–April 1990): 107–117.

Willenz, June. "Invisible Veterans." *Educational Record* 74 (Fall 1994): 41–46.

Wilson, Reginald. "G.I. Bill Expands Access for African Americans." *Educational Record* 74 (Fall 1994): 33–39.

PUBLIC TESTIMONY AND GOVERNMENT REPORTS

Federal Glass Ceiling Commission. *Good for Business: Making Full Use of the Nation's Human Capital*. March 1995.

National Advisory Commission on Civil Disorders. "Report of the National Advisory Commission on Civil Disorders." New York: Bantam Books, 1968.

National Council on Disability. *The Americans with Disabilities Act: Ensuring Equal Access to the American Dream*. January 26, 1995.

———. *Promises to Keep: A Decade of Federal Enforcement of the Americans with Disabilities Act*. June 2000.

President's Committee on Employment of People with Disabilities. *Fifty Years of Progress*. June 1997.

U.S. Commission on Civil Rights. *Civil Rights Issues of Handicapped Americans: Public Policy Implications. A Consultation*. Washington, DC, May 13–14, 1980.

GOVERNMENT DOCUMENTS

Congressional Record. Washington, DC: U.S. Government Printing Office.

Federal Register. Washington, DC: Office of the Federal Register, National Archives and Records Service.

Public Papers of the Presidents of the United States. Washington, DC: Office of the Federal Register, National Archives and Records Service.

U.S. Code of Federal Regulations. Washington, DC: Office of the Federal Register, National Archives and Records Service.

U.S. Reports. Washington, DC: U.S. Government Printing Office.

U.S. Statutes at Large. Washington, DC: U.S. Government Printing Office.

Index

Abolitionist movement, liv, lv, 3
Abrams, Morris, 272
Abramson, Joan, 224–225
ACCD. *See* American Coalition of Citizens with Disabilities (ACCD)
ACRC. *See* American Civil Rights Coalition (ACRC)
Action League for Physically Handicapped Adults (ALPHA), 216
ADA. *See* Americans with Disabilities Act (ADA)
Adams Order, 237
Adarand Constructors Inc. v. Pena (1995), 323–325, 326, 327, 328, 329, 344, 345, 361
Adkins v. Children's Hospital (1923), 29
Affirmative action, xlvii, 1; backlash against, 299; business acceptance of, 257–259, 313–314; Civil Rights Act of 1964 and, 94, 95; and civil rights movement, 375; class-based, 334–336; early use of the term, 32, 79; first time the concept was used to refer to disability, 174; first time women were entitled to, 281–283; proposed elimination of, 327, 353
African Americans: fair housing and, 78, 83; feminism and, 184; rights of, vis-à-vis Asian Americans, 317–318; rights of, vis-à-vis women, lv; 10–

12, 98, 99, 109, 113; Title IX and, 237; voting rights and, 46–47, 82. *See also* Education, race conscious admissions in; Employment, African Americans and
African Americans and Age Discrimination Act of 1975, 284
Alabama Christian Movement for Human Rights, 85
Albemarle Paper Co. v. Moody (1975), 197
Aleinikoff, T. Alexander, 301–302
Alexander v. Choate (1985), 305
Allan, Virginia, 136
Allen, Robert E., 314
ALPHA. *See* Action League for Physically Handicapped Adults
America, Richard, lxi
American Association of Medical Colleges (AAMC), 201
America OnLine (AOL), 365
American Civil Liberties Union (ACLU), lxi, 231; rejection by, of Judith Heumann's case, 137; Women's Rights Project of, 181
American Civil Rights Coalition (ACRC), 363, 364
American Coalition of Citizens with Disabilities (ACCD), 214–215, 217
American Disabled for Accessible Public Transit (ADAPT), 306

About the Editor

JO ANN OOIMAN ROBINSON is Professor of History at Morgan State University. She is the author of *Abraham Went Out: A Biography of A.J. Muste.*